THE GOLFERS

to the

West Country

By
Kevin Lee

Published by:

Travel Publishing Ltd
7a Apollo House, Calleva Park
Aldermaston, Berks, RG7 8TN

ISBN 1-902-00757-3

© Travel Publishing Ltd

First Published: 2001

Golfers Guides:

East Anglia	Ireland
Wales	West Country

Hidden Inns Series:

Central & Southern Scotland	Heart of England
Southeast England	South of England
Wales	Welsh Borders
West Country	Yorkshire

Regional Titles in the Hidden Places Series:

Cambridgeshire & Lincs	Chilterns
Cornwall	Derbyshire
Devon	Dorset, Hants & Isle of Wight
East Anglia	Gloucestershire & Wiltshire
Heart of England	Hereford, Worcs & Shropshire
Highlands & Islands	Kent
Lake District & Cumbria	Lancashire and Cheshire
Lincolnshire & Notts	Northumberland & Durham
Somerset	Sussex
Thames Valley	Yorkshire

National Titles in the Hidden Places Series:

England	Ireland
Scotland	Wales

Printing by: Scotprint, Haddington

Maps by: © MAPS IN MINUTES ™ 2001 © Crown Copyright, Ordnance Survey 2001

Editor: Kevin Lee

Cover Design: Lines & Words, Aldermaston

Cover Photographs: St Mellion Golf Course, Cornwall; Fieldhead Hotel, Cornwall; The Old
Barn Owl, Somerset; Hole Mill, Devon

Foreword

There are an increasing number of golfers from this country and overseas who are very happy to play away from their home courses to experience the many different types of terrain (and weather!) available in the British Isles. In fact in the U.K. each year well over 3 million trips, involving varying lengths of overnight stay, are made to play at least one game of golf. Golf and travel therefore are inextricably linked and this was a prime driving force behind the *Golfers Guide* series that will eventually cover the whole of the U.K. and Ireland and which was launched with the publication of the much acclaimed *Golfers Guide to Ireland* last year.

The *Golfers Guide to the West Country* is very much a comprehensive guide to playing 18-hole golf in Cornwall, Devon, Somerset and Dorset. But, for those golfers who wish to have time off from the rigours of the fairways the guide also offers an insight into the spectacular rugged coastline and secluded villages of Cornwall, the rolling hills, wooded valleys and bleak upland moors of Devon, the green undulating landscape and stone-built villages of Somerset and the rolling chalk downs and heathlands of Dorset. And importantly, it provides the golfing visitor with details of over 350 places to stay, eat and drink all of which have been linked to the nearest golf clubs whom we would like to thank for providing information and photographs. It is therefore, the ideal guide for planning every aspect of a golfing trip to the West Country.

Kevin Lee is a very experienced sports journalist with an excellent knowledge of golf in the West Country and his chapter introductions are packed with interesting information and stories whilst his golf course reviews are not only wonderfully descriptive but are spiced with witty (and sometimes acerbic!) remarks and anecdotes. He describes Mullion for instance as "intriguing, inviting, uplifting, cheeky, tricky and downright awkward in places" and at St Enedoc "anyone breaking 80 here has been smiled on by the golfing Gods!" Of Teignmouth he remarks "standing on the first tee high above the valley with the River Teign running through it and with the sea way below to the other side, you might think that Augusta isn't that special after all." We are sure therefore, that you will enjoy reading *The Golfers Guide to the West Country* but with the wide variety of wonderful courses and magnificent scenery on offer in this region you will want to visit Cornwall, Devon, Somerset and Dorset time and time again!

We are always interested to receive readers' comments on the contents of the book, on the golf courses covered (or not covered) and of course on the places to stay, eat and drink. This will help us refine and improve the future editions. Equally, if you wish to explore further the golfing opportunities or wide variety of countryside and many places of interest throughout the British Isles you may wish to read one of our other guides details of which can be found on the facing page or on our website www.travelpublishing.co.uk

Enjoy your golf!

Travel Publishing

Location Map of the West Country

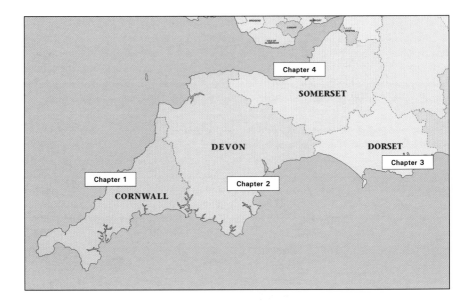

Contents

SECTION I: GOLF COURSE INFORMATION

SECTION II: ACCOMMODATION, FOOD AND DRINK

How to Use

The Golfers Guide to the West Country has been specifically designed as an easy-to-use guide so there is no need for complicated instructions. However the reader may find the following guidelines helpful in planning the perfect golfing holiday.

CHOOSING WHERE TO PLAY GOLF IN THE WEST COUNTRY

The golfing information for each county may be found as "chapters" in Section I of the guide. Use the *Contents Page* to find the area of your choice. Each "chapter" contains a review of golf in the county, useful information for players on each golf club and detailed reviews of selected courses. Use this information to decide where to play. Whether you are individuals or a society we do recommend that you contact the Golf Club in advance to avoid disappointment. The telephone number, fax number and e-mail address (where available) may be found under each golf club listing.

GOLFING ITINERARIES

If you wish to experience the varied terrains (links, parkland or heathland) on offer in the West Country without travelling long distances during your golfing holiday you should refer to the list of recommended golfing itineraries prepared by Kevin Lee. This can be found on the next page.

CHOOSING WHERE TO STAY, EAT AND DRINK

When you have decided on the golf courses you wish to play simply refer to the list of places to stay, eat and drink found after each golf course. Use the *red reference number* beside each listed entry to find more information (including a photograph) on the places of your choice in Section II of the guide. The telephone number, fax number and e-mail address (where available) are listed for each place should you wish to make a booking

INTERNATIONAL CALLING

Please note that callers from outside the United Kingdom should first dial the country code (00 44) followed by the number shown in the guide with the leading zero dropped.

LOCAL CURRENCY

All prices quoted in the guide are in *Pounds Sterling*.

Golfing Itineraries

For those golfers who want to enjoy a variety of golfing experiences in the West Country (links, parkland, heathland for example) during their visit without travelling the length and breadth of the region, Kevin Lee recommends you select a group from the following combination of courses:

CORNWALL

- China Fleet, St Mellion, Looe, Trethorne.
- St Enodoc, Bowood Park, Roserrow, Lanhydrock, Trevose.
- Newquay, Truro, Tehidy Park, Perranporth.
- Falmouth, Mullion, West Cornwall, Cape Cornwall.
- Carlyon Bay, Lostwithiel, Porthpean.

DEVON

- Ilfracombe, Saunton, Libbaton, Royal North Devon.
- Tiverton, Honiton, Axe Cliff, Sidmouth.
- Woodbury Park, Warren, Teignmouth, Teign Valley, Dartmouth.
- Okehampton, Manor House, Tavistock, Newton Abbot.
- Bigbury, Thurlestone, Staddon Heights, Yelverton, Wrangaton, Tavistock.

DORSET

- Bournemouth & Meyrick, Bournemouth Queen's Park, Crane Valley, Femdown.
- Broadstone, Canford Magna, Dudsbury, Parkstone, Ashley Wood.
- Wareham, Isle of Purbeck, East Dorset, Weymouth, Came Down.
- Bridport & West Dorset, Chedington Court, Lyme Regis.

SOMERSET

- Burnham & Berrow, Enmore Park, Minehead & West Somerset, Wells, Farrington.
- Clevedon, Weston-super-Mare, Mendip Spring, Worlebury, Tall Pines.
- Orchardleigh, Bath Sham Castle, The Mendip, Lansdown, Saltford.
- Oake Manor, Taunton& Pickeridge, Taunton Vale, Long Sutton, Windwhistle.·

Kevin Lee

We do hope you enjoy playing at these golf clubs but please do not hesitate to send us your own recommendations on the ideal combination of courses to play. We look forward to hearing from you!

Travel Publishing

CORNWALL

To cross the Tamar heading westwards is to cross a divide far wider than the swirling waters below, for it brings with it the distinct feeling that you have left England behind and entered a different land; that you have passed through some magical mist and found yourself in the pages of fantasy literature. The Tolkienesque place names such as Lostwithiel, Lanhydrock and Lanteglos seem to have come straight from the land of hobbits, dwarfs and orcs, while surely only a comic genius could have christened Portwrinkle, Mousehole, Goonhilly Downs and Twelveheads. But then, this is Cornwall, a land of diver-

sity and surprises, where not only history and legends have captured the imaginations of writers down the ages, but where even the golf courses have inspired poetic works from literary giants.

The county is a magnet for holidaymakers - grockles or emmets, they call them in these parts - because of that diversity, with Atlantic rollers crashing into the north coast, the far less torrid English Channel lapping the south, and the effects of the warming Gulf Stream creating a climate far milder than one would dare to expect on such an exposed peninsula. And sat in the middle

Golitha Falls, Bodmin Moor

is the brooding presence of Bodmin Moor, around 80 square miles of bleak and exposed upland which is peppered with prehistoric sites such as the Fernacre Stone Circle, dating back to the Bronze Age, and the Neolithic henge of Stripple Stones, not to mention the highest point in the county, the 1,377-foot hill called, believe it or not, "Brown Willy".

The northern outpost of the county is Bude, a pleasant little resort with a huge beach, and a seaside links course virtually in the town centre. The resort makes a good base for exploring the north Cornwall coast, with the picturesque harbour of Boscastle worth visiting, and, a few miles further south, Tintagel, with its ruined castle on Tintagel Head, which is said by many to be the

birthplace of King Arthur and/or the site of the legendary Camelot. But, again, this is Cornwall, so pick a legend you fancy believing in and go with it. The rest of the towns in the eastern part of the county sit around the edges of Bodmin Moor. To the north east is Launceston, the old regional capital with a crumbling castle built by William The Conqueror's half-brother, and to the south east is the market town of Liskeard, once one of Cornwall's five Stannery towns, which were licensed to weigh and stamp the tin mined in vast quantities throughout the county.

Boscastle Harbour

Padstow Village

Further west is the old county town of Bodmin, home to 11 holy wells, some allegedly with restorative powers, where the old jail has been converted into a hotel and whose dungeons now form one of the town's several interesting museums. Another unusual museum is to be found at nearby Wadebridge - the John Betjeman Centre. The former Poet Laureate is buried a couple of miles away at Rock, in a church yard next to the **St Enodoc** golf course, where a three at one hole moved him to verse - whether it was a par or a birdie is not, alas, recorded. The Camel estuary separates St Enodoc from Padstow, a lively little old harbour town put in the spotlight in recent times with the opening of TV chef Rick Stein's restaurant and cookery school. Golfing grockles might also like to have a look at the course at St Minver, called **Roserrow**, which opened in 1997 and offers nearly 7,000 yards of parkland track.

From Padstow and on down to Land's End, the rugged coastline is famous for its surfing, with Newquay the epicentre for the wave riders, who often appear to come perilously close to the resort's golf course, which runs just behind the beach. Once you get beyond the busy little resort of St Ives, you may be running out of land but you haven't quite run out of golf courses, for at St Just is **Cape Cornwall**, only a handful of miles from Land's End. Across the promontory from Land's End stands the aforementioned Mousehole (don't pronounce it like that, though. It's more Mou'zul) at the western end of the Cornish Riviera, where tiny fishing harbours nestle in natural coves, and where every village seems to have its own story of pirates and smugglers.

Across Mount's Bay is the oldest charter town in Cornwall, Marazion, once the most important trading centre in the area, and which overlooks one of the most unusual places in this sceptered isle, St Michael's Mount, now owned by the National Trust. This odd rocky outcrop, which is connected to the shore by a causeway visible at low tide, was so named when fishermen in the 8th Century saw a vision of St Michael on it.

The ancient port and market town of Penzance pays homage to its maritime heritage with a museum of artefacts from shipwrecks around the Cornish coast, and also boasts the birthplace of Marie Branwell, mother of the Bronte sisters, while both Helston and Falmouth also have fascinating museums.

At Helston, home of the Floral Dance of Terry Wogan's vocal infamy, the Folk Museum pays tribute to local man Henry Trengrouse, who developed the rocket-propelled safety line, while at Falmouth, the Cornwall Maritime Museum is housed in the **St Denys**, an old steam tug which is the centrepiece of the conservation area around the Custom House Quay. It is at Falmouth that seven river estuaries merge to form the Carrick Roads, a deep water anchorage thought so important by Henry VIII that he built a pair of fortresses either side of the har-

Mousehole Harbour

St Michael's Mount

bour mouth to protect it from attack. Much of Falmouth's rise as the main seaport in this area was down to Truro's decline as one, as the estuary that had served it well began to silt up. Today, Truro is the administrative centre of the county but evidence of its former glory, as a port still remains, not least in the number of quaint and narrow alleys, one with the splendid name of "Squeezeguts Alley".

The excellent plant-growing climate of this part of south Cornwall is reflected in the number of large gardens that can be visited. Trelissick Gardens, north of St Mawes, was recently joined by the Lost Gardens of Heligan, an enormous restoration project that now draws even more tourists to the area south of St Austell. Here, too, is the fishing port of Mevagissey, which relies more now on holidaymakers than fish, but which still retains its original charm. Another "gardening" project, but this one with a difference, is the Eden Project, where the differing climatic regions of the world have been recreated under massive domes. The project cost the best part of £75 million and is likely to become the county's biggest single tourist attraction once word gets around.

This whistle-stop tour of Cornwall began with a literary connection, and it ends with one. To the south east of the bustling old harbour town of Fowey lies the former home of novelist Daphne du Maurier, who used the area for the setting of her book Rebecca, although she renamed the towns Manderley for her purposes.

Lost Gardens of Heligan

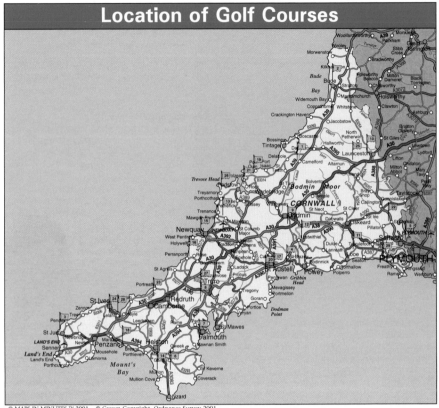

Location of Golf Courses

© MAPS IN MINUTES ™ 2001   © Crown Copyright, Ordnance Survey 2001

Bowood Park Golf Club

Valley Truckle, Lanteglos, Camelford,
Cornwall PL32 9RT

Tel: 01840 213017 Fax: 01840 212622

This Cornish course should not be confused with the European Challenge Tour venue of Bowood in Wiltshire, although those who have played both will not have failed to notice the great similarities in the countryside that graces each track. Lovers of Cornwall's golf courses will understand if I say that Bowood doesn't *feel* like a Cornish course - much like parts of Carlyon Bay - because there is a general absence of ruggedness, of that rough-and-readiness that one would associate with the county.

Perhaps that is not surprising when you consider that the course is set in hundreds of acres of what was once the largest deer park in Cornwall, with the front nine set around rolling hills while the back nine meanders through the valley of the River Allen.

On numerous holes you can shut your eyes and imagine a mounted medieval hunting party chasing some hapless stag through this very same countryside, possibly even King Arthur himself, given the proximity of Tintagel.

Difficult, at times, to appreciate that the course is not quite yet a teenager, although it can be as awkward as one, playing at a maximum of almost 6,700 yards and with obstacles that include not only the mature trees and natural water hazards, but also the wildlife that abounds in the valley.

It is certainly not a course to be missed, and one, which regularly crops up in the golfing trade press as a consistently high scorer for its all-round ambience and charm.

Sec/Manager:	Ian Young
Professional:	None
Directions:	¾ mile south of Camelford From the centre take the A39 (Helston). The entrance is after ¾ mile close to Shell Service Station.
Date Founded:	1992
Type of Course:	Parkland
No of Holes:	18
Length:	6692 yds (6177 mtrs)
Par:	72
SSS:	72
Green Fees:	Weekdays: £25; Weekends/ Bank Holidays: £25
Visitors:	Welcome: Advisable to ring in Advance. Unable to play Sunday mornings to 11.00 am
Societies:	Welcome: Contact Club in Advance. Unable to play Sunday mornings to 11.00 am
Facilities:	Putting Green, Chipping Green, Driving Range, Club Hire, Trolley Hire, Buggy Hire, Bar, Restaurant, Private Rooms

Accommodation, Food and Drink

Reference numbers below refer to detailed information provided in section 2

Accommodation

Bennetts Court Cottages, Whitstone, Holsworthy, Devon EX22 6UD

Tel: 01288 341370 Fax: 01288 341370
e-mail: helen@ bennettscourt.co.uk
website: www.bennettscourt.co.uk
Five, well-equipped self-catering cottages, converted from former farm buildings, sleeping between two and six people. Within the grounds there is a outdoor heated pool and other facilities.   246

The Camelot Hotel and Hawkers Restaurant, Downs View, Bude, Cornwall EX23 8RE

Tel: 01288 352361 Fax: 01288 355470
e-mail: stay@camelot-hotel.co.uk
website: www.camelot-hotel.co.uk
Super location on the edge of Bude Golf Course and five minutes from sea. High standards throughout, with relaxed comfortable ambience. 24 en-suite rooms. Popular restaurant.   106

Mayrose Farm Holiday Cottages, Helstone, Camelford, Cornwall PL32 9RN

Tel: 01840 213509 Fax: 01840 213509
e-mail: mayrosefarm@hotmail.com
Five, very different properties converted from former

farm buildings, decorated and furnished to a very high standard. Outdoor pool. Super holiday base. 105

Trethin Manor Holiday Cottages, Advent, Camelford, Cornwall PL32 9QW

Tel: 01840 213522 Fax: 01840 212898
A collection of former farm buildings which have been converted into comfortable self-catering accommodation. Ten cottages surrounded by landscaped grounds. Children's play area, barbecue, laundry. 120

The Wilsey Down, Hallworthy, Camelford, Cornwall PL32 9SH

Tel: 01840 261205
e-mail: jane@greatbidlake.farmcom.net
Comfortable, welcoming establishment with two bars and separate restaurant. Six guest rooms, 2 of which are en-suite, of varying sizes. 104

Food and Drink

The Brendon Arms, Vicarage Road, Bude, Cornwall EX23 8SD

Tel: 01288 354542 Fax: 01288 354542
e-mail: sophia@sophiafrbrendon.demon.co.uk
website: www.north-cornwall.co.uk/client/brendon-arms/
Traditional Cornish inn situated in a picturesque part of town. Serves a good selection of seafood while the bar stocks a range of real ales. Seven en-suite guest rooms. 109

Bude Haven Hotel, Flexbury Avenue, Bude, Cornwall EX23 8NS

Tel: 01288 352305 Fax: 01288 352305
e-mail: enquiries@budehavenhotel.co.uk
website: www.budehavenhotel.co.uk
Attractive Georgian building offering a comfortable, relaxed atmosphere. Eleven individually furnished en-suite bedrooms of varying sizes. Super residents' restaurant. 127

The Camelot Hotel and Hawkers Restaurant, Downs View, Bude, Cornwall EX23 8RE

Tel: 01288 352361 Fax: 01288 355470
e-mail: stay@camelot-hotel.co.uk
website: www.camelot-hotel.co.uk
Super location on the edge of Bude Golf Course and five minutes from sea. High standards throughout, with relaxed comfortable ambience. 24 en-suite rooms. Popular restaurant. 106

Inn on the Green, Crooklets Beach, Bude, Cornwall EX23 8NF

Tel: 01288 356013 Fax: 01288 356244
e-mail: innonthegreen46@btinternet.com
website: www.innonthegreen46.co.uk
Family-run Victorian hotel offering comfort, service and value for money. Fine restaurant serves wholesome food with bar open all day. 107

The Wilsey Down, Hallworthy, Camelford, Cornwall PL32 9SH

Tel: 01840 261205
e-mail: jane@greatbidlake.farmcom.net
Comfortable, welcoming establishment with two bars

and separate restaurant. Six guest rooms, 2 of which are en-suite, of varying sizes. 104

Bude and North Cornwall Golf Club

Burn View, Burn View, Bude, Cornwall EX23 8DA
Tel: 01288 352006 Fax: 01288 356855

Sec/Manager:	Pauline Ralph
Professional:	John Yeo
Directions:	300 yds north of the centre of Bude. The entrance is on Golf Course Road (road to Flexbury)
Date Founded:	1891
Type of Course:	Links
No of Holes:	18
Length:	6057 yds (5591 mtrs)
Par:	71
SSS:	70
Green Fees:	Weekdays: £25; Weekends/ Bank Holidays: £30
Visitors:	Welcome: Tee times bookable. Contact Club in Advance. Limited time weekends
Societies:	Welcome: Book in Advance. Limited time weekends
Facilities:	Putting Green, Driving Range, Trolley Hire, Bar, Restaurant

Accommodation, Food and Drink

Reference numbers below refer to detailed information provided in section 2

Accommodation

Bennetts Court Cottages, Whitstone, Holsworthy, Devon EX22 6UD

Tel: 01288 341370 Fax: 01288 341370
e-mail: helen@ bennettscourt.co.uk

website: www.bennettscourt.co.uk
Five, well-equipped self-catering cottages, converted from former farm buildings, sleeping between two and six people. Within the grounds there is a outdoor heated pool and other facilities. 246

The Brendon Arms, Vicarage Road, Bude, Cornwall EX23 8SD

Tel: 01288 354542 Fax: 01288 354542
e-mail: sophia@sophiafrbrendon.demon.co.uk
website: www.north-cornwall.co.uk/client/
brendon-arms/
Traditional Cornish inn situated in a picturesque part of town. Serves a good selection of seafood while the bar stocks a range of real ales. Seven en-suite guest rooms. 109

Bude Haven Hotel, Flexbury Avenue, Bude, Cornwall EX23 8NS

Tel: 01288 352305 Fax: 01288 352305
e-mail: enquiries@budehavenhotel.co.uk
website: www.budehavenhotel.co.uk
Attractive Georgian building offering a comfortable, relaxed atmosphere. Eleven individually furnished en-suite bedrooms of varying sizes. Super residents' restaurant. 127

The Camelot Hotel and Hawkers Restaurant, Downs View, Bude, Cornwall EX23 8RE

Tel: 01288 352361 Fax: 01288 355470
e-mail: stay@camelot-hotel.co.uk
website: www.camelot-hotel.co.uk
Super location on the edge of Bude Golf Course and five minutes from sea. High standards throughout, with relaxed comfortable ambience. 24 en-suite rooms. Popular restaurant. 106

Inn on the Green, Crooklets Beach, Bude, Cornwall EX23 8NF

Tel: 01288 356013 Fax: 01288 356244
e-mail: innonthegreen46@btinternet.com
website: www.innonthegreen46.co.uk
Family-run Victorian hotel offering comfort, service and value for money. Fine restaurant serves wholesome food with bar open all day. 107

Links Side, 7 Burn View, Bude, Cornwall EX23 8BY

Tel: 01288 352410
Small, cosy bed and breakfast with warm, friendly atmosphere. Rooms of varying sizes, most with en-suite facilities. 108

Wyvern House, 7 Downs View, Bude, Cornwall EX23 8RF

Tel: 01288 352205 Fax: 01288 356802
e-mail: eileen@wyvernhouse.co.uk
website: www.wyvernhouse.co.uk
Attractive house in pleasant situation just five minutes from the beach. Six guest rooms, some with en-suite facilities. Evening meals available. 114

Food and Drink

The Brendon Arms, Vicarage Road, Bude, Cornwall EX23 8SD

Tel: 01288 354542 Fax: 01288 354542

e-mail: sophia@sophiafrbrendon.demon.co.uk
website: www.north-cornwall.co.uk/client/
brendon-arms/
Traditional Cornish inn situated in a picturesque part of town. Serves a good selection of seafood while the bar stocks a range of real ales. Seven en-suite guest rooms. 109

Bude Haven Hotel, Flexbury Avenue, Bude, Cornwall EX23 8NS

Tel: 01288 352305 Fax: 01288 352305
e-mail: enquiries@budehavenhotel.co.uk
website: www.budehavenhotel.co.uk
Attractive Georgian building offering a comfortable, relaxed atmosphere. Eleven individually furnished en-suite bedrooms of varying sizes. Super residents' restaurant. 127

The Camelot Hotel and Hawkers Restaurant, Downs View, Bude, Cornwall EX23 8RE

Tel: 01288 352361 Fax: 01288 355470
e-mail: stay@camelot-hotel.co.uk
website: www.camelot-hotel.co.uk
Super location on the edge of Bude Golf Course and five minutes from sea. High standards throughout, with relaxed comfortable ambience. 24 en-suite rooms. Popular restaurant. 106

Inn on the Green, Crooklets Beach, Bude, Cornwall EX23 8NF

Tel: 01288 356013 Fax: 01288 356244
e-mail: innonthegreen46@btinternet.com
website: www.innonthegreen46.co.uk
Family-run Victorian hotel offering comfort, service and value for money. Fine restaurant serves wholesome food with bar open all day. 107

Cape Cornwall Golf Club

St. Just, Penzance, Cornwall TR19 7NL
Tel: 01736 788611 Fax: 01736 788611

Sec/Manager:	Tina Payne
Professional:	Mr. Atherton
Directions:	9 miles west of Penzance. From centre take St. Just Rd (A3071), then B road (Cape Cornwall). The entrance is on the left about 1 mile west of St. Just.

Date Founded: 1990
Type of Course: Coastal Links
No of Holes: 18
Length: 5632 yds (5198 mtrs)
Par: 69
SSS: 68
Green Fees: Weekdays: £20; Weekends/ Bank Holidays: £20
Visitors: Welcome: Contact Club in Advance. Unable to play weekend mornings.
Societies: Welcome: Contact Club in Advance. Unable to play weekends
Facilities: Practice Area, Putting Green, Chipping Green, Driving Range, Club Hire, Trolley Hire, Buggy Hire, Bar, Restaurant and Accommodation

Accommodation, Food and Drink

Reference numbers below refer to detailed information provided in section 2

Accommodation

Chy-Garth Guest House, Sea View Meadows, St. Ives Road, Carbis Bay, St. Ives, Cornwall TR26 2JX

Tel: 01736 795677
e-mail: ann@chy-garth.demon.co.uk
A delightful, detached house surrounded by colourful gardens and enjoying some beautiful sea views. A non-smoking establishment, there are eight guest rooms, nearly all with en-suite or private facilities. Ample car parking.

Dunmar Hotel, Pednolver Terrace, St. Ives, Cornwall TR26 2EL

Tel: 01736 796117 Fax: 01736 796053
Friendly, family-run 'olde worlde' hotel offering a warm welcome and traditional Cornish hospitality. 17 en-suite bedrooms of varying sizes with bar and restaurant available to guests.

Meudon Hotel, Mawnan Smith, Near Falmouth, Cornwall TR11 5HT

Tel: 01326 250541 Fax: 01326 250543
website: www.meudon.co.uk
Superb, family-run country house hotel, set in a sub-tropical garden paradise with private beach. Elegant restaurant specialising in local seafood. Free golf included in high- and mid-season rates.   119

Regent Hotel, Fern Lea Terrace, St. Ives, Cornwall TR26 2BH

Tel: 01736 796195 Fax: 01736 794641
e-mail: enquiries@regenthotel.com
website: www.regenthotel.com
Friendly, family-run hotel with AA and RAC 4 Diamond Grading. The nine en-suite guest bedrooms are tastefully decorated and comfortably furnished and many have spectacular views over the picturesque harbour.

Food and Drink

The Brookdale Hotel, Tregolls Road, Truro, Cornwall TR1 1JZ

Tel: 01872 273513 Fax: 01872 272400
e-mail: brookdale@hotelstruro.com
website: www.hotelstruro.com/brookdale
Good sized hotel set in its own beautifully landscaped grounds. Popular Italian Ristorante open Monday to Saturday. Comfortable, elegantly furnished en-suite rooms of varying types.   113

Meudon Hotel, Mawnan Smith, Near Falmouth, Cornwall TR11 5HT

Tel: 01326 250541 Fax: 01326 250543
website: www.meudon.co.uk
Superb, family-run country house hotel, set in a sub-tropical garden paradise with private beach. Elegant restaurant specialising in local seafood. Free golf included in high- and mid-season rates.   119

Carolyn Bay Golf Club

Carolyn Bay, St. Austell, Cornwall PL25 3RD
Tel: 01726 814250/812304 Fax: 01726 814250

It is perhaps no coincidence that the awesome Eden Project, where the world's differing climates are recreated under enormous domes and the relevant plant life allowed to thrive, is no more than a couple of miles away from a golf course which,

in parts, seems itself to have copied parts of the Garden of Eden. This championship-length course - just short of 6,600 yards - has such lush fairways and manicured greens, surrounded by an abundance of vegetation, that it is more reminiscent of the Carolinas than Cornwall.

But that is only half the story of this unusual course, for it starts off as a clifftop track with magnificent views of the rugged coastline before cloaking its fangs in some luxurious foliage. It is a dramatic change around the turn, when suddenly the wide-open spaces vanish and accuracy becomes the name of the game through the tree- and vegetation-lined back nine. Designer Hamilton Stutt must have been mischievously smug about this one back in the 1920s.

It's another one of those Cornish devils that holds your interest right up to the 18th green, with the last hole, a par three 230-yarder, offering a railway line and a road as out-of-bounds.

This being a hotel course, visitors will find the green fees substantially cheaper in the low season than in the middle of summer, although you might miss the naturists who apparently use one of the beaches overlooked by the course - just one of the many worthwhile views!

Sec/Manager:	Yvonne Lister
Professional:	Mark Rowe
Directions:	1½ miles southeast of St. Austell. From the A390 take Crinnis Road, then Sea Road (Carolyn Bay). The entrance is on the right hand side at Carolyn Bay Hotel.
Date Founded:	1926
Type of Course:	Coastal Clifftop
No of Holes:	18
Length:	6597 yds (6089 mtrs)
Par:	72
SSS:	71
Green Fees:	Weekdays: £35 (summer) £25-£28 (winter); Weekends/Bank Holidays: £35 (summer) £25-£28 (winter)
Visitors:	Welcome: Contact Club in Advance, Handicap Certificate required
Societies:	Welcome: Contact Club in Advance. Unable to play Saturdays
Facilities:	Putting Green, Chipping Green, Driving Range, Club Hire, Trolley Hire, Buggy Hire, Bar, Restaurant

Accommodation, Food and Drink

Reference numbers below refer to detailed information provided in section 2

Accommodation

The Brookdale Hotel, Tregolls Road, Truro, Cornwall TR1 1JZ

Tel: 01872 273513 Fax: 01872 272400
e-mail: brookdale@hotelstruro.com
website: www.hotelstruro.com/brookdale
Good sized hotel set in its own beautifully landscaped grounds. Popular Italian Ristorante open Monday to Saturday. Comfortable, elegantly furnished en-suite rooms of varying types.   113

Fieldhead Hotel, Portuan Road, Hannafore, West Looe, Cornwall PL13 2DR

Tel: 01503 262689 Fax: 01503 264114
e-mail: field.head@virgin.net
website: www.fieldheadhotel.co.uk
Elegant country house style hotel offering high standard of comfort and service. Comfortable en-suite rooms, many with sea views.   115

Marcorrie Hotel, 20 Falmouth Road, Truro, Cornwall TR1 2HX

Tel: 01872 277374 Fax: 01872 241666
e-mail: marcorrie@aol.com
website: www.cornwall.net/marcorrie
Small, charming family-run hotel on a delightful Victorian and Edwardian street near to the city centre, offering traditional Cornish hospitality.   103

Ruthern Valley Holidays, Ruthern Bridge, Nr. Bodmin, Cornwall PL30 5LU

Tel: 01208 831395 Fax: 01208 832324
website: self-catering-ruthern.co.uk
Peaceful, relaxing holiday retreat developed from former mining area. Range of holiday accommodation with bungalows, lodges, caravans and camping facilities. Well-stocked shop and children's play area.   101

Food and Drink

The Brookdale Hotel, Tregolls Road, Truro, Cornwall TR1 1JZ

Tel: 01872 273513 Fax: 01872 272400
e-mail: brookdale@hotelstruro.com
website: www.hotelstruro.com/brookdale
Good sized hotel set in its own beautifully landscaped grounds. Popular Italian Ristorante open Monday to Saturday. Comfortable, elegantly furnished en-suite rooms of varying types.   113

The Globe Inn, 3 North Street, Lostwithiel, Cornwall PL22 0EG

Tel: 01208 872501
Cosy, friendly, traditional inn offering a warm welcome to all. Open plan bar, restaurant area, patio and beer garden. Good menu of tasty home-cooked, freshly-prepared food.   102

The Sundeck, East Quay, Mevagissy, Cornwall PL26 6QQ

Tel: 01726 843051
A surprising find. Stylish decor in Mediterranean theme with picture windows looking out to sea. High quality home-cooked food.   112

Three Pilchards, The Quay, Polperro, Looe, Cornwall PL13 2QZ

Tel: 01503 272233
Traditional Cornish pub located on the sea front. Home-cooked food served each day.   116

Trewithen Restaurant, 3 Fore Street, Lostwithiel, Cornwall PL22 0BP

Tel: 01208 872373
Award-winning restaurant with cosy, cottagey style in the heart of the pretty town of Lostwithiel. Traditional, English cuisine.   110

China Fleet
Golf Club

Saltash, Cornwall PL12 6LJ

Tel: 01752 848668 Fax: 01752 848456

There is something about a famous and majestic river that lifts the heart - it must be a primeval feeling buried deep in the human psyche - and that is precisely what happens here on the banks of the River Tamar estuary.

This splendid course set in the grounds of the country club of the same name, stands no more than a mile from the Tamar Bridge separating Saltash from Plymouth, and Cornwall from Devon. And although the Martin Hawtree-designed parkland track was opened only a decade ago, its maturity belies that youthfulness.

It is getting a bit longish, at 6,500 yards, although because of the surroundings, it doesn't seem to play that distance - at least not until you look at your scorecard.

The opening par-four first takes you downwards the water, then the estuary accompanies you up the par-five second, also providing unexpected little creeks that creep across the course at various points.

Elevated tees, shots over trees and awkward greens cut into slopes are a feature of the front nine, while water is the obstacle on the back nine in the form of two lakes, which are the centre of a triangle created by holes 14, 15 and 16.

The 14th will test your nerve with a carry of about 150 yards over the lake from tee to fairway, while anyone with anything approaching a habitual hook will be in deep trouble - and deep water - on the 16th.

Sec/Manager:	David Sullivan
Professional:	Nick Cook

Directions:	2¾ miles northwest of Plymouth Hoe. From the centre take the A38 (Cornwall). From the west side of the Tamar Bridge take North Road (Old A38) for ½ mile, then turn right and follow signs to China Fleet Club. The entrance is after 600 yds.
Date Founded:	1991
Type of Course:	Parkland
No of Holes:	18
Length:	6551 yds (6046 mtrs)
Par:	72
SSS:	72
Green Fees:	Weekdays: £25; Weekends/ Bank Holidays: £30
Visitors:	Welcome: Contact Club in Advance. No restrictions
Societies:	Welcome: Contact Club in Advance. Unable to play weekends
Facilities:	Putting Green, Driving Range, Club Hire, Trolley Hire, Buggy Hire, Bar, Restaurant, Private Rooms

Accommodation, Food and Drink

Reference numbers below refer to detailed information provided in section 2

Accommodation

The Carpenters Arms, Metherell, Nr. Callington, Cornwall PL17 8BJ

Tel: 01579 350242 Fax: 01579 350242
A picturesque Cornish pub with friendly and welcoming service. Wide-ranging menu of home-cooked bar meals and snacks.   117

Cawsand Bay Hotel & Galleon Restaurant, The Bound, Cawsand, Nr. Torpoint, Cornwall PL10 1PG

Tel: 01752 822425 Fax: 01752 823527
e-mail: sales@cawsandbay.co.uk
website: www.cawsandbay.co.uk
Located directly on the sea front and with superb views across the Sound towards Plymouth. Ten

comfortable en-suite rooms of varying sizes. Popular bar and restaurant. 130

The Halfway House Inn, Grenofen, Tavistock, Devon PL19 9ER

Tel: 01822 612960 Fax: 01822 617697
A large, sprawling black and white 16th-century building with friendly atmosphere. Excellent reputation for high quality food with two restaurants serving an a la carte menu. Four guest rooms. 206

The Laurels, Huckworthy Bridge, Yelverton, Devon PL20 6LP

Tel: 01822 853622
Charming old cottage in riverside setting, recently restored and converted into a self-catering cottage and private home, in which bed and breakfast is available. Ideal holiday base. 239

Tavistock Arms, Fore Street, Gunnislake, Cornwall PL18 9BN

Tel: 01822 832217
Traditional, country pub located directly on the Devon/Cornwall border. Food is served all day. Bed and breakfast accommodation available. 118

Food and Drink

The Carpenters Arms, Metherell, Nr. Callington, Cornwall PL17 8BJ

Tel: 01579 350242 Fax: 01579 350242
A picturesque Cornish pub with friendly and welcoming service. Wide-ranging menu of home-cooked bar meals and snacks. 117

Cawsand Bay Hotel & Galleon Restaurant, The Bound, Cawsand, Nr. Torpoint, Cornwall PL10 1PG

Tel: 01752 822425 Fax: 01752 823527
e-mail: sales@cawsandbay.co.uk
website: www.cawsandbay.co.uk
Located directly on the sea front and with superb views across the Sound towards Plymouth. Ten comfortable en-suite rooms of varying sizes. Popular bar and restaurant. 130

The Halfway House Inn, Grenofen, Tavistock, Devon PL19 9ER

Tel: 01822 612960 Fax: 01822 617697
A large, sprawling black and white 16th-century building with friendly atmosphere. Excellent reputation for high quality food with two restaurants serving an a la carte menu. Four guest rooms. 206

Tavistock Arms, Fore Street, Gunnislake, Cornwall PL18 9BN

Tel: 01822 832217
Traditional, country pub located directly on the Devon/Cornwall border. Food is served all day. Bed and breakfast accommodation available. 118

The Walkhampton Inn, Walkhampton, Nr. Yelverton, Devon PL20 6JY

Tel: 01822 855556 Fax: 01822 855556
e-mail: info@walkhamptoninn.co.uk
Historic establishment, popular in the area for serving a good range of beer and traditional pub fayre. Two

guest rooms both of which are en-suite. 238

Culdrose Golf Club

Royal Naval Air Station, Culdrose,
Cornwall TR12 8QY
Tel: 01326 574121 extn. 2413

Sec/Manager:	VC Williams
Professional:	none
Directions:	2½ miles south of Helston on the Lizard road.(A3083)
Date Founded:	1962
Type of Course:	Parkland, Heathland
No of Holes:	11 (18 tees)
Length:	6432 yds (5936 mtrs)
Par:	72
SSS:	71
Green Fees:	Weekdays: Contact Club in Advance. for fees and restrictions; Weekends/Bank Holidays: Contact Club in Advance. for fees and restrictions
Visitors:	Play restricted to weekends and evenings Contact Secretary
Societies:	Contact Club Secretary.
Facilities:	Putting Green, Chipping Green, Trolley Hire, Bar, Restaurant

Accommodation, Food and Drink

Reference numbers below refer to detailed information provided in section 2

Accommodation

The Brookdale Hotel, Tregolls Road, Truro, Cornwall TR1 1JZ

Tel: 01872 273513 Fax: 01872 272400
e-mail: brookdale@hotelstruro.com
website: www.hotelstruro.com/brookdale
Good sized hotel set in its own beautifully landscaped grounds. Popular Italian Ristorante open Monday to Saturday. Comfortable, elegantly furnished en-suite rooms of varying types. 113

Chy-Garth Guest House, Sea View Meadows, St. Ives Road, Carbis Bay, St. Ives, Cornwall TR26 2JX

Tel: 01736 795677
e-mail: ann@chy-garth.demon.co.uk
A delightful, detached house surrounded by colourful gardens and enjoying some beautiful sea views. A non-smoking establishment, there are eight guest rooms, nearly all with en-suite or private facilities. Ample car parking.

Dunmar Hotel, Pednolver Terrace, St. Ives, Cornwall TR26 2EL

Tel: 01736 796117 Fax: 01736 796053
Friendly, family-run 'olde worlde' hotel offering a warm welcome and traditional Cornish hospitality. 17 en-suite bedrooms of varying sizes with bar and restaurant available to guests.

Marcorrie Hotel, 20 Falmouth Road, Truro, Cornwall TR1 2HX

Tel: 01872 277374 Fax: 01872 241666
e-mail: marcorrie@aol.com
website: www.cornwall.net/marcorrie
Small, charming family-run hotel on a delightful Victorian and Edwardian street near to the city centre, offering traditional Cornish hospitality.   103

Meudon Hotel, Mawnan Smith, Near Falmouth, Cornwall TR11 5HT

Tel: 01326 250541 Fax: 01326 250543
website: www.meudon.co.uk
Superb, family-run country house hotel, set in a sub-tropical garden paradise with private beach. Elegant restaurant specialising in local seafood. Free golf included in high- and mid-season rates.   119

Regent Hotel, Fern Lea Terrace, St. Ives, Cornwall TR26 2BH

Tel: 01736 796195 Fax: 01736 794641
e-mail: enquiries@regenthotel.com
website: www.regenthotel.com
Friendly, family-run hotel with AA and RAC 4 Diamond Grading. The nine en-suite guest bedrooms are tastefully decorated and comfortably furnished and many have spectacular views over the picturesque harbour.

White House Court Holiday Cottages, c/o 1 Middle Leigh, Newton Ferrers, Plymouth, Devon PL8 1DS

Tel: 01752 873128 Fax: 01752 873128
e-mail: whitehouse.cotts@barclay.net
website: www.whitehousecourt.co.uk
Eleven well-equipped self-catering cottages created from traditional, stone-built farm buildings. Two miles from the coast.   111

Food and Drink

The Brookdale Hotel, Tregolls Road, Truro, Cornwall TR1 1JZ

Tel: 01872 273513 Fax: 01872 272400
e-mail: brookdale@hotelstruro.com
website: www.hotelstruro.com/brookdale
Good sized hotel set in its own beautifully landscaped grounds. Popular Italian Ristorante open Monday to Saturday. Comfortable, elegantly furnished en-suite rooms of varying types.   113

Meudon Hotel, Mawnan Smith, Near Falmouth, Cornwall TR11 5HT

Tel: 01326 250541 Fax: 01326 250543
website: www.meudon.co.uk
Superb, family-run country house hotel, set in a sub-tropical garden paradise with private beach. Elegant restaurant specialising in local seafood. Free golf included in high- and mid-season rates.   119

The Sundeck, East Quay, Mevagissy, Cornwall PL26 6QQ

Tel: 01726 843051
A surprising find. Stylish decor in Mediterranean theme with picture windows looking out to sea. High quality home-cooked food.   112

Falmouth Golf Club

Swanpool Road, Falmouth, Cornwall TR11 5BQ
Tel: 01326 314296 Fax: 01326 317783

Sec/Manager:	Bob Wooldridge
Professional:	Brian Patterson
Directions:	1¼ miles south of Falmouth. From centre take Mawnan Smith Road On the outskirts take Swanpool Rd and the entrance is ½ mile west of Falmouth Bay on south side of road.
Date Founded:	1894
Type of Course:	Parkland
No of Holes:	18
Length:	5982 yds (5521 mtrs)
Par:	71
SSS:	70
Green Fees:	Weekdays: £25 (£35 for 36 holes); Weekends/Bank Holidays: £25 (£35 for 36 holes)
Visitors:	Welcome: Contact Club in Advance. No restrictions
Societies:	Welcome: Contact Club in Advance
Facilities:	Putting Green, Chipping Green, Driving Range, Club Hire, Trolley Hire, Buggy Hire, Bar, Restaurant

Accommodation, Food and Drink

Reference numbers below refer to detailed information provided in section 2

Accommodation

The Brookdale Hotel, Tregolls Road, Truro, Cornwall TR1 1JZ

Tel: 01872 273513 Fax: 01872 272400
e-mail: brookdale@hotelstruro.com
website: www.hotelstruro.com/brookdale
Good sized hotel set in its own beautifully landscaped grounds. Popular Italian Ristorante open Monday to Saturday. Comfortable, elegantly furnished en-suite rooms of varying types.   113

Chy-Garth Guest House, Sea View Meadows, St. Ives Road, Carbis Bay, St. Ives, Cornwall TR26 2JX

Tel: 01736 795677
e-mail: ann@chy-garth.demon.co.uk
A delightful, detached house surrounded by colourful gardens and enjoying some beautiful sea views. A non-smoking establishment, there are eight guest rooms, nearly all with en-suite or private facilities. Ample car parking.

Dunmar Hotel, Pednolver Terrace, St. Ives, Cornwall TR26 2EL

Tel: 01736 796117 Fax: 01736 796053
Friendly, family-run 'olde worlde' hotel offering a warm welcome and traditional Cornish hospitality. 17 en-suite bedrooms of varying sizes with bar and restaurant available to guests.

Marcorrie Hotel, 20 Falmouth Road, Truro, Cornwall TR1 2HX

Tel: 01872 277374 Fax: 01872 241666
e-mail: marcorrie@aol.com
website: www.cornwall.net/marcorrie
Small, charming family-run hotel on a delightful Victorian and Edwardian street near to the city centre, offering traditional Cornish hospitality.   103

Meudon Hotel, Mawnan Smith, Near Falmouth, Cornwall TR11 5HT

Tel: 01326 250541 Fax: 01326 250543
website: www.meudon.co.uk
Superb, family-run country house hotel, set in a sub-tropical garden paradise with private beach. Elegant restaurant specialising in local seafood. Free golf included in high- and mid-season rates.   119

Regent Hotel, Fern Lea Terrace, St. Ives, Cornwall TR26 2BH

Tel: 01736 796195 Fax: 01736 794641
e-mail: enquiries@regenthotel.com
website: www.regenthotel.com
Friendly, family-run hotel with AA and RAC 4 Diamond Grading. The nine en-suite guest bedrooms are tastefully decorated and comfortably furnished and many have spectacular views over the picturesque harbour.

White House Court Holiday Cottages, c/o 1 Middle Leigh, Newton Ferrers, Plymouth, Devon PL8 1DS

Tel: 01752 873128 Fax: 01752 873128
e-mail: whitehouse.cotts@barclay.net
website: www.whitehousecourt.co.uk
Eleven well-equipped self-catering cottages created from traditional, stone-built farm buildings. Two miles from the coast.   111

Food and Drink

The Brookdale Hotel, Tregolls Road, Truro, Cornwall TR1 1JZ

Tel: 01872 273513 Fax: 01872 272400
e-mail: brookdale@hotelstruro.com
website: www.hotelstruro.com/brookdale
Good sized hotel set in its own beautifully landscaped grounds. Popular Italian Ristorante open Monday to Saturday. Comfortable, elegantly furnished en-suite rooms of varying types.   113

Meudon Hotel, Mawnan Smith, Near Falmouth, Cornwall TR11 5HT

Tel: 01326 250541 Fax: 01326 250543
website: www.meudon.co.uk
Superb, family-run country house hotel, set in a sub-tropical garden paradise with private beach. Elegant restaurant specialising in local seafood. Free golf included in high- and mid-season rates.   119

The Sundeck, East Quay, Mevagissy, Cornwall PL26 6QQ

Tel: 01726 843051
A surprising find. Stylish decor in Mediterranean theme with picture windows looking out to sea. High quality home-cooked food.   112

Killiow Golf Club

Killiow, Kea, Truro, Cornwall TR3 6AG
Tel: 01872 240415 Fax: 01872 240415

Sec/Manager:	John Crowson
Professional:	None
Directions:	2¼ miles southwest of Truro. From centre take A38 (Helston). After 2 miles turn right at Playing Place into Chyreen Lane. After 700 yds turn right and the entrance is ½ mile on the left hand side.
Date Founded:	1987
Type of Course:	Parkland
No of Holes:	18
Length:	5274 yds (4868 mtrs)
Par:	69
SSS:	68
Green Fees:	Weekdays: £17.50 (Summer) £17.50 (Winter); Weekends/

	Bank Holidays: £15 (Summer) £15 (Winter)
Visitors:	Welcome: Contact Club in Advance
Societies:	Welcome: Contact Club in Advance
Facilities:	Putting Green, Driving Range, Club Hire, Trolley Hire, Bar, Restaurant

Accommodation, Food and Drink

Reference numbers below refer to detailed information provided in section 2

Accommodation

The Brookdale Hotel, Tregolls Road, Truro, Cornwall TR1 1JZ

Tel: 01872 273513 Fax: 01872 272400
e-mail: brookdale@hotelstruro.com
website: www.hotelstruro.com/brookdale
Good sized hotel set in its own beautifully landscaped grounds. Popular Italian Ristorante open Monday to Saturday. Comfortable, elegantly furnished en-suite rooms of varying types. 113

Hole Mill, Branscombe, Seaton, Devon EX12 3BX

Tel: 01297 680314
website: www.users.globalnet.co.uk/~branscombe/
hole1.htm
Former working watermill, located in pretty valley, converted into a charming house on many levels. Surrounded by colourful gardens. 3 guest rooms. 267

Marcorrie Hotel, 20 Falmouth Road, Truro, Cornwall TR1 2HX

Tel: 01872 277374 Fax: 01872 241666
e-mail: marcorrie@aol.com
website: www.cornwall.net/marcorrie
Small, charming family-run hotel on a delightful Victorian and Edwardian street near to the city centre, offering traditional Cornish hospitality. 103

Meudon Hotel, Mawnan Smith, Near Falmouth, Cornwall TR11 5HT

Tel: 01326 250541 Fax: 01326 250543
website: www.meudon.co.uk
Superb, family-run country house hotel, set in a sub-tropical garden paradise with private beach. Elegant restaurant specialising in local seafood. Free golf included in high- and mid-season rates. 119

White House Court Holiday Cottages, c/o 1 Middle Leigh, Newton Ferrers, Plymouth, Devon PL8 1DS

Tel: 01752 873128 Fax: 01752 873128
e-mail: whitehouse.cotts@barclay.net
website: www.whitehousecourt.co.uk
Eleven well-equipped self-catering cottages created from traditional, stone-built farm buildings. Two miles from the coast. 111

Woodlands Hotel, 38-40 Pentire Crescent, Newquay, Cornwall TR7 1PU

Tel: 01637 852229 Fax: 01637 852227
Quiet setting, just outside Newquay, with spectacular views over the river and open countryside. 54 bedrooms. Excellent facilities including outdoor pool, sauna, solarium, sunbed and bowling green. 131

Food and Drink

The Brookdale Hotel, Tregolls Road, Truro, Cornwall TR1 1JZ

Tel: 01872 273513 Fax: 01872 272400
e-mail: brookdale@hotelstruro.com
website: www.hotelstruro.com/brookdale
Good sized hotel set in its own beautifully landscaped grounds. Popular Italian Ristorante open Monday to Saturday. Comfortable, elegantly furnished en-suite rooms of varying types. 113

Meudon Hotel, Mawnan Smith, Near Falmouth, Cornwall TR11 5HT

Tel: 01326 250541 Fax: 01326 250543
website: www.meudon.co.uk
Superb, family-run country house hotel, set in a sub-tropical garden paradise with private beach. Elegant restaurant specialising in local seafood. Free golf included in high- and mid-season rates. 119

Smugglers Den Inn, Cubert, Newquay, Cornwall TR8 5PY

Tel: 01637 830209 Fax: 01637 830580
Quaint, 400-year old hostelry with a popular reputation for serving fine food and well-kept ale. Reputedly haunted! 126

The Sundeck, East Quay, Mevagissy, Cornwall PL26 6QQ

Tel: 01726 843051
A surprising find. Stylish decor in Mediterranean theme with picture windows looking out to sea. High quality home-cooked food. 112

Lanhydrock Golf Club

Lostwithiel Road, Bodmin Cornwall PL20 5AQ
Tel: 01208 73600 Fax: 01208 77325

Nestling in a delightfully-wooded valley just a mile south of Bodmin lies Lanhydrock, cunningly designed originally by Hamilton Stutt in the 1890s, and which could quite easily be the template for the phrase, 'A good walk spoiled.'

Although more than 100 years old, the course gained a new lease of life in the 1990s when it came under the auspices of the Bond family - they of St Mellion fame and of whom more later - and is as much a test of character and low cunning as it is golfing technique.

When the sun shines on what is probably, along with close neighbour Lostwithiel, one of the most charming inland courses in the county, the lush green of the fairways contrasted with the white sand of the bunkers can be breathtaking. You could be on the Algarve, in the Carolinas - it's only the trees that give the game away.

You get an early introduction to water - and there are a number of devilishly-placed ponds about - with your second to the par four first, which must clear it and not roll back into it, as this green, like several others, slopes from back to front.

Signature holes you will long remember are the sixth, a downhill par three over a lake to an elevated green; and the 12th through Tregullan Moor, whose ancient trees seem to have stepped from the pages of Tolkein's Middle Earth.

And if you are holidaying and missing the beach, fear not, a large part of it is here between the ninth and 18th greens, an awesome bunker of Hell's Half Acre proportions. Sand wedge, bucket and spade recommended!

Sec/Manager:	Graham Bond
Professional:	Jason Broadway
Directions:	1½ mile south of Bodmin. From centre take B3268 (Lostwithiel). Turn right about ½ mile from outskirts (junction with grass triangle). The entrance is on the left hand side after 400 yds

Date Founded:	1990
Type of Course:	Parkland
No of Holes:	18
Length:	6100 yds (5630 mtrs)
Par:	70
SSS:	70
Green Fees:	Weekdays: £29 (Summer) £20 (Winter); Weekends/Bank Holidays: £29 (Summer) £20 (Winter)
Visitors:	Welcome: Contact Club in Advance. No restrictions
Societies:	Welcome: Contact Club in Advance. No restrictions
Facilities:	Putting Green, Chipping Green, Driving Range, Club Hire, Trolley Hire, Buggy Hire, Bar, Restaurant

Accommodation, Food and Drink

Reference numbers below refer to detailed information provided in section 2

Accommodation

Fieldhead Hotel, Portuan Road, Hannafore, West Looe, Cornwall PL13 2DR

Tel: 01503 262689 Fax: 01503 264114
e-mail: field.head@virgin.net
website: www.fieldheadhotel.co.uk
Elegant country house style hotel offering high standard of comfort and service. Comfortable en-suite rooms, many with sea views. 115

Mayrose Farm Holiday Cottages, Helstone, Camelford, Cornwall PL32 9RN

Tel: 01840 213509 Fax: 01840 213509
e-mail: mayrosefarm@hotmail.com
Five, very different properties converted from former farm buildings, decorated and furnished to a very high standard. Outdoor pool. Super holiday base. 105

Ruthern Valley Holidays, Ruthern Bridge, Nr. Bodmin, Cornwall PL30 5LU

Tel: 01208 831395 Fax: 01208 832324
website: self-catering-ruthern.co.uk
Peaceful, relaxing holiday retreat developed from former mining area. Range of holiday accommodation with bungalows, lodges, caravans and camping facilities. Shop and children's play area. 101

Trethin Manor Holiday Cottages, Advent, Camelford, Cornwall PL32 9QW

Tel: 01840 213522 Fax: 01840 212898
A collection of former farm buildings which have been converted into comfortable self-catering accommodation. Ten cottages surrounded by landscaped grounds. Children's play area, barbecue, laundry. 120

Food and Drink

Fieldhead Hotel, Portuan Road, Hannafore, West Looe, Cornwall PL13 2DR

Tel: 01503 262689 Fax: 01503 264114
e-mail: field.head@virgin.net
website: www.fieldheadhotel.co.uk
Elegant country house style hotel offering high standard of comfort and service. Comfortable en-suite rooms, many with sea views.   115

The Globe Inn, 3 North Street, Lostwithiel, Cornwall PL22 0EG

Tel: 01208 872501
Cosy, friendly, traditional inn offering a warm welcome to all. Open plan bar, restaurant area, patio and beer garden. Good menu of tasty home-cooked, freshly-prepared food.   102

Three Pilchards, The Quay, Polperro, Looe, Cornwall PL13 2QZ

Tel: 01503 272233
Traditional Cornish pub located on the sea front. Home-cooked food served each day.   116

Trewithen Restaurant, 3 Fore Street, Lostwithiel, Cornwall PL22 0BP

Tel: 01208 872373
Award-winning restaurant with cosy, cottagey style in the heart of the pretty town of Lostwithiel. Traditional, English cuisine.   110

Launceston Golf Club

St. Stephen, Launceston, Cornwall PL15 8HF
Tel: 01566 773442 Fax: 01566 777056

On the rolling greenery on the north side of the old town is to be found one of best examples around the region of an undulating parkland course with more than enough to occupy the mind of golfers of any handicap. It is another one of Hamilton Stutt's little challenges, which makes best use of what nature provided, and in this case nature provided "The Hill".

This Cornish uprising - one of the more peaceful in the county's turbulent history, it must be said - dominates the course around the turn and affords great views across the Tamar Valley, with Bodmin Moor and Dartmoor as backdrops, and also of Launceston Castle.

Both the eighth and 11th fairways climb this troublesome knoll, atop which are perched the greens for holes eight, nine, 11 and 12, so don't get distracted while putting. These holes are, without doubt, the highlights of the course, with the ninth perhaps being the pick of the bunch, with its green not much more than a seven- or eight-iron away, set in among trees, and looking eminently like par material.

Like the nearby but far newer Trethorne course, Launceston offers plenty of shot-grabbing trees and gorse and a couple of elevated tees, which always make you feel better for no real reason, but at 6,400 yards, and with "The Hill" to overcome, it's as good an examination as most will require of their game.

Sec/Manager:	Charles Hicks
Professional:	John Tozer
Directions:	¾ mile northwest of Launceston. From centre take A388 then B3254 at mini roundabout. Turn left at Stephen's Church into Duke St. The entrance is after 150 yds on the right hand side on T junction
Date Founded:	1927
Type of Course:	Parkland
No of Holes:	18
Length:	6415 yds (5921 mtrs)
Par:	70
SSS:	71
Green Fees:	Weekdays: £20; Weekends/ Bank Holidays: £20
Visitors:	Welcome: Contact Club in Advance. Unable to play weekends Handicap certificates required

Societies:	Welcome: Contact Club in Advance
Facilities:	Putting Green, Club Hire, Trolley Hire, Bar, Restaurant

Accommodation, Food and Drink

Reference numbers below refer to detailed information provided in section 2

Accommodation

The Carpenters Arms, Metherell, Nr. Callington, Cornwall PL17 8BJ

Tel: 01579 350242 Fax: 01579 350242
A picturesque Cornish pub with friendly and welcoming service. Wide-ranging menu of home-cooked bar meals and snacks. 117

Inn on the Green, Crooklets Beach, Bude, Cornwall EX23 8NF

Tel: 01288 356013 Fax: 01288 356244
e-mail: innonthegreen46@btinternet.com
website: www.innonthegreen46.co.uk
Family-run Victorian hotel offering comfort, service and value for money. Fine restaurant serves wholesome food with bar open all day. 107

Lifton Hall Hotel, Lifton, Devon PL16 0DR

Tel: 01566 784863 Fax: 01566 784770
e-mail mail@liftonhall.co.uk
Traditional 250-year old Country House hotel in peaceful village location with ten en-suite rooms. Formal restaurant and a bistro, both specialising in local fish. 240

Links Side, 7 Burn View, Bude, Cornwall EX23 8BY

Tel: 01288 352410
Small, cosy bed and breakfast with warm, friendly atmosphere. Rooms of varying sizes, most with en-suite facilities. 108

The Wilsey Down, Hallworthy, Camelford, Cornwall PL32 9SH

Tel: 01840 261205
e-mail: jane@greatbidlake.farmcom.net
Comfortable, welcoming establishment with two bars and separate restaurant. Six guest rooms, 2 of which are en-suite, of varying sizes. 104

Food and Drink

The Carpenters Arms, Metherell, Nr. Callington, Cornwall PL17 8BJ

Tel: 01579 350242 Fax: 01579 350242
A picturesque Cornish pub with friendly and welcoming service. Wide-ranging menu of home-cooked bar meals and snacks. 117

Inn on the Green, Crooklets Beach, Bude, Cornwall EX23 8NF

Tel: 01288 356013 Fax: 01288 356244
e-mail: innonthegreen46@btinternet.com
website: www.innonthegreen46.co.uk

Family-run Victorian hotel offering comfort, service and value for money. Fine restaurant serves wholesome food with a fully stocked bar open all day.

107

Lifton Hall Hotel, Lifton, Devon PL16 0DR

Tel: 01566 784863 Fax: 01566 784770
e-mail mail@liftonhall.co.uk
Traditional 250-year old Country House hotel in peaceful village location with ten en-suite rooms. Formal restaurant and a bistro, both specialising in local fish. 240

The Wilsey Down, Hallworthy, Camelford, Cornwall PL32 9SH

Tel: 01840 261205
e-mail: jane@greatbidlake.farmcom.net
Comfortable, welcoming establishment with two bars and separate restaurant. Six guest rooms, 2 of which are en-suite, of varying sizes. 104

Looe Golf Club

Bin Down, Looe, Cornwall PL13 1PX
Tel: 01503 240239 Fax: 01503 240864

When you have won the Open half-a-dozen times, and claimed the US Open as well, then golf must start to come quite easily to you. No doubt that was what Harry Vardon was thinking when he set about the task of designing this hill-top course in the 1930s.

But perhaps the legendary Harry designed it more with his own abilities in mind rather than those of the average club golfer, for although the walking is easy enough around its 5,940 yards,

Date Founded:	1935
Type of Course:	Parkland
No of Holes:	18
Length:	5940 yds (5483 mtrs)
Par:	70
SSS:	69
Green Fees:	Weekdays: £25; Weekends/ Bank Holidays: £25
Visitors:	Welcome: Contact Club in Advance. No restrictions
Societies:	Welcome: Contact Club in Advance. No restrictions
Facilities:	Putting Green, Chipping Green, Club Hire, Trolley Hire, Buggy Hire, Bar, Restaurant

playing it is a different matter altogether.

Take, for instance, the first. At first glance it would appear to be a pleasant little 143-yarder to ease you into the round - except, that is, for a rather large oak tree that stands slap-bang in the middle of the fairway. Oh, and there are two more, one either side of the green, to keep you on your toes. Thanks, Harry!

Or take the seventh, another par three, but 233 yards from the tee and with a green like an up-turned saucer, making a par difficult enough, never mind a share in the twos kitty. Cheers, Harry!

And even right at the end, when you may have hoped that the struggle was finally coming to an end, there is the 18th, with an elevated tee and little margin for error as you aim for a narrow fairway that dog-legs right, although the view out to sea and Looe Island is pleasant enough, as are various other vistas across south east Cornwall and the coastline around this mixture of downland and parkland.

Sec/Manager:	Peter Street
Professional:	Alistair Macdonald
Directions:	3 miles northeast of Looe. From centre take B3253 (Widegates). After 2 miles turn left onto B road (Nomansland). The entrance is on the right hand side after 250 yds

Accommodation, Food and Drink

Reference numbers below refer to detailed information provided in section 2

Accommodation

The Carpenters Arms, Metherell, Nr. Callington, Cornwall PL17 8BJ

Tel: 01579 350242 Fax: 01579 350242
A picturesque Cornish pub with friendly and welcoming service. Wide-ranging menu of home-cooked bar meals and snacks.   117

Cawsand Bay Hotel & Galleon Restaurant, The Bound, Cawsand, Nr. Torpoint, Cornwall PL10 1PG

Tel: 01752 822425 Fax: 01752 823527
e-mail: sales@cawsandbay.co.uk
website: www.cawsandbay.co.uk
Located directly on the sea front and with superb views across the Sound towards Plymouth. Ten comfortable en-suite rooms of varying sizes. Popular bar and restaurant.   130

Fieldhead Hotel, Portuan Road, Hannafore, West Looe, Cornwall PL13 2DR

Tel: 01503 262689 Fax: 01503 264114
e-mail: field.head@virgin.net
website: www.fieldheadhotel.co.uk
Elegant country house style hotel offering high standard of comfort and service. Comfortable en-suite rooms, many with sea views.   115

Food and Drink

Cawsand Bay Hotel & Galleon Restaurant, The Bound, Cawsand, Nr. Torpoint, Cornwall PL10 1PG

Tel: 01752 822425 Fax: 01752 823527
e-mail: sales@cawsandbay.co.uk
website: www.cawsandbay.co.uk
Located directly on the sea front and with superb views across the Sound towards Plymouth. Ten comfortable en-suite rooms of varying sizes. Popular

bar and restaurant. 130

Fieldhead Hotel, Portuan Road, Hannafore, West Looe, Cornwall PL13 2DR

Tel: 01503 262689 Fax: 01503 264114
e-mail: field.head@virgin.net
website: www.fieldheadhotel.co.uk
Elegant country house style hotel offering high
standard of comfort and service. Comfortable en-suite
rooms, many with sea views. 115

The Globe Inn, 3 North Street, Lostwithiel, Cornwall PL22 0EG

Tel: 01208 872501
Cosy, friendly, traditional inn offering a warm
welcome to all. Open plan bar, restaurant area, patio
and beer garden. Good menu of tasty home-cooked,
freshly-prepared food. 102

Three Pilchards, The Quay, Polperro, Looe, Cornwall PL13 2QZ

Tel: 01503 272233
Traditional Cornish pub located on the sea front.
Home-cooked food served each day. 116

Trewithen Restaurant, 3 Fore Street, Lostwithiel, Cornwall PL22 0BP

Tel: 01208 872373
Award-winning restaurant with cosy, cottagey style in
the heart of the pretty town of Lostwithiel.
Traditional, English cuisine. 110

Lostwithiel Golf Club

Lower Polscoe, Lostwithiel,
Cornwall PL22 0HQ
Tel: 01208 873500 Fax: 01208 873479

Sec/Manager:	David Higman
Professional:	Tony Nash
Directions:	½ mile north of Lostwithiel. From centre take A390 (Liskeard). After crossing River Fowey and the railway turn left into Coll Road The entrance is on the left hand side after ¼ mile.
Date Founded:	1990

Type of Course:	Parkland
No of Holes:	18
Length:	5984 yds (5523 mtrs)
Par:	72
SSS:	70
Green Fees:	Weekdays: £25 (Summer) £15 (Winter); Weekends/Bank Holidays: £29 (Summer) £18 (Winter)
Visitors:	Welcome: Contact Club in Advance. No restrictions
Societies:	Welcome: Contact Club in Advance
Facilities:	Hotel, Putting Green, Chipping Green, Driving Range, Club Hire, Trolley Hire, Buggy Hire, Bar, Restaurant

Accommodation, Food and Drink

Reference numbers below refer to detailed
information provided in section 2

Accommodation

Cawsand Bay Hotel & Galleon Restaurant, The Bound, Cawsand, Nr. Torpoint, Cornwall PL10 1PG

Tel: 01752 822425 Fax: 01752 823527
e-mail: sales@cawsandbay.co.uk
website: www.cawsandbay.co.uk
Located directly on the sea front and with superb
views across the Sound towards Plymouth. Ten
comfortable en-suite rooms of varying sizes. Popular
bar and restaurant. 130

Fieldhead Hotel, Portuan Road, Hannafore, West Looe, Cornwall PL13 2DR

Tel: 01503 262689 Fax: 01503 264114
e-mail: field.head@virgin.net
website: www.fieldheadhotel.co.uk
Elegant country house style hotel offering high
standard of comfort and service. Comfortable en-suite
rooms, many with sea views. 115

Mayrose Farm Holiday Cottages, Helstone, Camelford, Cornwall PL32 9RN

Tel: 01840 213509 Fax: 01840 213509
e-mail: mayrosefarm@hotmail.com
Five, very different properties converted from former farm buildings, decorated and furnished to a very high standard. Outdoor pool. Super holiday base. 105

Ruthern Valley Holidays, Ruthern Bridge, Nr. Bodmin, Cornwall PL30 5LU

Tel: 01208 831395 Fax: 01208 832324
website: self-catering-ruthern.co.uk
Peaceful, relaxing holiday retreat developed from former mining area. Range of holiday accommodation with bungalows, lodges, caravans and camping facilities. Shop and children's play area. 101

Trethin Manor Holiday Cottages, Advent, Camelford, Cornwall PL32 9QW

Tel: 01840 213522 Fax: 01840 212898
A collection of former farm buildings which have been converted into comfortable self-catering accommodation. Ten cottages surrounded by landscaped grounds. Children's play area, barbecue, laundry. 120

Food and Drink

Cawsand Bay Hotel & Galleon Restaurant, The Bound, Cawsand, Nr. Torpoint, Cornwall PL10 1PG

Tel: 01752 822425 Fax: 01752 823527
e-mail: sales@cawsandbay.co.uk
website: www.cawsandbay.co.uk
Located directly on the sea front and with superb views across the Sound towards Plymouth. Ten comfortable en-suite rooms of varying sizes. Popular bar and restaurant. 130

Fieldhead Hotel, Portuan Road, Hannafore, West Looe, Cornwall PL13 2DR

Tel: 01503 262689 Fax: 01503 264114
e-mail: field.head@virgin.net
website: www.fieldheadhotel.co.uk
Elegant country house style hotel offering high standard of comfort and service. Comfortable en-suite rooms, many with sea views. 115

The Globe Inn, 3 North Street, Lostwithiel, Cornwall PL22 0EG

Tel: 01208 872501
Cosy, friendly, traditional inn offering a warm welcome to all. Open plan bar, restaurant area, patio and beer garden. Good menu of tasty home-cooked, freshly-prepared food. 102

Three Pilchards, The Quay, Polperro, Looe, Cornwall PL13 2QZ

Tel: 01503 272233
Traditional Cornish pub located on the sea front. Home-cooked food served each day. 116

Trewithen Restaurant, 3 Fore Street, Lostwithiel, Cornwall PL22 0BP

Tel: 01208 872373
Award-winning restaurant with cosy, cottagey style in

the heart of the pretty town of Lostwithiel. Traditional, English cuisine. 110

Merlin Golf Club

Mawgan Porth, Newquay, Cornwall TR8 4DN
Tel: 01841 540222 Fax: 01841 541031

Sec/Manager:	Margaret Oliver
Professional:	None
Directions:	4½ miles northeast of Newquay. From the centre take B3276 (Padstow). Just before Trenance turn right onto minor road (St. Eval). The entrance is on the right hand side after 300 yds
Date Founded:	1991
Type of Course:	Heathland
No of Holes:	18
Length:	6210 yds (5732 mtrs)
Par:	71
SSS:	71
Green Fees:	Weekdays: £13; Weekends/ Bank Holidays: £13
Visitors:	Welcome: Contact Club in Advance. No restrictions
Societies:	Welcome: Contact Club in Advance
Facilities:	Putting Green, Chipping Green, Driving Range, Club Hire, Trolley Hire, Buggy Hire, Bar, Restaurant

Accommodation, Food and Drink

Reference numbers below refer to detailed information provided in section 2

Accommodation

The Beaconsfield Hotel, The Crescent, Newquay, Cornwall TR7 1DT

Tel: 01637 872172 Fax: 01637 850711
Stylish hotel in fine location overlooking the sandy

beach and open sea beyond. Comfortable accommodation with 58 en-suite bedrooms. Several lounge areas, bar and restaurant for guests only. 128

Bewdley Hotel, Pentire Road, Newquay, Cornwall TR7 1NX

Tel: 01637 872883 Fax: 01637 872883
Friendly, family-run hotel overlooking links golf course and beach. 29 en-suite rooms of varying sizes. Evening entertainment through the summer. Heated outdoor pool. 122

The Brookdale Hotel, Tregolls Road, Truro, Cornwall TR1 1JZ

Tel: 01872 273513 Fax: 01872 272400
e-mail: brookdale@hotelstruro.com
website: www.hotelstruro.com/brookdale
Good sized hotel set in its own beautifully landscaped grounds. Popular Italian Ristorante open Monday to Saturday. Comfortable, elegantly furnished en-suite rooms of varying types. 113

Chynoweth Lodge Hotel, 1 Eliot Gardens, Newquay, Cornwall TR7 2QE

Tel: 01637 876684
e-mail: reg@chynowethlodge.co.uk
website: www.chynowethlodge.co.uk
Comfortable accommodation, with nine en-suite rooms, personally run by resident owners. Comfortable lounge area and attractive dining room. Home-cooked food served in ample portions. 121

The Cumberland Hotelm, Henver Road, Newquay, Cornwall TR7 3BJ

Tel: 01637 873025 Fax: 01637 873097
Friendly seaside hotel with facilities including an outdoor pool and spacious ballroom. 32 rooms of varying sizes, all en-suite. Restaurant serves mainly English cuisine each evening, with lunches available on request.

The Glen Court Hotel, Mellanvrane Lane, Newquay, Cornwall TR7 2LB

Tel: 01637 874848
An 11-bedroom, family-run hotel ideal for those wanting a relaxing holiday. Restaurant serves superb home-cooked meals. Also a comfortable lounge and separate bar area.

Marcorrie Hotel, 20 Falmouth Road, Truro, Cornwall TR1 2HX

Tel: 01872 277374 Fax: 01872 241666
e-mail: marcorrie@aol.com
website: www.cornwall.net/marcorrie
Small, charming family-run hotel on a delightful Victorian and Edwardian street near to the city centre, offering traditional Cornish hospitality. 103

Pendeen Hotel, 7 Alexandra Road, Porth, Newquay, Cornwall TR7 3ND

Tel: 01637 873521 Fax: 01637 873521
e-mail: pendeen@cornwall.net
Relaxing and peaceful hotel where you will find friendly service. 15 en-suite rooms. Restaurant serves traditional English and international cuisine focusing on fresh fish and seafood. 129

Porth Lodge Hotel, Porthbean Road, Newquay, Cornwall TR7 3TL

Tel: 01637 874483
Popular hostelry, with two bar areas, serving good food, with beer garden and children's room. 20 en-suite rooms and six self-catering apartments. Also a 10-pin bowling alley. 123

Porth Veor Manor, Porth Way, Nr. Newquay, Cornwall TR7 3LW

Tel: 01637 873274 Fax: 01637 873274
Friendly hotel offering the best in traditional Cornish hospitality. Elevated location offers superb views in all directions. 22 en-suite rooms. Award-winning restaurant open to non-residents. 125

Ruthern Valley Holidays, Ruthern Bridge, Nr. Bodmin, Cornwall PL30 5LU

Tel: 01208 831395 Fax: 01208 832324
website: self-catering-ruthern.co.uk
Peaceful, relaxing holiday retreat developed from former mining area. Range of holiday accommodation with bungalows, lodges, caravans and camping facilities. Shop and children's play area. 101

Treheveras Guest House, 2a Dane Road, Newquay, Cornwall TR7 1HL

Tel: 01637 874079
e-mail: treheveras@aol.com
A small guest house located on Newquay's Towan headland. Seven cosy rooms, five double, two single, most with en-suite facilities. Traditional cooked English breakfast. Reasonable rates.

Trenance Lodge Hotel and Restaurant, Trenance Road, Newquay, Cornwall TR7 2HW

Tel: 01637 876702 Fax: 01637 878772
e-mail: info@trenance-lodge.co.uk
website: www.trenance-lodge.co.uk
A fine restaurant with excellent reputation for serving fine local produce in a modern British style. Also 5 en-suite bedrooms, stylishly furnished and well-appointed. 124

White House Court Holiday Cottages, c/o 1 Middle Leigh, Newton Ferrers, Plymouth, Devon PL8 1DS

Tel: 01752 873128 Fax: 01752 873128
e-mail: whitehouse.cotts@barclay.net
website: www.whitehousecourt.co.uk
Eleven well-equipped self-catering cottages created from traditional, stone-built farm buildings. Two miles from the coast. 111

Woodlands Hotel, 38-40 Pentire Crescent, Newquay, Cornwall TR7 1PU

Tel: 01637 852229 Fax: 01637 852227
Quiet setting, just outside Newquay, with spectacular views over the river and open countryside. 54 bedrooms. Excellent facilities including outdoor pool, sauna, solarium, sunbed and bowling green. 131

Food and Drink

The Brookdale Hotel, Tregolls Road, Truro, Cornwall TR1 1JZ

Tel: 01872 273513 Fax: 01872 272400
e-mail: brookdale@hotelstruro.com
website: www.hotelstruro.com/brookdale
Good sized hotel set in its own beautifully landscaped
grounds. Popular Italian Ristorante open Monday to
Saturday. Comfortable, elegantly furnished en-suite
rooms of varying types. 113

The Globe Inn, 3 North Street, Lostwithiel, Cornwall PL22 0EG

Tel: 01208 872501
Cosy, friendly, traditional inn offering a warm
welcome to all. Open plan bar, restaurant area, patio
and beer garden. Good menu of tasty home-cooked,
freshly-prepared food. 102

Legonna Farm, Lane, Newquay, Cornwall TR8 4NJ

Tel: 01637 872272
A traditional Cornish welcome awaits all who visit
Legonna Farm where you will find comfortable bed
and breakfast accommodation. Nine en-suite rooms of
varying sizes. Packed lunches and evening meals
available on request.

Pendeen Hotel, 7 Alexandra Road, Porth, Newquay, Cornwall TR7 3ND

Tel: 01637 873521 Fax: 01637 873521
e-mail: pendeen@cornwall.net
Relaxing and peaceful hotel where you will find
friendly service. 15 en-suite rooms. Restaurant serves
traditional English and international cuisine focusing
on fresh fish and seafood. 129

Porth Lodge Hotel, Porthbean Road, Newquay, Cornwall TR7 3TL

Tel: 01637 874483
Popular hostelry, with two bar areas, serving good
food, with beer garden and children's room. 20 en-
suite rooms and six self-catering apartments. Also a
10-pin bowling alley. 123

Porth Veor Manor, Porth Way, Nr. Newquay, Cornwall TR7 3LW

Tel: 01637 873274 Fax: 01637 873274
Friendly hotel offering the best in traditional Cornish
hospitality. Elevated location offers superb views in
all directions. 22 en-suite rooms. Award-winning
restaurant open to non-residents. 125

Smugglers Den Inn, Cubert, Newquay, Cornwall TR8 5PY

Tel: 01637 830209 Fax: 01637 830580
Quaint, 400-year old hostelry with a popular
reputation for serving fine food and well-kept ale.
Reputedly haunted! 126

Trenance Lodge Hotel and Restaurant, Trenance Road, Newquay, Cornwall TR7 2HW

Tel: 01637 876702 Fax: 01637 878772
e-mail: info@trenance-lodge.co.uk
website: www.trenance-lodge.co.uk
A fine restaurant with excellent reputation for serving
fine local produce in a modern British style. Also 5
en-suite bedrooms, stylishly furnished and well-
appointed. 124

Tywarnhayle Hotel, The Square, Perranporth, Cornwall TR6 0ER

Tel: 01872 572215 Fax: 01872 571773
Friendly, family-run hostelry serving a good range of
food and drink. The menu is typically English cuisine
and the traditional Sunday Roast lunches are very
popular. Restaurant seats 60.

Mullion Golf Club

Cury, Helston, Cornwall TR12 7BP
Tel: 01326 240685 Fax: 01326 240685

Mullion has been variously described as quaint,
cute and short but sweet. And it cannot be de-
nied that this, the most southerly course on the
mainland, is all of these. But to leave it at that is
to do it a disservice, and such adjectives as intriguing, inviting, uplifting, cheeky, tricky and
downright awkward in places also need to be applied to this out-of-the-way gem. Indeed, it is
difficult to imagine from where it conjures up a
membership of some 650 souls, situated as it is
between Goonhilly Downs and Mounts Bay, some
seven or eight miles south of Helston, itself hardly
a metropolis.

This 6,000-yard track really is a delight as it
clambers unceremoniously and purposefully up

and down the cliffs between the old smugglers' coves, from the high-up fourth tee to the beachside greens at eight and 10.It was from this same cliff, incidentally, that Marconi sent his first transatlantic radio signal, which is probably why BT's main satellite receiving station is nearby.

There are some fascinating and enchanting holes, like the seventh and eighth to Gunwalloe Cove, where a slice at the latter will be gone on the tide; the scenic 10th, where your approach to the elevated green must carry a ravine separating it from the shoreline; and the 17th, where the tee has been described as 'the warmest spot in England.'AP Herbert once wrote:

'Go on old ball, we are but two,
We may be down in three,
Or nine or ten or 25, it matters not!
To be alive at Mullion
In the summer time
Is good enough for me.'

Sec/Manager:	Gerry Fitter
Professional:	Philip Blundell
Directions:	4½ miles south of Helston. From centre take A3083 (Lizard). After 4½ miles turn right to Cury. The entrance is ½ mile beyond Cury Village.
Date Founded:	1895
Type of Course:	Links
No of Holes:	18
Length:	6037 yds (5572 mtrs)
Par:	70
SSS:	70
Green Fees:	Weekdays: £23; Weekends/ Bank Holidays: £28
Visitors:	Welcome: Contact Club in Advance. Handicap Certificates required. Unable to play during competitions.
Societies:	Welcome: Contact Club in Advance
Facilities:	Teaching Acadamy, Putting Green, Chipping Green, Driving Range, Club Hire, Trolley Hire, Buggy Hire, Bar, Restaurant

Accommodation, Food and Drink

Reference numbers below refer to detailed information provided in section 2

Accommodation

The Brookdale Hotel, Tregolls Road, Truro, Cornwall TR1 1JZ

Tel: 01872 273513 Fax: 01872 272400
e-mail: brookdale@hotelstruro.com
website: www.hotelstruro.com/brookdale
Good sized hotel set in its own beautifully landscaped grounds. Popular Italian Ristorante open Monday to Saturday. Comfortable, elegantly furnished en-suite rooms of varying types. 113

Chy-Garth Guest House, Sea View Meadows, St. Ives Road, Carbis Bay, St. Ives, Cornwall TR26 2JX

Tel: 01736 795677
e-mail: ann@chy-garth.demon.co.uk
A delightful, detached house surrounded by colourful gardens and enjoying some beautiful sea views. A non-smoking establishment, there are eight guest rooms, nearly all with en-suite or private facilities. Ample car parking.

Dunmar Hotel, Pednolver Terrace, St. Ives, Cornwall TR26 2EL

Tel: 01736 796117 Fax: 01736 796053
Friendly, family-run 'olde worlde' hotel offering a warm welcome and traditional Cornish hospitality. 17 en-suite bedrooms of varying sizes with bar and restaurant available to guests.

Marcorrie Hotel, 20 Falmouth Road, Truro, Cornwall TR1 2HX

Tel: 01872 277374 Fax: 01872 241666
e-mail: marcorrie@aol.com
website: www.cornwall.net/marcorrie
Small, charming family-run hotel on a delightful Victorian and Edwardian street near to the city centre, offering traditional Cornish hospitality. 103

Meudon Hotel, Mawnan Smith, Near Falmouth, Cornwall TR11 5HT

Tel: 01326 250541 Fax: 01326 250543
website: www.meudon.co.uk
Superb, family-run country house hotel, set in a sub-tropical garden paradise with private beach. Elegant restaurant specialising in local seafood. Free golf included in high- and mid-season rates. 119

Regent Hotel, Fern Lea Terrace, St. Ives, Cornwall TR26 2BH

Tel: 01736 796195 Fax: 01736 794641
e-mail: enquiries@regenthotel.com
website: www.regenthotel.com
Friendly, family-run hotel with AA and RAC 4 Diamond Grading. The nine en-suite guest bedrooms are tastefully decorated and comfortably furnished and many have spectacular views over the picturesque harbour.

White House Court Holiday Cottages, c/o 1 Middle Leigh, Newton Ferrers, Plymouth, Devon PL8 1DS

Tel: 01752 873128 Fax: 01752 873128
e-mail: whitehouse.cotts@barclay.net
website: www.whitehousecourt.co.uk
Eleven well-equipped self-catering cottages created from traditional, stone-built farm buildings. Two miles from the coast. 111

Food and Drink

The Brookdale Hotel, Tregolls Road, Truro, Cornwall TR1 1JZ

Tel: 01872 273513 Fax: 01872 272400
e-mail: brookdale@hotelstruro.com
website: www.hotelstruro.com/brookdale
Good sized hotel set in its own beautifully landscaped grounds. Popular Italian Ristorante open Monday to Saturday. Comfortable, elegantly furnished en-suite rooms of varying types.   113

Meudon Hotel, Mawnan Smith, Near Falmouth, Cornwall TR11 5HT

Tel: 01326 250541 Fax: 01326 250543
website: www.meudon.co.uk
Superb, family-run country house hotel, set in a sub-tropical garden paradise with private beach. Elegant restaurant specialising in local seafood. Free golf included in high- and mid-season rates.   119

The Sundeck, East Quay, Mevagissy, Cornwall PL26 6QQ

Tel: 01726 843051
A surprising find. Stylish decor in Mediterranean theme with picture windows looking out to sea. High quality home-cooked food.   112

on this excellent seaside course, whose gently-undulating fairways are right on Fistral Beach, and therefore at the mercy of the prevailing winds but with the almost-obligatory breathtaking sea views.

The course was one of the earliest to be re-designed - by HS Colt - at a greater length following the introduction of the rubber-cored ball and one of Colt's favourite ploys, the dog-leg fairway, remains a chief feature of this wide-open and somewhat unusual landscape.

At 6,140 yards, and a par of only 69, allied to all that space, the course looks a bit of a pushover but, with natural and man-made sand traps littering the track and that wind doing its best to spoil your day, anything under a 90 for mid-handicappers would be a decent result.

Newquay Golf Club

Tower Road, Newquay, Cornwall TR7 1LT
Tel: 01637 874354 Fax: 01637 874066

One of the great pleasures of golf is that, very much like cricket, it is steeped in history and folklore, with many hundreds of clubs having notched up more than a century. Another great pleasure is browsing through the inevitable centenary year books that are produced because they innocently supply some marvellous insights into bygone days.

Newquay's centenary booklet offers this little gem from the club rules of 1896 (my italics): "Should a ball be driven over the cliffs, another ball must be dropped *a club length from the edge of the cliff* in a line where it went over, the player or side losing one stroke."

For those of a nervous disposition, it should be pointed out that the cliffs are not very high

Sec/Manager:	G. Binnie
Professional:	Mark Bevan
Directions:	¾ miles west of Newquay. From centre follow signs to Fistral Beach. Tower Road is off Forest to the left. The entrance is on the right hand side after 200 yds. If coming from outside Newquay follow A392 to its last roundabout. Straight on is Tower Road. The entrance is on the left hand side after 500 yds.
Date Founded:	1890
Type of Course:	Links
No of Holes:	18
Length:	6150 yds (5676 mtrs)
Par:	69
SSS:	69
Green Fees:	Weekdays: £25; Weekends/ Bank Holidays: £25
Visitors:	Welcome: Contact Club in Advance. Handicap Certificate required. No restrictions
Societies:	Welcome: Contact Club in

Advance. Unable to play weekends.

Facilities: Putting Green, Chipping Green, Trolley Hire, Bar, Restaurant

Accommodation, Food and Drink

Reference numbers below refer to detailed information provided in section 2

Accommodation

The Beaconsfield Hotel, The Crescent, Newquay, Cornwall TR7 1DT

Tel: 01637 872172 Fax: 01637 850711
Stylish hotel in fine location overlooking the sandy beach and open sea beyond. Comfortable accommodation with 58 en-suite bedrooms. Several lounge areas, bar and restaurant for guests only. 128

Bewdley Hotel, Pentire Road, Newquay, Cornwall TR7 1NX

Tel: 01637 872883 Fax: 01637 872883
Friendly, family-run hotel overlooking links golf course and beach. 29 en-suite rooms of varying sizes. Evening entertainment through the summer. Heated outdoor pool. 122

The Brookdale Hotel, Tregolls Road, Truro, Cornwall TR1 1JZ

Tel: 01872 273513 Fax: 01872 272400
e-mail: brookdale@hotelstruro.com
website: www.hotelstruro.com/brookdale
Good sized hotel set in its own beautifully landscaped grounds. Popular Italian Ristorante open Monday to Saturday. Comfortable, elegantly furnished en-suite rooms of varying types. 113

Chynoweth Lodge Hotel, 1 Eliot Gardens, Newquay, Cornwall TR7 2QE

Tel: 01637 876684
e-mail: reg@chynowethlodge.co.uk
website: www.chynowethlodge.co.uk
Comfortable accommodation, with nine en-suite rooms, personally run by resident owners. Comfortable lounge area and attractive dining room. Home-cooked food served in ample portions. 121

The Cumberland Hotelm, Henver Road, Newquay, Cornwall TR7 3BJ

Tel: 01637 873025 Fax: 01637 873097
Friendly seaside hotel with facilities including an outdoor pool and spacious ballroom. 32 rooms of varying sizes, all en-suite. Restaurant serves mainly English cuisine each evening, with lunches available on request.

The Glen Court Hotel, Mellanvrane Lane, Newquay, Cornwall TR7 2LB

Tel: 01637 874848
An 11-bedroom, family-run hotel ideal for those wanting a relaxing holiday. Restaurant serves superb home-cooked meals. Also a comfortable lounge and separate bar area.

Marcorrie Hotel, 20 Falmouth Road, Truro, Cornwall TR1 2HX

Tel: 01872 277374 Fax: 01872 241666
e-mail: marcorrie@aol.com
website: www.cornwall.net/marcorrie
Small, charming family-run hotel on a delightful Victorian and Edwardian street near to the city centre, offering traditional Cornish hospitality. 103

Pendeen Hotel, 7 Alexandra Road, Porth, Newquay, Cornwall TR7 3ND

Tel: 01637 873521 Fax: 01637 873521
e-mail: pendeen@cornwall.net
Relaxing and peaceful hotel where you will find friendly service. 15 en-suite rooms. Restaurant serves traditional English and international cuisine focusing on fresh fish and seafood. 129

Porth Lodge Hotel, Porthbean Road, Newquay, Cornwall TR7 3TL

Tel: 01637 874483
Popular hostelry, with two bar areas, serving good food, with beer garden and children's room. 20 en-suite rooms and six self-catering apartments. Also a 10-pin bowling alley.^ 123

Porth Veor Manor, Porth Way, Nr. Newquay, Cornwall TR7 3LW

Tel: 01637 873274 Fax: 01637 873274
Friendly hotel offering the best in traditional Cornish hospitality. Elevated location offers superb views in all directions. 22 en-suite rooms. Award-winning restaurant open to non-residents. 125

Ruthern Valley Holidays, Ruthern Bridge, Nr. Bodmin, Cornwall PL30 5LU

Tel: 01208 831395 Fax: 01208 832324
website: self-catering-ruthern.co.uk
Peaceful, relaxing holiday retreat developed from former mining area. Range of holiday accommodation with bungalows, lodges, caravans and camping facilities. Shop and children's play area. 101

Treheveras Guest House, 2a Dane Road, Newquay, Cornwall TR7 1HL

Tel: 01637 874079
e-mail: treheveras@aol.com
A small guest house located on Newquay's Towan headland. Seven cosy rooms, five double, two single, most with en-suite facilities. Traditional cooked English breakfast. Reasonable rates.

Trenance Lodge Hotel and Restaurant, Trenance Road, Newquay, Cornwall TR7 2HW

Tel: 01637 876702 Fax: 01637 878772
e-mail: info@trenance-lodge.co.uk
website: www.trenance-lodge.co.uk
A fine restaurant with excellent reputation for serving fine local produce in a modern British style. Also 5 en-suite bedrooms, stylishly furnished and well-appointed. 124

White House Court Holiday Cottages, c/o 1 Middle Leigh, Newton Ferrers, Plymouth, Devon PL8 1DS

Tel: 01752 873128 Fax: 01752 873128

e-mail: whitehouse.cotts@barclay.net
website: www.whitehousecourt.co.uk
Eleven well-equipped self-catering cottages created
from traditional, stone-built farm buildings. Two
miles from the coast.   111

Woodlands Hotel, 38-40 Pentire Crescent, Newquay, Cornwall TR7 1PU

Tel: 01637 852229 Fax: 01637 852227
Quiet setting, just outside Newquay, with spectacular
views over the river and open countryside. 54
bedrooms. Excellent facilities including outdoor pool,
sauna, solarium, sunbed and bowling green.   131

Food and Drink

The Brookdale Hotel, Tregolls Road, Truro, Cornwall TR1 1JZ

Tel: 01872 273513 Fax: 01872 272400
e-mail: brookdale@hotelstruro.com
website: www.hotelstruro.com/brookdale
Good sized hotel set in its own beautifully landscaped
grounds. Popular Italian Ristorante open Monday to
Saturday. Comfortable, elegantly furnished en-suite
rooms of varying types.   113

The Globe Inn, 3 North Street, Lostwithiel, Cornwall PL22 0EG

Tel: 01208 872501
Cosy, friendly, traditional inn offering a warm
welcome to all. Open plan bar, restaurant area, patio
and beer garden. Good menu of tasty home-cooked,
freshly-prepared food.   102

Legonna Farm, Lane, Newquay, Cornwall TR8 4NJ

Tel: 01637 872272
A traditional Cornish welcome awaits all who visit
Legonna Farm where you will find comfortable bed
and breakfast accommodation. Nine en-suite rooms of
varying sizes. Packed lunches and evening meals
available on request.

Pendeen Hotel, 7 Alexandra Road, Porth, Newquay, Cornwall TR7 3ND

Tel: 01637 873521 Fax: 01637 873521
e-mail: pendeen@cornwall.net
Relaxing and peaceful hotel where you will find
friendly service. 15 en-suite rooms. Restaurant serves
traditional English and international cuisine focusing
on fresh fish and seafood.   129

Porth Lodge Hotel, Porthbean Road, Newquay, Cornwall TR7 3TL

Tel: 01637 874483
Popular hostelry, with two bar areas, serving good
food, with beer garden and children's room. 20 en-
suite rooms and six self-catering apartments. Also a
10-pin bowling alley.   123

Porth Veor Manor, Porth Way, Nr. Newquay, Cornwall TR7 3LW

Tel: 01637 873274 Fax: 01637 873274
Friendly hotel offering the best in traditional Cornish
hospitality. Elevated location offers superb views in
all directions. 22 en-suite rooms. Award-winning

restaurant open to non-residents.   125

Smugglers Den Inn, Cubert, Newquay, Cornwall TR8 5PY

Tel: 01637 830209 Fax: 01637 830580
Quaint, 400-year old hostelry with a popular
reputation for serving fine food and well-kept ale.
Reputedly haunted!   126

Trenance Lodge Hotel and Restaurant, Trenance Road, Newquay, Cornwall TR7 2HW

Tel: 01637 876702 Fax: 01637 878772
e-mail: info@trenance-lodge.co.uk
website: www.trenance-lodge.co.uk
A fine restaurant with excellent reputation for serving
fine local produce in a modern British style. Also 5
en-suite bedrooms, stylishly furnished and well-
appointed.   124

Tywarnhayle Hotel, The Square, Perranporth, Cornwall TR6 0ER

Tel: 01872 572215 Fax: 01872 571773
Friendly, family-run hostelry serving a good range of
food and drink. The menu is typically English cuisine
and the traditional Sunday Roast lunches are very
popular. Restaurant seats 60.

Perranporth Golf Club

Budnic Hill, Perranporth, Cornwall TR6 0AB
Tel: 01872 572454 Fax: 01872 573701

Sec/Manager:	Dave Mugford
Professional:	Derek Mitchell
Directions:	½ mile northeast of Perranporth. From the centre take B3285. The entrance is on the left hand side 300 yds after a sign to Beach Dunes Hotel.
Date Founded:	1927
Type of Course:	Links
No of Holes:	18

Length:	6286 yds (5802 mtrs)
Par:	72
SSS:	72
Green Fees:	Weekdays: £25; Weekends/ Bank Holidays: £30
Visitors:	Welcome: Contact Club in Advance. Unable to play mornings at weekends. Handicap Certificate required
Societies:	Welcome: Contact Club in Advance
Facilities:	Putting Green, Chipping Green, Driving Range, Club Hire, Trolley Hire, Bar, Restaurant

Accommodation, Food and Drink

Reference numbers below refer to detailed information provided in section 2

Accommodation

The Beaconsfield Hotel, The Crescent, Newquay, Cornwall TR7 1DT

Tel: 01637 872172 Fax: 01637 850711
Stylish hotel in fine location overlooking the sandy beach and open sea beyond. Comfortable accommodation with 58 en-suite bedrooms. Several lounge areas, bar and restaurant for guests only. 128

Bewdley Hotel, Pentire Road, Newquay, Cornwall TR7 1NX

Tel: 01637 872883 Fax: 01637 872883
Friendly, family-run hotel overlooking links golf course and beach. 29 en-suite rooms of varying sizes. Evening entertainment through the summer. Heated outdoor pool. 122

The Brookdale Hotel, Tregolls Road, Truro, Cornwall TR1 1JZ

Tel: 01872 273513 Fax: 01872 272400
e-mail: brookdale@hotelstruro.com
website: www.hotelstruro.com/brookdale
Good sized hotel set in its own beautifully landscaped grounds. Popular Italian Ristorante open Monday to Saturday. Comfortable, elegantly furnished en-suite rooms of varying types. 113

Chynoweth Lodge Hotel, 1 Eliot Gardens, Newquay, Cornwall TR7 2QE

Tel: 01637 876684
e-mail: reg@chynowethlodge.co.uk
website: www.chynowethlodge.co.uk
Comfortable accommodation, with nine en-suite rooms, personally run by resident owners. Comfortable lounge area and attractive dining room. Home-cooked food served in ample portions. 121

The Cumberland Hotelm, Henver Road, Newquay, Cornwall TR7 3BJ

Tel: 01637 873025 Fax: 01637 873097
Friendly seaside hotel with facilities including an

outdoor pool and spacious ballroom. 32 rooms of varying sizes, all en-suite. Restaurant serves mainly English cuisine each evening, with lunches available on request.

The Glen Court Hotel, Mellanvrane Lane, Newquay, Cornwall TR7 2LB

Tel: 01637 874848
An 11-bedroom, family-run hotel ideal for those wanting a relaxing holiday. Restaurant serves superb home-cooked meals. Also a comfortable lounge and separate bar area.

Marcorrie Hotel, 20 Falmouth Road, Truro, Cornwall TR1 2HX

Tel: 01872 277374 Fax: 01872 241666
e-mail: marcorrie@aol.com
website: www.cornwall.net/marcorrie
Small, charming family-run hotel on a delightful Victorian and Edwardian street near to the city centre, offering traditional Cornish hospitality. 103

Pendeen Hotel, 7 Alexandra Road, Porth, Newquay, Cornwall TR7 3ND

Tel: 01637 873521 Fax: 01637 873521
e-mail: pendeen@cornwall.net
Relaxing and peaceful hotel where you will find friendly service. 15 en-suite rooms. Restaurant serves traditional English and international cuisine focusing on fresh fish and seafood. 129

Porth Lodge Hotel, Porthbean Road, Newquay, Cornwall TR7 3TL

Tel: 01637 874483
Popular hostelry, with two bar areas, serving good food, with beer garden and children's room. 20 en-suite rooms and six self-catering apartments. Also a 10-pin bowling alley. 123

Porth Veor Manor, Porth Way, Nr. Newquay, Cornwall TR7 3LW

Tel: 01637 873274 Fax: 01637 873274
Friendly hotel offering the best in traditional Cornish hospitality. Elevated location offers superb views in all directions. 22 en-suite rooms. Award-winning restaurant open to non-residents. 125

Ruthern Valley Holidays, Ruthern Bridge, Nr. Bodmin, Cornwall PL30 5LU

Tel: 01208 831395 Fax: 01208 832324
website: self-catering-ruthern.co.uk
Peaceful, relaxing holiday retreat developed from former mining area. Range of holiday accommodation with bungalows, lodges, caravans and camping facilities. Shop and children's play area. 101

Treheveras Guest House, 2a Dane Road, Newquay, Cornwall TR7 1HL

Tel: 01637 874079
e-mail: treheveras@aol.com
A small guest house located on Newquay's Towan headland. Seven cosy rooms, five double, two single, most with en-suite facilities. Traditional cooked English breakfast. Reasonable rates.

Trenance Lodge Hotel and Restaurant, Trenance Road, Newquay, Cornwall TR7 2HW

Tel: 01637 876702 Fax: 01637 878772
e-mail: info@trenance-lodge.co.uk
website: www.trenance-lodge.co.uk
A fine restaurant with excellent reputation for serving
fine local produce in a modern British style. Also 5
en-suite bedrooms, stylishly furnished and well-
appointed.   124

**White House Court Holiday Cottages,
c/o 1 Middle Leigh, Newton Ferrers,
Plymouth, Devon PL8 1DS**

Tel: 01752 873128 Fax: 01752 873128
e-mail: whitehouse.cotts@barclay.net
website: www.whitehousecourt.co.uk
Eleven well-equipped self-catering cottages created
from traditional, stone-built farm buildings. Two
miles from the coast.   111

**Woodlands Hotel, 38-40 Pentire Crescent,
Newquay, Cornwall TR7 1PU**

Tel: 01637 852229 Fax: 01637 852227
Quiet setting, just outside Newquay, with spectacular
views over the river and open countryside. 54
bedrooms. Excellent facilities including outdoor pool,
sauna, solarium, sunbed and bowling green.   131

Food and Drink

**The Brookdale Hotel, Tregolls Road, Truro,
Cornwall TR1 1JZ**

Tel: 01872 273513 Fax: 01872 272400
e-mail: brookdale@hotelstruro.com
website: www.hotelstruro.com/brookdale
Good sized hotel set in its own beautifully landscaped
grounds. Popular Italian Ristorante open Monday to
Saturday. Comfortable, elegantly furnished en-suite
rooms of varying types.   113

**The Globe Inn, 3 North Street, Lostwithiel,
Cornwall PL22 0EG**

Tel: 01208 872501
Cosy, friendly, traditional inn offering a warm
welcome to all. Open plan bar, restaurant area, patio
and beer garden. Good menu of tasty home-cooked,
freshly-prepared food.   102

**Legonna Farm, Lane, Newquay,
Cornwall TR8 4NJ**

Tel: 01637 872272
A traditional Cornish welcome awaits all who visit
Legonna Farm where you will find comfortable bed
and breakfast accommodation. Nine en-suite rooms of
varying sizes. Packed lunches and evening meals
available on request.

**Pendeen Hotel, 7 Alexandra Road, Porth,
Newquay, Cornwall TR7 3ND**

Tel: 01637 873521 Fax: 01637 873521
e-mail: pendeen@cornwall.net
Relaxing and peaceful hotel where you will find
friendly service. 15 en-suite rooms. Restaurant serves
traditional English and international cuisine focusing
on fresh fish and seafood.   129

**Porth Lodge Hotel, Porthbean Road, Newquay,
Cornwall TR7 3TL**

Tel: 01637 874483

Popular hostelry, with two bar areas, serving good
food, with beer garden and children's room. 20 en-
suite rooms and six self-catering apartments. Also a
10-pin bowling alley.   123

**Porth Veor Manor, Porth Way, Nr. Newquay,
Cornwall TR7 3LW**

Tel: 01637 873274 Fax: 01637 873274
Friendly hotel offering the best in traditional Cornish
hospitality. Elevated location offers superb views in
all directions. 22 en-suite rooms. Award-winning
restaurant open to non-residents.   125

**Smugglers Den Inn, Cubert, Newquay,
Cornwall TR8 5PY**

Tel: 01637 830209 Fax: 01637 830580
Quaint, 400-year old hostelry with a popular
reputation for serving fine food and well-kept ale.
Reputedly haunted!   126

**Trenance Lodge Hotel and Restaurant,
Trenance Road, Newquay, Cornwall TR7 2HW**

Tel: 01637 876702 Fax: 01637 878772
e-mail: info@trenance-lodge.co.uk
website: www.trenance-lodge.co.uk
A fine restaurant with excellent reputation for serving
fine local produce in a modern British style. Also 5
en-suite bedrooms, stylishly furnished and well-
appointed.   124

**Tywarnhayle Hotel, The Square, Perranporth,
Cornwall TR6 0ER**

Tel: 01872 572215 Fax: 01872 571773
Friendly, family-run hostelry serving a good range of
food and drink. The menu is typically English cuisine
and the traditional Sunday Roast lunches are very
popular. Restaurant seats 60.

Porthpean Golf Club

Porthpean, St. Austell PL26 6AY
Tel: 01726 64613 Fax: 01276 716143

Sec/Manager:	Mrs. Tucker
Professional:	Tony Nash
Directions:	1½ miles south of St. Austell. Follow signs to Porthpean from the A390 St. Austell by-pass.

Date Founded: 1992

Type of Course: Parkland

No of Holes: 18

Length: 4928 yds (4548 mtrs)

Par: 67

SSS: 67

Green Fees: Weekdays & Weekends: £7.50
(9 holes) £12.50 (18 holes)

Visitors: Welcome: Contact Club in
Advance. No Restrictions

Societies: Welcome: Contact Club in
Advance

Facilities: Putting Green, Driving Range,
Club Hire, Trolley Hire, Bar,
Restaurant, Self Catering
Accommodation

Accommodation, Food and Drink

Reference numbers below refer to detailed
information provided in section 2

Accommodation

The Brookdale Hotel, Tregolls Road, Truro, Cornwall TR1 1JZ

Tel: 01872 273513 Fax: 01872 272400
e-mail: brookdale@hotelstruro.com
website: www.hotelstruro.com/brookdale
Good sized hotel set in its own beautifully landscaped
grounds. Popular Italian Ristorante open Monday to
Saturday. Comfortable, elegantly furnished en-suite
rooms of varying types. 113

Fieldhead Hotel, Portuan Road, Hannafore, West Looe, Cornwall PL13 2DR

Tel: 01503 262689 Fax: 01503 264114
e-mail: field.head@virgin.net
website: www.fieldheadhotel.co.uk
Elegant country house style hotel offering high
standard of comfort and service. Comfortable en-suite
rooms, many with sea views. 115

Marcorrie Hotel, 20 Falmouth Road, Truro, Cornwall TR1 2HX

Tel: 01872 277374 Fax: 01872 241666
e-mail: marcorrie@aol.com
website: www.cornwall.net/marcorrie
Small, charming family-run hotel on a delightful

Victorian and Edwardian street near to the city centre,
offering traditional Cornish hospitality. 103

Ruthern Valley Holidays, Ruthern Bridge, Nr. Bodmin, Cornwall PL30 5LU

Tel: 01208 831395 Fax: 01208 832324
website: self-catering-ruthern.co.uk
Peaceful, relaxing holiday retreat developed from
former mining area. Range of holiday accommodation
with bungalows, lodges, caravans and camping
facilities. Shop and children's play area. 101

Food and Drink

The Brookdale Hotel, Tregolls Road, Truro, Cornwall TR1 1JZ

Tel: 01872 273513 Fax: 01872 272400
e-mail: brookdale@hotelstruro.com
website: www.hotelstruro.com/brookdale
Good sized hotel set in its own beautifully landscaped
grounds. Popular Italian Ristorante open Monday to
Saturday. Comfortable, elegantly furnished en-suite
rooms of varying types. 113

The Globe Inn, 3 North Street, Lostwithiel, Cornwall PL22 0EG

Tel: 01208 872501
Cosy, friendly, traditional inn offering a warm
welcome to all. Open plan bar, restaurant area, patio
and beer garden. Good menu of tasty home-cooked,
freshly-prepared food. 102

The Sundeck, East Quay, Mevagissy, Cornwall PL26 6QQ

Tel: 01726 843051
A surprising find. Stylish decor in Mediterranean
theme with picture windows looking out to sea. High
quality home-cooked food. 112

Three Pilchards, The Quay, Polperro, Looe, Cornwall PL13 2QZ

Tel: 01503 272233
Traditional Cornish pub located on the sea front.
Home-cooked food served each day. 116

Trewithen Restaurant, 3 Fore Street, Lostwithiel, Cornwall PL22 0BP

Tel: 01208 872373
Award-winning restaurant with cosy, cottagey style in
the heart of the pretty town of Lostwithiel.
Traditional, English cuisine. 110

Praa Sands Golf Club

Praa Sands Penzance, Cornwall TR20 9TQ
Tel: 01736 763445 Fax: 01736 763399

Sec/Manager:	David Phillips
Professional:	none
Directions:	5½ miles west of Helston. From centre take A394 (Penzance).

At St. Germoe turn left into Pengersick Lane. The entrance is after ½ mile.

Date Founded:	1971
Type of Course:	Parkland
No of Holes:	9 x 2
Length:	4122 yds (3805 mtrs)
Par:	62
SSS:	60
Green Fees:	Weekdays: £10; Weekends/ Bank Holidays: £15
Visitors:	Welcome: Contact Club in Advance. Unable to play Sunday mornings
Societies:	Welcome: Contact Club in Advance.
Facilities:	Putting Green, Club Hire, Trolley Hire, Bar, Restaurant

Accommodation, Food and Drink

Reference numbers below refer to detailed information provided in section 2

Accommodation

The Brookdale Hotel, Tregolls Road, Truro, Cornwall TR1 1JZ

Tel: 01872 273513 Fax: 01872 272400
e-mail: brookdale@hotelstruro.com
website: www.hotelstruro.com/brookdale
Good sized hotel set in its own beautifully landscaped grounds. Popular Italian Ristorante open Monday to Saturday. Comfortable, elegantly furnished en-suite rooms of varying types.   113

Chy-Garth Guest House, Sea View Meadows, St. Ives Road, Carbis Bay, St. Ives, Cornwall TR26 2JX

Tel: 01736 795677
e-mail: ann@chy-garth.demon.co.uk
A delightful, detached house surrounded by colourful gardens and enjoying some beautiful sea views. A non-smoking establishment, there are eight guest rooms, nearly all with en-suite or private facilities. Ample car parking.

Dunmar Hotel, Pednolver Terrace, St. Ives, Cornwall TR26 2EL

Tel: 01736 796117 Fax: 01736 796053
Friendly, family-run 'olde worlde' hotel offering a warm welcome and traditional Cornish hospitality. 17 en-suite bedrooms of varying sizes with bar and restaurant available to guests.

Marcorrie Hotel, 20 Falmouth Road, Truro, Cornwall TR1 2HX

Tel: 01872 277374 Fax: 01872 241666
e-mail: marcorrie@aol.com
website: www.cornwall.net/marcorrie
Small, charming family-run hotel on a delightful Victorian and Edwardian street near to the city centre, offering traditional Cornish hospitality.   103

Meudon Hotel, Mawnan Smith, Near Falmouth, Cornwall TR11 5HT

Tel: 01326 250541 Fax: 01326 250543
website: www.meudon.co.uk
Superb, family-run country house hotel, set in a sub-tropical garden paradise with private beach. Elegant restaurant specialising in local seafood. Free golf included in high- and mid-season rates.   119

Regent Hotel, Fern Lea Terrace, St. Ives, Cornwall TR26 2BH

Tel: 01736 796195 Fax: 01736 794641
e-mail: enquiries@regenthotel.com
website: www.regenthotel.com
Friendly, family-run hotel with AA and RAC 4 Diamond Grading. The nine en-suite guest bedrooms are tastefully decorated and comfortably furnished and many have spectacular views over the picturesque harbour.

White House Court Holiday Cottages, c/o 1 Middle Leigh, Newton Ferrers, Plymouth, Devon PL8 1DS

Tel: 01752 873128 Fax: 01752 873128
e-mail: whitehouse.cotts@barclay.net
website: www.whitehousecourt.co.uk
Eleven well-equipped self-catering cottages created from traditional, stone-built farm buildings. Two miles from the coast.   111

Food and Drink

The Brookdale Hotel, Tregolls Road, Truro, Cornwall TR1 1JZ

Tel: 01872 273513 Fax: 01872 272400
e-mail: brookdale@hotelstruro.com
website: www.hotelstruro.com/brookdale
Good sized hotel set in its own beautifully landscaped grounds. Popular Italian Ristorante open Monday to Saturday. Comfortable, elegantly furnished en-suite rooms of varying types.   113

Meudon Hotel, Mawnan Smith, Near Falmouth, Cornwall TR11 5HT

Tel: 01326 250541 Fax: 01326 250543
website: www.meudon.co.uk
Superb, family-run country house hotel, set in a sub-tropical garden paradise with private beach. Elegant restaurant specialising in local seafood. Free golf included in high- and mid-season rates.   119

The Sundeck, East Quay, Mevagissy, Cornwall PL26 6QQ

Tel: 01726 843051
A surprising find. Stylish decor in Mediterranean theme with picture windows looking out to sea. High quality home-cooked food.   112

Roserrow Golf Club

Roserrow, St. Minver, Cornwall PL27 6QT
Tel: 01208 863000 Fax: 01208 863002

Sec/Manager:	WJJ Blewitt
Professional:	Andrew Cullen
Directions:	5 miles north of Wadebridge off the B3314 to Polzeath
Date Founded:	1997
Type of Course:	Heathland
No of Holes:	18
Length:	6551 yds (6047 mtrs)
Par:	72
SSS:	70
Green Fees:	Weekdays: £25; Weekends/ Bank Holidays: £25
Visitors:	Welcome: Contact Club in Advance. Unable to play Sunday mornings and Bank Holidays, Tuesday & Friday mornings
Societies:	Welcome: Contact Club in Advance. Unable to play Sun, Tue, Fri mornings.
Facilities:	Putting Green, Driving Range, Club Hire, Trolley Hire, Buggy Hire, Caddy Service, Bar, Restaurant, Leisure Club, Self Catering Accommodation

Accommodation, Food and Drink

Reference numbers below refer to detailed information provided in section 2

Accommodation

The Beaconsfield Hotel, The Crescent, Newquay, Cornwall TR7 1DT

Tel: 01637 872172 Fax: 01637 850711
Stylish hotel in fine location overlooking the sandy beach and open sea beyond. Comfortable accommodation with 58 en-suite bedrooms. Several lounge areas, bar and restaurant for guests only.   128

Bewdley Hotel, Pentire Road, Newquay, Cornwall TR7 1NX

Tel: 01637 872883 Fax: 01637 872883
Friendly, family-run hotel overlooking links golf course and beach. 29 en-suite rooms of varying sizes. Evening entertainment through the summer. Heated outdoor pool.   122

The Brookdale Hotel, Tregolls Road, Truro, Cornwall TR1 1JZ

Tel: 01872 273513 Fax: 01872 272400
e-mail: brookdale@hotelstruro.com
website: www.hotelstruro.com/brookdale
Good sized hotel set in its own beautifully landscaped grounds. Popular Italian Ristorante open Monday to Saturday. Comfortable, elegantly furnished en-suite rooms of varying types.   113

Chynoweth Lodge Hotel, 1 Eliot Gardens, Newquay, Cornwall TR7 2QE

Tel: 01637 876684
e-mail: reg@chynowethlodge.co.uk
website: www.chynowethlodge.co.uk
Comfortable accommodation, with nine en-suite rooms, personally run by resident owners. Comfortable lounge area and attractive dining room. Home-cooked food served in ample portions.   121

The Cumberland Hotelm, Henver Road, Newquay, Cornwall TR7 3BJ

Tel: 01637 873025 Fax: 01637 873097
Friendly seaside hotel with facilities including an outdoor pool and spacious ballroom. 32 rooms of varying sizes, all en-suite. Restaurant serves mainly English cuisine each evening, with lunches available on request.

The Glen Court Hotel, Mellanvrane Lane,

Newquay, Cornwall TR7 2LB

Tel: 01637 874848
An 11-bedroom, family-run hotel ideal for those
wanting a relaxing holiday. Restaurant serves superb
home-cooked meals. Also a comfortable lounge and
separate bar area.

Marcorrie Hotel, 20 Falmouth Road, Truro, Cornwall TR1 2HX

Tel: 01872 277374 Fax: 01872 241666
e-mail: marcorrie@aol.com
website: www.cornwall.net/marcorrie
Small, charming family-run hotel on a delightful
Victorian and Edwardian street near to the city centre,
offering traditional Cornish hospitality.   103

Mayrose Farm Holiday Cottages, Helstone, Camelford, Cornwall PL32 9RN

Tel: 01840 213509 Fax: 01840 213509
e-mail: mayrosefarm@hotmail.com
Five, very different properties converted from former
farm buildings, decorated and furnished to a very
high standard. Outdoor pool. Super holiday base. 105

Pendeen Hotel, 7 Alexandra Road, Porth, Newquay, Cornwall TR7 3ND

Tel: 01637 873521 Fax: 01637 873521
e-mail: pendeen@cornwall.net
Relaxing and peaceful hotel where you will find
friendly service. 15 en-suite rooms. Restaurant serves
traditional English and international cuisine focusing
on fresh fish and seafood.   129

Porth Lodge Hotel, Porthbean Road, Newquay, Cornwall TR7 3TL

Tel: 01637 874483
Popular hostelry, with two bar areas, serving good
food, with beer garden and children's room. 20 en-
suite rooms and six self-catering apartments. Also a
10-pin bowling alley.   123

Porth Veor Manor, Porth Way, Nr. Newquay, Cornwall TR7 3LW

Tel: 01637 873274 Fax: 01637 873274
Friendly hotel offering the best in traditional Cornish
hospitality. Elevated location offers superb views in
all directions. 22 en-suite rooms. Award-winning
restaurant open to non-residents.   125

Ruthern Valley Holidays, Ruthern Bridge, Nr. Bodmin, Cornwall PL30 5LU

Tel: 01208 831395 Fax: 01208 832324
website: self-catering-ruthern.co.uk
Peaceful, relaxing holiday retreat developed from
former mining area. Range of holiday accommodation
with bungalows, lodges, caravans and camping
facilities. Shop and children's play area.   101

Treheveras Guest House, 2a Dane Road, Newquay, Cornwall TR7 1HL

Tel: 01637 874079
e-mail: treheveras@aol.com
A small guest house located on Newquay's Towan
headland. Seven cosy rooms, five double, two single,
most with en-suite facilities. Traditional cooked
English breakfast. Reasonable rates.

Trenance Lodge Hotel and Restaurant, Trenance Road, Newquay, Cornwall TR7 2HW

Tel: 01637 876702 Fax: 01637 878772
e-mail: info@trenance-lodge.co.uk
website: www.trenance-lodge.co.uk
A fine restaurant with excellent reputation for serving
fine local produce in a modern British style. Also 5
en-suite bedrooms, stylishly furnished and well-
appointed.   124

Trethin Manor Holiday Cottages, Advent, Camelford, Cornwall PL32 9QW

Tel: 01840 213522 Fax: 01840 212898
A collection of former farm buildings which have
been converted to comfortable self-catering
accommodation. Ten cottages surrounded by
landscaped grounds. Children's play area, barbecue,
laundry.   120

White House Court Holiday Cottages, c/o 1 Middle Leigh, Newton Ferrers, Plymouth, Devon PL8 1DS

Tel: 01752 873128 Fax: 01752 873128
e-mail: whitehouse.cotts@barclay.net
website: www.whitehousecourt.co.uk
Eleven well-equipped self-catering cottages created
from traditional, stone-built farm buildings. Two
miles from the coast.   111

The Wilsey Down, Hallworthy, Camelford, Cornwall PL32 9SH

Tel: 01840 261205
e-mail: jane@greatbidlake.farmcom.net
Comfortable, welcoming establishment with two bars
and separate restaurant. Six guest rooms, 2 of which
are en-suite, of varying sizes.   104

Woodlands Hotel, 38-40 Pentire Crescent, Newquay, Cornwall TR7 1PU

Tel: 01637 852229 Fax: 01637 852227
Quiet setting, just outside Newquay, with spectacular
views over the river and open countryside. 54
bedrooms. Excellent facilities including outdoor pool,
sauna, solarium, sunbed and bowling green.   131

Food and Drink

The Brookdale Hotel, Tregolls Road, Truro, Cornwall TR1 1JZ

Tel: 01872 273513 Fax: 01872 272400
e-mail: brookdale@hotelstruro.com
website: www.hotelstruro.com/brookdale
Good sized hotel set in its own beautifully landscaped
grounds. Popular Italian Ristorante open Monday to
Saturday. Comfortable, elegantly furnished en-suite
rooms of varying types.   113

The Cumberland Hotelm, Henver Road, Newquay, Cornwall TR7 3BJ

Tel: 01637 873025 Fax: 01637 873097
Friendly seaside hotel with facilities including an
outdoor pool and spacious ballroom. 32 rooms of
varying sizes, all en-suite. Restaurant serves mainly
English cuisine each evening, with lunches available
on request.

The Globe Inn, 3 North Street, Lostwithiel, Cornwall PL22 0EG

Tel: 01208 872501
Cosy, friendly, traditional inn offering a warm welcome to all. Open plan bar, restaurant area, patio and beer garden. Good menu of tasty home-cooked, freshly-prepared food.   102

Legonna Farm, Lane, Newquay, Cornwall TR8 4NJ

Tel: 01637 872272
A traditional Cornish welcome awaits all who visit Legonna Farm where you will find comfortable bed and breakfast accommodation. Nine en-suite rooms of varying sizes. Packed lunches and evening meals available on request.

Pendeen Hotel, 7 Alexandra Road, Porth, Newquay, Cornwall TR7 3ND

Tel: 01637 873521 Fax: 01637 873521
e-mail: pendeen@cornwall.net
Relaxing and peaceful hotel where you will find friendly service. 15 en-suite rooms. Restaurant serves traditional English and international cuisine focusing on fresh fish and seafood.   129

Porth Lodge Hotel, Porthbean Road, Newquay, Cornwall TR7 3TL

Tel: 01637 874483
Popular hostelry, with two bar areas, serving good food, with beer garden and children's room. 20 en-suite rooms and six self-catering apartments. Also a 10-pin bowling alley.   123

Porth Veor Manor, Porth Way, Nr. Newquay, Cornwall TR7 3LW

Tel: 01637 873274 Fax: 01637 873274
Friendly hotel offering the best in traditional Cornish hospitality. Elevated location offers superb views in all directions. 22 en-suite rooms. Award-winning restaurant open to non-residents.   125

Smugglers Den Inn, Cubert, Newquay, Cornwall TR8 5PY

Tel: 01637 830209 Fax: 01637 830580
Quaint, 400-year old hostelry with a popular reputation for serving fine food and well-kept ale. Reputedly haunted!   126

Trenance Lodge Hotel and Restaurant, Trenance Road, Newquay, Cornwall TR7 2HW

Tel: 01637 876702 Fax: 01637 878772
e-mail: info@trenance-lodge.co.uk
website: www.trenance-lodge.co.uk
A fine restaurant with excellent reputation for serving fine local produce in a modern British style. Also 5 en-suite bedrooms, stylishly furnished and well-appointed.   124

Tywarnhayle Hotel, The Square, Perranporth, Cornwall TR6 0ER

Tel: 01872 572215 Fax: 01872 571773
Friendly, family-run hostelry serving a good range of food and drink. The menu is typically English cuisine and the traditional Sunday Roast lunches are very popular. Restaurant seats 60.

The Wilsey Down, Hallworthy, Camelford, Cornwall PL32 9SH

Tel: 01840 261205
e-mail: jane@greatbidlake.farmcom.net
Comfortable, welcoming establishment with two bars and separate restaurant. Six guest rooms, 2 of which are en-suite, of varying sizes.   104

St. Austell Golf Club

Tregongeeves Lane, St. Austell,
Cornwall PL26 7DS
Tel: 01726 74756 Fax: 01726 74756

Sec/Manager:	K. Trehair
Professional:	Tony Pitts
Directions:	1¼ miles southwest of St. Austell. From the centre take Truro Road (B3274) and join A390 (Truro). After ½ mile turn left onto Tregongeeves Lane. The entrance is on the right hand side.
Date Founded:	1911
Type of Course:	Parkland, Heathland
No of Holes:	18
Length:	6091 yds (5621 mtrs)
Par:	69
SSS:	69
Green Fees:	Weekdays: £20; Weekends/ Bank Holidays: £22

Visitors:	Welcome: Contact Club in Advance. Play at weekends by arrangement
Societies:	Welcome: Contact Club in Advance. Unable to play Tuesday, Thursday and weekends.
Facilities:	Putting Green, Chipping Green, Driving Range, Trolley Hire, Bar, Restaurant

Accommodation, Food and Drink

Reference numbers below refer to detailed information provided in section 2

Accommodation

The Brookdale Hotel, Tregolls Road, Truro, Cornwall TR1 1JZ

Tel: 01872 273513 Fax: 01872 272400
e-mail: brookdale@hotelstruro.com
website: www.hotelstruro.com/brookdale
Good sized hotel set in its own beautifully landscaped grounds. Popular Italian Ristorante open Monday to Saturday. Comfortable, elegantly furnished en-suite rooms of varying types.   113

Fieldhead Hotel, Portuan Road, Hannafore, West Looe, Cornwall PL13 2DR

Tel: 01503 262689 Fax: 01503 264114
e-mail: field.head@virgin.net
website: www.fieldheadhotel.co.uk
Elegant country house style hotel offering high standard of comfort and service. Comfortable en-suite rooms, many with sea views.   115

Marcorrie Hotel, 20 Falmouth Road, Truro, Cornwall TR1 2HX

Tel: 01872 277374 Fax: 01872 241666
e-mail: marcorrie@aol.com
website: www.cornwall.net/marcorrie
Small, charming family-run hotel on a delightful Victorian and Edwardian street near to the city centre, offering traditional Cornish hospitality.   103

Ruthern Valley Holidays, Ruthern Bridge, Nr. Bodmin, Cornwall PL30 5LU

Tel: 01208 831395 Fax: 01208 832324
website: self-catering-ruthern.co.uk
Peaceful, relaxing holiday retreat developed from former mining area. Range of holiday accommodation with bungalows, lodges, caravans and camping facilities. Well-stocked shop and children's play area.
                                                        101

Food and Drink

The Brookdale Hotel, Tregolls Road, Truro, Cornwall TR1 1JZ

Tel: 01872 273513 Fax: 01872 272400
e-mail: brookdale@hotelstruro.com
website: www.hotelstruro.com/brookdale
Good sized hotel set in its own beautifully landscaped

grounds. Popular Italian Ristorante open Monday to Saturday. Comfortable, elegantly furnished en-suite rooms of varying types.   113

The Globe Inn, 3 North Street, Lostwithiel, Cornwall PL22 0EG

Tel: 01208 872501
Cosy, friendly, traditional inn offering a warm welcome to all. Open plan bar, restaurant area, patio and beer garden. Good menu of tasty home-cooked, freshly-prepared food.   102

The Sundeck, East Quay, Mevagissy, Cornwall PL26 6QQ

Tel: 01726 843051
A surprising find. Stylish decor in Mediterranean theme with picture windows looking out to sea. High quality home-cooked food.   112

Three Pilchards, The Quay, Polperro, Looe, Cornwall PL13 2QZ

Tel: 01503 272233
Traditional Cornish pub located on the sea front. Home-cooked food served each day.   116

Trewithen Restaurant, 3 Fore Street, Lostwithiel, Cornwall PL22 0BP

Tel: 01208 872373
Award-winning restaurant with cosy, cottagey style in the heart of the pretty town of Lostwithiel. Traditional, English cuisine.   110

St. Enodoc Golf Club

Rock, Wadebridge, Cornwall PL27 6LD
Tel: 01208 863216 Fax: 01208 862976

Look, are you really certain you want to do this? There are other courses to play, even other games to take up. Remember, you don't have to do it. You don't need to prove anything. Still going ahead? OK, just remember that you can take with you a maximum of 14 clubs, but on golf balls there appears to be no restriction on numbers. Perhaps just as well, for the course which moved Poet Laureate John Betjamin to verse could well move you to tears of frustration.

St Enodoc is one of the most celebrated courses in the country. As a links course, it has every-

thing you would expect, like meandering, difficult fairways; humps, lumps and bumps; a persistent wind; and lightning-fast greens - and that's just for starters.

Aficionados will know that St Enodoc is also famous for its sixth hole, or at least what is generally regarded as the biggest 'bunker' on a golf course, the aptly-named Himalayas sand hill.

Sadly, history fails to record whether designer James Braid was in a particularly bad mood when he incorporated this monumental obstacle into the course or if he was merely being mischievous.

You might think that life would get a little easier after overcoming that, but alas, no. The card says 6,200 yards, par 69. Right! Anybody breaking 80 here has been smiled on by the golfing Gods.

Betjamen, who is buried in the graveyard adjacent to the sunken church near the 10th, was so overjoyed by a rare birdie - at the 13th - that he wrote:

*'It lay content
Two paces from the pin.
A steady putt and then it went
Oh, most securely in.
The very turf rejoiced to see
That quite unprecedented three.'*

Better get your own poetic homily prepared, or stick to the far shorter and less hazardous Holywell course.

Sec/Manager:	Ian Waters
Professional:	Nick Williams
Directions:	5 miles northwest of Wadebridge. Take the B3314 from Wadebridge to St. Miniver. Turn left to Rock and follow signs to the Course.
Visitors:	Welcome: Contact Club in Advance. Handicap Certificates required. Unable to play before 2.30 pm Saturdays.
Societies:	Welcome: Contact Club by writing in Advance.
Facilities:	Practice Ground Chipping Green, Club Hire, Trolley Hire, Buggy Hire, Bar, Restaurant, Driving Range

Church

Date Founded:	1890
Type of Course:	Links
No of Holes:	18
Length:	6207 yds (5729 mtrs)
Par:	69
SSS:	69
Green Fees:	Weekdays: £35; Weekends/ Bank Holidays: £40

Holywell

Date Founded:	1935
Type of Course:	Links
No of Holes:	18
Length:	4142 yds (3823 mtrs)
Par:	63
SSS:	61
Green Fees:	Weekdays: £15; Weekends/ Bank Holidays: £15

Accommodation, Food and Drink

Reference numbers below refer to detailed information provided in section 2

Accommodation

The Beaconsfield Hotel, The Crescent, Newquay, Cornwall TR7 1DT

Tel: 01637 872172 Fax: 01637 850711
Stylish hotel in fine location overlooking the sandy beach and open sea beyond. Comfortable accommodation with 58 en-suite bedrooms. Several lounge areas, bar and restaurant for guests only. 128

Bewdley Hotel, Pentire Road, Newquay, Cornwall TR7 1NX

Tel: 01637 872883 Fax: 01637 872883
Friendly, family-run hotel overlooking links golf
course and beach. 29 en-suite rooms of varying sizes.
Evening entertainment through the summer. Heated
outdoor pool. 122

The Brookdale Hotel, Tregolls Road, Truro, Cornwall TR1 1JZ

Tel: 01872 273513 Fax: 01872 272400
e-mail: brookdale@hotelstruro.com
website: www.hotelstruro.com/brookdale
Good sized hotel set in its own beautifully landscaped
grounds. Popular Italian Ristorante open Monday to
Saturday. Comfortable, elegantly furnished en-suite
rooms of varying types. 113

Chynoweth Lodge Hotel, 1 Eliot Gardens, Newquay, Cornwall TR7 2QE

Tel: 01637 876684
e-mail: reg@chynowethlodge.co.uk
website: www.chynowethlodge.co.uk
Comfortable accommodation, with nine en-suite
rooms, personally run by resident owners.
Comfortable lounge area and attractive dining room.
Home-cooked food served in ample portions. 121

The Cumberland Hotelm, Henver Road, Newquay, Cornwall TR7 3BJ

Tel: 01637 873025 Fax: 01637 873097
Friendly seaside hotel with facilities including an
outdoor pool and spacious ballroom. 32 rooms of
varying sizes, all en-suite. Restaurant serves mainly
English cuisine each evening, with lunches available
on request.

The Glen Court Hotel, Mellanvrane Lane, Newquay, Cornwall TR7 2LB

Tel: 01637 874848
An 11-bedroom, family-run hotel ideal for those
wanting a relaxing holiday. Restaurant serves superb
home-cooked meals. Also a comfortable lounge and
separate bar area.

Marcorrie Hotel, 20 Falmouth Road, Truro, Cornwall TR1 2HX

Tel: 01872 277374 Fax: 01872 241666
e-mail: marcorrie@aol.com
website: www.cornwall.net/marcorrie
Small, charming family-run hotel on a delightful
Victorian and Edwardian street near to the city centre,
offering traditional Cornish hospitality. 103

Mayrose Farm Holiday Cottages, Helstone, Camelford, Cornwall PL32 9RN

Tel: 01840 213509 Fax: 01840 213509
e-mail: mayrosefarm@hotmail.com
Five, very different properties converted from former
farm buildings, decorated and furnished to a very
high standard. Outdoor pool. Super holiday base. 105

Pendeen Hotel, 7 Alexandra Road, Porth, Newquay, Cornwall TR7 3ND

Tel: 01637 873521 Fax: 01637 873521
e-mail: pendeen@cornwall.net

Relaxing and peaceful hotel where you will find
friendly service. 15 en-suite rooms. Restaurant serves
traditional English and international cuisine focusing
on fresh fish and seafood. 129

Porth Lodge Hotel, Porthbean Road, Newquay, Cornwall TR7 3TL

Tel: 01637 874483
Popular hostelry, with two bar areas, serving good
food, with beer garden and children's room. 20 en-
suite rooms and six self-catering apartments. Also a
10-pin bowling alley. 123

Porth Veor Manor, Porth Way, Nr. Newquay, Cornwall TR7 3LW

Tel: 01637 873274 Fax: 01637 873274
Friendly hotel offering the best in traditional Cornish
hospitality. Elevated location offers superb views in
all directions. 22 en-suite rooms. Award-winning
restaurant open to non-residents. 125

Ruthern Valley Holidays, Ruthern Bridge, Nr. Bodmin, Cornwall PL30 5LU

Tel: 01208 831395 Fax: 01208 832324
website: self-catering-ruthern.co.uk
Peaceful, relaxing holiday retreat developed from
former mining area. Range of holiday accommodation
with bungalows, lodges, caravans and camping
facilities. Shop and children's play area. 101

Treheveras Guest House, 2a Dane Road, Newquay, Cornwall TR7 1HL

Tel: 01637 874079
e-mail: treheveras@aol.com
A small guest house located on Newquay's Towan
headland. Seven cosy rooms, five double, two single,
most with en-suite facilities. Traditional cooked
English breakfast. Reasonable rates.

Trenance Lodge Hotel and Restaurant, Trenance Road, Newquay, Cornwall TR7 2HW

Tel: 01637 876702 Fax: 01637 878772
e-mail: info@trenance-lodge.co.uk
website: www.trenance-lodge.co.uk
A fine restaurant with excellent reputation for serving
fine local produce in a modern British style. Also 5
en-suite bedrooms, stylishly furnished and well-
appointed. 124

Trethin Manor Holiday Cottages, Advent, Camelford, Cornwall PL32 9QW

Tel: 01840 213522 Fax: 01840 212898
A collection of former farm buildings which have
been converted into comfortable self-catering
accommodation. Ten cottages surrounded by
landscaped grounds. Children's play area, barbecue,
laundry. 120

White House Court Holiday Cottages, c/o 1 Middle Leigh, Newton Ferrers, Plymouth, Devon PL8 1DS

Tel: 01752 873128 Fax: 01752 873128
e-mail: whitehouse.cotts@barclay.net
website: www.whitehousecourt.co.uk
Eleven well-equipped self-catering cottages created
from traditional, stone-built farm buildings. Two

miles from the coast. 111

The Wilsey Down, Hallworthy, Camelford, Cornwall PL32 9SH

Tel: 01840 261205
e-mail: jane@greatbidlake.farmcom.net
Comfortable, welcoming establishment with two bars and separate restaurant. Six guest rooms, 2 of which are en-suite, of varying sizes. 104

Woodlands Hotel, 38-40 Pentire Crescent, Newquay, Cornwall TR7 1PU

Tel: 01637 852229 Fax: 01637 852227
Quiet setting, just outside Newquay, with spectacular views over the river and open countryside. 54 bedrooms. Excellent facilities including outdoor pool, sauna, solarium, sunbed and bowling green. 131

Food and Drink

The Brookdale Hotel, Tregolls Road, Truro, Cornwall TR1 1JZ

Tel: 01872 273513 Fax: 01872 272400
e-mail: brookdale@hotelstruro.com
website: www.hotelstruro.com/brookdale
Good sized hotel set in its own beautifully landscaped grounds. Popular Italian Ristorante open Monday to Saturday. Comfortable, elegantly furnished en-suite rooms of varying types. 113

The Globe Inn, 3 North Street, Lostwithiel, Cornwall PL22 0EG

Tel: 01208 872501
Cosy, friendly, traditional inn offering a warm welcome to all. Open plan bar, restaurant area, patio and beer garden. Good menu of tasty home-cooked, freshly-prepared food. 102

Legonna Farm, Lane, Newquay, Cornwall TR8 4NJ

Tel: 01637 872272
A traditional Cornish welcome awaits all who visit Legonna Farm where you will find comfortable bed and breakfast accommodation. Nine en-suite rooms of varying sizes. Packed lunches and evening meals available on request.

Pendeen Hotel, 7 Alexandra Road, Porth, Newquay, Cornwall TR7 3ND

Tel: 01637 873521 Fax: 01637 873521
e-mail: pendeen@cornwall.net
Relaxing and peaceful hotel where you will find friendly service. 15 en-suite rooms. Restaurant serves traditional English and international cuisine focusing on fresh fish and seafood. 129

Porth Lodge Hotel, Porthbean Road, Newquay, Cornwall TR7 3TL

Tel: 01637 874483
Popular hostelry, with two bar areas, serving good food, with beer garden and children's room. 20 en-suite rooms and six self-catering apartments. Also a 10-pin bowling alley. 123

Porth Veor Manor, Porth Way, Nr. Newquay, Cornwall TR7 3LW

Tel: 01637 873274 Fax: 01637 873274

Friendly hotel offering the best in traditional Cornish hospitality. Elevated location offers superb views in all directions. 22 en-suite rooms. Award-winning restaurant open to non-residents. 125

Smugglers Den Inn, Cubert, Newquay, Cornwall TR8 5PY

Tel: 01637 830209 Fax: 01637 830580
Quaint, 400-year old hostelry with a popular reputation for serving fine food and well-kept ale. Reputedly haunted! 126

Trenance Lodge Hotel and Restaurant, Trenance Road, Newquay, Cornwall TR7 2HW

Tel: 01637 876702 Fax: 01637 878772
e-mail: info@trenance-lodge.co.uk
website: www.trenance-lodge.co.uk
A fine restaurant with excellent reputation for serving fine local produce in a modern British style. Also 5 en-suite bedrooms, stylishly furnished and well-appointed. 124

Tywarnhayle Hotel, The Square, Perranporth, Cornwall TR6 0ER

Tel: 01872 572215 Fax: 01872 571773
Friendly, family-run hostelry serving a good range of food and drink. The menu is typically English cuisine and the traditional Sunday Roast lunches are very popular. Restaurant seats 60.

The Wilsey Down, Hallworthy, Camelford, Cornwall PL32 9SH

Tel: 01840 261205
e-mail: jane@greatbidlake.farmcom.net
Comfortable, welcoming establishment with two bars and separate restaurant. Six guest rooms, 2 of which are en-suite, of varying sizes. 104

St. Mellion Golf Club

St. Mellion, Saltash, Cornwall PL12 6SD
Tel: 01579 351351 Fax: 01579 350537

For St Mellion, read St Enodoc and add Jack Nicklaus, then double it. Here in the magical Tamar Valley you are given a choice of two routes to hell and back. Do you go with our old friend Hamilton Stutt, who designed the Old Course, or follow the tracks of the Golden Bear on the Nicklaus Course?

Both were the dream of farming brothers Martin and Hermon Bond, the Godfathers of Cornish golf in the last quarter of the 20th century, and the original 18, now the Old Course, put St Mellion on the map.

So what of the Nicklaus track? Well, and you must bear in mind here that we are in the land of legend, it is said that the brothers wanted to create the best course in Europe and decided Nicklaus was the only man for the job. But how to get him interested? How about a letter outlining the plan, folded around a cheque for £1 million?

True or not, it's a good tale and, whatever happened, Nicklaus eventually came, saw and concurred. Thus was created the 'Augusta of Cornwall,' a little poetic, perhaps, although one or two holes do closely resemble the home of the US Masters. Suffice to say the course was good enough to attract the B&H International Open in the early 1990s - Ballesteros, Olazabal and Langer all proving winners in different years.

The courses are now owned by a multi-national company, but the test remains at its most severe. Those with handicaps above the mid-teens might be better leaving well enough alone.

Sec/Manager:	Richard Burrows
Professional:	David Moon
Directions:	8½ miles northwest of Plymouth City Centre. From the Tamar Bridge on A38 continue for 1½ miles and turn right onto the A388 (Callington). After 4¼ miles the entrance is on the left hand side just after St. Mellion
Visitors:	Welcome: Contact Club in Advance. Handicap certificates required. No restrictions
Societies:	Welcome: Contact Club in Advance
Facilities:	Putting Green, Chipping Green, Club Hire, Trolley Hire, Buggy Hire, Bar, Restaurant, Driving Range, Private Rooms

Nicklaus Course

Date Founded:	1998
Type of Course:	Parkland
No of Holes:	18
Length:	6651 yds (6139 mtrs)
Par:	72
SSS:	72
Green Fees:	Weekdays: £50; Weekends/ Bank Holidays: £50

Old Course

Date Founded:	1998
Type of Course:	Parkland
No of Holes:	18
Length:	5927 yds (5471 mtrs)
Par:	70
SSS:	70
Green Fees:	Weekdays: £35; Weekends/ Bank Holidays: £35

Accommodation, Food and Drink

Reference numbers below refer to detailed information provided in section 2

Accommodation

The Brendon Arms, Vicarage Road, Bude, Cornwall EX23 8SD

Tel: 01288 354542 Fax: 01288 354542
e-mail: sophia@sophiafrbrendon.demon.co.uk
website: www.north-cornwall.co.uk/client/ brendon-arms/
Traditional Cornish inn situated in a picturesque part of town. Serves a good selection of seafood while the bar stocks a range of real ales. Seven en-suite guest rooms.   109

The Camelot Hotel and Hawkers Restaurant, Downs View, Bude, Cornwall EX23 8RE

Tel: 01288 352361 Fax: 01288 355470
e-mail: stay@camelot-hotel.co.uk
website: www.camelot-hotel.co.uk
Super location on the edge of Bude Golf Course and five minutes from sea. High standards throughout, with relaxed comfortable ambience. 24 en-suite rooms. Popular restaurant.   106

The Carpenters Arms, Metherell, Nr. Callington, Cornwall PL17 8BJ

Tel: 01579 350242 Fax: 01579 350242
A picturesque Cornish pub with friendly and welcoming service. Wide-ranging menu of home-cooked bar meals and snacks.   117

Cawsand Bay Hotel & Galleon Restaurant, The Bound, Cawsand, Nr. Torpoint, Cornwall PL10 1PG

Tel: 01752 822425 Fax: 01752 823527
e-mail: sales@cawsandbay.co.uk
website: www.cawsandbay.co.uk
Located directly on the sea front and with superb views across the Sound towards Plymouth. Ten comfortable en-suite rooms of varying sizes. Popular bar and restaurant.   130

Fieldhead Hotel, Portuan Road, Hannafore, West Looe, Cornwall PL13 2DR

Tel: 01503 262689 Fax: 01503 264114
e-mail: field.head@virgin.net
website: www.fieldheadhotel.co.uk
Elegant country house style hotel offering high

standard of comfort and service. Comfortable en-suite
rooms, many with sea views. 115

The Halfway House Inn, Grenofen, Tavistock, Devon PL19 9ER

Tel: 01822 612960 Fax: 01822 617697
A large, sprawling black and white 16th-century
building with friendly atmosphere. Excellent
reputation for high quality food with two restaurants
serving an a la carte menu. Four guest rooms. 206

The Old Coach House, Ottery, Tavistock, Devon PL19 8NS

Tel: 01822 617515 Fax: 01822 617515
e-mail eddie@coachhouseone.supanet.com
Old coach house which was substantially renovated
in 1989 to create a delightful hotel and restaurant.
Comfortable accommodation and superb a la carte
restaurant. 236

Royal Standard Inn, Mary Tavy, Nr. Tavistock, Devon PL19 9QB

Tel: 01822 810289 Fax: 01822 810615
Former coaching inn with an atmosphere of character
and charm. The inn claims to serve the best beer in
the area while the food comprises a good selection of
traditional meals and snacks. 235

Tavistock Arms, Fore Street, Gunnislake, Cornwall PL18 9BN

Tel: 01822 832217
Traditional, country pub located directly on the
Devon/Cornwall border. Food is served all day. Bed
and breakfast accommodation available. 118

Three Pilchards, The Quay, Polperro, Looe, Cornwall PL13 2QZ

Tel: 01503 272233
Traditional Cornish pub located on the sea front.
Home-cooked food served each day. 116

Tehidy Park Golf Club

Cambourne, Cornwall TR14 0HH
Tel: 01209 842208 Fax: 01209 843680

Sec/Manager: Ray Parker
Professional: James Dumbreck

Directions:	2 miles north of Cambourne centre. From the A30 take the A3047 turning right under dual carriageway. Follow brown signs to Tehidy Park
Date Founded:	1922
Type of Course:	Parkland
No of Holes:	18
Length:	6241 yds (5761 mtrs)
Par:	71
SSS:	71
Green Fees:	Weekdays: £25; Weekends/ Bank Holidays: £30
Visitors:	Welcome: Tee times bookable ring in advance. Handicap certificate required
Societies:	Welcome: Contact Club in Advance. Unable to play Tuesday, Thursday and weekends.
Facilities:	Putting Green, Club Hire, Trolley Hire, Bar, Restaurant

Accommodation, Food and Drink

Reference numbers below refer to detailed
information provided in section 2

Accommodation

The Brookdale Hotel, Tregolls Road, Truro, Cornwall TR1 1JZ

Tel: 01872 273513 Fax: 01872 272400
e-mail: brookdale@hotelstruro.com
website: www.hotelstruro.com/brookdale
Good sized hotel set in its own beautifully landscaped
grounds. Popular Italian Ristorante open Monday to
Saturday. Comfortable, elegantly furnished en-suite
rooms of varying types. 113

Chy-Garth Guest House, Sea View Meadows, St. Ives Road, Carbis Bay, St. Ives, Cornwall TR26 2JX

Tel: 01736 795677
e-mail: ann@chy-garth.demon.co.uk

A delightful, detached house surrounded by colourful gardens and enjoying some beautiful sea views. A non-smoking establishment, there are eight guest rooms, nearly all with en-suite or private facilities. Ample car parking.

Dunmar Hotel, Pednolver Terrace, St. Ives, Cornwall TR26 2EL

Tel: 01736 796117 Fax: 01736 796053
Friendly, family-run 'olde worlde' hotel offering a warm welcome and traditional Cornish hospitality. 17 en-suite bedrooms of varying sizes with bar and restaurant available to guests.

Marcorrie Hotel, 20 Falmouth Road, Truro, Cornwall TR1 2HX

Tel: 01872 277374 Fax: 01872 241666
e-mail: marcorrie@aol.com
website: www.cornwall.net/marcorrie
Small, charming family-run hotel on a delightful Victorian and Edwardian street near to the city centre, offering traditional Cornish hospitality. 103

Meudon Hotel, Mawnan Smith, Near Falmouth, Cornwall TR11 5HT

Tel: 01326 250541 Fax: 01326 250543
website: www.meudon.co.uk
Superb, family-run country house hotel, set in a sub-tropical garden paradise with private beach. Elegant restaurant specialising in local seafood. Free golf included in high- and mid-season rates. 119

Regent Hotel, Fern Lea Terrace, St. Ives, Cornwall TR26 2BH

Tel: 01736 796195 Fax: 01736 794641
e-mail: enquiries@regenthotel.com
website: www.regenthotel.com
Friendly, family-run hotel with AA and RAC 4 Diamond Grading. The nine en-suite guest bedrooms are tastefully decorated and comfortably furnished and many have spectacular views over the picturesque harbour.

White House Court Holiday Cottages, c/o 1 Middle Leigh, Newton Ferrers, Plymouth, Devon PL8 1DS

Tel: 01752 873128 Fax: 01752 873128
e-mail: whitehouse.cotts@barclay.net
website: www.whitehousecourt.co.uk
Eleven well-equipped self-catering cottages created from traditional, stone-built farm buildings. Two miles from the coast. 111

Food and Drink

The Brookdale Hotel, Tregolls Road, Truro, Cornwall TR1 1JZ

Tel: 01872 273513 Fax: 01872 272400
e-mail: brookdale@hotelstruro.com
website: www.hotelstruro.com/brookdale
Good sized hotel set in its own beautifully landscaped grounds. Popular Italian Ristorante open Monday to Saturday. Comfortable, elegantly furnished en-suite rooms of varying types. 113

Meudon Hotel, Mawnan Smith, Near Falmouth, Cornwall TR11 5HT

Tel: 01326 250541 Fax: 01326 250543
website: www.meudon.co.uk
Superb, family-run country house hotel, set in a sub-tropical garden paradise with private beach. Elegant restaurant specialising in local seafood. Free golf included in high- and mid-season rates. 119

The Sundeck, East Quay, Mevagissy, Cornwall PL26 6QQ

Tel: 01726 843051
A surprising find. Stylish decor in Mediterranean theme with picture windows looking out to sea. High quality home-cooked food. 112

Tregenna Castle Golf Club

St. Ives, Cornwall TR26 2DE

Tel: 01736 797381 (Shop) 01736 795254 (Hotel)

Sec/Manager:	Ian Pleasence
Professional:	None
Directions:	¼ mile southeast of St. Ives centre. Opposite the Jet Service Station on Trelyon Avenue (A3074)
Date Founded:	1982
Type of Course:	Parkland
No of Holes:	18
Length:	3418 yds (3155 mtrs)
Par:	60
SSS:	58
Green Fees:	Weekdays: £15; Weekends/ Bank Holidays: £15
Visitors:	Welcome: No restrictions
Societies:	Welcome: Contact Club in Advance. No restrictions.
Facilities:	Putting Green, Club Hire, Trolley Hire, Bar, Restaurant, Private Rooms

Accommodation, Food and Drink

Reference numbers below refer to detailed
information provided in section 2

Accommodation

**The Brookdale Hotel, Tregolls Road, Truro,
Cornwall TR1 1JZ**

Tel: 01872 273513 Fax: 01872 272400
e-mail: brookdale@hotelstruro.com
website: www.hotelstruro.com/brookdale
Good sized hotel set in its own beautifully landscaped
grounds. Popular Italian Ristorante open Monday to
Saturday. Comfortable, elegantly furnished en-suite
rooms of varying types.   113

**Chy-Garth Guest House, Sea View Meadows,
St. Ives Road, Carbis Bay, St. Ives,
Cornwall TR26 2JX**

Tel: 01736 795677
e-mail: ann@chy-garth.demon.co.uk
A delightful, detached house surrounded by colourful
gardens and enjoying some beautiful sea views. A
non-smoking establishment, there are eight guest
rooms, nearly all with en-suite or private facilities.
Ample car parking.

**Dunmar Hotel, Pednolver Terrace, St. Ives,
Cornwall TR26 2EL**

Tel: 01736 796117 Fax: 01736 796053
Friendly, family-run 'olde worlde' hotel offering a
warm welcome and traditional Cornish hospitality. 17
en-suite bedrooms of varying sizes with bar and
restaurant available to guests.

**Marcorrie Hotel, 20 Falmouth Road, Truro,
Cornwall TR1 2HX**

Tel: 01872 277374 Fax: 01872 241666
e-mail: marcorrie@aol.com
website: www.cornwall.net/marcorrie
Small, charming family-run hotel on a delightful
Victorian and Edwardian street near to the city centre,
offering traditional Cornish hospitality.   103

**Meudon Hotel, Mawnan Smith, Near Falmouth,
Cornwall TR11 5HT**

Tel: 01326 250541 Fax: 01326 250543
website: www.meudon.co.uk
Superb, family-run country house hotel, set in a sub-
tropical garden paradise with private beach. Elegant
restaurant specialising in local seafood. Free golf
included in high- and mid-season rates.   119

**Regent Hotel, Fern Lea Terrace, St. Ives,
Cornwall TR26 2BH**

Tel: 01736 796195 Fax: 01736 794641
e-mail: enquiries@regenthotel.com
website: www.regenthotel.com
Friendly, family-run hotel with AA and RAC 4
Diamond Grading. The nine guest bedrooms
are tastefully decorated and comfortably furnished
and many have spectacular views over the picturesque
harbour.

**White House Court Holiday Cottages,
c/o 1 Middle Leigh, Newton Ferrers,**

Plymouth, Devon PL8 1DS

Tel: 01752 873128 Fax: 01752 873128
e-mail: whitehouse.cotts@barclay.net
website: www.whitehousecourt.co.uk
Eleven well-equipped self-catering cottages created
from traditional, stone-built farm buildings. Two
miles from the coast.   111

Food and Drink

**The Brookdale Hotel, Tregolls Road, Truro,
Cornwall TR1 1JZ**

Tel: 01872 273513 Fax: 01872 272400
e-mail: brookdale@hotelstruro.com
website: www.hotelstruro.com/brookdale
Good sized hotel set in its own beautifully landscaped
grounds. Popular Italian Ristorante open Monday to
Saturday. Comfortable, elegantly furnished en-suite
rooms of varying types.   113

**Meudon Hotel, Mawnan Smith, Near Falmouth,
Cornwall TR11 5HT**

Tel: 01326 250541 Fax: 01326 250543
website: www.meudon.co.uk
Superb, family-run country house hotel, set in a sub-
tropical garden paradise with private beach. Elegant
restaurant specialising in local seafood. Free golf
included in high- and mid-season rates.   119

**The Sundeck, East Quay, Mevagissy,
Cornwall PL26 6QQ**

Tel: 01726 843051
A surprising find. Stylish decor in Mediterranean
theme with picture windows looking out to sea. High
quality home-cooked food.   112

Trethorne Golf Club

Kennards House, Launceston,
Cornwall PL15 8QE

Tel: 01566 86903 Fax: 01566 86981

Sec/Manager:	Colin Willis
Professional:	Mark Boundy
Directions:	2½ miles west of Launceston. From the centre of Launceston take the A30 (Bodmin) and turn right onto A395

(Davidstow). The entrance is on the right hand side.

Date Founded:	1993
Type of Course:	Parkland
No of Holes:	18
Length:	6432 yds (5937 mtrs)
Par:	71
SSS:	71
Green Fees:	Weekdays: £24; Weekends/ Bank Holidays: £24
Visitors:	Welcome: Contact Club in Advance. No restrictions
Societies:	Welcome: Contact Club in Advance
Facilities:	Putting Green, Chipping Green, Driving Range, Club Hire, Trolley Hire, Buggy Hire, Bar, Restaurant

Accommodation, Food and Drink

Reference numbers below refer to detailed information provided in section 2

Accommodation

Bennetts Court Cottages, Whitstone, Holsworthy, Devon EX22 6UD

Tel: 01288 341370 Fax: 01288 341370
e-mail: helen@ bennettscourt.co.uk

website: www.bennettscourt.co.uk
Five, well-equipped self-catering cottages, converted from former farm buildings, sleeping between two and six people. Within the grounds there is a outdoor heated pool and other facilities. 246

The Carpenters Arms, Metherell, Nr. Callington, Cornwall PL17 8BJ

Tel: 01579 350242 Fax: 01579 350242
A picturesque Cornish pub with friendly and welcoming service. Wide-ranging menu of home-cooked bar meals and snacks. 117

Lifton Hall Hotel, Lifton, Devon PL16 0DR

Tel: 01566 784863 Fax: 01566 784770
e-mail mail@liftonhall.co.uk
Traditional 250-year old Country House hotel in peaceful village location with ten en-suite rooms. Formal restaurant and a bistro, both specialising in local fish. 240

Mayrose Farm Holiday Cottages, Helstone, Camelford, Cornwall PL32 9RN

Tel: 01840 213509 Fax: 01840 213509
e-mail: mayrosefarm@hotmail.com
Five, very different properties converted from former farm buildings, decorated and furnished to a very high standard. Outdoor pool. Super holiday base. 105

Trethin Manor Holiday Cottages, Advent, Camelford, Cornwall PL32 9QW

Tel: 01840 213522 Fax: 01840 212898
A collection of former farm buildings which have been converted into comfortable self-catering accommodation. Ten cottages surrounded by landscaped grounds. Children's play area, barbecue, laundry. 120

The Wilsey Down, Hallworthy, Camelford, Cornwall PL32 9SH

Tel: 01840 261205
e-mail: jane@greatbidlake.farmcom.net
Comfortable, welcoming establishment with two bars and separate restaurant. Six guest rooms, 2 of which are en-suite, of varying sizes. 104

Food and Drink

The Carpenters Arms, Metherell, Nr. Callington, Cornwall PL17 8BJ

Tel: 01579 350242 Fax: 01579 350242
A picturesque Cornish pub with friendly and welcoming service. Wide-ranging menu of home-cooked bar meals and snacks. 117

Lifton Hall Hotel, Lifton, Devon PL16 0DR

Tel: 01566 784863 Fax: 01566 784770
e-mail mail@liftonhall.co.uk
Traditional 250-year old Country House hotel in peaceful village location with ten en-suite rooms. Formal restaurant and a bistro, both specialising in local fish. 240

The Wilsey Down, Hallworthy, Camelford, Cornwall PL32 9SH

Tel: 01840 261205

e-mail: jane@greatbidlake.farmcom.net
Comfortable, welcoming establishment with two bars
and separate restaurant. Six guest rooms, 2 of which
are en-suite, of varying sizes. 104

Trevose Golf Club

Constantine Bay, Padstow, Cornwall PL28 8JB
Tel: 01841 520208 Fax: 01841 521057

Despite its proximity to the fearsome St Enodoc, Trevose offers a completely different type of links golf on a course where, unlike its neighbour, even the high handicapper has every chance of a decent score.

This is far more of a holiday golf destination, offering enjoyment without pretty much all the hassle and aggravation that can descend on the golfer who has bitten off more than his ability can chew. The contrast in landscapes is dramatic, with Trevose being far flatter and more wide open, without the intimidating sandhills and worryingly narrow fairways. This is one to enjoy. It goes without saying that any course on the north coast of Cornwall offers spectacular scenery and backdrops, but they don't come any more dramatic than at the fourth green.

After negotiating a couple of gentle par four openers and a short par three played over a little valley, the fourth tee offers you the chance to open your shoulders to hit the apex of a left-hand dogleg, and then on towards the green. Beyond the flag, huge Atlantic breakers crash into the shore

of Booby's Bay. In a stiff on-shore wind you can taste the salty spray, and may even have to duck the odd distressed surfer! Another unusual feature is the green at the seventh. Only on a truly wild links course could you find a putting surface with a hog's back ridge running across it.

But the springy turf and generally short rough makes this a popular venue and, although straight and accurate shots will bring their usual rewards, there is just enough leeway for errors to be made and rectified without it all ending in tears.

Sec/Manager:	Patrick O'Shea
Professional:	Gary Allis
Directions:	3 miles west of Padstow. From centre take the B3276 (St. Merryn) and turn right into Constantine Bay. The entrance is after 1 mile on the right hand side
Visitors:	Welcome: Contact Club in Advance. Handicap Certificate required
Societies:	Welcome: Contact Club in Advance.
Facilities:	Putting Green, Chipping Green, Club Hire, Trolley Hire, Buggy Hire, Bar, Restaurant, Driving Range

Championship Course

Date Founded: 1925
Type of Course: Links
No of Holes: 18
Length: 6608 yds (6099 mtrs)
Par: 71
SSS: 71
Green Fees: Weekdays: £35-£38 (summer) £35 (winter); Weekends/Bank Holidays: £38-£38 (summer) £25 (winter)

New Course

Date Founded: 1993
Type of Course: Links
No of Holes: 9
Length: 3031 yds (2798 mtrs)
Par: 35
SSS: None
Green Fees: Weekdays: £25 (summer) £18 (winter); Weekends/Bank Holidays: £25 (summer) £18 (winter)

Short Course

Date Founded: 1970
Type of Course: Links
No of Holes: 9
Length: 1690 yds (1560 mtrs)
Par: 29
SSS: None
Green Fees: Weekdays: £10; Weekends/ Bank Holidays: £10

Accommodation, Food and Drink

Reference numbers below refer to detailed information provided in section 2

Accommodation

The Beaconsfield Hotel, The Crescent, Newquay, Cornwall TR7 1DT

Tel: 01637 872172 Fax: 01637 850711
Stylish hotel in fine location overlooking the sandy beach and open sea beyond. Comfortable accommodation with 58 en-suite bedrooms. Several lounge areas, bar and restaurant for guests only. 128

Bewdley Hotel, Pentire Road, Newquay, Cornwall TR7 1NX

Tel: 01637 872883 Fax: 01637 872883
Friendly, family-run hotel overlooking links golf

course and beach. 29 en-suite rooms of varying sizes. Evening entertainment through the summer. Heated outdoor pool. 122

The Brookdale Hotel, Tregolls Road, Truro, Cornwall TR1 1JZ

Tel: 01872 273513 Fax: 01872 272400
e-mail: brookdale@hotelstruro.com
website: www.hotelstruro.com/brookdale
Good sized hotel set in its own beautifully landscaped grounds. Popular Italian Ristorante open Monday to Saturday. Comfortable, elegantly furnished en-suite rooms of varying types. 113

Chynoweth Lodge Hotel, 1 Eliot Gardens, Newquay, Cornwall TR7 2QE

Tel: 01637 876684
e-mail: reg@chynowethlodge.co.uk
website: www.chynowethlodge.co.uk
Comfortable accommodation, with nine en-suite rooms, personally run by resident owners. Comfortable lounge area and attractive dining room. Home-cooked food served in ample portions. 121

The Cumberland Hotelm, Henver Road, Newquay, Cornwall TR7 3BJ

Tel: 01637 873025 Fax: 01637 873097
Friendly seaside hotel with facilities including an outdoor pool and spacious ballroom. 32 rooms of varying sizes, all en-suite. Restaurant serves mainly English cuisine each evening, with lunches available on request.

The Glen Court Hotel, Mellanvrane Lane, Newquay, Cornwall TR7 2LB

Tel: 01637 874848
An 11-bedroom, family-run hotel ideal for those wanting a relaxing holiday. Restaurant serves superb home-cooked meals. Also a comfortable lounge and separate bar area.

Marcorrie Hotel, 20 Falmouth Road, Truro, Cornwall TR1 2HX

Tel: 01872 277374 Fax: 01872 241666
e-mail: marcorrie@aol.com
website: www.cornwall.net/marcorrie
Small, charming family-run hotel on a delightful Victorian and Edwardian street near to the city centre, offering traditional Cornish hospitality. 103

Mayrose Farm Holiday Cottages, Helstone, Camelford, Cornwall PL32 9RN

Tel: 01840 213509 Fax: 01840 213509
e-mail: mayrosefarm@hotmail.com
Five, very different properties converted from former farm buildings, decorated and furnished to a very high standard. Outdoor pool. Super holiday base. 105

Pendeen Hotel, 7 Alexandra Road, Porth, Newquay, Cornwall TR7 3ND

Tel: 01637 873521 Fax: 01637 873521
e-mail: pendeen@cornwall.net
Relaxing and peaceful hotel where you will find friendly service. 15 en-suite rooms. Restaurant serves traditional English and international cuisine focusing on fresh fish and seafood. 129

Porth Lodge Hotel, Porthbean Road, Newquay, Cornwall TR7 3TL

Tel: 01637 874483
Popular hostelry, with two bar areas, serving good food, with beer garden and children's room. 20 en-suite rooms and six self-catering apartments. Also a 10-pin bowling alley.   123

Porth Veor Manor, Porth Way, Nr. Newquay, Cornwall TR7 3LW

Tel: 01637 873274 Fax: 01637 873274
Friendly hotel offering the best in traditional Cornish hospitality. Elevated location offers superb views in all directions. 22 en-suite rooms. Award-winning restaurant open to non-residents.   125

Ruthern Valley Holidays, Ruthern Bridge, Nr. Bodmin, Cornwall PL30 5LU

Tel: 01208 831395 Fax: 01208 832324
website: self-catering-ruthern.co.uk
Peaceful, relaxing holiday retreat developed from former mining area. Range of holiday accommodation with bungalows, lodges, caravans and camping facilities. Shop and children's play area.   101

Treheveras Guest House, 2a Dane Road, Newquay, Cornwall TR7 1HL

Tel: 01637 874079
e-mail: treheveras@aol.com
A small guest house located on Newquay's Towan headland. Seven cosy rooms, five double, two single, most with en-suite facilities. Traditional cooked English breakfast. Reasonable rates.

Trenance Lodge Hotel and Restaurant, Trenance Road, Newquay, Cornwall TR7 2HW

Tel: 01637 876702 Fax: 01637 878772
e-mail: info@trenance-lodge.co.uk
website: www.trenance-lodge.co.uk
A fine restaurant with excellent reputation for serving fine local produce in a modern British style. Also 5 en-suite bedrooms, stylishly furnished and well-appointed.   124

Trethin Manor Holiday Cottages, Advent, Camelford, Cornwall PL32 9QW

Tel: 01840 213522 Fax: 01840 212898
A collection of former farm buildings which have been converted into comfortable self-catering accommodation. Ten cottages surrounded by landscaped grounds. Children's play area, barbecue, laundry. 120

White House Court Holiday Cottages, c/o 1 Middle Leigh, Newton Ferrers, Plymouth, Devon PL8 1DS

Tel: 01752 873128 Fax: 01752 873128
e-mail: whitehouse.cotts@barclay.net
website: www.whitehousecourt.co.uk
Eleven well-equipped self-catering cottages created from traditional, stone-built farm buildings. Two miles from the coast.   111

The Wilsey Down, Hallworthy, Camelford, Cornwall PL32 9SH

Tel: 01840 261205
e-mail: jane@greatbidlake.farmcom.net

Comfortable, welcoming establishment with two bars and separate restaurant. Six guest rooms, 2 of which are en-suite, of varying sizes.   104

Woodlands Hotel, 38-40 Pentire Crescent, Newquay, Cornwall TR7 1PU

Tel: 01637 852229 Fax: 01637 852227
Quiet setting, just outside Newquay, with spectacular views over the river and open countryside. 54 bedrooms. Excellent facilities including outdoor pool, sauna, solarium, sunbed and bowling green.   131

Food and Drink

The Brookdale Hotel, Tregolls Road, Truro, Cornwall TR1 1JZ

Tel: 01872 273513 Fax: 01872 272400
e-mail: brookdale@hotelstruro.com
website: www.hotelstruro.com/brookdale
Good sized hotel set in its own beautifully landscaped grounds. Popular Italian Ristorante open Monday to Saturday. Comfortable, elegantly furnished en-suite rooms of varying types.   113

The Globe Inn, 3 North Street, Lostwithiel, Cornwall PL22 0EG

Tel: 01208 872501
Cosy, friendly, traditional inn offering a warm welcome to all. Open plan bar, restaurant area, patio and beer garden. Good menu of tasty home-cooked, freshly-prepared food.   102

Legonna Farm, Lane, Newquay, Cornwall TR8 4NJ

Tel: 01637 872272
A traditional Cornish welcome awaits all who visit Legonna Farm where you will find comfortable bed and breakfast accommodation. Nine en-suite rooms of varying sizes. Packed lunches and evening meals available on request.

Pendeen Hotel, 7 Alexandra Road, Porth, Newquay, Cornwall TR7 3ND

Tel: 01637 873521 Fax: 01637 873521
e-mail: pendeen@cornwall.net
Relaxing and peaceful hotel where you will find friendly service. 15 en-suite rooms. Restaurant serves traditional English and international cuisine focusing on fresh fish and seafood.   129

Porth Lodge Hotel, Porthbean Road, Newquay, Cornwall TR7 3TL

Tel: 01637 874483
Popular hostelry, with two bar areas, serving good food, with beer garden and children's room. 20 en-suite rooms and six self-catering apartments. Also a 10-pin bowling alley.   123

Porth Veor Manor, Porth Way, Nr. Newquay, Cornwall TR7 3LW

Tel: 01637 873274 Fax: 01637 873274
Friendly hotel offering the best in traditional Cornish hospitality. Elevated location offers superb views in all directions. 22 en-suite rooms. Award-winning restaurant open to non-residents.   125

Smugglers Den Inn, Cubert, Newquay, Cornwall TR8 5PY

Tel: 01637 830209 Fax: 01637 830580
Quaint, 400-year old hostelry with a popular
reputation for serving fine food and well-kept ale.
Reputedly haunted! 126

Trenance Lodge Hotel and Restaurant, Trenance Road, Newquay, Cornwall TR7 2HW

Tel: 01637 876702 Fax: 01637 878772
e-mail: info@trenance-lodge.co.uk
website: www.trenance-lodge.co.uk
A fine restaurant with excellent reputation for serving
fine local produce in a modern British style. Also 5
en-suite bedrooms, stylishly furnished and well-
appointed. 124

Tywarnhayle Hotel, The Square, Perranporth, Cornwall TR6 0ER

Tel: 01872 572215 Fax: 01872 571773
Friendly, family-run hostelry serving a good range of
food and drink. The menu is typically English cuisine
and the traditional Sunday Roast lunches are very
popular. Restaurant seats 60.

The Wilsey Down, Hallworthy, Camelford, Cornwall PL32 9SH

Tel: 01840 261205
e-mail: jane@greatbidlake.farmcom.net
Comfortable, welcoming establishment with two bars
and separate restaurant. Six guest rooms, 2 of which
are en-suite, of varying sizes. 104

Truro Golf Club

Treliske, Truro, Cornwall TR1 3LG
Tel: **01872 278684** Fax: **01872 278684**

Sec/Manager:	Hugh Lester
Professional:	Nigel Bicknell
Directions:	1½ mile west of Truro. Turn right on second roundabout on A390.

Date Founded: 1937
Type of Course: Parkland

No of Holes:	18
Length:	5306 yds (4897 mtrs)
Par:	66
SSS:	66
Green Fees:	Weekdays: £20; Weekends/ Bank Holidays: £25
Visitors:	Welcome: Contact Club in Advance. No restrictions
Societies:	Welcome: Contact Club in Advance
Facilities:	Putting Green, Chipping Green, Trolley Hire, Buggy Hire, Bar, Restaurant

Accommodation, Food and Drink

Reference numbers below refer to detailed
information provided in section 2

Accommodation

The Brookdale Hotel, Tregolls Road, Truro, Cornwall TR1 1JZ

Tel: 01872 273513 Fax: 01872 272400
e-mail: brookdale@hotelstruro.com
website: www.hotelstruro.com/brookdale
Good sized hotel set in its own beautifully landscaped
grounds. Popular Italian Ristorante open Monday to
Saturday. Comfortable, elegantly furnished en-suite
rooms of varying types. 113

Hole Mill, Branscombe, Seaton, Devon EX12 3BX

Tel: 01297 680314
website: www.users.globalnet.co.uk/~branscombe/
hole1.htm
Former working watermill, located in pretty valley,
converted into a charming house on many levels.
Surrounded by colourful gardens. Three guest rooms.
267

Marcorrie Hotel, 20 Falmouth Road, Truro, Cornwall TR1 2HX

Tel: 01872 277374 Fax: 01872 241666
e-mail: marcorrie@aol.com
website: www.cornwall.net/marcorrie
Small, charming family-run hotel on a delightful
Victorian and Edwardian street near to the city centre,
offering traditional Cornish hospitality. 103

Meudon Hotel, Mawnan Smith, Near Falmouth, Cornwall TR11 5HT

Tel: 01326 250541 Fax: 01326 250543
website: www.meudon.co.uk
Superb, family-run country house hotel, set in a sub-
tropical garden paradise with private beach. Elegant
restaurant specialising in local seafood. Free golf
included in high- and mid-season rates. 119

White House Court Holiday Cottages, c/o 1 Middle Leigh, Newton Ferrers, Plymouth, Devon PL8 1DS

Tel: 01752 873128 Fax: 01752 873128
e-mail: whitehouse.cotts@barclay.net

website: www.whitehousecourt.co.uk
Eleven well-equipped self-catering cottages created
from traditional, stone-built farm buildings. Two
miles from the coast.   111

Woodlands Hotel, 38-40 Pentire Crescent, Newquay, Cornwall TR7 1PU

Tel: 01637 852229 Fax: 01637 852227
Quiet setting, just outside Newquay, with spectacular
views over the river and open countryside. 54
bedrooms. Excellent facilities including outdoor pool,
sauna, solarium, sunbed and bowling green.   131

Food and Drink

The Brookdale Hotel, Tregolls Road, Truro, Cornwall TR1 1JZ

Tel: 01872 273513 Fax: 01872 272400
e-mail: brookdale@hotelstruro.com
website: www.hotelstruro.com/brookdale
Good sized hotel set in its own beautifully landscaped
grounds. Popular Italian Ristorante open Monday to
Saturday. Comfortable, elegantly furnished en-suite
rooms of varying types.   113

Meudon Hotel, Mawnan Smith, Near Falmouth, Cornwall TR11 5HT

Tel: 01326 250541 Fax: 01326 250543
website: www.meudon.co.uk
Superb, family-run country house hotel, set in a sub-
tropical garden paradise with private beach. Elegant
restaurant specialising in local seafood. Free golf
included in high- and mid-season rates.   119

Smugglers Den Inn, Cubert, Newquay, Cornwall TR8 5PY

Tel: 01637 830209 Fax: 01637 830580
Quaint, family, 400-year old hostelry with a popular
reputation for serving fine food and well-kept ale.
Reputedly haunted!   126

The Sundeck, East Quay, Mevagissey, Cornwall PL26 6QQ

Tel: 01726 843051
A surprising find. Stylish decor in Mediterranean
theme with picture windows looking out to sea. High
quality home-cooked food.   112

Tywarnhayle Hotel, The Square, Perranporth, Cornwall TR6 0ER

Tel: 01872 572215 Fax: 01872 571773
Friendly, family-run hostelry serving a good range of
food and drink. The menu is typically English cuisine
and the traditional Sunday Roast lunches are very
popular. Restaurant seats 60.

West Cornwall Golf Club

Lelant, St. Ives, Cornwall TR26 3DZ

Tel: 01736 753401 Fax: 01736 735401

It would be a reasonable expectation that a golf

course designed by a man of the cloth would perhaps be gentle and forgiving, possibly even a little
charitable and cognisant of the shortcomings of
others. Or none of these, as the case may be.

But when you stand on the first tee at Lelant -
as West Cornwall is commonly known - facing a
par three of 229 yards before you have even had a
chance to loosen up, you may well cast a disap-
proving glance Heavenwards from beneath a
furrowed brow. It doesn't help much that you
need to aim your tee shot at the tower of St Uny
Church to get the best line into the green.

To be fair to the Rev Tyack, who no doubt designed the course in the late 1880s on a wing and
a prayer, things do gradually get easier, although
the second, with its raised and well-guarded green,
has to be negotiated first.

A single-line railway track offers a novel boundary, which has to be crossed to play holes five, six
and seven - known locally as "Calamity Corner",
but which could equally be entitled the "Unholy
Trinity" - before crossing back to the right side of
the tracks for the remainder of the round.

As you might expect on this, one of the most
westerly courses on the UK mainland, there are
more fine views, which start to appear at the blind
11th and come to the fore at the 12th. It's a tough
ending, too, with a par five at the 16th, another

190-yard three next, followed by the best part of 400 yards to a pocket handkerchief green at the last.

Sec/Manager:	Malcolm Lack
Professional:	Paul Atherton
Directions:	Take A30 to Hayle turning onto the A3074 to St. Ives
Date Founded:	1889
Type of Course:	Links
No of Holes:	18
Length:	5884 yds (5431 mtrs)
Par:	69
SSS:	69
Green Fees:	Weekdays: £25; Weekends/ Bank Holidays: £30
Visitors:	Welcome: Contact Club in Advance. Handicap Certificates required. No restrictions
Societies:	Welcome: Contact Club in Advance. Unable to play weekends
Facilities:	Putting Green, Chipping Green, Practice Fairway, Club Hire, Trolley Hire, Bar, Restaurant

Accommodation, Food and Drink

Reference numbers below refer to detailed information provided in section 2

Accommodation

The Brookdale Hotel, Tregolls Road, Truro, Cornwall TR1 1JZ

Tel: 01872 273513 Fax: 01872 272400
e-mail: brookdale@hotelstruro.com
website: www.hotelstruro.com/brookdale
Good sized hotel set in its own beautifully landscaped grounds. Popular Italian Ristorante open Monday to Saturday. Comfortable, elegantly furnished en-suite rooms of varying types.   113

Chy-Garth Guest House, Sea View Meadows, St. Ives Road, Carbis Bay, St. Ives, Cornwall TR26 2JX

Tel: 01736 795677
e-mail: ann@chy-garth.demon.co.uk
A delightful, detached house surrounded by colourful gardens and enjoying some beautiful sea views. A non-smoking establishment, there are eight guest rooms, nearly all with en-suite or private facilities. Ample car parking.

Dunmar Hotel, Pednolver Terrace, St. Ives, Cornwall TR26 2EL

Tel: 01736 796117 Fax: 01736 796053
Friendly, family-run 'olde worlde' hotel offering a

warm welcome and traditional Cornish hospitality. 17 en-suite bedrooms of varying sizes with bar and restaurant available to guests.

Marcorrie Hotel, 20 Falmouth Road, Truro, Cornwall TR1 2HX

Tel: 01872 277374 Fax: 01872 241666
e-mail: marcorrie@aol.com
website: www.cornwall.net/marcorrie
Small, charming family-run hotel on a delightful Victorian and Edwardian street near to the city centre, offering traditional Cornish hospitality.   103

Meudon Hotel, Mawnan Smith, Near Falmouth, Cornwall TR11 5HT

Tel: 01326 250541 Fax: 01326 250543
website: www.meudon.co.uk
Superb, family-run country house hotel, set in a sub-tropical garden paradise with private beach. Elegant restaurant specialising in local seafood. Free golf included in high- and mid-season rates.   119

Regent Hotel, Fern Lea Terrace, St. Ives, Cornwall TR26 2BH

Tel: 01736 796195 Fax: 01736 794641
e-mail: enquiries@regenthotel.com
website: www.regenthotel.com
Friendly, family-run hotel with AA and RAC 4 Diamond Grading. The nine en-suite guest bedrooms are tastefully decorated and comfortably furnished and many have spectacular views over the picturesque harbour.

White House Court Holiday Cottages, c/o 1 Middle Leigh, Newton Ferrers, Plymouth, Devon PL8 1DS

Tel: 01752 873128 Fax: 01752 873128
e-mail: whitehouse.cotts@barclay.net
website: www.whitehousecourt.co.uk
Eleven well-equipped self-catering cottages created from traditional, stone-built farm buildings. Two miles from the coast.   111

Food and Drink

The Brookdale Hotel, Tregolls Road, Truro, Cornwall TR1 1JZ

Tel: 01872 273513 Fax: 01872 272400
e-mail: brookdale@hotelstruro.com
website: www.hotelstruro.com/brookdale
Good sized hotel set in its own beautifully landscaped grounds. Popular Italian Ristorante open Monday to Saturday. Comfortable, elegantly furnished en-suite rooms of varying types.   113

Meudon Hotel, Mawnan Smith, Near Falmouth, Cornwall TR11 5HT

Tel: 01326 250541 Fax: 01326 250543
website: www.meudon.co.uk
Superb, family-run country house hotel, set in a sub-tropical garden paradise with private beach. Elegant restaurant specialising in local seafood. Free golf included in high- and mid-season rates.   119

The Sundeck, East Quay, Mevagissy, Cornwall PL26 6QQ

Tel: 01726 843051
A surprising find. Stylish decor in Mediterranean
theme with picture windows looking out to sea. High
quality home-cooked food. 112

Whitsand Bay Golf Club

Portwrinkle, Torpoint, Cornwall PL11 3BU
Tel: 01503 230470 Fax: 01503 230329

Sec/Manager:	Mr. Dyer
Professional:	Steven Poole
Directions:	7 miles west of Plymouth. From the A374 at Hessenford take the B3247 to Portwrinkle
Date Founded:	1905
Type of Course:	Clifftop
No of Holes:	18
Length:	5645 yds (5210 mtrs)
Par:	69
SSS:	69
Green Fees:	Weekdays: £25; Weekends/ Bank Holidays: £25
Visitors:	Welcome: Contact Club in Advance. No restrictions
Societies:	Welcome: Contact Club in Advance
Facilities:	Putting Green, Club Hire,

Trolley Hire, Buggy Hire, Bar,
Restaurant

Accommodation, Food and Drink

Reference numbers below refer to detailed
information provided in section 2

Accommodation

**The Carpenters Arms, Metherell,
Nr. Callington, Cornwall PL17 8BJ**

Tel: 01579 350242 Fax: 01579 350242
A picturesque Cornish pub with friendly and
welcoming service. Wide-ranging menu of home-
cooked bar meals and snacks. 117

**Cawsand Bay Hotel & Galleon Restaurant,
The Bound, Cawsand, Nr. Torpoint,
Cornwall PL10 1PG**

Tel: 01752 822425 Fax: 01752 823527
e-mail: sales@cawsandbay.co.uk
website: www.cawsandbay.co.uk
Located directly on the sea front and with superb
views across the Sound towards Plymouth. Ten
comfortable en-suite rooms of varying sizes. Popular
bar and restaurant. 130

**Fieldhead Hotel, Portuan Road, Hannafore,
West Looe, Cornwall PL13 2DR**

Tel: 01503 262689 Fax: 01503 264114
e-mail: field.head@virgin.net
website: www.fieldheadhotel.co.uk
Elegant country house style hotel offering high
standard of comfort and service. Comfortable en-suite
rooms, many with sea views. 115

**The Halfway House Inn, Grenofen, Tavistock,
Devon PL19 9ER**

Tel: 01822 612960 Fax: 01822 617697
A large, sprawling black and white 16th-century
building with friendly atmosphere. Excellent
reputation for high quality food with two restaurants
serving an a la carte menu. Four guest rooms. 206

**The Laurels, Huckworthy Bridge, Yelverton,
Devon PL20 6LP**

Tel: 01822 853622
Charming old cottage in riverside setting, recently
restored and converted into a self-catering cottage
and private home, in which bed and breakfast is
available. Ideal holiday base. 239

**Tavistock Arms, Fore Street, Gunnislake,
Cornwall PL18 9BN**

Tel: 01822 832217
Traditional, country pub located directly on the
Devon/Cornwall border. Food is served all day. Bed
and breakfast accommodation available. 118

Food and Drink

**The Carpenters Arms, Metherell,
Nr. Callington, Cornwall PL17 8BJ**

Tel: 01579 350242 Fax: 01579 350242

A picturesque Cornish pub with friendly and welcoming service. Wide-ranging menu of home-cooked bar meals and snacks. 117

Cawsand Bay Hotel & Galleon Restaurant, The Bound, Cawsand, Nr. Torpoint, Cornwall PL10 1PG

Tel: 01752 822425 Fax: 01752 823527
e-mail: sales@cawsandbay.co.uk
website: www.cawsandbay.co.uk
Located directly on the sea front and with superb views across the Sound towards Plymouth. Ten comfortable en-suite rooms of varying sizes. Popular bar and restaurant. 130

Fieldhead Hotel, Portuan Road, Hannafore, West Looe, Cornwall PL13 2DR

Tel: 01503 262689 Fax: 01503 264114
e-mail: field.head@virgin.net
website: www.fieldheadhotel.co.uk
Elegant country house style hotel offering high standard of comfort and service. Comfortable en-suite rooms, many with sea views. 115

The Globe Inn, 3 North Street, Lostwithiel, Cornwall PL22 0EG

Tel: 01208 872501
Cosy, friendly, traditional inn offering a warm welcome to all. Open plan bar, restaurant area, patio and beer garden. Good menu of tasty home-cooked, freshly-prepared food. 102

The Halfway House Inn, Grenofen, Tavistock, Devon PL19 9ER

Tel: 01822 612960 Fax: 01822 617697
A large, sprawling black and white 16th-century building with friendly atmosphere. Excellent reputation for high quality food with two restaurants serving an a la carte menu. Four guest rooms. 206

Tavistock Arms, Fore Street, Gunnislake, Cornwall PL18 9BN

Tel: 01822 832217
Traditional, country pub located directly on the Devon/Cornwall border. Food is served all day. Bed and breakfast accommodation available. 118

Three Pilchards, The Quay, Polperro, Looe, Cornwall PL13 2QZ

Tel: 01503 272233
Traditional Cornish pub located on the sea front. Home-cooked food served each day. 116

Trewithen Restaurant, 3 Fore Street, Lostwithiel, Cornwall PL22 0BP

Tel: 01208 872373
Award-winning restaurant with cosy, cottagey style in the heart of the pretty town of Lostwithiel. Traditional, English cuisine. 110

The Walkhampton Inn, Walkhampton, Nr. Yelverton, Devon PL20 6JY

Tel: 01822 855556 Fax: 01822 855556
e-mail: info@walkhamptoninn.co.uk
Historic establishment, popular in the area for serving a good range of beer and traditional pub fayre. Two guest rooms both of which are en-suite. 238

DEVON

'When Adam and Eve were dispossessed
Of the garden hard by Heaven,
They planted another one down in the West,
'Twas Devon, glorious Devon!'

- Sir Harold Edwin Boulton.

No matter what are the counter claims and the disagreements - and there will no doubt be many - Devon can rightly claim to be the cradle of golf in England, and the county can forward plenty of arguments in support of the title. Not least of these are that the county boasts the oldest links course in the country (**Royal North Devon**), the oldest club still playing on its original track (**Royal North Devon**), and the oldest ladies' club (at, erm, **Royal North Devon**). And if you throw in the birthplace of the first Englishman to win The Open, John Henry Taylor, who just happened to come from Northam, near, you've guessed it, Royal North Devon, you begin to get a taste of the sort of golfing history the county is steeped in. Members at **Torquay Golf Club** will have no hesitation in telling you that theirs was the first course to be constructed on the south coast of England; while over in **Tiverton** they will talk of the legendary Joyce Wethered, lionised by no less an authority than Bobby Jones, and who re-wrote the record books of the women's game several times in the 1920s by winning just about everything there was to win, then retiring, presumably bored, at an amazingly early age. There is even a course designed by the man who went on to sculpt the contours of Augusta, home of the US Masters.

But what the historical debate doesn't put into perspective is that magical amalgam of glorious Devon to which Boulton's words quoted above referred. The richness of the rolling green hills and contrast with the ploughed red soil seem to dress much of the east and south of the county in a lushness which can be in stark contrast to the utter wildness of Dartmoor and the rugged nature of the county's northern coastline. They say that in Devon, you can find everything you ever wanted, and it's another argument that is hard to rebut.

Plymouth Hoe

Most visitors heading for the English Riviera tend to bypass Exeter, which is a pity because they are missing out on a thriving little city whose history pre-dates the arrival of the Romans, and which hides a number of fascinating museums and the intriguing Underground Passages, stone-vaulted caverns built more than 600 years ago to get spring water into the city from outside the fortified walls. And very few of the millions of annual holidaymakers ever get as far as Plymouth, a modern city steeped in naval history, whose centre was bombed into oblivion during World War Two and which was completely rebuilt in the 1950s. Those who do venture to this western boundary of Devon will be rewarded with tales of Sir Francis Drake and the Pilgrim Fathers, views of the distant

The Guildhall, Totnes

Eddystone Lighthouse (at least, on a good day - it is 12 miles out to sea) and the much closer Drake's Island, and the majestic breakwater, built in the early part of the 1800s, which protects the Sound from the worst of the wind and waves. But what most of the summer visitors are heading for is the self-styled "English Riviera", that busy stretch from the western banks of the Exe Estuary down to the South Hams, bounded by the sea on one side and Dartmoor on the other.

The coastline here can, in places, be just as dramatic and breathtaking as the stretch from the Dorset border westwards, and all along its length it is peppered with golf courses, which got there first - many more than a hundred years ago - and hog all the best views. From Dawlish and Teignmouth, to the big resorts of Torquay and Paignton, Brixham, Dartmouth and beyond, this is holiday Devon, and everything associated with it that you would expect. But there are quieter spots, even in this hedonistic environment. One is the charming little town of Totnes on the River Dart, whose one great claim to fame is that its once-great pilchard trade produced the money for Sir Thomas Bodley to found and fund Oxford University's renowned Bodleian Library. The other gem is Dartmouth, a huge favourite with the sailing fraternity, but an ancient port bursting with lore and legend in its own right. Some parts of the quayside may look vaguely familiar to television viewers who remember the series called The Onedin Line. Not surprising, as Dartmouth was the location used for many of the adventures.

The north coast of the county is somewhat less commercialised, possibly because it is not as easy to get to, although the North Devon Link road from the M5 has made the trip far less of an ordeal than it was some years ago. If you pass that way, you will get a taste of rural Devon and some wonderful countryside to view before reaching busy Barnstaple, with its 16-arch bridge across the Taw estuary and its large indoor Pannier Market. This is Tarka country, where the literary otter lends its name to a countryside trail and a railway link, The Tarka Line. Tourism in North Devon has a lot to thank author Henry Williamson for. The Tarka Trail, a 180-mile long figure-of-eight circuit centred on Barnstaple, attracts thousands of walkers to normally-unseen areas of beautiful countryside, and does the local economy no harm whatsoever.

The Old Front, Dartmouth

The coastline from Ilfracombe - the biggest coastal resort in the area - running south around Bideford Bay (or Barnstaple Bay, as some prefer it) past Westward Ho! (named, would you believe, after Charles Kingsley's novel, and not the other way around) and across to Hartland Point provides some spectacular scenery, as well as the golf courses of **Royal North Devon** and **Saunton**, the latter probably the best in England to never have hosted The Open, but that's a matter addressed elsewhere in this guide. One of the musts for nature lovers in this part of the region, almost as a warm-

Steep Cobbled Road, Clovelly

up act to the main attraction, is the country park at Northam Burrows. The park covers more than 600 acres and is a magnet for migratory birds, as well as teeming with animals, plants and insects of all varieties. Another must for every visitor has to be the tiny cliffside village of Clovelly. It is almost indescribably gorgeous. Make sure you take a camera with you, because unless you show them the evidence, your friends won't believe you.

Clapper Bridge, Dartmoor

That covers the outer ring of the doughnut of Devon but, unlike a normal doughnut, the best bit of this one is in the middle. Dartmoor, national park and national treasure, is several hundred square miles of wild, wild countryside in the raw, and an enormous draw for those who want to escape the trappings of the modern world and wander with nature. The most striking aspects of this breathtaking area are the tors, granite fingers and knuckles scattered throughout the landscape, and which give their name to the annual test of endurance known as the "Ten Tors Race". This, then, is where Adam and Eve made their second home. It must be said, they made a pretty good job of it.

Location of Golf Courses

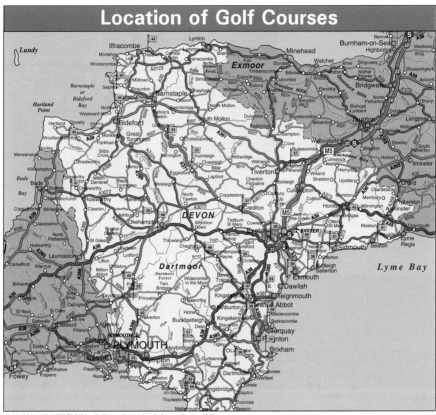

© MAPS IN MINUTES ™ 2001   © Crown Copyright, Ordnance Survey 2001

Ashbury Golf Club

Fowley Cross, Okehampton, Devon EX20 4NL
Tel: 01837 55453 Fax: 01837 55468

Sec/Manager:	Simon Brothers
Professional:	Reg Cade
Directions:	2½ miles west of Okehampton centre. From centre take New Road (B3260 Tavistock) for 3 miles to the junction of the A30 dual carriageway and the A386. Take the A386 (Great Torrington) for 2 miles and turn left into Dry Lane (Southcott), turning right after 1 mile. The entrance is after ¼ mile on the right hand side.
Visitors:	Welcome: Contact Club in Advance
Societies:	No Societies
Facilities:	Putting Green, Chipping Green, Club Hire, Trolley Hire, Buggy Hire, Bar, Restaurant, Driving Range

Oakwood

Date Founded:	1995
Type of Course:	Parkland
No of Holes:	18
Length:	5343 yds (4932 mtrs)
Par:	68
SSS:	66
Green Fees:	Weekdays: £15-£20; Weekends/Bank Holidays: £15-£20

Ashbury Courses
(Pines, Beeches, Willows)

Date Founded:	1995
Type of Course:	Parkland
No of Holes:	9 x3 (Pines & Beeches)

(Beeches and Willows) (Willows and Pines)	
Length:	5343 yds (4932 mtrs)
Par:	68
SSS:	66
Green Fees:	Weekdays: £15-£20; Weekends/Bank Holidays: £15-£20

Acorns Par 3

Date Founded:	1995
Type of Course:	Parkland
No of Holes:	18
Length:	2018 yds (1863 mtrs)
Par:	68
SSS:	66
Green Fees:	Weekdays: £15-£20; Weekends/Bank Holidays: £15-£20

Accommodation, Food and Drink

Reference numbers below refer to detailed information provided in section 2

Accommodation

The Bridge Inn, Bridge Street, Hatherleigh, Nr. Okehampton, Devon EX20 3JA

Tel: 01837 810947 Fax: 01837 810614
The Bridge Inn dates from the 16th century and is one of the oldest buildings in the area. Cosy interior with bar and separate restaurant. Six en-suite guest rooms of varying sizes. 231

The Coffee Pot, 14 St. James Street, Okehampton, Devon EX20 1DA

Tel: 01837 52988
Traditional coffee shop, open daily serving early breakfast, coffee, lunches and afternoon teas. Conveniently located close to the town centre. 233

Lifton Hall Hotel, Lifton, Devon PL16 0DR

Tel: 01566 784863 Fax: 01566 784770
e-mail mail@liftonhall.co.uk
Traditional 250-year old Country House hotel in peaceful village location with ten en-suite rooms. Formal restaurant and a bistro, both specialising in local fish. 240

Pressland Country House Hotel, Hatherleigh, Nr. Okehampton, Devon EX20 3LW

Tel: 01837 810871 Fax: 01837 810303
e-mail graham@presslandhouse.co.uk
website www.presslandhouse.co.uk
Victorian manor house surrounded by lawns and woodland. Five spacious guest rooms, most with en-suite facilities, and superb residents' restaurant. 230

The Royal Oak, The Square, Dolton, Winkleigh, Devon EX19 8QF

Tel: 01805 804288

Friendly country pub with spacious interior. Superb restaurant offering an excellent menu with live jazz twice monthly. Five guest rooms, some en-suite. 258

The Torrs, Belstone, Okehampton, Devon EX20 1QZ

Tel: 01837 840689
Small, cosy pub, popular with locals and visitors. Refreshing ales and tasty, home-cooked meals. Bed and breakfast accommodation available with three en-suite guest rooms. 232

Food and Drink

The Bridge Inn, Bridge Street, Hatherleigh, Nr. Okehampton, Devon EX20 3JA

Tel: 01837 810947 Fax: 01837 810614
The Bridge Inn dates from the 16th century and is one of the oldest buildings in the area. Cosy interior with bar and separate restaurant. Six en-suite guest rooms of varying sizes. 231

Lifton Hall Hotel, Lifton, Devon PL16 0DR

Tel: 01566 784863 Fax: 01566 784770
e-mail mail@liftonhall.co.uk
Traditional 250-year old Country House hotel in peaceful village location with ten en-suite rooms. Formal restaurant and a bistro, both specialising in local fish. 240

The Royal Oak, The Square, Dolton, Winkleigh, Devon EX19 8QF

Tel: 01805 804288
Friendly country pub with spacious interior. Superb restaurant offering an excellent menu with live jazz twice monthly. Five guest rooms, some en-suite. 258

The Torrs, Belstone, Okehampton, Devon EX20 1QZ

Tel: 01837 840689
Small, cosy pub, popular with locals and visitors. Refreshing ales and tasty, home-cooked meals. Bed and breakfast accommodation available with three en-suite guest rooms. 232

Victorian Pantry, Museum Courtyard, West Street, Okehampton, Devon EX20 1HQ

Tel: 01837 53988
Housed within an historic building not far from the Dartmoor Museum. Open daily serving a good selection of drinks, home-cooked cakes and hot meals. 229

Axe Cliff Golf Club

Squires Lane, Axmouth, Seaton, Devon EX12 4AB

Tel: 01297 24371 Fax: 01297 24371

How much would it cost a club these days to get a modern-day five-times winner of The Open (say, Tom Watson, for instance) to pop along for the day, walk around the course and offer a few sug-

gestions on redesigning it to make it a more interesting and challenging prospect for the members?

Axe Cliff lashed out the princely sum of nine guineas - plus expenses - as demanded by James Braid in 1928 to do just that when it had acquired two fields to expand into. It was money well spent.

There are two things you should ask before attempting to play this spectacular cliff-top course. The first is how many holes there are, for in its chequered history it has been a nine-holer, then 15, then 18, and then back to 15 again. It wasn't until 1979 that it regained its full 18-hole length. It remains that today unless, that is, the odd green or fairway has slipped into the bay below.

With that in mind, therefore, it is a wise golfer who stocks up with plenty of balls before tackling the 15th and 16th holes of this scenic course. The 15th has out of bounds all along its length, out of bounds in this case meaning a drop of more than 200 feet over the edge of the cliff!

The second question is how much are the green fees. Tradition has it that the standard reply is that the golf is free - you pay for the views. And boy, have they got views for you!

Sec/Manager:	John Davies
Professional:	Mark Dack
Directions:	1 mile south of Axmouth. From the A3052 Sidmouth to Lyme Regis road take the B3172 (Axmouth) Continue for ¾ mile past Axmouth and turn left before crossing the bridge to Seaton. The entrance is after 200 yds at the end.
Date Founded:	1894
Type of Course:	Clifftop
No of Holes:	18
Length:	5969 yds (5509 mtrs)
Par:	70
SSS:	70

Green Fees:	Weekdays: £20; Weekends/ Bank Holidays: £24
Visitors:	Welcome: Contact Club in Advance. No restrictions
Societies:	Welcome: Contact Club in Advance
Facilities:	Putting Green, Club Hire, Trolley Hire, Bar, Restaurant

Accommodation, Food and Drink

Reference numbers below refer to detailed information provided in section 2

Accommodation

Coverdale Guest House, Woodmead Road, Lyme Regis, Dorset DT7 3AB

Tel: 01297 442882 Fax: 01297 444673
e-mail: coverdale@tinyworld.co.uk
Spacious non-smoking accommodation enjoying spectacular views to the coast and overlooking woodland. Eight comfortable bedrooms. **306**

Hole Mill, Branscombe, Seaton, Devon EX12 3BX

Tel: 01297 680314
website: www.users.globalnet.co.uk/~branscombe/hole1.htm
Former working watermill, located in pretty valley, converted into a charming house on many levels. Surrounded by colourful gardens. 3 guest rooms. **267**

Home Farm Hotel and Restaurant, Wilmington, Honiton, Devon EX14 9JR

Tel: 01404 831278 Fax: 01404 831411
e-mail: homefarmhotel@breathe-mail.net
website: www.homefarmhotel.co.uk
Sixteenth century farmhouse which has been converted into an intimate hotel and restaurant. 13 individually-styled, en-suite bedrooms of varying sizes. The restaurant has a far-reaching reputation for the high quality of its food and service. **223**

Kent House Hotel, Silver Street, Lyme Regis, Dorset DT7 3HT

Tel: 01297 443442 Fax: 01297 444626
e-mail: thekenthouse@talk21.com
Large Victorian property providing bright, airy and well-appointed accommodation. Nine rooms, varying sizes, most en-suite. Restaurant specialises in seafood dishes. **305**

Kersbrook Hotel, Pound Road, Lyme Regis, Dorset DT7 3HX

Tel: 01297 442596 Fax: 01297 442596
A family-run bed and breakfast establishment housed within an historic, listed building. Ten en-suite guest bedrooms with many enjoying fine views.

Mariners Hotel, Silver Street, Lyme Regis, Dorset DT7 3HS

Tel: 01297 442753 Fax: 01297 442431
e-mail: mariners@ukgateway.net

This former 17th-century coaching inn retains much of its original character, while offering a comfortable and stylish place to stay. 12 en-suite bedrooms, relaxing lounge and cosy restaurant.

Marlborough Hotel, The Esplanade, Sidmouth, Devon EX10 8AR

Tel: 01395 513320
Super sea front property just a stone's throw from the beach. Popular pub and hotel, offering fine food all day. 18 en-suite rooms. **224**

Mermaid House, 32 Coombe Street, Lyme Regis, Dorset DT7 3PP

Tel: 01297 445351
website: www.smoothhound.co.uk/hotels/mermaid
Charming, relaxing house in old part of Lyme Regis, three minutes walk from the sea. Superb breakfast using free range produce. Free parking nearby.

Springfield House, Woodmead Road, Lyme Regis, Dorset DT7 3LJ

Tel: 01297 443409 Fax: 01297 443685
e-mail: springfield@lymeregis.com
website: www.lymeregis.com/springfield
An elegant Georgian town house, tastefully converted to provide guest house accommodation with five en-suite rooms of varying sizes, all with sea views. Residents benefit from reduced fees at Lyme Regis Golf Club.

Food and Drink

Home Farm Hotel and Restaurant, Wilmington, Honiton, Devon EX14 9JR

Tel: 01404 831278 Fax: 01404 831411
e-mail: homefarmhotel@breathe-mail.net
website: www.homefarmhotel.co.uk
Sixteenth century farmhouse which has been converted into an intimate hotel and restaurant. 13 individually-styled, en-suite bedrooms of varying sizes. The restaurant has a far-reaching reputation for the high quality of its food and service. **223**

Kent House Hotel, Silver Street, Lyme Regis, Dorset DT7 3HT

Tel: 01297 443442 Fax: 01297 444626
e-mail: thekenthouse@talk21.com
Large Victorian property providing bright, airy and well-appointed accommodation. Nine rooms, varying sizes, most en-suite. Restaurant specialises in seafood dishes. **305**

Mariners Hotel, Silver Street, Lyme Regis, Dorset DT7 3HS

Tel: 01297 442753 Fax: 01297 442431
e-mail: mariners@ukgateway.net
This former 17th-century coaching inn retains much of its original character, while offering a comfortable and stylish place to stay. 12 en-suite bedrooms, relaxing lounge and cosy restaurant.

Marlborough Hotel, The Esplanade, Sidmouth, Devon EX10 8AR

Tel: 01395 513320
Super sea front property just a stone's throw from the

beach. Popular pub and hotel, offering fine food all day. 18 en-suite rooms. 224

The Volunteer Inn, Broad Street, Lyme Regis, Dorset DT7 3QS

Tel: 01297 442214
Historic, town centre free house serving a good selection of real ales, including draught Guinness. Also offers a full range of freshly cooked meals with seafood being a speciality.

Bigbury Golf Club

Bigbury, Kingsbridge, Devon TQ7 4BB
Tel: 01548 810055 Fax: 01548 810207

Sec/Manager:	Martin Lowry
Professional:	Simon Lloyd
Directions:	Take the A379 Plymouth, Kingsbridge road. Turn right at Harraton Cross to Brigbury-on-Sea.
Date Founded:	1926
Type of Course:	Clifftop
No of Holes:	18
Length:	6048 yds (5582 mtrs)
Par:	70
SSS:	69
Green Fees:	Weekdays: £25; Weekends/ Bank Holidays: £27
Visitors:	Welcome: Contact Club in Advance. No restrictions Handicap Certificate required
Societies:	Welcome: Contact Club in Advance. Unable to play Mon, Tue, Fri, Sat, Sun.
Facilities:	Putting Green, Chipping Green, Club Hire, Trolley Hire, Buggy Hire, Bar, Restaurant

Accommodation, Food and Drink

Reference numbers below refer to detailed information provided in section 2

Accommodation

Campbells, 5 Mount Boone, Dartmouth, Devon TQ6 9PB

Tel: 01803 833438 Fax: 01803 833438
Award-winning bed and breakfast enjoying stunning views over the town of Dartmouth. Two elegant, en-suite, double bedrooms. Superb breakfasts with excellent choice. 264

Chuckle Too, Blackawton, Totnes, Devon TQ9 7BG

Tel: 01803 712455

Modern, self-catering cottage offering cosy cottage-style accommodation. Sleeps up to three adults. Very well equipped. 262

The Floating Bridge and Floaters Restaurant, Sandquay, Dartmouth, Devon TQ6 9PQ

Tel: 01803 832354 Fax: 01803 832354
Popular riverside hostelry serving fine refreshment and award-winning food. Fresh local fish a speciality. Well worth a detour. 266

The Steam Packet Inn, St. Peter's Quay, Totnes, Devon TQ9 5EN

Tel: 01803 863880 Fax: 01803 862754
Elegant riverside inn with open plan lounge bar and elegant, conservatory Restaurant. Ten en-suite guest bedrooms. Private river moorings available. 261

Tides Reach Hotel, South Sands, Salcombe, Devon TQ8 8LJ

Tel: 01548 843466 Fax: 01548 843954
e-mail: enquire@tidesreach.com
website: www.tidesreach.com
Elegant, luxurious hotel with a good reputation for high standards of service. Superb, south-facing location and excellent residents' facilities. High quality restaurant. 234

The White House, Chillington, Nr. Kingsbridge, Devon TQ7 2JX

Tel: 01548 580580 Fax: 01548 581124
A small, high quality hotel and restaurant offering seven luxuriously furnished bedrooms including two suites. 203

Yealm Holidays, 8 Whittingham Road, Collaton Park, Yealmpton, Plymouth, Devon PL8 2NF

Tel: 01752 872712 Fax: 01752 873173
e-mail: info@yealm-holidays.co.uk
website: www.yealm-holidays.co.uk
Selection of cottages, houses and flats all situated around the estuary of the River Yealm, sleeping between two and nine. Pets welcome in some properties. 265

Food and Drink

The Laughing Monk Restaurant, Totnes Road, Strete, Nr. Dartmouth, Devon TQ6 0RN

Tel: 01803 770639
Award-winning restaurant, including "Best Restaurant in the West" Gold Award. Housed within a 160-year old former church school. Open for dinner throughout the year. 227

Old Mother Hubbards, 35 Market Street, Yealmpton, Devon PL8 2EA

Tel: 01752 880085
Thought to be the original home of Old Mother Hubbard, as immortalised in the traditional nursery rhyme. Now a cosy and intimate restaurant open for a la carte lunches and evening meals. Ring for opening details.

The Singing Kettle, 6 Smith Street, Dartmouth, Devon TQ6 9QR

Tel: 01803 832624

Traditional English tea room tucked away on a side street in the centre of Dartmouth. Open all day for food and drink, mostly home-made.   263

The Steam Packet Inn, St. Peter's Quay, Totnes, Devon TQ9 5EN

Tel: 01803 863880 Fax: 01803 862754
Elegant riverside inn with open plan lounge bar and elegant, conservatory Restaurant. Ten en-suite guest bedrooms. Private river moorings available.   261

Tides Reach Hotel, South Sands, Salcombe, Devon TQ8 8LJ

Tel: 01548 843466 Fax: 01548 843954
e-mail: enquire@tidesreach.com
website: www.tidesreach.com
Elegant, luxurious hotel with a good reputation for high standards of service. Superb, south-facing location and excellent residents' facilities. High quality restaurant.   234

The White House, Chillington, Nr. Kingsbridge, Devon TQ7 2JX

Tel: 01548 580580 Fax: 01548 581124
A small, high quality hotel and restaurant offering seven luxuriously furnished bedrooms including two suites.   203

Chulmleigh Golf Club

Leigh Road, Chulmleigh Devon EX18 7BL
Tel: 01769 580519 Fax: 01769 580519

Sec/Manager:	Howard Meadows
Professional:	John Phillips
Directions:	¼ mile northwest of Chulmleigh centre. From the centre take Fore St. (B3096, Taw Valley). The entrance is after ¼ mile on the right hand side in Leigh Road
Date Founded:	1976
Type of Course:	Undulating Parkland
No of Holes:	18 (Summer) 9 (Winter)
Length:	2310 yds (2132 mtrs)
Par:	54
SSS:	54
Green Fees:	Weekdays: £6.50; Weekends/ Bank Holidays: £6.50
Visitors:	Welcome: Contact Club in Advance. No restrictions
Societies:	Welcome: Contact Club in Advance
Facilities:	Putting Green, Chipping Green, Club Hire, Trolley Hire, Hire, Bar, Restaurant

Accommodation, Food and Drink

Reference numbers below refer to detailed information provided in section 2

Accommodation

'Oaklands', Black Dog, Nr. Crediton, Devon EX17 4QJ

Tel: 01884 860645 Fax: 01884 861030
A super house built to very high standards of craftsmanship. Three en-suite rooms. Stunning views and gardens.   247

Mole Cottage, Chittlehamholt, Devon EX37 9HF

Tel: 01769 540471 Fax: 01769 540471
e-mail: relax@moley.uk.com
website: www.moley.uk.com
17th century thatched cottage enjoying a riverside location within the magical Mole Valley. Also a working pottery and gallery. Residential Pottery courses available.   218

The Royal Oak, The Square, Dolton, Winkleigh, Devon EX19 8QF

Tel: 01805 804288
Friendly country pub with spacious interior. Superb restaurant offering an excellent menu with live jazz twice monthly. Five guest rooms, some en-suite. 258

Waterfront Inn, Golf Links Road, Westward Ho!, Devon EX39 1LH

Tel: 01237 474737 Fax: 01237 471719
Modern, friendly inn with much to offer to visitors to the area. Large bar areas, stylish restaurant and comfortable, newly furnished accommodation. 220

Yeolden House Hotel, Durrant Lane, Northam, Nr. Bideford, Devon EX39 2RL

Tel: 01237 474400 Fax: 01237 476618
e-mail: yeoldonhouse@aol.com
website: www.yeoldonhousehotel.co.uk
An imposing house surrounded by lawns and colourful flower beds that slope gently down to the river. Ten en-suite rooms that have each been individually designed. Elegant restaurant. 216

Food and Drink

The Duchess Restaurant, Duke Street, South Molton, Devon EX36 3AL

Tel: 01769 573123
Small charming restaurant with a calm, relaxing atmosphere. Open for lunch and dinner, with fully licensed bar.   241

The Royal Oak, The Square, Dolton, Winkleigh, Devon EX19 8QF

Tel: 01805 804288
Friendly country pub with spacious interior. Superb restaurant offering an excellent menu with live jazz twice monthly. Five guest rooms, some en-suite. 258

Waterfront Inn, Golf Links Road, Westward Ho!, Devon EX39 1LH

Tel: 01237 474737 Fax: 01237 471719

Modern, friendly inn with much to offer to visitors to the area. Large bar areas, stylish restaurant and comfortable, newly furnished accommodation. 220

Yeolden House Hotel, Durrant Lane, Northam, Nr. Bideford, Devon EX39 2RL

Tel: 01237 474400 Fax: 01237 476618
e-mail: yeoldonhouse@aol.com
website: www.yeoldonhousehotel.co.uk
An imposing house surrounded by lawns and colourful flower beds that slope gently down to the river. Ten en-suite rooms that have each been individually designed. Elegant restaurant. 216

Churston Golf Club

Churston, Brixham, Devon TQ5 0LA

Tel: 01803 842751 Fax: 01803 845738

You have to hand it to these golf course architects. They take one look at what might be simple open countryside and, in their mind's eye, picture a golf course as the finished article. So it was with this particular corner of Devon when HS 'Harry' Colt's opinion was canvassed back in 1921.

His views are recorded in the club's official centenary handbook thus: "From a great portion of the ground are obtained magnificent views of Torbay, and the situation and surroundings are admirable in every way. I consider that it will be feasible with sufficient money available to construct a very attractive course on the ground selected."

That, of course, was Harry's sales pitch to the Churston Golf Club, which had found it necessary to look for a new course because the good citizens of the area where becoming less than enamoured of golf balls whizzing around their top hats and parasols as they strolled on Galmpton Common, the site of the original course.

Old Harry was spot on, though, and the downland course offers marvellous views over Brixham harbour and the bay, particularly on the back nine. A variety of shots are required to combat the gorse and occasional wooded areas.

Holes to watch include the opener, which, in the summer, plays 242 yards as a par three, and the 13th, an elevated tee with superb views over Torbay, but a tight par 4 with plenty of trouble awaiting you.

Sec/Manager:	Simon Bawden
Professional:	Neil Holman
Directions:	2 miles west of Brixham centre. From the junction of the A380 (Torbay ring road) and the A385 (Totnes road) take the A3022 (Brixham). The entrance is after 2¾ miles on the left, just after Warborough Road
Date Founded:	1890
Type of Course:	Downland Clifftop
No of Holes:	18
Length:	6200 yds (5722 mtrs)
Par:	70
SSS:	70
Green Fees:	Weekdays: £30; Weekends/ Bank Holidays: £35
Visitors:	Welcome: Contact Club in Advance. Handicap Certificate required. No restrictions
Societies:	Welcome: Contact Club in Advance. Unable to play Sat – Wed
Facilities:	Putting Green, Chipping Green, Trolley Hire, Bar, Restaurant

Accommodation, Food and Drink

Reference numbers below refer to detailed information provided in section 2

Accommodation

Alexandra Lodge Holiday Apartments, Grafton Road, Torquay, South Devon TQ1 1QJ

Tel: 01803 213465 Fax: 01803 390933
e-mail: almes@fsbdial.co.uk
website: www.alexandra-lodge.co.uk
Lovely detached Georgian villa in secluded grounds

offering seven self-catering apartments sleeping
between two and eight people.   249

The Anchorage Guest House, 170 New Road, Brixham, Devon TQ5 8DA

Tel/Fax: 01803 852960
A comfortable, friendly guest house with a fabulous
award-winning garden. Seven guest rooms.   257

Babbacombe Hall Hotel, 17 Manor Road, Babbacombe, Torquay, Devon TQ1 3JX

Tel: 01803 325668 Fax: 01803 325668
Victorian seaside hotel with six en-suite rooms. Bar
and restaurant open to residents only.   253

Campbells, 5 Mount Boone, Dartmouth, Devon TQ6 9PB

Tel: 01803 833438 Fax: 01803 833438
Award-winning bed and breakfast enjoying stunning
views over the town of Dartmouth. Two elegant, en-
suite, double bedrooms. Superb breakfasts with
excellent choice.   264

Chuckle Too, Blackawton, Totnes, Devon TQ9 7BG

Tel: 01803 712455
Modern, self-catering cottage offering cosy cottage-
style accommodation. Sleeps up to three adults. Very
well equipped.   262

Exmouth View Hotel, St. Albans Road, Babbacombe, Torquay, Devon TQ1 3LQ

Tel: 0800 7817817/01803 327307 Fax: 01803 329967
e-mail: relax@exmouth-view.co.uk
website: www.exmouth-view.co.uk
A modern hotel offering comfortable accommodation
at an affordable price. Licensed bar and restaurant.250

The Floating Bridge and Floaters Restaurant, Sandquay, Dartmouth, Devon TQ6 9PQ

Tel: 01803 832354 Fax: 01803 832354
Popular riverside hostelry serving fine refreshment
and award-winning food. Fresh local fish a speciality.
Well worth a detour.   266

The Steam Packet Inn, St. Peter's Quay, Totnes, Devon TQ9 5EN

Tel: 01803 863880 Fax: 01803 862754
Elegant riverside inn with open plan lounge bar and
elegant, conservatory Restaurant. Ten en-suite guest
bedrooms. Private river moorings available.   261

Westbury, 51 New Road, Brixham, Devon TQ5 8NL

Tel/Fax: 01803 851684
e-mail: ann.burt@lineone.net
A charming Georgian house offering stylish
accommodation with six guest rooms. Private
parking.   255

The White House, Chillington, Nr. Kingsbridge, Devon TQ7 2JX

Tel: 01548 580580 Fax: 01548 581124
A small, high quality hotel and restaurant offering
seven luxuriously furnished bedrooms including two
suites.   203

Food and Drink

The Laughing Monk Restaurant, Totnes Road, Strete, Nr. Dartmouth, Devon TQ6 0RN

Tel: 01803 770639
Award-winning restaurant, including "Best Restaurant
in the West" Gold Award. Housed within a 160-year
old former church school. Open for dinner
throughout the year.   227

The Plough Inn, Fore Street, Ipplepen, Devon TQ12 5RP

Tel: 01808 812118 Fax: 01803 814278
website: www.ipplepen.com
An attractive old inn with a great deal of character.
Good range of drinks and home-cooked food.   259

The Singing Kettle, 6 Smith Street, Dartmouth, Devon TQ6 9QR

Tel: 01803 832624
Traditional English tea room tucked away on a side
street in the centre of Dartmouth. Open all day for
food and drink, mostly home-made.   263

The Steam Packet Inn, St. Peter's Quay, Totnes, Devon TQ9 5EN

Tel: 01803 863880 Fax: 01803 862754
Elegant riverside inn with open plan lounge bar and
elegant, conservatory Restaurant. Ten en-suite guest
bedrooms. Private river moorings available.   261

The White House, Chillington, Nr. Kingsbridge, Devon TQ7 2JX

Tel: 01548 580580 Fax: 01548 581124
A small, high quality hotel and restaurant offering
seven luxuriously furnished bedrooms including two
suites.   203

Dainton Park Golf Club

Totnes Road, Ipplepen, Newton Abbot,
Devon TQ12 5TN

Tel: 01803 815000 Fax: 01803 815009

Sec/Manager:	Mike Pennington
Professional:	Martin Tyson
Directions:	2¾ miles southwest of Newton Abbot centre. From centre take the A381 (Totnes) for 2¾ miles. The entrance is on the left hand side, just after the garden centre on the right hand side.
Date Founded:	1993
Type of Course:	Parkland
No of Holes:	18
Length:	6237 yds (5757 mtrs)
Par:	71

SSS:	72
Green Fees:	Weekdays: £18; Weekends/ Bank Holidays: £20
Visitors:	Welcome: Contact Club in Advance. No restrictions
Societies:	Welcome: Contact Club in Advance. Unable to play weekends before 12 midday
Facilities:	Putting Green, Chipping Green, Driving Range, Club Hire, Trolley Hire, Bar, Restaurant

Accommodation, Food and Drink

Reference numbers below refer to detailed information provided in section 2

Accommodation

Alexandra Lodge Holiday Apartments, Grafton Road, Torquay, South Devon TQ1 1QJ

Tel: 01803 213465 Fax: 01803 390933
e-mail: almes@fsbdial.co.uk
website: www.alexandra-lodge.co.uk
Lovely detached Georgian villa in secluded grounds offering seven self-catering apartments sleeping between two and eight people.   249

The Anchorage Guest House, 170 New Road, Brixham, Devon TQ5 8DA

Tel/Fax: 01803 852960
A comfortable, friendly guest house with a fabulous award-winning garden. Seven guest rooms.   257

Babbacombe Hall Hotel, 17 Manor Road, Babbacombe, Torquay, Devon TQ1 3JX

Tel: 01803 325668 Fax: 01803 325668
Victorian seaside hotel with six en-suite rooms. Bar and restaurant open to residents only.   253

Brunswick House, 5 Brunswick Street, Teignmouth, Devon TQ14 8AE

Tel: 01626 774102
e-mail: peterhockings@hotmail.com
Bed and breakfast housed within Victorian terrace just 100 metres from sea front. Spacious accommodation with eight, en-suite guest rooms.   212

Chuckle Too, Blackawton, Totnes, Devon TQ9 7BG

Tel: 01803 712455
Modern, self-catering cottage offering cosy cottage-style accommodation. Sleeps up to three adults. Very well equipped.   262

Collingwood Hotel, Braddons Hill Road East, Torquay, Devon TQ1 1HB

Tel: 01803 293448 Fax: 01626 400221
e-mail: bookings@collingwood-hotel.co.uk
An elegant Georgian Hotel located a short distance from the sea front. Regular themed breaks.   256

The Halfway Inn, Sidmouth Road, Aylesbeare,

Devon EX5 2JP

Tel: 01395 232273 Fax: 01395 516398
Former coaching inn offering a fine selection of refreshments with very extensive food menu. Four guest rooms for bed and breakfast, two en-suite.   243

Hole Mill, Branscombe, Seaton, Devon EX12 3BX

Tel: 01297 680314
website: www.users.globalnet.co.uk/~branscombe/ hole1.htm
Former working watermill, located in pretty valley, converted into a charming house on many levels. Surrounded by colourful gardens. 3 guest rooms.   267

Marlborough Hotel, The Esplanade, Sidmouth, Devon EX10 8AR

Tel: 01395 513320
Super sea front property just a stone's throw from the beach. Popular pub and hotel, offering fine food all day. 18 en-suite rooms.   224

Sir Walter Raleigh, 22 High Street, East Budleigh, Devon EX9 7EB

Tel: 01395 442510
A charming, traditional, thatched building serving fine local ales and freshly prepared food. Bed and breakfast accommodation available.   252

The Steam Packet Inn, St. Peter's Quay, Totnes, Devon TQ9 5EN

Tel: 01803 863880 Fax: 01803 862754
Elegant riverside inn with open plan lounge bar and elegant, conservatory Restaurant. Ten en-suite guest bedrooms. Private river moorings available.   261

The Welcome Stranger, Liverton, Nr. Newton Abbott, Devon TQ12 6JA

Tel: 01626 821224
e-mail: welcomestranger@talk21.com
A friendly, country pub offering a good variety of sensibly priced, home-cooked food. Two twin en-suite rooms.   260

Westbury, 51 New Road, Brixham, Devon TQ5 8NL

Tel/Fax: 01803 851684
e-mail: ann.burt@lineone.net
A charming Georgian house offering stylish accommodation with six guest rooms. Private parking.   255

Woodlands Hotel, 51 Barnpark Road, Teignmouth, Devon TQ14 8PN

Tel: 01626 773094
Delightful Regency-style hotel retaining a great deal of period elegance. Comfortable guest rooms with many having superb views out to sea. Half- or Full-board available.   221

Food and Drink

Collingwood Hotel, Braddons Hill Road East, Torquay, Devon TQ1 1HB

Tel: 01803 293448 Fax: 01626 400221
e-mail: bookings@collingwood-hotel.co.uk

An elegant Georgian Hotel located a short distance from the sea front. Regular themed breaks.

The Halfway Inn, Sidmouth Road, Aylesbeare, Devon EX5 2JP

Tel: 01395 232273 Fax: 01395 516398
Former coaching inn offering a fine selection of refreshments with very extensive food menu. Four guest rooms for bed and breakfast, two en-suite.

Marlborough Hotel, The Esplanade, Sidmouth, Devon EX10 8AR

Tel: 01395 513320
Super sea front property just a stone's throw from the beach. Popular pub and hotel, offering fine food all day. 18 en-suite rooms.

The Plough Inn, Fore Street, Ipplepen, Devon TQ12 5RP

Tel: 01808 812118 Fax: 01803 814278
website: www.ipplepen.com
An attractive old inn with a great deal of character. Good range of drinks and home-cooked food.

Sir Walter Raleigh, 22 High Street, East Budleigh, Devon EX9 7EB

Tel: 01395 442510
A charming, traditional, thatched building serving fine local ales and freshly prepared food. Bed and breakfast accommodation available.

The Steam Packet Inn, St. Peter's Quay, Totnes, Devon TQ9 5EN

Tel: 01803 863880 Fax: 01803 862754
Elegant riverside inn with open plan lounge bar and elegant, conservatory Restaurant. Ten en-suite guest bedrooms. Private river moorings available.

The Welcome Stranger, Liverton, Nr. Newton Abbott, Devon TQ12 6JA

Tel: 01626 821224
e-mail: welcomestranger@talk21.com
A friendly, country pub offering a good variety of sensibly priced, home-cooked food. Two twin en-suite rooms.

One of the more pleasant aspects of the course is that, although less than 10 years old, it gives the impression of being a far older, more traditional course, winding its way through mature trees and almost undisturbed countryside. The fairways are undulating, fairly narrow at times, and often surrounded by mounds, making it in many ways reminiscent of St Mellion, but without being quite as fearsome if your tee shot misses the mown surface. Whereas at St Mellion you might well lose your ball, here you should still have a second shot, albeit perhaps not the one you would have chosen.

There are an alarming number of bunkers peppered about, and water, in the form of natural streams or man-made ponds, comes into play on seven holes. One that you will undoubtedly remember, and not necessarily for the right reasons, is the fourth, a 450-yard par five which dog-legs right to left, then left to right, has water threatening all down one side and unpleasant mounds down the other - and a pond next to the green for good measure.

The 18th provides a delightfully-challenging finale, a par three of 200 yards or so, but most of it a carry over more water.

Dartmouth Golf Club

Blackawton, Totnes, Devon TQ9 7DE
Tel: 01803 712686 Fax: 01803 712628

You never know quite who you might bump into hacking their way around the prodigious 7,000-plus yards of this country club course about five miles inland from the picturesque harbour. But if the owner is around, he may well have with him some showbiz stars that share his love of golf.

The club, which opened in 1992, belongs to the Director General of the BBC, Greg Dyke, and the championship course measures an awesome 7,190 yards off the back markers, although lesser mortals can trim about 500 yards off that from the blue tees.

Sec/Manager:	Brian Munroe
Professional:	Steve Dougan
Directions:	2¾ miles west of Dartmouth centre. From Dartmouth higher ferry take the A3122 (Halwell, Totnes) for 2¾ miles. The entrance is on the right hand side near Woodlands Leisure Park.
Visitors:	Welcome: Contact Club in Advance. No restrictions. Handicap certificates required
Societies:	Welcome: By arrangement with Club
Facilities:	Hotel, Self Catering Cottages, Private Rooms, Putting Green, Chipping Green, Club Hire, Trolley Hire, Buggy Hire, Bar, Restaurant, Driving Range

Championship

Date Founded:	1992
Type of Course:	Parkland
No of Holes:	18
Length:	7200 yds (6646 mtrs)
Par:	72
SSS:	72
Green Fees:	Weekdays: £27; Weekends/ Bank Holidays: £35

Club

Date Founded:	1992
Type of Course:	Parkland
No of Holes:	9
Length:	2539 yds (2343 mtrs)
Par:	33
SSS:	64
Green Fees:	Weekdays: Price varies; Weekends/Bank Holidays: Price varies

Accommodation, Food and Drink

Reference numbers below refer to detailed information provided in section 2

Accommodation

Campbells, 5 Mount Boone, Dartmouth, Devon TQ6 9PB

Tel: 01803 833438 Fax: 01803 833438
Award-winning bed and breakfast enjoying stunning views over the town of Dartmouth. Two elegant, en-suite, double bedrooms. Superb breakfasts with

excellent choice. 264

Chuckle Too, Blackawton, Totnes, Devon TQ9 7BG

Tel: 01803 712455
Modern, self-catering cottage offering cosy cottage-style accommodation. Sleeps up to three adults. Very well equipped. 262

The Floating Bridge and Floaters Restaurant, Sandquay, Dartmouth, Devon TQ6 9PQ

Tel: 01803 832354 Fax: 01803 832354
Popular riverside hostelry serving fine refreshment and award-winning food. Fresh local fish a speciality. Well worth a detour. 266

Tides Reach Hotel, South Sands, Salcombe, Devon TQ8 8LJ

Tel: 01548 843466 Fax: 01548 843954
e-mail: enquire@tidesreach.com
website: www.tidesreach.com
Elegant, luxurious hotel with a good reputation for high standards of service. Superb, south-facing location and excellent residents' facilities. High quality restaurant. 234

The White House, Chillington, Nr. Kingsbridge, Devon TQ7 2JX

Tel: 01548 580580 Fax: 01548 581124
A small, high quality hotel and restaurant offering seven luxuriously furnished bedrooms including two suites. 203

Food and Drink

The Laughing Monk Restaurant, Totnes Road, Strete, Nr. Dartmouth, Devon TQ6 0RN

Tel: 01803 770639
Award-winning restaurant, including "Best Restaurant in the West" Gold Award. Housed within a 160-year old former church school. Open for dinner throughout the year. 227

The Singing Kettle, 6 Smith Street, Dartmouth, Devon TQ6 9QR

Tel: 01803 832624
Traditional English tea room tucked away on a side street in the centre of Dartmouth. Open all day for food and drink, mostly home-made. 263

Tides Reach Hotel, South Sands, Salcombe, Devon TQ8 8LJ

Tel: 01548 843466 Fax: 01548 843954
e-mail: enquire@tidesreach.com
website: www.tidesreach.com
Elegant, luxurious hotel with a good reputation for high standards of service. Superb, south-facing location and excellent residents' facilities. High quality restaurant. 234

The White House, Chillington, Nr. Kingsbridge, Devon TQ7 2JX

Tel: 01548 580580 Fax: 01548 581124
A small, high quality hotel and restaurant offering seven luxuriously furnished bedrooms including two suites. 203

Downes Crediton Golf Club

Hookway, Crediton, Devon EX17 3PT
Tel: 01363 773025 Fax: 01363 775060

Sec/Manager:	Phillip Lee
Professional:	Howard Finch
Directions:	8 miles northwest of Exeter. At Crediton railway station turn left off the A377 and follow signs to Hookway
Date Founded:	1976
Type of Course:	Parkland
No of Holes:	18
Length:	5954 yds (5495 mtrs)
Par:	70
SSS:	69
Green Fees:	Weekdays: £22; Weekends/ Bank Holidays: £25
Visitors:	Welcome: Contact Club in Advance. No restrictions
Societies:	Welcome: Contact Club in Advance. Unable to play weekends
Facilities:	Putting Green, Club Hire, Trolley Hire Bar, Restaurant

Accommodation, Food and Drink

Reference numbers below refer to detailed information provided in section 2

Accommodation

'Oaklands', Black Dog, Nr. Crediton, Devon EX17 4QJ

Tel: 01884 860645 Fax: 01884 861030
A super house built to very high standards of craftsmanship. Three en-suite rooms. Stunning views and gardens. 247

Dartmoor Railway Inn, Station Road, Crediton, Devon EX17 3BX

Tel: 01363 724989
Traditional hostelry offering a warm, friendly welcome to all. Home-cooked food with popular Sunday roast lunches. Three en-suite rooms. 248

Mole Cottage, Chittlehamholt, Devon EX37 9HF

Tel: 01769 540471 Fax: 01769 540471
e-mail: relax@moley.uk.com
website: www.moley.uk.com
17th century thatched cottage enjoying a riverside location within the magical Mole Valley. Also a working pottery and gallery. Residential Pottery courses available. 218

'The Oyster', Colebrooke, Devon EX17 5JQ

Tel: 01363 84576
Cosy modern bungalow taking its unusual name from the owner, Pearl. Three bedrooms, each en-suite or with private facilities. Many guests have returned several times - what better recommendation! 245

The Red Lion, Shobrooke, Nr. Crediton, Devon EX17 1AT

Tel: 01363 772340
Friendly country pub run by popular couple. Cosy bars with a separate 50-seater restaurant. Three, double, en-suite rooms. 244

Food and Drink

Dartmoor Railway Inn, Station Road, Crediton, Devon EX17 3BX

Tel: 01363 724989
Traditional hostelry offering a warm, friendly welcome to all. Home-cooked food with popular Sunday roast lunches. Three en-suite rooms. 248

The Duchess Restaurant, Duke Street, South Molton, Devon EX36 3AL

Tel: 01769 573123
Small charming restaurant with a calm, relaxing atmosphere. Open for lunch and dinner, with fully licensed bar. 241

The Red Lion, Shobrooke, Nr. Crediton, Devon EX17 1AT

Tel: 01363 772340
Friendly country pub run by popular couple. Cosy bars with a separate 50-seater restaurant. Three, double, en-suite rooms. 244

East Devon
Golf Club

North View Road, Budleigh Salterton,
Devon EX9 6DQ

Tel: 01395 443370 Fax: 01395 445547

Elsewhere in this guide there has been mention of clubs, which are fairly new to the scene, and others which have celebrated their centenaries years ago. East Devon offers golfers the chance to get in on the 100th birthday celebrations, as the course comes of age in 2002.

It might best be described as a cliff-top downland course, but that doesn't really do it full justice. The turf has that links feel to it, but with a heathland look, not very Devon-ish at all, but more like the courses you might find in the Home Counties countryside.

What you won't find in the Home Counties, however, are, yes, you've guessed it, yet more breathtaking views. They say that on a clear day you can see from the mouth of the River Exe in the west to the distant Portland Bill, on the far side of Lyme Bay in the east, and that's a long carry in anybody's book.

But don't get all misty-eyed and whimsical with this course, or you will be brought back to reality with a hefty bump. You will need your wits about you from the word go, with Stroke Index 1 popping up as early as the third, a tough uphill par

four, while the seventh is a tight little dog-leg through the pines.

But East Devon leaves the best until almost last, the signature 17th which you will love and loathe. A 450-yard downhill par four may sound simple enough in cold print, but the reality is that this one can bite you just when you think you are home and dry. You'll need to hit an island fairway amidst the gorse and heather, before playing across a big ravine to try and find the elevated green. Not one to forget in a hurry.

Sec/Manager:	None
Professional:	Trevor Underwood
Directions:	¾ mile southwest of Budleigh Salterton centre. From the centre (East Budleigh Rd) take the B3178 for 1 mile and turn left into Sharbrook Hill on the outskirts. The entrance is after 300 yds at the end in North View Road
Date Founded:	1902
Type of Course:	Heathland
No of Holes:	18
Length:	6240 yds (5759 mtrs)
Par:	70
SSS:	70
Green Fees:	Weekdays: £28; Weekends/ Bank Holidays: £36
Visitors:	Welcome: Contact Club in Advance. Unable to play Tuesday & Thursday Handicap certificates
Societies:	Welcome: Contact Club in Advance.
Facilities:	Practice Area, Putting Green, Chipping Green, Club Hire, Trolley Hire, Hire, Bar, Restaurant

Accommodation, Food and Drink

Reference numbers below refer to detailed information provided in section 2

Accommodation

Chimneys of Starcross, Starcross, Nr. Exeter, Devon EX6 8PA

Tel: 01626 890813
A characterful, detached house situated overlooking the Exe estuary. Built in 1888, many of the original features have been preserved. Seven rooms with five en-suite.   202

The Devon Arms, Kenton, Nr. Exeter, Devon EX6 8LD

Tel: 01626 890213 Fax: 01626 891678
e-mail: devon.arms@ukgateway.net
Next to Powderham Castle, The Exeter Arms is a
family-run hostelry serving home-cooked food. Six
en-suite rooms available for bed and breakfast.   254

The Halfway Inn, Sidmouth Road, Aylesbeare, Devon EX5 2JP

Tel: 01395 232273 Fax: 01395 516398
Former coaching inn offering a fine selection of
refreshments with very extensive food menu. Four
guest rooms for bed and breakfast, two en-suite.   243

Langstone Cliff Hotel, Dawlish, Devon EX7 0NA

Tel: 01626 868000 Fax: 01626 868006
e-mail: reception@langstone-hotel.co.uk
One of Dorset's premier hotels in superb location
overlooking the sea. Excellent facilities including
tennis, practice golf and indoor and outdoor pools.
Popular restaurant.   237

Lower Southbrook Farm, Southbrook Lane, Whimple, Exeter, Devon EX5 2PG

Tel: 01404 822989 Fax: 01404 822989
Modern, comfortable self-catering cottages converted
from former farm buildings. Each sleeps six.   242

Marlborough Hotel, The Esplanade, Sidmouth, Devon EX10 8AR

Tel: 01395 513320
Super sea front property just a stone's throw from the
beach. Popular pub and hotel, offering fine food all
day. 18 en-suite rooms.   224

Sir Walter Raleigh, 22 High Street, East Budleigh, Devon EX9 7EB

Tel: 01395 442510
A charming, traditional, thatched building serving
fine local ales and freshly prepared food. Bed and
breakfast accommodation available.   252

Food and Drink

The Devon Arms, Kenton, Nr. Exeter, Devon EX6 8LD

Tel: 01626 890213 Fax: 01626 891678
e-mail: devon.arms@ukgateway.net
Next to Powderham Castle, The Exeter Arms is a
family-run hostelry serving home-cooked food. Six
en-suite rooms available for bed and breakfast.   254

Langstone Cliff Hotel, Dawlish, Devon EX7 0NA

Tel: 01626 868000 Fax: 01626 868006
e-mail: reception@langstone-hotel.co.uk
One of Dorset's premier hotels in superb location
overlooking the sea. Excellent facilities including
tennis, practice golf and indoor and outdoor pools.
Popular restaurant.   237

Marlborough Hotel, The Esplanade, Sidmouth, Devon EX10 8AR

Tel: 01395 513320
Super sea front property just a stone's throw from the
beach. Popular pub and hotel, offering fine food all
day. 18 en-suite rooms.   224

Sir Walter Raleigh, 22 High Street, East Budleigh, Devon EX9 7EB

Tel: 01395 442510
A charming, traditional, thatched building serving
fine local ales and freshly prepared food. Bed and
breakfast accommodation available.   252

Exeter Golf Club

Countess Wear, Exeter Devon EX2 7AE
Tel: 01392 874139 Fax: 01392 874914

Sec/Manager:	Keith Ham
Professional:	Mike Rowett
Directions:	4 miles southeast of Exeter City centre. From the centre take Topsham Rd (B3182). The entrance is after 2¼ miles on the left hand side, ¼ mile after crossing roundabout junction of A379 and B3181. From M5 junction 30 take the A379 leading to the B3181 (Countess Wear) and turn left at roundabout onto B3182. The entrance is after ¼ mile on the left hand side.
Date Founded:	1929
Type of Course:	Parkland
No of Holes:	18
Length:	6008 yds (5545 mtrs)
Par:	69
SSS:	69
Green Fees:	Weekdays: £30 (round) £35 (day); Weekends/Bank Holidays: £35 (round) £42 (day)
Visitors:	Welcome: Contact Club in Advance. Unable to play before 2.30 pm Tuesday

Societies: Welcome: Contact Club in Advance. Restrictions

Facilities: Putting Green, Club Hire, Trolley Hire, Bar, Restaurant

Accommodation, Food and Drink

Reference numbers below refer to detailed information provided in section 2

Accommodation

Chimneys of Starcross, Starcross, Nr. Exeter, Devon EX6 8PA

Tel: 01626 890813
A characterful, detached house situated overlooking the Exe estuary. Built in 1888, many of the original features have been preserved. Seven rooms with five en-suite.   202

Dartmoor Railway Inn, Station Road, Crediton, Devon EX17 3BX

Tel: 01363 724989
Traditional hostelry offering a warm, friendly welcome to all. Home-cooked food with popular Sunday roast lunches. Three en-suite rooms.   248

The Devon Arms, Kenton, Nr. Exeter, Devon EX6 8LD

Tel: 01626 890213 Fax: 01626 891678
e-mail: devon.arms@ukgateway.net
Next to Powderham Castle, The Exeter Arms is a family-run hostelry serving home-cooked food. Six en-suite rooms available for bed and breakfast.   254

The Halfway Inn, Sidmouth Road, Aylesbeare, Devon EX5 2JP

Tel: 01395 232273 Fax: 01395 516398
Former coaching inn offering a fine selection of refreshments with very extensive food menu. Four guest rooms for bed and breakfast, two en-suite.   243

Langstone Cliff Hotel, Dawlish, Devon EX7 0NA

Tel: 01626 868000 Fax: 01626 868006
e-mail: reception@langstone-hotel.co.uk
One of Dorset's premier hotels in superb location overlooking the sea. Excellent facilities including tennis, practice golf and indoor and outdoor pools. Popular restaurant.   237

'The Oyster', Colebrooke, Devon EX17 5JQ

Tel: 01363 84576
Cosy modern bungalow taking its unusual name from the owner, Pearl. Three bedrooms, each en-suite or with private facilities. Many guests have returned several times - what better recommendation!   245

The Red Lion, Shobrooke, Nr. Crediton, Devon EX17 1AT

Tel: 01363 772340
Friendly country pub run by popular couple. Cosy bars with a separate 50-seater restaurant. Three, double, en-suite rooms.   244

South Farm Holiday Cottages, South Farm, Blackborough, Cullompton, Devon EX15 2JE

Tel: 01823 681078 Fax: 01823 680483
e-mail: chapmans@southfarm.co.uk
website: www.southfarm.co.uk
Delightful complex of five cottages in the heart of the Devonshire countryside. Excellent facilities include four coarse fishing lakes, tennis courts, outdoor pool and games barn. Open all year round for short breaks and longer stays.

Food and Drink

Dartmoor Railway Inn, Station Road, Crediton, Devon EX17 3BX

Tel: 01363 724989
Traditional hostelry offering a warm, friendly welcome to all. Home-cooked food with popular Sunday roast lunches. Three en-suite rooms.   248

The Devon Arms, Kenton, Nr. Exeter, Devon EX6 8LD

Tel: 01626 890213 Fax: 01626 891678
e-mail: devon.arms@ukgateway.net
Next to Powderham Castle, The Exeter Arms is a family-run hostelry serving home-cooked food. Six en-suite rooms available for bed and breakfast.   254

The Halfway Inn, Sidmouth Road, Aylesbeare, Devon EX5 2JP

Tel: 01395 232273 Fax: 01395 516398
Former coaching inn offering a fine selection of refreshments with very extensive food menu. Four guest rooms for bed and breakfast, two en-suite.   243

Langstone Cliff Hotel, Dawlish, Devon EX7 0NA

Tel: 01626 868000 Fax: 01626 868006
e-mail: reception@langstone-hotel.co.uk
One of Dorset's premier hotels in superb location overlooking the sea. Excellent facilities including tennis, practice golf and indoor and outdoor pools. Popular restaurant.   237

The Red Lion, Shobrooke, Nr. Crediton, Devon EX17 1AT

Tel: 01363 772340
Friendly country pub run by popular couple. Cosy bars with a separate 50-seater restaurant. Three, double, en-suite rooms.   244

Hartland Forest Golf Club

Hartland Forest Leisure Park, Bideford, Devon EX39 5RA

Tel: 01237 531441 Fax: 01237 431734

Sec/Manager: Bill Jamieson

Professional: None

Directions: 11 miles southwest of Bideford centre. From Bideford take the A39 (Bude). After 14 miles from Bideford, or 4 miles after

Clovelly Cross, turn left onto minor road with brown sign to Golf Course. The entrance is after 1½ miles.

Date Founded: 1979

Type of Course: Parkland

No of Holes: 18

Length: 6015 yds (5552 mtrs)

Par: 71

SSS: 69

Green Fees: Weekdays: £15 (round) £20 (day); Weekends/Bank Holidays: £15 (round) £20 (day)

Visitors: Welcome: Contact Club in Advance. No restrictions

Societies: Welcome: Contact Club in Advance

Facilities: Putting Green, Club Hire, Trolley Hire, Buggy Hire, Bar, Restaurant

Accommodation, Food and Drink

Reference numbers below refer to detailed information provided in section 2

Accommodation

Bennetts Court Cottages, Whitstone, Holsworthy, Devon EX22 6UD

Tel: 01288 341370 Fax: 01288 341370
e-mail: helen@ bennettscourt.co.uk
website: www.bennettscourt.co.uk
Five, well-equipped self-catering cottages, converted from former farm buildings, sleeping between two and six people. Within the grounds there is a outdoor heated pool and other facilities. 246

The Brendon Arms, Vicarage Road, Bude, Cornwall EX23 8SD

Tel: 01288 354542 Fax: 01288 354542
e-mail: sophia@sophiafrbrendon.demon.co.uk
website: www.north-cornwall.co.uk/client/brendon-arms/
Traditional Cornish inn situated in a picturesque part of town. Serves a good selection of seafood while the bar stocks a range of real ales. Seven en-suite guest rooms. 109

Bude Haven Hotel, Flexbury Avenue, Bude, Cornwall EX23 8NS

Tel: 01288 352305 Fax: 01288 352305
e-mail: enquiries@budehavenhotel.co.uk
website: www.budehavenhotel.co.uk
Attractive Georgian building offering a comfortable, relaxed atmosphere. Eleven individually furnished en-suite bedrooms of varying sizes. Super residents' restaurant. 127

The Camelot Hotel and Hawkers Restaurant, Downs View, Bude, Cornwall EX23 8RE

Tel: 01288 352361 Fax: 01288 355470
e-mail: stay@camelot-hotel.co.uk
website: www.camelot-hotel.co.uk
Super location on the edge of Bude Golf Course and five minutes from sea. High standards throughout, with relaxed comfortable ambience. 24 en-suite rooms. Popular restaurant. 106

Inn on the Green, Crooklets Beach, Bude, Cornwall EX23 8NF

Tel: 01288 356013 Fax: 01288 356244
e-mail: innonthegreen46@btinternet.com
website: www.innonthegreen46.co.uk
Family-run Victorian hotel offering comfort, service and value for money. Fine restaurant serves wholesome food with bar open all day. 107

Links Side, 7 Burn View, Bude, Cornwall EX23 8BY

Tel: 01288 352410
Small, cosy bed and breakfast with warm, friendly atmosphere. Rooms of varying sizes, most with en-suite facilities. 108

The Village Inn, Youngaton Road, Westward Ho!, Bideford, Devon EX39 1HU

Tel: 01237 477331 Fax: 01237 425183
Family-run free house in popular area of north Devon. Food served from extensive menu of meals and snacks, available in bar or separate restaurant. Newly built en-suite bed and breakfast accommodation. 217

Waterfront Inn, Golf Links Road, Westward Ho!, Devon EX39 1LH

Tel: 01237 474737 Fax: 01237 471719
Modern, friendly inn with much to offer to visitors to the area. Large bar areas, stylish restaurant and comfortable, newly furnished accommodation. 220

Wyvern House, 7 Downs View, Bude, Cornwall EX23 8RF

Tel: 01288 352205 Fax: 01288 356802
e-mail: eileen@wyvernhouse.co.uk
website: www.wyvernhouse.co.uk
Attractive house in pleasant situation just five minutes from the beach. Six guest rooms, some with en-suite facilities. Evening meals available. 114

Yeolden House Hotel, Durrant Lane, Northam, Nr. Bideford, Devon EX39 2RL

Tel: 01237 474400 Fax: 01237 476618
e-mail: yeoldonhouse@aol.com
website: www.yeoldonhousehotel.co.uk
An imposing house surrounded by lawns and colourful flower beds that slope gently down to the river. Ten en-suite rooms that have each been individually designed. Elegant restaurant. 216

Food and Drink

The Brendon Arms, Vicarage Road, Bude, Cornwall EX23 8SD

Tel: 01288 354542 Fax: 01288 354542
e-mail: sophia@sophiafrbrendon.demon.co.uk
website: www.north-cornwall.co.uk/client/
brendon-arms/
Traditional Cornish inn situated in a picturesque part of town. Serves a good selection of seafood while the bar stocks a range of real ales. Seven en-suite guest rooms. 109

Bude Haven Hotel, Flexbury Avenue, Bude, Cornwall EX23 8NS

Tel: 01288 352305 Fax: 01288 352305
e-mail: enquiries@budehavenhotel.co.uk
website: www.budehavenhotel.co.uk
Attractive Georgian building offering a comfortable, relaxed atmosphere. Eleven individually furnished en-suite bedrooms of varying sizes. Super residents' restaurant. 127

The Camelot Hotel and Hawkers Restaurant, Downs View, Bude, Cornwall EX23 8RE

Tel: 01288 352361 Fax: 01288 355470
e-mail: stay@camelot-hotel.co.uk
website: www.camelot-hotel.co.uk
Super location on the edge of Bude Golf Course and five minutes from sea. High standards throughout, with relaxed comfortable ambience. 24 en-suite rooms. Popular restaurant. 106

Inn on the Green, Crooklets Beach, Bude, Cornwall EX23 8NF

Tel: 01288 356013 Fax: 01288 356244
e-mail: innonthegreen46@btinternet.com
website: www.innonthegreen.co.uk
Family-run Victorian hotel offering comfort, service and value for money. Fine restaurant serves wholesome food with bar open all day. 107

The Village Inn, Youngaton Road, Westward Ho!, Bideford, Devon EX39 1HU

Tel: 01237 477331 Fax: 01237 425183
Family-run free house in popular area of north Devon. Food served from extensive menu of meals and snacks, available in bar or separate restaurant. Newly built en-suite bed and breakfast accommodation. 217

Waterfront Inn, Golf Links Road, Westward Ho!, Devon EX39 1LH

Tel: 01237 474737 Fax: 01237 471719
Modern, friendly inn with much to offer to visitors to the area. Large bar areas, stylish restaurant and comfortable, newly furnished accommodation. 220

Yeolden House Hotel, Durrant Lane, Northam, Nr. Bideford, Devon EX39 2RL

Tel: 01237 474400 Fax: 01237 476618
e-mail: yeoldonhouse@aol.com
website: www.yeoldonhousehotel.co.uk
An imposing house surrounded by lawns and colourful flower beds that slope gently down to the river. Ten en-suite rooms that have each been individually designed. Elegant restaurant. 216

Holsworthy Golf Club

Kilatree, Holsworthy, Devon EX22 6LP
Tel: 01409 253177 Fax: 01409 253177

Sec/Manager:	Barry Megson
Professional:	Graham Webb
Directions:	1 mile west of Holsworthy centre. From centre take the A3072 (Stratton, Bude). After 1¼ miles turn left (next after Rydon turn). The entrance is after ½ mile on left hand side.
Date Founded:	1937
Type of Course:	Parkland
No of Holes:	18
Length:	6250 yds (5769 mtrs)
Par:	70
SSS:	69
Green Fees:	Weekdays: £20 (day); Weekends/Bank Holidays: £20 (day)
Visitors:	Welcome: Contact Club in Advance. No restrictions
Societies:	Welcome: Contact Club in Advance
Facilities:	Practice Area, Putting Green, Driving Range, Club Hire, Trolley Hire, Bar, Restaurant

Accommodation, Food and Drink

Reference numbers below refer to detailed information provided in section 2

Accommodation

Bennetts Court Cottages, Whitstone, Holsworthy, Devon EX22 6UD

Tel: 01288 341370 Fax: 01288 341370

e-mail: helen@ bennettscourt.co.uk
website: www.bennettscourt.co.uk
Five, well-equipped self-catering cottages, converted from former farm buildings, sleeping between two and six people. Within the grounds there is a outdoor heated pool and other facilities. 246

The Brendon Arms, Vicarage Road, Bude, Cornwall EX23 8SD

Tel: 01288 354542 Fax: 01288 354542
e-mail: sophia@sophiafrbrendon.demon.co.uk
website: www.north-cornwall.co.uk/client/ brendon-arms/
Traditional Cornish inn situated in a picturesque part of town. Serves a good selection of seafood while the bar stocks a range of real ales. Seven en-suite guest rooms. 109

The Bridge Inn, Bridge Street, Hatherleigh, Nr. Okehampton, Devon EX20 3JA

Tel: 01837 810947 Fax: 01837 810614
The Bridge Inn dates from the 16th century and is one of the oldest buildings in the area. Cosy interior with bar and separate restaurant. Six en-suite guest rooms of varying sizes. 231

Bude Haven Hotel, Flexbury Avenue, Bude, Cornwall EX23 8NS

Tel: 01288 352305 Fax: 01288 352305
e-mail: enquiries@budehavenhotel.co.uk
website: www.budehavenhotel.co.uk
Attractive Georgian building offering a comfortable, relaxed atmosphere. Eleven individually furnished en-suite bedrooms of varying sizes. Super residents' restaurant. 127

The Camelot Hotel and Hawkers Restaurant, Downs View, Bude, Cornwall EX23 8RE

Tel: 01288 352361 Fax: 01288 355470
e-mail: stay@camelot-hotel.co.uk
website: www.camelot-hotel.co.uk
Super location on the edge of Bude Golf Course and five minutes from sea. High standards throughout, with relaxed comfortable ambience. 24 en-suite rooms. Popular restaurant. 106

Inn on the Green, Crooklets Beach, Bude, Cornwall EX23 8NF

Tel: 01288 356013 Fax: 01288 356244
e-mail: innonthegreen46@btinternet.com
website: www.innonthegreen46.co.uk
Family-run Victorian hotel offering comfort, service and value for money. Fine restaurant serves wholesome food with a bar open all day. 107

Links Side, 7 Burn View, Bude, Cornwall EX23 8BY

Tel: 01288 352410
Small, cosy bed and breakfast with warm, friendly atmosphere. Rooms of varying sizes, most with en-suite facilities. 108

Pressland Country House Hotel, Hatherleigh, Nr. Okehampton, Devon EX20 3LW

Tel: 01837 810871 Fax: 01837 810303
e-mail graham@presslandhouse.co.uk
website www.presslandhouse.co.uk

Victorian manor house surrounded by lawns and woodland. Five spacious guest rooms, most with en-suite facilities, and superb residents' restaurant. 230

The Royal Oak, The Square, Dolton, Winkleigh, Devon EX19 8QF

Tel: 01805 804288
Friendly country pub with spacious interior. Superb restaurant offering an excellent menu with live jazz twice monthly. Five guest rooms, some en-suite. 258

The Village Inn, Youngaton Road, Westward Ho!, Bideford, Devon EX39 1HU

Tel: 01237 477331 Fax: 01237 425183
Family-run free house in popular area of north Devon. Food served from extensive menu of meals and snacks, available in bar or separate restaurant. Newly built en-suite bed and breakfast accommodation. 217

Waterfront Inn, Golf Links Road, Westward Ho!, Devon EX39 1LH

Tel: 01237 474737 Fax: 01237 471719
Modern, friendly inn with much to offer to visitors to the area. Large bar areas, stylish restaurant and comfortable, newly furnished accommodation. 220

Wyvern House, 7 Downs View, Bude, Cornwall EX23 8RF

Tel: 01288 352205 Fax: 01288 356802
e-mail: eileen@wyvernhouse.co.uk
website: www.wyvernhouse.co.uk
Attractive house in pleasant situation just five minutes from the beach. Six guest rooms, some with en-suite facilities. Evening meals available. 114

Yeolden House Hotel, Durrant Lane, Northam, Nr. Bideford, Devon EX39 2RL

Tel: 01237 474400 Fax: 01237 476618
e-mail: yeoldonhouse@aol.com
website: www.yeoldonhousehotel.co.uk
An imposing house surrounded by lawns and colourful flower beds that slope gently down to the river. Ten en-suite rooms that have each been individually designed. Elegant restaurant. 216

Food and Drink

The Brendon Arms, Vicarage Road, Bude, Cornwall EX23 8SD

Tel: 01288 354542 Fax: 01288 354542
e-mail: sophia@sophiafrbrendon.demon.co.uk
website: www.north-cornwall.co.uk/client/ brendon-arms/
Traditional Cornish inn situated in a picturesque part of town. Serves a good selection of seafood while the bar stocks a range of real ales. Seven en-suite guest rooms. 109

The Bridge Inn, Bridge Street, Hatherleigh, Nr. Okehampton, Devon EX20 3JA

Tel: 01837 810947 Fax: 01837 810614
The Bridge Inn dates from the 16th century and is one of the oldest buildings in the area. Cosy interior with bar and separate restaurant. Six en-suite guest rooms of varying sizes. 231

Bude Haven Hotel, Flexbury Avenue, Bude, Cornwall EX23 8NS

Tel: 01288 352305 Fax: 01288 352305
e-mail: enquiries@budehavenhotel.co.uk
website: www.budehavenhotel.co.uk
Attractive Georgian building offering a comfortable, relaxed atmosphere. Eleven individually furnished en-suite bedrooms of varying sizes. Super residents' restaurant.   127

The Camelot Hotel and Hawkers Restaurant, Downs View, Bude, Cornwall EX23 8RE

Tel: 01288 352361 Fax: 01288 355470
e-mail: stay@camelot-hotel.co.uk
website: www.camelot-hotel.co.uk
Super location on the edge of Bude Golf Course and five minutes from sea. High standards throughout, with relaxed comfortable ambience. 24 en-suite rooms. Popular restaurant.   106

Inn on the Green, Crooklets Beach, Bude, Cornwall EX23 8NF

Tel: 01288 356013 Fax: 01288 356244
e-mail: innonthegreen46@btinternet.com
website: www.innonthegreen46.co.uk
Family-run Victorian hotel offering comfort, service and value for money. Fine restaurant serves wholesome food with a bar open all day.   107

The Royal Oak, The Square, Dolton, Winkleigh, Devon EX19 8QF

Tel: 01805 804288
Friendly country pub with spacious interior. Superb restaurant offering an excellent menu with live jazz twice monthly. Five guest rooms, some en-suite. 258

The Village Inn, Youngaton Road, Westward Ho!, Bideford, Devon EX39 1HU

Tel: 01237 477331 Fax: 01237 425183
Family-run free house in popular area of north Devon. Food served from extensive menu of meals and snacks, available in bar or separate restaurant. Newly built en-suite bed and breakfast accommodation.   217

Waterfront Inn, Golf Links Road, Westward Ho!, Devon EX39 1LH

Tel: 01237 474737 Fax: 01237 471719
Modern, friendly inn with much to offer to visitors to the area. Large bar areas, stylish restaurant and comfortable, newly furnished accommodation.   220

Yeolden House Hotel, Durrant Lane, Northam, Nr. Bideford, Devon EX39 2RL

Tel: 01237 474400 Fax: 01237 476618
e-mail: yeoldonhouse@aol.com
website: www.yeoldonhousehotel.co.uk
An imposing house surrounded by lawns and colourful flower beds that slope gently down to the river. Ten en-suite rooms that have each been individually designed. Elegant restaurant.   216

Honiton Golf Club

Middlehills, Honiton, Devon EX14 8TR
Tel: 01404 44422 Fax: 01404 46383

Sec/Manager:	Brian Young
Professional:	Adrian Cave
Directions:	1½ miles southeast of Honiton centre. From the A30 Honiton by-pass take the A35 (Bridport). After 1¼ miles turn right into Tower Road The entrance is after 1 mile at junction with Northleigh Hill Road
Date Founded:	1896
Type of Course:	Hilltop
No of Holes:	18
Length:	5940 yds (5483 mtrs)
Par:	69
SSS:	68
Green Fees:	Weekdays: £23; Weekends/ Bank Holidays: £28
Visitors:	Welcome: Contact Club in Advance. No restrictions. Handicap certificates required
Societies:	Welcome: Contact Club for availability
Facilities:	Putting Green, Chipping Green, Club Hire, Trolley Hire, Restaurant

Accommodation, Food and Drink

Reference numbers below refer to detailed information provided in section 2

Accommodation

The Halfway Inn, Sidmouth Road, Aylesbeare, Devon EX5 2JP

Tel: 01395 232273 Fax: 01395 516398
Former coaching inn offering a fine selection of
refreshments with very extensive food menu. Four
guest rooms for bed and breakfast, two en-suite. 243

Hole Mill, Branscombe, Seaton,Devon EX12 3BX

Tel: 01297 680314
website: www.users.globalnet.co.uk/~branscombe/
hole1.htm
Former working watermill, located in pretty valley,
converted into a charming house on many levels.
Surrounded by colourful gardens. 3 guest rooms. 267

Home Farm Hotel and Restaurant, Wilmington, Honiton, Devon EX14 9JR

Tel: 01404 831278 Fax: 01404 831411
e-mail: homefarmhotel@breathe-mail.net
website: www.homefarmhotel.co.uk
Sixteenth century farmhouse which has been
converted into an intimate hotel and restaurant. 13
individually-styled, en-suite bedrooms of varying
sizes. The restaurant has a far-reaching reputation for
the high quality of its food and service. 223

Lower Southbrook Farm, Southbrook Lane, Whimple, Exeter, Devon EX5 2PG

Tel: 01404 822989 Fax: 01404 822989
Modern, comfortable self-catering cottages converted
from former farm buildings. Each sleeps six. 242

Mariners Hotel, Silver Street, Lyme Regis, Dorset DT7 3HS

Tel: 01297 442753 Fax: 01297 442431
e-mail: mariners@ukgateway.net
This former 17th-century coaching inn retains much
of its original character, while offering a comfortable
and stylish place to stay. 12 en-suite bedrooms,
relaxing lounge and cosy restaurant.

Marlborough Hotel, The Esplanade, Sidmouth, Devon EX10 8AR

Tel: 01395 513320
Super sea front property just a stone's throw from the
beach. Popular pub and hotel, offering fine food all
day. 18 en-suite rooms. 224

Sir Walter Raleigh, 22 High Street, East Budleigh, Devon EX9 7EB

Tel: 01395 442510
A charming, traditional, thatched building serving
fine local ales and freshly prepared food. Bed and
breakfast accommodation available. 252

South Farm Holiday Cottages, South Farm, Blackborough, Cullompton, Devon EX15 2JE

Tel: 01823 681078 Fax: 01823 680483
e-mail: chapmans@southfarm.co.uk
website: www.southfarm.co.uk
Delightful complex of five cottages in the heart of the
Devonshire countryside. Excellent facilities include
four coarse fishing lakes, tennis courts, outdoor pool
and games barn. Open all year round for short breaks
and longer stays.

Springfield House, Woodmead Road, Lyme Regis, Dorset DT7 3LJ

Tel: 01297 443409 Fax: 01297 443685
e-mail: springfield@lymeregis.com
website: www.lymeregis.com/springfield
An elegant Georgian town house, tastefully converted
to provide guest house accommodation with five en-
suite rooms of varying sizes, all with sea views.
Residents benefit from reduced fees at Lyme Regis
Golf Club.

Whidborne Manor, Ashill, Bishopsteignton, Devon TQ14 9PY

Tel: 01626 870177
e-mail: nicky.dykes@btinternet.com
Cosy 15th-century thatched cottage, attractively
furnished, with many original beams and timbers
throughout. Two double rooms. Evening meals by
arrangement. 201

Food and Drink

Home Farm Hotel and Restaurant, Wilmington, Honiton, Devon EX14 9JR

Tel: 01404 831278 Fax: 01404 831411
e-mail: homefarmhotel@breathe-mail.net
website: www.homefarmhotel.co.uk
Sixteenth century farmhouse which has been
converted into an intimate hotel and restaurant. 13
individually-styled, en-suite bedrooms of varying
sizes. The restaurant has a far-reaching reputation for
the high quality of its food and service. 223

Mariners Hotel, Silver Street, Lyme Regis, Dorset DT7 3HS

Tel: 01297 442753 Fax: 01297 442431
e-mail: mariners@ukgateway.net
This former 17th-century coaching inn retains much
of its original character, while offering a comfortable
and stylish place to stay. 12 en-suite bedrooms,
relaxing lounge and cosy restaurant.

Marlborough Hotel, The Esplanade, Sidmouth, Devon EX10 8AR

Tel: 01395 513320
Super sea front property just a stone's throw from the
beach. Popular pub and hotel, offering fine food all
day. 18 en-suite rooms. 224
Sir Walter Raleigh,

22 High Street, East Budleigh, Devon EX9 7EB

Tel: 01395 442510
A charming, traditional, thatched building serving
fine local ales and freshly prepared food. Bed and
breakfast accommodation available. 252

The Volunteer Inn, Broad Street, Lyme Regis, Dorset DT7 3QS

Tel: 01297 442214
Historic, town centre free house serving a good
selection of real ales, including draught Guinness.
Also offers a full range of freshly cooked meals with
seafood being a speciality.

Hurdwick Golf Club

Tavistock Hamlets, Tavistock, Devon PL19 8PZ
Tel: 01822 612746

Sec/Manager:	Major Cullen
Professional:	Andrew Milton
Directions:	1¼ miles north of Tavistock centre. From centre take the Brentor, Coryton road (narrow road out of main square). The entrance is after 1¼ miles on the right hand side.
Date Founded:	1988
Type of Course:	Parkland
No of Holes:	18
Length:	5217 yds (4815 mtrs)
Par:	68
SSS:	67
Green Fees:	Weekdays: £15; Weekends/ Bank Holidays £15:
Visitors:	Welcome: Contact Club in Advance
Societies:	Welcome: Contact Club in Advance
Facilities:	Putting Green, Chipping Green, Club Hire, Trolley Hire, Buggy Hire, Bar, Restaurant

Accommodation, Food and Drink

Reference numbers below refer to detailed
information provided in section 2

Accommodation

The Carpenters Arms, Metherell, Nr. Callington, Cornwall PL17 8BJ

Tel: 01579 350242 Fax: 01579 350242
A picturesque Cornish pub with friendly and
welcoming service. Wide-ranging menu of home-
cooked bar meals and snacks.   117

The Halfway House Inn, Grenofen, Tavistock, Devon PL19 9ER

Tel: 01822 612960 Fax: 01822 617697
A large, sprawling black and white 16th-century
building with friendly atmosphere. Excellent
reputation for high quality food with two restaurants
serving an a la carte menu. Four guest rooms.   206

The Laurels, Huckworthy Bridge, Yelverton, Devon PL20 6LP

Tel: 01822 853622
Charming old cottage in riverside setting, recently
restored and converted into a self-catering cottage
and private home, in which bed and breakfast is
available. Ideal holiday base.   239

Lifton Hall Hotel, Lifton, Devon PL16 0DR

Tel: 01566 784863 Fax: 01566 784770
e-mail mail@liftonhall.co.uk
Traditional 250-year old Country House hotel in
peaceful village location with ten en-suite rooms.
Formal restaurant and a bistro, both specialising in
local fish.   240

The Old Coach House, Ottery, Tavistock, Devon PL19 8NS

Tel: 01822 617515 Fax: 01822 617515
e-mail eddie@coachhouseone.supanet.com
Old coach house which was substantially renovated
in 1989 to create a delightful hotel and restaurant.
Comfortable accommodation and superb a la carte
restaurant.   236

Tavistock Arms, Fore Street, Gunnislake, Cornwall PL18 9BN

Tel: 01822 832217
Traditional, country pub located directly on the
Devon/Cornwall border. Food is served all day. Bed
and breakfast accommodation available.   118

Food and Drink

The Carpenters Arms, Metherell, Nr. Callington, Cornwall PL17 8BJ

Tel: 01579 350242 Fax: 01579 350242
A picturesque Cornish pub with friendly and
welcoming service. Wide-ranging menu of home-
cooked bar meals and snacks.   117

The Halfway House Inn, Grenofen, Tavistock, Devon PL19 9ER

Tel: 01822 612960 Fax: 01822 617697
A large, sprawling black and white 16th-century
building with friendly atmosphere. Excellent
reputation for high quality food with two restaurants
serving an a la carte menu. Four guest rooms.   206

Lifton Hall Hotel, Lifton, Devon PL16 0DR

Tel: 01566 784863 Fax: 01566 784770
e-mail mail@liftonhall.co.uk
Traditional 250-year old Country House hotel in
peaceful village location with ten en-suite rooms.
Formal restaurant and a bistro, both specialising in
local fish.   240

The Old Coach House, Ottery, Tavistock, Devon PL19 8NS

Tel: 01822 617515 Fax: 01822 617515
e-mail eddie@coachhouseone.supanet.com
Old coach house which was substantially renovated
in 1989 to create a delightful hotel and restaurant.
Comfortable accommodation and superb a la carte
restaurant.   236

Royal Standard Inn, Mary Tavy, Nr. Tavistock, Devon PL19 9QB

Tel: 01822 810289 Fax: 01822 810615
Former coaching inn with an atmosphere of character
and charm. The inn claims to serve the best beer in
the area while the food comprises a good selection of
traditional meals and snacks.   235

Tavistock Arms, Fore Street, Gunnislake, Cornwall PL18 9BN

Tel: 01822 832217
Traditional, country pub located directly on the Devon/Cornwall border. Food is served all day. Bed and breakfast accommodation available. 118

The Walkhampton Inn, Walkhampton, Nr. Yelverton, Devon PL20 6JY

Tel: 01822 855556 Fax: 01822 855556
e-mail: info@walkhamptoninn.co.uk
Historic establishment, popular in the area for serving a good range of beer and traditional pub fayre. Two guest rooms both of which are en-suite. 238

Illfracombe Golf Club

Hele Bay, Illfracombe, Devon EX34 9RT

Tel: 01271 862176, 863328 Fax: 01271 863328

Sec/Manager:	Brian Wright
Professional:	Mark Davies
Directions:	1½ miles northeast of Ilfracombe centre. From centre take the A399 (Combe Martin) coast road. The entrance is 600 yds after passing Evoco Service Station on right hand side.
Date Founded:	1892
Type of Course:	Parkland
No of Holes:	18
Length:	5795 yds (5348 mtrs)
Par:	69
SSS:	68
Green Fees:	Weekdays: £20; Weekends/ Bank Holidays: £24
Visitors:	Welcome: Contact Club in Advance. Handicap certificates required
Societies:	Welcome: Contact Club in Advance
Facilities:	Practice Area, Putting Green,

Chipping Green, Club Hire, Trolley Hire, Bar, Restaurant

Accommodation, Food and Drink

Reference numbers below refer to detailed information provided in section 2

Accommodation

Autumn Lodge, Victoria Street, Combe Martin, Devon EX34 0JS

Tel: 01271 883558
e-mail: lespallatt@supanet.com
Friendly, comfortable hotel with eight bedrooms. Licensed cocktail bar and residents' restaurant. Large heated, outdoor pool. 219

The Beaufort Hotel, Torrs Park, Ilfracombe, Devon EX34 8AY

Tel: 01271 866556
Elegant hotel situated in the delightful Torrs Park area of Ilfracombe with outdoor heated pool, solarium and mini-gymnasium. 12 en-suite rooms. 204

Cliffe Hydro Hotel, Hillsborough Road, Ilfracombe, Devon EX34 9NP

Tel: 01271 863606 Fax: 01271 879019
Medium-sized hotel offering sensibly priced accommodation in superb location looking down onto Ilfracombe harbour. Excellent indoor leisure complex. 228

The Collingdale Hotel, Larkstone Terrace, Ilfracombe, Devon EX34 9NU

Tel: 01271 863770 Fax: 01271 863770
e-mail: collingdale@onet.co.uk
A small, comfortable hotel enjoying a central location within Ilfracombe. Eight en-suite rooms of varying sizes. 211

The Dorchester Hotel, 59 St. Brannocks Road, Ilfracombe, Devon EX34 8EQ

Tel: 01271 865472 Fax: 01271 866949
Family-run hotel with six double, en-suite guest rooms. Fully licensed bar and TV lounge. Children and pets welcome.

Epchris Hotel, Torrs Park, Ilfracombe, Devon EX34 8AZ

Tel: 01271 862751 Fax: 01271 879077
e-mail: epchris-hotel@ic24.net
website: www.epchris-hotel.co.uk
Family-run hotel, set within two acres of private grounds, overlooking Ilfracombe. Nine spacious bedrooms. Within the grounds is a heated outdoor swimming pool and popular games room. 209

Glen Tor Hotel, Torrs Park, Ilfracombe, Devon EX34 8AZ

Tel: 01271 862403 Fax: 01271 862403
e-mail: info@glentorhotel.co.uk
website: www.glentorhotel.co.uk
Small, family-run establishment in a quiet corner of Ilfracombe. Seven en-suite guest bedrooms. Evening meals available on request. 208

The Ilfracombe Regal Hotel, 19 Gilbert Grove, Ilfracombe, Devon EX34 9BG

Tel: 01271 866799
The Ilfracombe Regal is a small, privately-run hotel in the heart of the town of Ilfracombe. All the rooms are en-suite and provided with tea and coffee making facilities and a colour TV. There is a licensed bar and all food is freshly prepared to order. 225

Leadengate House, Croyde, Nr. Braunton, Devon EX33 1PN

Tel: 01271 890373
A family-run, comfortable bed and breakfast with friendly personal service. 1 single, 1 twin and 3 double rooms, all en-suite. Packed lunches available.

Marlborough Hotel, 7 Market Street, Ilfracombe, Devon EX34 9AY

Tel: 01271 863580
Centrally located hotel with 17 comfortable rooms of varying sizes. Licensed bar and dance floor. Restaurant open to residents only. Private outdoor pool.

Preston House Hotel, Saunton, Braunton, Devon EX33 1LG

Tel: 01271 890472 Fax: 01271 890555
Unrivalled location looking down on open sea and the two mile stretch of Saunton Sands. 12 en-suite guest rooms. Stylish restaurant also open to non-residents. 215

Sherborne Lodge, Torrs Park, Ilfracombe, Devon EX34 8AY

Tel: 01271 862297
e-mail: 113121.222@compuserve.com
Friendly, family-run licensed hotel. Eleven en-suite rooms. Drying facilities, flexible bar and dining. Groups welcome.

Shuna Guest House, Downend, Croyde, Devon EX33 1QE

Tel: 01271 890537 Fax: 01271 890537
Small, luxurious, family-run guest house enjoying spectacular views. Five en-suite rooms including a 'Penthouse' suite with balcony.

South Leigh Hotel, Runnacleave Road, Ilfracombe, Devon EX34 8AQ

Tel: 01271 863976 Fax: 01271 863322
Friendly, family-run hotel, situated in its own grounds close to the beach. 26 bedrooms. Live entertainment most nights. 205

St. Brannocks House Hotel, 61-62 St. Brannocks Road, Ilfracombe, Devon EX34 8EQ

Tel: 01271 863873 Fax: 01271 863873
Comfortable guest house accommodation offering good home-cooking and service with a smile.14 tastefully decorated bedrooms, most with en-suite facilities. 213

Sunnymeade Country Hotel, Dean Cross, West Down, Nr. Ilfracombe, Devon EX34 8NT

Tel: 01271 863668
e-mail: info@sunnymeade.co.uk
website: www.sunnymeade.co.uk

Small, friendly hotel with award-winning chef. Shooting breaks are a speciality. six en-suite guest rooms. 207

The Village Inn, Youngaton Road, Westward Ho!, Bideford, Devon EX39 1HU

Tel: 01237 477331 Fax: 01237 425183
Family-run free house in popular area of north Devon. Food served from extensive menu of meals and snacks, available in bar or separate restaurant. Newly built en-suite bed and breakfast accommodation. 217

Waterloo House Hotel, Waterloo Terrace, Fore Street, Ilfracombe, Devon EX34 9DJ

Tel: 01271 863060 Fax: 01272 863060
e-mail info@waterloohousehotel.co.uk
website www.waterloohousehotel.co.uk
Dating back to 1820 the hotel was originally three cottages built to commemorate the Battle of Waterloo and many original period features have been retained. Ten individually styled guest rooms, mostly en-suite, and a superb restaurant. 226

Wentworth House Hotel, 2 Belmont Road, Ilfracombe, Devon EX34 8DR

Tel: 01271 863048 Fax: 01271 863048
A former gentleman's residence converted to offer comfortable accommodation. Nine spacious guest rooms. 210

Wheel Farm Country Cottages, Wheel Farm, Berry Down, Combe Martin, Devon EX34 0NT

Tel: 01271 882100 Fax: 01271 883120
website: www.wheelfarmcottages.co.uk
Award-winning complex of ten self-catering cottages converted from old stone farm buildings into comfortable, well equipped accommodation. Heated indoor swimming pool, tennis courts, sauna and fitness room. 222

Food and Drink

Preston House Hotel, Saunton, Braunton, Devon EX33 1LG

Tel: 01271 890472 Fax: 01271 890555
Unrivalled location looking down on open sea and the two mile stretch of Saunton Sands. 12 en-suite guest rooms. Stylish restaurant also open to non-residents. 215

The Red Barn Restaurant, Woolacombe, Devon EX34 7DF

Tel: 01271 870264
A family-run restaurant and bar just 100 metres from a popular surfing beach. Wide ranging menu catering to all tastes. Ideal for families. 214

Sunnymeade Country Hotel, Dean Cross, West Down, Nr. Ilfracombe, Devon EX34 8NT

Tel: 01271 863668
e-mail: info@sunnymeade.co.uk
website: www.sunnymeade.co.uk
Small, friendly hotel with award-winning chef. Shooting breaks are a speciality. Six en-suite guest rooms. 207

The Village Inn, Youngaton Road, Westward Ho!, Bideford, Devon EX39 1HU

Tel: 01237 477331 Fax: 01237 425183
Family-run free house in popular area of north Devon. Food served from extensive menu of meals and snacks, available in bar or separate restaurant. Newly built en-suite bed and breakfast accommodation.   217

Waterloo House Hotel, Waterloo Terrace, Fore Street, Ilfracombe, Devon EX34 9DJ

Tel: 01271 863060 Fax: 01272 863060
e-mail info@waterloohousehotel.co.uk
website www.waterloohousehotel.co.uk
Dating back to 1820 the hotel was originally three cottages built to commemorate the Battle of Waterloo and many original period features have been retained. Ten individually styled guest rooms, mostly en-suite, and a superb restaurant.   226

Libbaton Golf Club

High Bickington, Umberleigh, Devon EX37 9BS

Tel: 01769 560269, 560167 Fax: 01769 560342

Sec/Manager:	J. Brough
Professional:	Sarah Burnell (visiting)
Directions:	9 miles south of Barnstaple centre. From centre take the A377 (Exeter). After 5 miles turn right onto the B3217 (High Bickington, Dolton). The entrance is 1 mile past High Bickington on the right hand side.
Date Founded:	1988
Type of Course:	Parkland
No of Holes:	18
Length:	6198 yds (5721 mtrs)
Par:	73
SSS:	72
Green Fees:	Weekdays: £18; Weekends/ Bank Holidays: £22
Visitors:	Welcome: Contact Club in Advance
Societies:	Welcome: Contact Club in Advance
Facilities:	Putting Green, Chipping Green, Driving Range, Club Hire, Trolley Hire, Bar, Restaurant

Accommodation, Food and Drink

Reference numbers below refer to detailed information provided in section 2

Accommodation

'Oaklands', Black Dog, Nr. Crediton, Devon EX17 4QJ

Tel: 01884 860645 Fax: 01884 861030
A super house built to very high standards of craftsmanship. Three en-suite rooms. Stunning views and gardens.   247

Mole Cottage, Chittlehamholt, Devon EX37 9HF

Tel: 01769 540471 Fax: 01769 540471
e-mail: relax@moley.uk.com
website: www.moley.uk.com
17th century thatched cottage enjoying a riverside location within the magical Mole Valley. Also a working pottery and gallery. Residential Pottery courses available.   218

The Royal Oak, The Square, Dolton, Winkleigh, Devon EX19 8QF

Tel: 01805 804288
Friendly country pub with spacious interior. Superb restaurant offering an excellent menu with live jazz twice monthly. Five guest rooms, some en-suite. 258

Waterfront Inn, Golf Links Road, Westward Ho!, Devon EX39 1LH

Tel: 01237 474737 Fax: 01237 471719
Modern, friendly inn with much to offer to visitors to the area. Large bar areas, stylish restaurant and comfortable, newly furnished accommodation. 220

Yeolden House Hotel, Durrant Lane, Northam, Nr. Bideford, Devon EX39 2RL

Tel: 01237 474400 Fax: 01237 476618
e-mail: yeoldonhouse@aol.com
website: www.yeoldonhousehotel.co.uk
An imposing house surrounded by lawns and colourful flower beds that slope gently down to the river. Ten en-suite rooms that have each been individually designed. Elegant restaurant.   216

Food and Drink

The Duchess Restaurant, Duke Street, South Molton, Devon EX36 3AL

Tel: 01769 573123
Small charming restaurant with a calm, relaxing atmosphere. Open for lunch and dinner, with fully licensed bar.   241

The Royal Oak, The Square, Dolton, Winkleigh, Devon EX19 8QF

Tel: 01805 804288

Friendly country pub with spacious interior. Superb restaurant offering an excellent menu with live jazz twice monthly. Five guest rooms, some en-suite. 258

Waterfront Inn, Golf Links Road, Westward Ho!, Devon EX39 1LH

Tel: 01237 474737 Fax: 01237 471719
Modern, friendly inn with much to offer to visitors to the area. Large bar areas, stylish restaurant and comfortable, newly furnished accommodation. 220

Yeolden House Hotel, Durrant Lane, Northam, Nr. Bideford, Devon EX39 2RL

Tel: 01237 474400 Fax: 01237 476618
e-mail: yeoldonhouse@aol.com
website: www.yeoldonhousehotel.co.uk
An imposing house surrounded by lawns and colourful flower beds that slope gently down to the river. Ten en-suite rooms that have each been individually designed. Elegant restaurant. 216

Manor House Golf Club

Moretonhampstead, Devon TQ13 8RE
Tel: 01647 440998 Fax: 01647 440961

The hugely impressive and enormous Jacobean mansion dominates one of the most beautiful golf courses you are likely to find. Set in the 270 acres of Dartmoor countryside, on the edge of the National Park, the course is redolent with history. The mansion was built in 1880 by a bookseller

who turned out to be quite successful - William Henry (WH) Smith - as a country retreat, and the golf course followed about 40 years later.

One of the regular visitors was Henry Cotton, who described the seventh hole as "the finest inland par-four in England," and well he might. The very tight fairway has a river running down each side and, at 384 yards off the back tees; keeping your first two long and straight are your only hope.

The Rivers Bovey and Bowden meander in a sort of aimless fashion throughout the front nine, and there is hardly an approach shot where one or other isn't making a nuisance of itself. The back nine is mercifully drier, although the aforementioned Mr Cotton has had the final say, and it could ruin your round.

In 1968 he redesigned the 18th hole, which now has a nasty little slope, and if you miss the green with your approach on this par-four, you really are a gonner. Having said that, this is a must-play course for anyone visiting the region, and one that will stick in the memory long after you've double-bogeyed that last hole.

Sec/Manager:	R. Lewis
Professional:	None
Directions:	2 miles southwest of Moretonhampstead centre. From centre take the B3212 (Princetown). The entrance is after 2 miles, just after the turning to North Bovey, on the left hand side through imposing stone pillars.
Date Founded:	1934
Type of Course:	Parkland
No of Holes:	18
Length:	6016 yds (5553 mtrs)
Par:	69
SSS:	69
Green Fees:	Weekdays: £25 (round) £30 (day); Weekends/Bank Holidays: £30 (round) £37 (day)
Visitors:	Welcome: Contact Club in Advance. No restrictions
Societies:	Welcome: Contact Club in Advance. Unable to play weekends
Facilities:	Putting Green, Chipping Green, Club Hire, Trolley Hire, Buggy Hire, Bar, Restaurant

Accommodation, Food and Drink

Reference numbers below refer to detailed information provided in section 2

Accommodation

The Coffee Pot, 14 St. James Street, Okehampton, Devon EX20 1DA

Tel: 01837 52988
Traditional coffee shop, open daily serving early breakfast, coffee, lunches and afternoon teas. Conveniently located close to the town centre. 233

Dartmoor Railway Inn, Station Road, Crediton, Devon EX17 3BX

Tel: 01363 724989
Traditional hostelry offering a warm, friendly welcome to all. Home-cooked food with popular Sunday roast lunches. Three en-suite rooms. 248

The Red Lion, Shobrooke, Nr. Crediton, Devon EX17 1AT

Tel: 01363 772340
Friendly country pub run by popular couple. Cosy bars with a separate 50-seater restaurant. Three, double, en-suite rooms. 244

The Torrs, Belstone, Okehampton, Devon EX20 1QZ

Tel: 01837 840689
Small, cosy pub, popular with locals and visitors. Refreshing ales and tasty, home-cooked meals. Bed and breakfast accommodation available with three en-suite guest rooms. 232

The Welcome Stranger, Liverton, Nr. Newton Abbott, Devon TQ12 6JA

Tel: 01626 821224
e-mail: welcomestranger@talk21.com
A friendly, country pub offering a good variety of sensibly priced, home-cooked food. Two twin en-suite rooms. 260

Food and Drink

Dartmoor Railway Inn, Station Road, Crediton, Devon EX17 3BX

Tel: 01363 724989
Traditional hostelry offering a warm, friendly welcome to all. Home-cooked food with popular Sunday roast lunches. Three en-suite rooms. 248

The Plough Inn, Fore Street, Ipplepen, Devon TQ12 5RP

Tel: 01808 812118 Fax: 01803 814278
website: www.ipplepen.com
An attractive old inn with a great deal of character. Good range of drinks and home-cooked food. 259

The Red Lion, Shobrooke, Nr. Crediton, Devon EX17 1AT

Tel: 01363 772340
Friendly country pub run by popular couple. Cosy bars with a separate 50-seater restaurant. Three, double, en-suite rooms. 244

The Torrs, Belstone, Okehampton, Devon EX20 1QZ

Tel: 01837 840689
Small, cosy pub, popular with locals and visitors. Refreshing ales and tasty, home-cooked meals. Bed and breakfast accommodation available with three en-suite guest rooms. 232

Victorian Pantry, Museum Courtyard, West Street, Okehampton, Devon EX20 1HQ

Tel: 01837 53988
Housed within an historic building not far from the Dartmoor Museum. Open daily serving a good selection of drinks, home-cooked cakes and hot meals. 229

The Welcome Stranger, Liverton, Nr. Newton Abbott, Devon TQ12 6JA

Tel: 01626 821224
e-mail: welcomestranger@talk21.com
A friendly, country pub offering a good variety of sensibly priced, home-cooked food. Two twin en-suite rooms. 260

Newton Abbot Golf Club

Bovey Road, Newton Abbot, Devon TQ12 6QQ
Tel: **01626 352460** Fax: 01626 330210

Sec/Manager:	Geoff Rees
Professional:	Malcolm Craig
Directions:	3 miles northwest of Newton Abbot centre. From A38 Heathfield junction take the A382 (Newton Abbot). The entrance is after ½ mile on the right hand side, just past Trago Mills roundabout.
Date Founded:	1930
Type of Course:	Parkland
No of Holes:	18
Length:	5764 yds (5320 mtrs)
Par:	69
SSS:	68
Green Fees:	Weekdays: £25 (round) £30 (day); Weekends/Bank Holidays: £28 (round) £32 (day)
Visitors:	Welcome: Contact Club in Advance. Handicap certificates required
Societies:	Welcome: Contact Club in Advance. Unable to play Mon-Wed Fri-Sun

Facilities: Putting Green, Club Hire, Trolley Hire, Bar, Restaurant

Accommodation, Food and Drink

Reference numbers below refer to detailed information provided in section 2

Accommodation

Alexandra Lodge Holiday Apartments, Grafton Road, Torquay, South Devon TQ1 1QJ

Tel: 01803 213465 Fax: 01803 390933
e-mail: almes@fsbdial.co.uk
website: www.alexandra-lodge.co.uk
Lovely detached Georgian villa in secluded grounds offering seven self-catering apartments sleeping between two and eight people.   249

The Anchorage Guest House, 170 New Road, Brixham, Devon TQ5 8DA

Tel/Fax: 01803 852960
A comfortable, friendly guest house with a fabulous award-winning garden. Seven guest rooms.   257

Babbacombe Hall Hotel, 17 Manor Road, Babbacombe, Torquay, Devon TQ1 3JX

Tel: 01803 325668 Fax: 01803 325668
Victorian seaside hotel with six en-suite rooms. Bar and restaurant open to residents only.   253

Brunswick House, 5 Brunswick Street, Teignmouth, Devon TQ14 8AE

Tel: 01626 774102
e-mail: peterhockings@hotmail.com
Bed and breakfast housed within Victorian terrace just 100 metres from sea front. Spacious accommodation with eight, en-suite guest rooms.   212

Chuckle Too, Blackawton, Totnes, Devon TQ9 7BG

Tel: 01803 712455
Modern, self-catering cottage offering cosy cottage-style accommodation. Sleeps up to three adults. Very well equipped.   262

Collingwood Hotel, Braddons Hill Road East, Torquay, Devon TQ1 1HB

Tel: 01803 293448 Fax: 01626 400221
e-mail: bookings@collingwood-hotel.co.uk
An elegant Georgian Hotel located a short distance from the sea front. Regular themed breaks.   256

The Halfway Inn, Sidmouth Road, Aylesbeare, Devon EX5 2JP

Tel: 01395 232273 Fax: 01395 516398
Former coaching inn offering a fine selection of refreshments with very extensive food menu. Four guest rooms for bed and breakfast, two en-suite.   243

Hole Mill, Branscombe, Seaton, Devon EX12 3BX

Tel: 01297 680314
website: www.users.globalnet.co.uk/~branscombe/hole1.htm
Former working watermill, located in pretty valley, converted into a charming house on many levels. Surrounded by colourful gardens. 3 guest rooms.   267

Marlborough Hotel, The Esplanade, Sidmouth, Devon EX10 8AR

Tel: 01395 513320
Super sea front property just a stone's throw from the beach. Popular pub and hotel, offering fine food all day. 18 en-suite rooms.   224

Shell Cove House, Old Teignmouth Road, Dawlish, Devon EX7 0NJ

Tel: 01626 862523 Fax: 01626 862523
A Georgian house converted into a number of self-contained, self-catering apartments. Also a luxurious cottage available. Excellent facilities on site.   251

Sir Walter Raleigh, 22 High Street, East Budleigh, Devon EX9 7EB

Tel: 01395 442510
A charming, traditional, thatched building serving fine local ales and freshly prepared food. Bed and breakfast accommodation available.   252

The Steam Packet Inn, St. Peter's Quay, Totnes, Devon TQ9 5EN

Tel: 01803 863880 Fax: 01803 862754
Elegant riverside inn with open plan lounge bar and elegant, conservatory Restaurant. Ten en-suite guest bedrooms. Private river moorings available.   261

The Welcome Stranger, Liverton, Nr. Newton Abbott, Devon TQ12 6JA

Tel: 01626 821224
e-mail: welcomestranger@talk21.com
A friendly, country pub offering a good variety of sensibly priced, home-cooked food. Two twin en-suite rooms.   260

Westbury, 51 New Road, Brixham, Devon TQ5 8NL

Tel/Fax: 01803 851684
e-mail: ann.burt@lineone.net
A charming Georgian house offering stylish accommodation with six guest rooms. Private parking.   255

Woodlands Hotel, 51 Barnpark Road, Teignmouth, Devon TQ14 8PN

Tel: 01626 773094
Delightful Regency-style hotel retaining a great deal of period elegance. Comfortable guest rooms with many having superb views out to sea. Half- or Full-board available.   221

Food and Drink

Collingwood Hotel, Braddons Hill Road East, Torquay, Devon TQ1 1HB

Tel: 01803 293448 Fax: 01626 400221
e-mail: bookings@collingwood-hotel.co.uk
An elegant Georgian Hotel located a short distance from the sea front. Regular themed breaks.   256

The Halfway Inn, Sidmouth Road, Aylesbeare, Devon EX5 2JP

Tel: 01395 232273 Fax: 01395 516398
Former coaching inn offering a fine selection of
refreshments with very extensive food menu. Four
guest rooms for bed and breakfast, two en-suite. 243

Marlborough Hotel, The Esplanade, Sidmouth, Devon EX10 8AR

Tel: 01395 513320
Super sea front property just a stone's throw from the
beach. Popular pub and hotel, offering fine food all
day. 18 en-suite rooms. 224

The Plough Inn, Fore Street, Ipplepen, Devon TQ12 5RP

Tel: 01808 812118 Fax: 01803 814278
website: www.ipplepen.com
An attractive old inn with a great deal of character.
Good range of drinks and home-cooked food. 259

Sir Walter Raleigh, 22 High Street, East Budleigh, Devon EX9 7EB

Tel: 01395 442510
A charming, traditional, thatched building serving
fine local ales and freshly prepared food. Bed and
breakfast accommodation available. 252

The Steam Packet Inn, St. Peter's Quay, Totnes, Devon TQ9 5EN

Tel: 01803 863880 Fax: 01803 862754
Elegant riverside inn with open plan lounge bar and
elegant, conservatory Restaurant. Ten en-suite guest
bedrooms. Private river moorings available. 261

The Welcome Stranger, Liverton, Nr. Newton Abbott, Devon TQ12 6JA

Tel: 01626 821224
e-mail: welcomestranger@talk21.com
A friendly, country pub offering a good variety of
sensibly priced, home-cooked food. Two twin en-suite
rooms. 260

Okehampton Golf Club

Okehampton, Devon Ex20 1EF
Tel: 01837 52113 Fax: 01837 53724

Sec/Manager:	Clive Yeo
Professional:	Simon Jefferies
Directions:	½ miles south of Okehampton centre. From centre (East St) take Station Road. After 700 yds bear right into Tors Road and the entrance is after 100 yds on the right hand side.
Date Founded:	1913
Type of Course:	Parkland
No of Holes:	18
Length:	5700 yds (5261 mtrs)

Par:	68
SSS:	66
Green Fees:	Weekdays: £17 (round £20 (day) Saturdays £20-£25
Visitors:	Welcome: Contact Club in Advance. Unable to play Sundays
Societies:	Welcome: Contact Club in Advance
Facilities:	Putting Green, Club Hire, Trolley Hire, Bar, Restaurant

Accommodation, Food and Drink

Reference numbers below refer to detailed
information provided in section 2

Accommodation

'Oaklands', Black Dog, Nr. Crediton, Devon EX17 4QJ

Tel: 01884 860645 Fax: 01884 861030
A super house built to very high standards of
craftsmanship. Three en-suite rooms. Stunning views
and gardens. 247

Bennetts Court Cottages, Whitstone, Holsworthy, Devon EX22 6UD

Tel: 01288 341370 Fax: 01288 341370
e-mail: helen@ bennettscourt.co.uk
website: www.bennettscourt.co.uk
Five, well-equipped self-catering cottages, converted
from former farm buildings, sleeping between two
and six people. Within the grounds there is a outdoor
heated pool and other facilities. 246

The Bridge Inn, Bridge Street, Hatherleigh, Nr. Okehampton, Devon EX20 3JA

Tel: 01837 810947 Fax: 01837 810614
The Bridge Inn dates from the 16th century and is
one of the oldest buildings in the area. Cosy interior
with bar and separate restaurant. Six en-suite guest
rooms of varying sizes. 231

The Coffee Pot, 14 St. James Street, Okehampton, Devon EX20 1DA

Tel: 01837 52988
Traditional coffee shop, open daily serving early

breakfast, coffee, lunches and afternoon teas. Conveniently located close to the town centre. 233

Dartmoor Railway Inn, Station Road, Crediton, Devon EX17 3BX

Tel: 01363 724989
Traditional hostelry offering a warm, friendly welcome to all. Home-cooked food with popular Sunday roast lunches. Three en-suite rooms. 248

Lifton Hall Hotel, Lifton, Devon PL16 0DR

Tel: 01566 784863 Fax: 01566 784770
e-mail mail@liftonhall.co.uk
Traditional 250-year old Country House hotel in peaceful village location with ten en-suite rooms. Formal restaurant and a bistro, both specialising in local fish. 240

'The Oyster', Colebrooke, Devon EX17 5JQ

Tel: 01363 84576
Cosy modern bungalow taking its unusual name from the owner, Pearl. Three bedrooms, each en-suite or with private facilities. Many guests have returned several times - what better recommendation! 245

Pressland Country House Hotel, Hatherleigh, Nr. Okehampton, Devon EX20 3LW

Tel: 01837 810871 Fax: 01837 810303
e-mail graham@presslandhouse.co.uk
website www.presslandhouse.co.uk
Victorian manor house surrounded by lawns and woodland. Five spacious guest rooms, most with en-suite facilities, and superb residents' restaurant. 230

The Red Lion, Shobrooke, Nr. Crediton, Devon EX17 1AT

Tel: 01363 772340
Friendly country pub run by popular couple. Cosy bars with a separate 50-seater restaurant. Three, double, en-suite rooms. 244

The Royal Oak, The Square, Dolton, Winkleigh, Devon EX19 8QF

Tel: 01805 804288
Friendly country pub with spacious interior. Superb restaurant offering an excellent menu with live jazz twice monthly. Five guest rooms, some en-suite. 258

The Torrs, Belstone, Okehampton, Devon EX20 1QZ

Tel: 01837 840689
Small, cosy pub, popular with locals and visitors. Refreshing ales and tasty, home-cooked meals. Bed and breakfast accommodation available with three en-suite guest rooms. 232

Food and Drink

The Bridge Inn, Bridge Street, Hatherleigh, Nr. Okehampton, Devon EX20 3JA

Tel: 01837 810947 Fax: 01837 810614
The Bridge Inn dates from the 16th century and is one of the oldest buildings in the area. Cosy interior with bar and separate restaurant. Six en-suite guest rooms of varying sizes. 231

Dartmoor Railway Inn, Station Road, Crediton, Devon EX17 3BX

Tel: 01363 724989
Traditional hostelry offering a warm, friendly welcome to all. Home-cooked food with popular Sunday roast lunches. Three en-suite rooms. 248

The Duchess Restaurant, Duke Street, South Molton, Devon EX36 3AL

Tel: 01769 573123
Small charming restaurant with a calm, relaxing atmosphere. Open for lunch and dinner, with fully licensed bar. 241

Lifton Hall Hotel, Lifton, Devon PL16 0DR

Tel: 01566 784863 Fax: 01566 784770
e-mail mail@liftonhall.co.uk
Traditional 250-year old Country House hotel in peaceful village location with ten en-suite rooms. Formal restaurant and a bistro, both specialising in local fish. 240

The Red Lion, Shobrooke, Nr. Crediton, Devon EX17 1AT

Tel: 01363 772340
Friendly country pub run by popular couple. Cosy bars with a separate 50-seater restaurant. Three, double, en-suite rooms. 244

The Royal Oak, The Square, Dolton, Winkleigh, Devon EX19 8QF

Tel: 01805 804288
Friendly country pub with spacious interior. Superb restaurant offering an excellent menu with live jazz twice monthly. Five guest rooms, some en-suite. 258

The Torrs, Belstone, Okehampton, Devon EX20 1QZ

Tel: 01837 840689
Small, cosy pub, popular with locals and visitors. Refreshing ales and tasty, home-cooked meals. Bed and breakfast accommodation available with three en-suite guest rooms. 232

Victorian Pantry, Museum Courtyard, West Street, Okehampton, Devon EX20 1HQ

Tel: 01837 53988
Housed within an historic building not far from the Dartmoor Museum. Open daily serving a good selection of drinks, home-cooked cakes and hot meals. 229

Royal North Devon

Golf Links Road, Westward Ho!, Bideford, Devon EX39 1HD

Tel: 01237 473817 Fax: 01237 423456

There is very little, if anything at all, left to say about the RND that hasn't already been said elsewhere.

If St Andrews is the heart and soul of golf in Scotland, then only Royal North Devon can lay

Visitors:	Welcome: Contact Club in Advance. Handicap certificates required
Societies:	Welcome: Contact Club in Advance. Unable to play Tuesday, Thursday and weekends
Facilities:	Putting Green, Chipping Green, Club Hire, Trolley Hire, Bar, Restaurant

serious claim to be its English counterpart. The historical role of honour simply speaks for itself.

The RND - or Westward Ho!, to give it its more common title - was founded in 1864, the first links course in England and the oldest English club which still plays over its original turf. It boasts the oldest ladies' club in the world - established in 1868 - was designed by Old Tom Morris, who could play a bit, as the record books show, and is where a little lad from the nearby village of Northam was first attracted to the game - by earning 6d (2.5p) a round caddying. The lad's name was John H Taylor, elected the club's president in 1957, but who also happened to have won the Open five times in the interim.

Oh, and the golf course is still there, too, despite having been used as a practice bombing range during World War Two, and it retains to this day its rough-hewn, natural look and feel, achingly gorgeous on a glorious summer day, but brooding and moody when the winds - they get a lot of winds here - whip in from the sea under leaden skies.

The pretty flat and wide open Burrows on which the course stands is common land where sheep still graze unfettered and unhindered, but don't worry, they are quite used to golfers. Apart from wishing you a marvellous experience, just two tips - avoid that cavernous "Cape" bunker on the fourth, and do try to stay well clear of those rather famous and equally vicious rushes!

Sec/Manager:	R.K. Fowler
Professional:	Richard Merring
Directions:	From Northam village road go down Bone Hill off the B3236
Date Founded:	1864
Type of Course:	Links
No of Holes:	18
Length:	6668 yds (6155 mtrs)
Par:	72
SSS:	72
Green Fees:	Weekdays: £30; Weekends/ Bank Holidays: £36

Accommodation, Food and Drink

Reference numbers below refer to detailed information provided in section 2

Accommodation

'Oaklands', Black Dog, Nr. Crediton, Devon EX17 4QJ

Tel: 01884 860645 Fax: 01884 861030
A super house built to very high standards of craftsmanship. Three en-suite rooms. Stunning views and gardens. 247

Autumn Lodge, Victoria Street, Combe Martin, Devon EX34 0JS

Tel: 01271 883558
e-mail: lespallatt@supanet.com
Friendly, comfortable hotel with eight bedrooms. Licensed cocktail bar and residents' restaurant. Large heated, outdoor pool. 219

The Beaufort Hotel, Torrs Park, Ilfracombe, Devon EX34 8AY

Tel: 01271 866556
Elegant hotel situated in the delightful Torrs Park area of Ilfracombe with outdoor heated pool, solarium and mini-gymnasium. 12 en-suite rooms. 204

Cliffe Hydro Hotel, Hillsborough Road, Ilfracombe, Devon EX34 9NP

Tel: 01271 863606 Fax: 01271 879019
Medium-sized hotel offering sensibly priced accommodation in superb location looking down onto Ilfracombe harbour. Excellent indoor leisure complex. 228

The Collingdale Hotel, Larkstone Terrace, Ilfracombe, Devon EX34 9NU

Tel: 01271 863770 Fax: 01271 863770
e-mail: collingdale@onet.co.uk
A small, comfortable hotel enjoying a central location within Ilfracombe. Eight en-suite rooms of varying sizes. 211

The Dorchester Hotel, 59 St. Brannocks Road, Ilfracombe, Devon EX34 8EQ

Tel: 01271 865472 Fax: 01271 866949
Family-run hotel with six double, en-suite guest rooms. Fully licensed bar and TV lounge. Children and pets welcome.

Epchris Hotel, Torrs Park, Ilfracombe, Devon EX34 8AZ

Tel: 01271 862751 Fax: 01271 879077
e-mail: epchris-hotel@ic24.net
website: www.epchris-hotel.co.uk
Family-run hotel, set within two acres of private
grounds, overlooking Ilfracombe. Nine spacious
bedrooms. Within the grounds is a heated outdoor
swimming pool and popular games room.   209

Exmouth View Hotel, St. Albans Road, Babbacombe, Torquay, Devon TQ1 3LQ

Tel: 0800 7817817/01803 327307 Fax: 01803 329967
e-mail: relax@exmouth-view.co.uk
website: www.exmouth-view.co.uk
A modern hotel offering comfortable accommodation
at an affordable price. Licensed bar and restaurant.250

Glen Tor Hotel, Torrs Park, Ilfracombe, Devon EX34 8AZ

Tel: 01271 862403 Fax: 01271 862403
e-mail: info@glentorhotel.co.uk
website: www.glentorhotel.co.uk
Small, family-run establishment in a quiet corner of
Ilfracombe. Seven en-suite guest bedrooms. Evening
meals available on request.   208

The Ilfracombe Regal Hotel, 19 Gilbert Grove, Ilfracombe, Devon EX34 9BG

Tel: 01271 866799
The Ilfracombe Regal is a small, privately-run hotel in
the heart of the town of Ilfracombe. All the rooms are
en-suite and provided with tea and coffee making
facilities and a colour TV. There is a licensed bar and
all food is freshly prepared to order.   225

Leadengate House, Croyde, Nr. Braunton, Devon EX33 1PN

Tel: 01271 890373
A family-run, comfortable bed and breakfast with
friendly personal service. 1 single, 1 twin and 3
double rooms, all en-suite. Packed lunches available.

Marlborough Hotel, 7 Market Street, Ilfracombe, Devon EX34 9AY

Tel: 01271 863580
Centrally located hotel with 17 comfortable rooms of
varying sizes. Licensed bar and dance floor. Restaurant
open to residents only. Private outdoor pool.

Mole Cottage, Chittlehamholt, Devon EX37 9HF

Tel: 01769 540471 Fax: 01769 540471
e-mail: relax@moley.uk.com
website: www.moley.uk.com
17th century thatched cottage enjoying a riverside
location within the magical Mole Valley. Also a
working pottery and gallery. Residential Pottery
courses available.   218

Preston House Hotel, Saunton, Braunton, Devon EX33 1LG

Tel: 01271 890472 Fax: 01271 890555
Unrivalled location looking down on open sea and
the two mile stretch of Saunton Sands. 12 en-suite
guest rooms. Stylish restaurant also open to non-
residents.   215

The Royal Oak, The Square, Dolton, Winkleigh, Devon EX19 8QF

Tel: 01805 804288
Friendly country pub with spacious interior. Superb
restaurant offering an excellent menu with live jazz
twice monthly. Five guest rooms, some en-suite.   258

Sherborne Lodge, Torrs Park, Ilfracombe, Devon EX34 8AY

Tel: 01271 862297
e-mail: 113121.222@compuserve.com
Friendly, family-run licensed hotel. Eleven en-suite
rooms. Drying facilities, flexible bar and dining.
Groups welcome.

Shuna Guest House, Downend, Croyde, Devon EX33 1QE

Tel: 01271 890537 Fax: 01271 890537
Small, luxurious, family-run guest house enjoying
spectacular views. Five en-suite rooms including a
'Penthouse' suite with balcony.

South Leigh Hotel, Runnacleave Road, Ilfracombe, Devon EX34 8AQ

Tel: 01271 863976 Fax: 01271 863322
Friendly, family-run hotel, situated in its own
grounds close to the beach. 26 bedrooms. Live
entertainment most nights.   205

St. Brannocks House Hotel, 61-62 St. Brannocks Road, Ilfracombe, Devon EX34 8EQ

Tel: 01271 863873 Fax: 01271 863873
Comfortable guest house accommodation offering
good home-cooking and service with a smile.14
tastefully decorated bedrooms, most with en-suite
facilities.   213

Sunnymeade Country Hotel, Dean Cross, West Down, Nr. Ilfracombe, Devon EX34 8NT

Tel: 01271 863668
e-mail: info@sunnymeade.co.uk
website: www.sunnymeade.co.uk
Small, friendly hotel with award-winning chef.
Shooting breaks are a speciality. Six en-suite guest
rooms.   207

The Village Inn, Youngaton Road, Westward Ho!, Bideford, Devon EX39 1HU

Tel: 01237 477331 Fax: 01237 425183
Family-run free house in popular area of north
Devon. Food served from extensive menu of meals
and snacks, available in bar or separate restaurant.
Newly built en-suite bed and breakfast
accommodation.   217

Waterfront Inn, Golf Links Road, Westward Ho!, Devon EX39 1LH

Tel: 01237 474737 Fax: 01237 471719
Modern, friendly inn with much to offer to visitors to
the area. Large bar areas, stylish restaurant and
comfortable, newly furnished accommodation.   220

Waterloo House Hotel, Waterloo Terrace, Fore Street, Ilfracombe, Devon EX34 9DJ

Tel: 01271 863060 Fax: 01272 863060
e-mail info@waterloohousehotel.com
website www.waterloohousehotel.co.uk
Dating back to 1820 the hotel was originally three

cottages built to commemorate the Battle of Waterloo and many original period features have been retained. Ten individually styled guest rooms, mostly en-suite, and a superb restaurant. 226

Wentworth House Hotel, 2 Belmont Road, Ilfracombe, Devon EX34 8DR

Tel: 01271 863048 Fax: 01271 863048
A former gentleman's residence converted to offer comfortable accommodation. Nine spacious guest rooms. 210

Wheel Farm Country Cottages, Wheel Farm, Berry Down, Combe Martin, Devon EX34 0NT

Tel: 01271 882100 Fax: 01271 883120
website: www.wheelfarmcottages.co.uk
Award-winning complex of ten self-catering cottages converted from old stone farm buildings into comfortable, well equipped accommodation. Heated indoor swimming pool, tennis courts, sauna and fitness room. 222

Yeolden House Hotel, Durrant Lane, Northam, Nr. Bideford, Devon EX39 2RL

Tel: 01237 474400 Fax: 01237 476618
e-mail: yeoldonhouse@aol.com
website: www.yeoldonhousehotel.co.uk
An imposing house surrounded by lawns and colourful flower beds that slope gently down to the river. Ten en-suite rooms that have each been individually designed. Elegant restaurant. 216

Food and Drink

The Duchess Restaurant, Duke Street, South Molton, Devon EX36 3AL

Tel: 01769 573123
Small charming restaurant with a calm, relaxing atmosphere. Open for lunch and dinner, with fully licensed bar. 241

Preston House Hotel, Saunton, Braunton, Devon EX33 1LG

Tel: 01271 890472 Fax: 01271 890555
Unrivalled location looking down on open sea and the two mile stretch of Saunton Sands. 12 en-suite guest rooms. Stylish restaurant also open to non-residents. 215

The Red Barn Restaurant, Woolacombe, Devon EX34 7DF

Tel: 01271 870264
A family-run restaurant and bar just 100 metres from a popular surfing beach. Wide ranging menu catering to all tastes. Ideal for families. 214

The Royal Oak, The Square, Dolton, Winkleigh, Devon EX19 8QF

Tel: 01805 804288
Friendly country pub with spacious interior. Superb restaurant offering an excellent menu with live jazz twice monthly. Five guest rooms, some en-suite. 258

Sunnymeade Country Hotel, Dean Cross, West Down, Nr. Ilfracombe, Devon EX34 8NT

Tel: 01271 863668

e-mail: info@sunnymeade.co.uk
website: www.sunnymeade.co.uk
Small, friendly hotel with award-winning chef. Shooting breaks are a speciality. Six en-suite guest rooms. 207

The Village Inn, Youngaton Road, Westward Ho!, Bideford, Devon EX39 1HU

Tel: 01237 477331 Fax: 01237 425183
Family-run free house in popular area of north Devon. Food served from extensive menu of meals and snacks, available in bar or separate restaurant. Newly built en-suite bed and breakfast accommodation. 217

Waterfront Inn, Golf Links Road, Westward Ho!, Devon EX39 1LH

Tel: 01237 474737 Fax: 01237 471719
Modern, friendly inn with much to offer to visitors to the area. Large bar areas, stylish restaurant and comfortable, newly furnished accommodation. 220

Waterloo House Hotel, Waterloo Terrace, Fore Street, Ilfracombe, Devon EX34 9DJ

Tel: 01271 863060 Fax: 01272 863060
e-mail info@waterloohousehotel.co.uk
website www.waterloohousehotel.co.uk
Dating back to 1820 the hotel was originally three cottages built to commemorate the Battle of Waterloo and many original period features have been retained. Ten individually styled guest rooms, mostly en-suite, and a superb restaurant. 226

Yeolden House Hotel, Durrant Lane, Northam, Nr. Bideford, Devon EX39 2RL

Tel: 01237 474400 Fax: 01237 476618
e-mail: yeoldonhouse@aol.com
website: www.yeoldonhousehotel.co.uk
An imposing house surrounded by lawns and colourful flower beds that slope gently down to the river. Ten en-suite rooms that have each been individually designed. Elegant restaurant. 216

Saunton Golf Club

Saunton, Braunton, Devon EX33 1LG
Tel: 01271 812436 Fax: 01271 814241

If there is ever a course in the South West that might, just might, one day stage the Open, then it will surely be Saunton. The only reason ever put forward, it seems, for the championship not to be held on this windswept stretch of the North Devon dunes - just across the estuary from the Royal North Devon club - is its geographical location, which seems a rather flimsy effort. Some of the Scottish courses are hardly snuggling in the Home Counties!

There are, in fact, two 18-hole courses here, the West course being added in the early 1970s, but it is the old, or East, course which captures the imagination. It is classic links territory, a course that invariably draws accolades in every

one of the industry's 'Top 100 Courses To Play,' and no wonder.

Although the course doesn't quite share the same kind of moonscape feeling of Burnham & Berrow, further up the coast in Somerset, there is that definite eerie links feel throughout, where beauty and bleakness seem as one.

Despite having only two par-five holes, there are few greater challenges on this island. The first four holes are all 400-yards plus, and there is little respite until the 13th, the first par three, and even then, getting on and staying on the awkward green is a task in itself.

Dunes, sandhills, narrow fairways, nasty dog-legs, cunningly-placed bunkers, natural ditches and hummocks all conspire to destroy your confidence. And if you have any left at all by the 16th - which has just about every one of the above mentioned hazards - you'll be a gibbering wreck by the time you get to the 17th tee.

Anybody with a handicap in double figures may well be better off on the West course, if only for their own sanity!

Sec/Manager:	Mr. Reynolds
Professional:	Albert Mackenzie
Directions:	7 miles northwest of Barnstaple. From centre take the A361 (Braunton). At Braunton turn left onto the B3231 (Saunton, Croyde). The entrance is just after Saunton on the left hand side, before the Saunton Sands Hotel.
Visitors:	Welcome: Contact Club in Advance. Handicap Certificates
Societies:	Welcome: Contact Club in Advance
Facilities:	Putting Green, Chipping Green, Club Hire, Trolley Hire, Buggy Hire, Bar, Restaurant, Driving Range

East

Date Founded:	1897
Type of Course:	Links
No of Holes:	18
Length:	6373 yds (5882 mtrs)
Par:	71
SSS:	71
Green Fees:	Weekdays: £45 (round) £65 (day); Weekends/Bank Holidays: £45 (round) £65 (day)

West

Date Founded:	1897
Type of Course:	Links
No of Holes:	18
Length:	6138 yds (5663 mtrs)
Par:	71
SSS:	70
Green Fees:	Weekdays: £45 (round) £65 (day); Weekends/Bank Holidays: £45 (round) £65 (day)

Accommodation, Food and Drink

Reference numbers below refer to detailed information provided in section 2

Accommodation

Autumn Lodge, Victoria Street, Combe Martin, Devon EX34 0JS

Tel: 01271 883558
e-mail: lespallatt@supanet.com
Friendly, comfortable hotel with eight bedrooms. Licensed cocktail bar and residents' restaurant. Large heated, outdoor pool. 219

The Beaufort Hotel, Torrs Park, Ilfracombe, Devon EX34 8AY

Tel: 01271 866556
Elegant hotel situated in the delightful Torrs Park area of Ilfracombe with outdoor heated pool, solarium and mini-gymnasium. 12 en-suite rooms. 204

Cliffe Hydro Hotel, Hillsborough Road, Ilfracombe, Devon EX34 9NP

Tel: 01271 863606 Fax: 01271 879019
Medium-sized hotel offering sensibly priced accommodation in superb location looking down onto Ilfracombe harbour. Excellent indoor leisure complex. 228

The Collingdale Hotel, Larkstone Terrace, Ilfracombe, Devon EX34 9NU

Tel: 01271 863770 Fax: 01271 863770

e-mail: collingdale@onet.co.uk
A small, comfortable hotel enjoying a central location within Ilfracombe. Eight en-suite rooms of varying sizes. 211

The Dorchester Hotel, 59 St. Brannocks Road, Ilfracombe, Devon EX34 8EQ

Tel: 01271 865472 Fax: 01271 866949
Family-run hotel with six double, en-suite guest rooms. Fully licensed bar and TV lounge. Children and pets welcome.

Epchris Hotel, Torrs Park, Ilfracombe, Devon EX34 8AZ

Tel: 01271 862751 Fax: 01271 879077
e-mail: epchris-hotel@ic24.net
website: www.epchris-hotel.co.uk
Family-run hotel, set within two acres of private grounds, overlooking Ilfracombe. Nine spacious bedrooms. Within the grounds is a heated outdoor swimming pool and popular games room. 209

Glen Tor Hotel, Torrs Park, Ilfracombe, Devon EX34 8AZ

Tel: 01271 862403 Fax: 01271 862403
e-mail: info@glentorhotel.co.uk
website: www.glentorhotel.co.uk
Small, family-run establishment in a quiet corner of Ilfracombe. Seven en-suite guest bedrooms. Evening meals available on request. 208

The Ilfracombe Regal Hotel, 19 Gilbert Grove, Ilfracombe, Devon EX34 9BG

Tel: 01271 866799
The Ilfracombe Regal is a small, privately-run hotel in the heart of the town of Ilfracombe. All the rooms are en-suite and provided with tea and coffee making facilities and a colour TV. There is a licensed bar and all food is freshly prepared to order. 225

Leadengate House, Croyde, Nr. Braunton, Devon EX33 1PN

Tel: 01271 890373
A family-run, comfortable bed and breakfast with friendly personal service. 1 single, 1 twin and 3 double rooms, all en-suite. Packed lunches available.

Marlborough Hotel, 7 Market Street, Ilfracombe, Devon EX34 9AY

Tel: 01271 863580
Centrally located hotel with 17 comfortable rooms of varying sizes. Licensed bar and dance floor. Restaurant open to residents only. Private outdoor pool.

Mole Cottage, Chittlehamholt, Devon EX37 9HF

Tel: 01769 540471 Fax: 01769 540471
e-mail: relax@moley.uk.com
website: www.moley.uk.com
17th century thatched cottage enjoying a riverside location within the magical Mole Valley. Also a working pottery and gallery. Residential Pottery courses available. 218

Preston House Hotel, Saunton, Braunton, Devon EX33 1LG

Tel: 01271 890472 Fax: 01271 890555
Unrivalled location looking down on open sea and the two mile stretch of Saunton Sands. 12 en-suite guest rooms. Stylish restaurant also open to non-residents. 215

Sherborne Lodge, Torrs Park, Ilfracombe, Devon EX34 8AY

Tel: 01271 862297
e-mail: 113121.222@compuserve.com
Friendly, family-run licensed hotel. Eleven en-suite rooms. Drying facilities, flexible bar and dining. Groups welcome.

Shuna Guest House, Downend, Croyde, Devon EX33 1QE

Tel: 01271 890537 Fax: 01271 890537
Small, luxurious, family-run guest house enjoying spectacular views. Five en-suite rooms including a 'Penthouse' suite with balcony.

South Leigh Hotel, Runnacleave Road, Ilfracombe, Devon EX34 8AQ

Tel: 01271 863976 Fax: 01271 863322
Friendly, family-run hotel, situated in its own grounds close to the beach. 26 bedrooms. Live entertainment most nights. 205

St. Brannocks House Hotel, 61-62 St. Brannocks Road, Ilfracombe, Devon EX34 8EQ

Tel: 01271 863873 Fax: 01271 863873
Comfortable guest house accommodation offering good home-cooking and service with a smile. 14 tastefully decorated bedrooms, most with en-suite facilities. 213

Sunnymeade Country Hotel, Dean Cross, West Down, Nr. Ilfracombe, Devon EX34 8NT

Tel: 01271 863668
e-mail: info@sunnymeade.co.uk
website: www.sunnymeade.co.uk
Small, friendly hotel with award-winning chef. Shooting breaks are a speciality. Six en-suite guest rooms. 207

The Village Inn, Youngaton Road, Westward Ho!, Bideford, Devon EX39 1HU

Tel: 01237 477331 Fax: 01237 425183
Family-run free house in popular area of north Devon. Food served from extensive menu of meals and snacks, available in bar or separate restaurant. Newly built en-suite bed and breakfast accommodation. 217

Waterfront Inn, Golf Links Road, Westward Ho!, Devon EX39 1LH

Tel: 01237 474737 Fax: 01237 471719
Modern, friendly inn with much to offer to visitors to the area. Large bar areas, stylish restaurant and comfortable, newly furnished accommodation. 220

Waterloo House Hotel, Waterloo Terrace, Fore Street, Ilfracombe, Devon EX34 9DJ

Tel: 01271 863060 Fax: 01272 863060
e-mail info@waterloohousehotel.co.uk
website www.waterloohousehotel.co.uk
Dating back to 1820 the hotel was originally three cottages built to commemorate the Battle of Waterloo and many original period features have been retained.

Ten individually styled guest rooms, mostly en-suite, and a superb restaurant. 226

Wentworth House Hotel, 2 Belmont Road, Ilfracombe, Devon EX34 8DR

Tel: 01271 863048 Fax: 01271 863048
A former gentleman's residence converted to offer comfortable accommodation. Nine spacious guest rooms. 210

Wheel Farm Country Cottages, Wheel Farm, Berry Down, Combe Martin, Devon EX34 0NT

Tel: 01271 882100 Fax: 01271 883120
website: www.wheelfarmcottages.co.uk
Award-winning complex of ten self-catering cottages converted from old stone farm buildings into comfortable, well equipped accommodation. Heated indoor swimming pool, tennis courts, sauna and fitness room. 222

Yeolden House Hotel, Durrant Lane, Northam, Nr. Bideford, Devon EX39 2RL

Tel: 01237 474400 Fax: 01237 476618
e-mail: yeoldonhouse@aol.com
website: www.yeoldonhousehotel.co.uk
An imposing house surrounded by lawns and colourful flower beds that slope gently down to the river. Ten en-suite rooms that have each been individually designed. Elegant restaurant. 216

Food and Drink

Preston House Hotel, Saunton, Braunton, Devon EX33 1LG

Tel: 01271 890472 Fax: 01271 890555
Unrivalled location looking down on open sea and the two mile stretch of Saunton Sands. 12 en-suite guest rooms. Stylish restaurant also open to non-residents. 215

The Red Barn Restaurant, Woolacombe, Devon EX34 7DF

Tel: 01271 870264
A family-run restaurant and bar just 100 metres from a popular surfing beach. Wide ranging menu catering to all tastes. Ideal for families. 214

Sunnymeade Country Hotel, Dean Cross, West Down, Nr. Ilfracombe, Devon EX34 8NT

Tel: 01271 863668
e-mail: info@sunnymeade.co.uk
website: www.sunnymeade.co.uk
Small, friendly hotel with award-winning chef. Shooting breaks are a speciality. Six en-suite guest rooms. 207

The Village Inn, Youngaton Road, Westward Ho!, Bideford, Devon EX39 1HU

Tel: 01237 477331 Fax: 01237 425183
Family-run free house in popular area of north Devon. Food served from extensive menu of meals and snacks, available in bar or separate restaurant. Newly built en-suite bed and breakfast accommodation. 217

Waterfront Inn, Golf Links Road, Westward Ho!, Devon EX39 1LH

Tel: 01237 474737 Fax: 01237 471719
Modern, friendly inn with much to offer to visitors to the area. Large bar areas, stylish restaurant and comfortable, newly furnished accommodation. 220

Waterloo House Hotel, Waterloo Terrace, Fore Street, Ilfracombe, Devon EX34 9DJ

Tel: 01271 863060 Fax: 01272 863060
e-mail info@waterloohousehotel.co.uk
website www.waterloohousehotel.co.uk
Dating back to 1820 the hotel was originally three cottages built to commemorate the Battle of Waterloo and many original period features have been retained. Ten individually styled guest rooms, mostly en-suite, and a superb restaurant. 226

Yeolden House Hotel, Durrant Lane, Northam, Nr. Bideford, Devon EX39 2RL

Tel: 01237 474400 Fax: 01237 476618
e-mail: yeoldonhouse@aol.com
website: www.yeoldonhousehotel.co.uk
An imposing house surrounded by lawns and colourful flower beds that slope gently down to the river. Ten en-suite rooms that have each been individually designed. Elegant restaurant. 216

Sidmouth Golf Club

Cotmaton Road, Sidmouth, Devon EX10 8SX
Tel: 01395 513023, 513451 Fax: 01395 514661

Sec/Manager:	Ian Smithy
Professional:	Gaele Tapper
Directions:	½ mile west of Sidmouth centre. From the seafront take the Esplanade (towards Beer) then Peak Hill Rd for ¼ mile and turn right into Cotmaton Road. The entrance is after 250 yds on left hand side.
Date Founded:	1889
Type of Course:	Parkland
No of Holes:	18
Length:	5100 yds (4707 mtrs)

Par:	66
SSS:	65

Green Fees:	Weekdays: £20 (round) £24 (day); Weekends/Bank Holidays: £20 (round) £24 (day)
Visitors:	Welcome: Contact Club in Advance. No Restrictions
Societies:	Welcome: Contact Club in Advance
Facilities:	Putting Green, Club Hire, Trolley Hire, Bar, Restaurant

Accommodation, Food and Drink

Reference numbers below refer to detailed information provided in section 2

Accommodation

The Halfway Inn, Sidmouth Road, Aylesbeare, Devon EX5 2JP

Tel: 01395 232273 Fax: 01395 516398
Former coaching inn offering a fine selection of refreshments with very extensive food menu. Four guest rooms for bed and breakfast, two en-suite. 243

Hole Mill, Branscombe, Seaton, Devon EX12 3BX

Tel: 01297 680314
website: www.users.globalnet.co.uk/~branscombe/hole1.htm
Former working watermill, located in pretty valley, converted to a charming house on many levels. Surrounded by colourful gardens. 3 guest rooms. 267

Home Farm Hotel and Restaurant, Wilmington, Honiton, Devon EX14 9JR

Tel: 01404 831278 Fax: 01404 831411
e-mail: homefarmhotel@breathe-mail.net
website: www.homefarmhotel.co.uk
Sixteenth century farmhouse which has been converted into an intimate hotel and restaurant. 13 individually-styled, en-suite bedrooms of varying sizes. The restaurant has a far-reaching reputation for the high quality of its food and service. 223

Lower Southbrook Farm, Southbrook Lane, Whimple, Exeter, Devon EX5 2PG

Tel: 01404 822989 Fax: 01404 822989
Modern, comfortable self-catering cottages converted from former farm buildings. Each sleeps six. 242

Marlborough Hotel, The Esplanade, Sidmouth, Devon EX10 8AR

Tel: 01395 513320
Super sea front property just a stone's throw from the beach. Popular pub and hotel, offering fine food all day. 18 en-suite rooms. 224

Sir Walter Raleigh, 22 High Street, East Budleigh, Devon EX9 7EB

Tel: 01395 442510

A charming, traditional, thatched building serving fine local ales and freshly prepared food. Bed and breakfast accommodation available. 252

Food and Drink

The Halfway Inn, Sidmouth Road, Aylesbeare, Devon EX5 2JP

Tel: 01395 232273 Fax: 01395 516398
Former coaching inn offering a fine selection of refreshments with very extensive food menu. Four guest rooms for bed and breakfast, two en-suite. 243

Hole Mill, Branscombe, Seaton, Devon EX12 3BX

Tel: 01297 680314
website: www.users.globalnet.co.uk/~branscombe/hole1.htm
Former working watermill, located in pretty valley, converted into a charming house on many levels. Surrounded by colourful gardens. 3 guest rooms. 267

Home Farm Hotel and Restaurant, Wilmington, Honiton, Devon EX14 9JR

Tel: 01404 831278 Fax: 01404 831411
e-mail: homefarmhotel@breathe-mail.net
website: www.homefarmhotel.co.uk
Sixteenth century farmhouse which has been converted into an intimate hotel and restaurant. 13 individually-styled, en-suite bedrooms of varying sizes. The restaurant has a far-reaching reputation for the high quality of its food and service. 223

Marlborough Hotel, The Esplanade, Sidmouth, Devon EX10 8AR

Tel: 01395 513320
Super sea front property just a stone's throw from the beach. Popular pub and hotel, offering fine food all day. 18 en-suite rooms. 224

Sir Walter Raleigh, 22 High Street, East Budleigh, Devon EX9 7EB

Tel: 01395 442510
A charming, traditional, thatched building serving fine local ales and freshly prepared food. Bed and breakfast accommodation available. 252

Staddon Heights Golf Club

Plymstock, Plymouth, Devon PL9 9SP
Tel: 01752 402475 Fax: 01752 401998

For a city of its size, Plymouth isn't overly well endowed with golf courses, most of them being congregated around the more popular holiday spots of south Devon, but four or five miles south east of the city stands Staddon Heights.

Finding your way to this course will give you a clue as to its name because, when you finally arrive, you will be rewarded with panoramic views across the city and Plymouth Sound, and away in the distance to Dartmoor and Bodmin Moor.

Despite its cliff-top position, this pleasant parkland course makes for easy going on the legs and, for high handicappers, there are no monstrous par-fives to confront; in fact, there are no par-fives at all.

What you do get, courtesy of designer Hamilton Stutt, is a constantly-changing and tricky little course of not much more than 5,800 yards, but with enough bunkers, bushes and clumps of trees to keep you on your toes all the way round.

The tone is set early on, with just about all the first half-a-dozen holes having greens which are well guarded by sand traps to catch those who are not paying attention, while the seventh green has a variation on this theme - a pond with an island.

Two of the most vaunted holes are the 14th - Staddon's very own "Road Hole" - which offers big hitters the temptation to drive across the dog-leg, and the tame-looking par-three 17th, with its green cut into a hillside. Woe betide anybody who misses it to the right - a nasty slope - or the left - thick scrubby bushes. Don't get complacent with this one.

Sec/Manager:	None
Professional:	Ian Marshall
Directions:	2 miles southeast of Plymouth City centre. From the centre take the A374 (Exeter). After 1 mile turn right onto the A379 (Plymstock, Elburton). After Elburton turn right 300 yds past BP Service Station onto minor road signed Staddiscombe. From Staddiscombe follow signs for Staddon Heights and Turnchapel. The entrance is after 1¼ miles on right hand side.
Date Founded:	1804
Type of Course:	Clifftop
No of Holes:	18
Length:	5751 yds (5308 mtrs)
Par:	68
SSS:	68
Green Fees:	Weekdays: £18; Weekends/ Bank Holidays: £22
Visitors:	Welcome: Contact Club in Advance. No Restrictions
Societies:	Welcome: Contact Club in Advance

Facilities:	Putting Green, Club Hire, Trolley Hire, Bar, Restaurant

Accommodation, Food and Drink

Reference numbers below refer to detailed information provided in section 2

Accommodation

The Carpenters Arms, Metherell, Nr. Callington, Cornwall PL17 8BJ

Tel: 01579 350242 Fax: 01579 350242
A picturesque Cornish pub with friendly and welcoming service. Wide-ranging menu of home-cooked bar meals and snacks.   117

Cawsand Bay Hotel & Galleon Restaurant, The Bound, Cawsand, Nr. Torpoint, Cornwall PL10 1PG

Tel: 01752 822425 Fax: 01752 823527
e-mail: sales@cawsandbay.co.uk
website: www.cawsandbay.co.uk
Located directly on the sea front and with superb views across the Sound towards Plymouth. Ten comfortable en-suite rooms of varying sizes. Popular bar and restaurant.   130

The Halfway House Inn, Grenofen, Tavistock, Devon PL19 9ER

Tel: 01822 612960 Fax: 01822 617697
A large, sprawling black and white 16th-century building with friendly atmosphere. Excellent reputation for high quality food with two restaurants serving an a la carte menu. Four guest rooms.   206

The Laurels, Huckworthy Bridge, Yelverton, Devon PL20 6LP

Tel: 01822 853622
Charming old cottage in riverside setting, recently restored and converted into a self-catering cottage and private home, in which bed and breakfast is available. Ideal holiday base.   239

Tavistock Arms, Fore Street, Gunnislake, Cornwall PL18 9BN

Tel: 01822 832217
Traditional, country pub located directly on the Devon/Cornwall border. Food is served all day. Bed and breakfast accommodation available.   118

Yealm Holidays, 8 Whittingham Road, Collaton Park, Yealmpton, Plymouth, Devon PL8 2NF

Tel: 01752 872712 Fax: 01752 873173
e-mail: info@yealm-holidays.co.uk
website: www.yealm-holidays.co.uk
Selection of cottages, houses and flats all situated around the estuary of the River Yealm, sleeping between two and nine. Pets welcome in some properties.   265

Food and Drink

The Carpenters Arms, Metherell, Nr. Callington, Cornwall PL17 8BJ

Tel: 01579 350242 Fax: 01579 350242
A picturesque Cornish pub with friendly and
welcoming service. Wide-ranging menu of home-
cooked bar meals and snacks.   117

Cawsand Bay Hotel & Galleon Restaurant, The Bound, Cawsand, Nr. Torpoint, Cornwall PL10 1PG

Tel: 01752 822425 Fax: 01752 823527
e-mail: sales@cawsandbay.co.uk
website: www.cawsandbay.co.uk
Located directly on the sea front and with superb
views across the Sound towards Plymouth. Ten
comfortable en-suite rooms of varying sizes. Popular
bar and restaurant.   130

The Halfway House Inn, Grenofen, Tavistock, Devon PL19 9ER

Tel: 01822 612960 Fax: 01822 617697
A large, sprawling black and white 16th-century
building with friendly atmosphere. Excellent
reputation for high quality food with two restaurants
serving an a la carte menu. Four guest rooms.   206

Old Mother Hubbards, 35 Market Street, Yealmpton, Devon PL8 2EA

Tel: 01752 880085
Thought to be the original home of Old Mother
Hubbard, as immortalised in the traditional nursery
rhyme. Now a cosy and intimate restaurant open for a
la carte lunches and evening meals. Ring for opening
details.

Tavistock Arms, Fore Street, Gunnislake, Cornwall PL18 9BN

Tel: 01822 832217
Traditional, country pub located directly on the
Devon/Cornwall border. Food is served all day. Bed
and breakfast accommodation available.   118

The Walkhampton Inn, Walkhampton, Nr. Yelverton, Devon PL20 6JY

Tel: 01822 855556 Fax: 01822 855556
e-mail: info@walkhamptoninn.co.uk
Historic establishment, popular in the area for serving
a good range of beer and traditional pub fayre. Two
guest rooms both of which are en-suite.   238

Tavistock Golf Club

Down road, Tavistock, Devon PL19 9AQ
Tel: 01822 612049 Fax: 01822 612049

Sec/Manager:	Mr. O'Dowd
Professional:	D. Rehagg
Directions:	1 mile southeast of centre of Tavistock. Take Whitchurch Road into Down Road.
Date Founded:	1890
Type of Course:	Moorland
No of Holes:	18

Length:	5898 yds (5444 mtrs)
Par:	70
SSS:	68
Green Fees:	Weekdays: £24; Weekends/ Bank Holidays: £30
Visitors:	Welcome: Contact Club in Advance. No restrictions
Societies:	Welcome: Contact Club in Advance. Unable to play at weekends
Facilities:	Practice Area, Putting Green, Trolley Hire Bar, Restaurant

Accommodation, Food and Drink

Reference numbers below refer to detailed
information provided in section 2

Accommodation

The Bridge Inn, Bridge Street, Hatherleigh, Nr. Okehampton, Devon EX20 3JA

Tel: 01837 810947 Fax: 01837 810614
The Bridge Inn dates from the 16th century and is
one of the oldest buildings in the area. Cosy interior
with bar and separate restaurant. Six en-suite guest
rooms of varying sizes.   231

The Carpenters Arms, Metherell, Nr. Callington, Cornwall PL17 8BJ

Tel: 01579 350242 Fax: 01579 350242
A picturesque Cornish pub with friendly and
welcoming service. Wide-ranging menu of home-
cooked bar meals and snacks.   117

The Coffee Pot, 14 St. James Street, Okehampton, Devon EX20 1DA

Tel: 01837 52988
Traditional coffee shop, open daily serving early breakfast, coffee, lunches and afternoon teas. Conveniently located close to the town centre. 233

The Halfway House Inn, Grenofen, Tavistock, Devon PL19 9ER

Tel: 01822 612960 Fax: 01822 617697
A large, sprawling black and white 16th-century building with friendly atmosphere. Excellent reputation for high quality food with two restaurants serving an a la carte menu. Four guest rooms. 206

The Laurels, Huckworthy Bridge, Yelverton, Devon PL20 6LP

Tel: 01822 853622
Charming old cottage in riverside setting, recently restored and converted into a self-catering cottage and private home, in which bed and breakfast is available. Ideal holiday base. 239

Lifton Hall Hotel, Lifton, Devon PL16 0DR

Tel: 01566 784863 Fax: 01566 784770
e-mail mail@liftonhall.co.uk
Traditional 250-year old Country House hotel in peaceful village location with ten en-suite rooms. Formal restaurant and a bistro, both specialising in local fish. 240

The Old Coach House, Ottery, Tavistock, Devon PL19 8NS

Tel: 01822 617515 Fax: 01822 617515
e-mail eddie@coachhouseone.supanet.com
Old coach house which was substantially renovated in 1989 to create a delightful hotel and restaurant. Comfortable accommodation and superb a la carte restaurant. 236

Pressland Country House Hotel, Hatherleigh, Nr. Okehampton, Devon EX20 3LW

Tel: 01837 810871 Fax: 01837 810303
e-mail graham@presslandhouse.co.uk
website www.presslandhouse.co.uk
Victorian manor house surrounded by lawns and woodland. Five spacious guest rooms, most with en-suite facilities, and superb residents' restaurant. 230

Tavistock Arms, Fore Street, Gunnislake, Cornwall PL18 9BN

Tel: 01822 832217
Traditional, country pub located directly on the Devon/Cornwall border. Food is served all day. Bed and breakfast accommodation available. 118

The Torrs, Belstone, Okehampton, Devon EX20 1QZ

Tel: 01837 840689
Small, cosy pub, popular with locals and visitors. Refreshing ales and tasty, home-cooked meals. Bed and breakfast accommodation available with three en-suite guest rooms. 232

Food and Drink

The Bridge Inn, Bridge Street, Hatherleigh, Nr. Okehampton, Devon EX20 3JA

Tel: 01837 810947 Fax: 01837 810614
The Bridge Inn dates from the 16th century and is one of the oldest buildings in the area. Cosy interior with bar and separate restaurant. Six en-suite guest rooms of varying sizes. 231

The Carpenters Arms, Metherell, Nr. Callington, Cornwall PL17 8BJ

Tel: 01579 350242 Fax: 01579 350242
A picturesque Cornish pub with friendly and welcoming service. Wide-ranging menu of home-cooked bar meals and snacks. 117

The Halfway House Inn, Grenofen, Tavistock, Devon PL19 9ER

Tel: 01822 612960 Fax: 01822 617697
A large, sprawling black and white 16th-century building with friendly atmosphere. Excellent reputation for high quality food with two restaurants serving an a la carte menu. Four guest rooms. 206

Lifton Hall Hotel, Lifton, Devon PL16 0DR

Tel: 01566 784863 Fax: 01566 784770
e-mail mail@liftonhall.co.uk
Traditional 250-year old Country House hotel in peaceful village location with ten en-suite rooms. Formal restaurant and a bistro, both specialising in local fish. 240

The Old Coach House, Ottery, Tavistock, Devon PL19 8NS

Tel: 01822 617515 Fax: 01822 617515
e-mail eddie@coachhouseone.supanet.com
Old coach house which was substantially renovated in 1989 to create a delightful hotel and restaurant. Comfortable accommodation and superb a la carte restaurant. 236

Royal Standard Inn, Mary Tavy, Nr. Tavistock, Devon PL19 9QB

Tel: 01822 810289 Fax: 01822 810615
Former coaching inn with an atmosphere of character and charm. The inn claims to serve the best beer in the area while the food comprises a good selection of traditional meals and snacks. 235

Tavistock Arms, Fore Street, Gunnislake, Cornwall PL18 9BN

Tel: 01822 832217
Traditional, country pub located directly on the Devon/Cornwall border. Food is served all day. Bed and breakfast accommodation available. 118

The Torrs, Belstone, Okehampton, Devon EX20 1QZ

Tel: 01837 840689
Small, cosy pub, popular with locals and visitors. Refreshing ales and tasty, home-cooked meals. Bed and breakfast accommodation available with three en-suite guest rooms. 232

Victorian Pantry, Museum Courtyard, West Street, Okehampton, Devon EX20 1HQ

Tel: 01837 53988
Housed within an historic building not far from the Dartmoor Museum. Open daily serving a good selection of drinks, home-cooked cakes and hot meals.   229

The Walkhampton Inn, Walkhampton, Nr. Yelverton, Devon PL20 6JY

Tel: 01822 855556 Fax: 01822 855556
e-mail: info@walkhamptoninn.co.uk
Historic establishment, popular in the area for serving a good range of beer and traditional pub fayre. Two guest rooms both of which are en-suite.   238

Teignmouth Golf Club

Exeter Road, Teignmouth, Devon TQ14 9NY

Tel: 01626 772894

Let's face it, you are never, in your wildest dreams, ever going to play the Masters course at Augusta and, with the trouble and strife it causes even the best professionals in the world, that's probably no bad thing for your sanity.

Dr Alister Mackenzie designed Augusta to test the best but, before he drew up those famous designs, he had a practice run - by designing Teignmouth. There might not be much in common between the immaculately manicured and coiffeured, lush green acres of Georgia and the wild and rugged Devon plateau around 900 feet up on Haldon Moor, but there may be more than you imagine.

When he set about Teignmouth in the early 1920s, Mackenzie employed two of his signature features, the two-tier green well guarded by bunkers, and the short hole over some natural hazard - in Teignmouth's case, that is old quarry workings.

There are six par threes here, five of them approached over quarries, and 11 of the 18 greens are two-tiered, so you have plenty to think about when it comes to club selection for approach shots.

Despite its elevated position, the course is reasonably flat and meanders pleasantly through the gorse and heather that you would expect on such heathland, and gives excellent views as far as Portland Bill in Dorset on a clear day - and being so high up, mist and fog can sometimes be a problem.

But standing on the first tee, high above a valley with the River Teign running through it and with the sea way below to the other side, you might think Augusta isn't all that special after all.

Sec/Manager:	S. Wright
Professional:	Peter Ward
Directions:	2 miles northwest of Teignmouth seafront. From seafront take Exeter Road (B3192) for 2¼ miles and turn left into Shepherds Lane where course is signed.
Date Founded:	1925
Type of Course:	Heathland
No of Holes:	18
Length:	6083 yds (5615 mtrs)
Par:	69
SSS:	71
Green Fees:	Weekdays: £25; Weekends/ Bank Holidays: £27.50
Visitors:	Welcome: By arrangement Contact Club
Societies:	Welcome: Contact Club in Advance. Unable to play Mon, Wed, Fri, Sat, Sun
Facilities:	Practice Area, Putting Green, Club Hire, Trolley Hire, Bar, Restaurant

Accommodation, Food and Drink

Reference numbers below refer to detailed information provided in section 2

Accommodation

Babbacombe Hall Hotel, 17 Manor Road, Babbacombe, Torquay, Devon TQ1 3JX

Tel: 01803 325668 Fax: 01803 325668
Victorian seaside hotel with six en-suite rooms. Bar and restaurant open to residents only.   253

Brunswick House, 5 Brunswick Street, Teignmouth, Devon TQ14 8AE

Tel: 01626 774102
e-mail: peterhockings@hotmail.com
Bed and breakfast located within Victorian terrace just 100 metres from sea front. Spacious accommodation with eight, en-suite guest rooms.   212

Chimneys of Starcross, Starcross, Nr. Exeter, Devon EX6 8PA

Tel: 01626 890813
A characterful, detached house situated overlooking the Exe estuary. Built in 1888, many of the original features have been preserved. Seven rooms with five en-suite.   202

Collingwood Hotel, Braddons Hill Road East, Torquay, Devon TQ1 1HB

Tel: 01803 293448 Fax: 01626 400221
e-mail: bookings@collingwood-hotel.co.uk
An elegant Georgian Hotel located a short distance from the sea front. Regular themed breaks.   256

The Devon Arms, Kenton, Nr. Exeter, Devon EX6 8LD

Tel: 01626 890213 Fax: 01626 891678
e-mail: devon.arms@ukgateway.net
Next to Powderham Castle, The Exeter Arms is a family-run hostelry serving home-cooked food. Six en-suite rooms available for bed and breakfast.   254

Langstone Cliff Hotel, Dawlish, Devon EX7 0NA

Tel: 01626 868000 Fax: 01626 868006
e-mail: reception@langstone-hotel.co.uk
One of Dorset's premier hotels in superb location overlooking the sea. Excellent facilities including tennis, practice golf and indoor and outdoor pools. Popular restaurant.   237

Shell Cove House, Old Teignmouth Road, Dawlish, Devon EX7 0NJ

Tel: 01626 862523 Fax: 01626 862523
A Georgian house converted into a number of self-contained, self-catering apartments. Also a luxurious cottage available. Excellent facilities on site.   251

The Welcome Stranger, Liverton, Nr. Newton Abbott, Devon TQ12 6JA

Tel: 01626 821224
e-mail: welcomestranger@talk21.com
A friendly, country pub offering a good variety of sensibly priced, home-cooked food. Two twin en-suite rooms.   260

Whidborne Manor, Ashill, Bishopsteignton, Devon TQ14 9PY

Tel: 01626 870177
e-mail: nicky.dykes@btinternet.com
Cosy 15th-century thatched cottage, attractively furnished, with many original beams and timbers throughout. Two double rooms. Evening meals by arrangement.   201

Woodlands Hotel, 51 Barnpark Road, Teignmouth, Devon TQ14 8PN

Tel: 01626 773094
Delightful Regency-style hotel retaining a great deal of period elegance. Comfortable guest rooms with many having superb views out to sea. Half- or Full-board available.   221

Food and Drink

Collingwood Hotel, Braddons Hill Road East, Torquay, Devon TQ1 1HB

Tel: 01803 293448 Fax: 01626 400221
e-mail: bookings@collingwood-hotel.co.uk
An elegant Georgian Hotel located a short distance from the sea front. Regular themed breaks.   256

The Devon Arms, Kenton, Nr. Exeter, Devon EX6 8LD

Tel: 01626 890213 Fax: 01626 891678
e-mail: devon.arms@ukgateway.net
Next to Powderham Castle, The Exeter Arms is a family-run hostelry serving home-cooked food. Six en-suite rooms available for bed and breakfast.   254

Langstone Cliff Hotel, Dawlish, Devon EX7 0NA

Tel: 01626 868000 Fax: 01626 868006
e-mail: reception@langstone-hotel.co.uk
One of Dorset's premier hotels in superb location overlooking the sea. Excellent facilities including tennis, practice golf and indoor and outdoor pools. Popular restaurant.   237

The Welcome Stranger, Liverton, Nr. Newton Abbott, Devon TQ12 6JA

Tel: 01626 821224
e-mail: welcomestranger@talk21.com
A friendly, country pub offering a good variety of sensibly priced, home-cooked food. Two twin en-suite rooms.   260

Teign Valley Golf Club

Cristow, Exeter, Devon EX6 7PA

Tel: 01647 253026

The fact that Teign Valley has been open for only half-a-dozen years may put off some people, who might assume that it is still peppered with saplings and that the surroundings are not yet as mature as on much longer-established courses. But don't be misled. This lovely course is set in the Dartmoor National Park, and offers a terrific wander through some spectacular countryside.

The course is cleverly designed to loop around rolling hills and through a couple of valleys, and there are some superb views peeking out from behind the ancient wild woodlands on this most natural of tracks.

Designer Dr Peter Nicholson has used what nature provided to create a challenge which is fair and not too strenuous, even for the average weekender, and, because of its location, and because the club maintains a fairly small membership, it has become ever-increasingly popular with holidaymakers, who always have an excellent chance of getting a suitable tee time.

There are five par-threes, which gives you a fighting chance to make up for all those bogeys, the most awkward of which is probably the 12th, with its green cheek-by-jowl with a small lake - the same lake you must avoid when playing up the adjacent 11th.

You have the early chance to make your mark on the River Teign with wayward shots on the fourth or fifth, and there is a teasing little finish, with the last two holes both dog-legs requiring a high degree of accuracy if you are to get a view of the green.

Sec/Manager: Mike Daniels

Professional: Scott Amiet

Directions:	7 miles southwest of Exeter City centre. From Exeter take the A38 (Plymouth). After 7 miles turn right onto the B3344 leading to the B3193 (Christow). After 3½ miles the entrance is on the left hand side just before Lower Ashton turning.
Date Founded:	1995
Type of Course:	Parkland
No of Holes:	18
Length:	5677 yds (5240 mtrs)
Par:	69
SSS:	67
Green Fees:	Weekdays: £14-£17; Weekends/Bank Holidays: £20
Visitors:	Welcome: Contact Club in Advance. No restrictions
Societies:	Welcome: Contact Club in Advance
Facilities:	Putting Green, Club Hire, Trolley Hire, Buggy Hire, Bar, Restaurant

Accommodation, Food and Drink

Reference numbers below refer to detailed information provided in section 2

Accommodation

Babbacombe Hall Hotel, 17 Manor Road, Babbacombe, Torquay, Devon TQ1 3JX

Tel: 01803 325668 Fax: 01803 325668
Victorian seaside hotel with six en-suite rooms. Bar and restaurant open to residents only. 253

Brunswick House, 5 Brunswick Street, Teignmouth, Devon TQ14 8AE

Tel: 01626 774102
e-mail: peterhockings@hotmail.com
Bed and breakfast housed within Victorian terrace just 100 metres from sea front. Spacious accommodation with eight, en-suite guest rooms. 212

Chimneys of Starcross, Starcross, Nr. Exeter, Devon EX6 8PA

Tel: 01626 890813
A characterful, detached house situated overlooking the Exe estuary. Built in 1888, many of the original features have been preserved. Seven rooms with five en-suite. 202

Collingwood Hotel, Braddons Hill Road East, Torquay, Devon TQ1 1HB

Tel: 01803 293448 Fax: 01626 400221
e-mail: bookings@collingwood-hotel.co.uk
An elegant Georgian Hotel located a short distance from the sea front. Regular themed breaks. 256

Dartmoor Railway Inn, Station Road, Crediton, Devon EX17 3BX

Tel: 01363 724989
Traditional hostelry offering a warm, friendly welcome to all. Home-cooked food with popular Sunday roast lunches. Three en-suite rooms. 248

The Devon Arms, Kenton, Nr. Exeter, Devon EX6 8LD

Tel: 01626 890213 Fax: 01626 891678
e-mail: devon.arms@ukgateway.net
Next to Powderham Castle, The Exeter Arms is a family-run hostelry serving home-cooked food. Six en-suite rooms available for bed and breakfast. 254

Langstone Cliff Hotel, Dawlish, Devon EX7 0NA

Tel: 01626 868000 Fax: 01626 868006
e-mail: reception@langstone-hotel.co.uk
One of Dorset's premier hotels in superb location overlooking the sea. Excellent facilities including tennis, practice golf and indoor and outdoor pools. Popular restaurant. 237

Shell Cove House, Old Teignmouth Road, Dawlish, Devon EX7 0NJ

Tel: 01626 862523 Fax: 01626 862523
A Georgian house converted into a number of self-contained, self-catering apartments. Also a luxurious cottage available. Excellent facilities on site. 251

The Welcome Stranger, Liverton, Nr. Newton Abbott, Devon TQ12 6JA

Tel: 01626 821224
e-mail: welcomestranger@talk21.com
A friendly, country pub offering a good variety of sensibly priced, home-cooked food. Two twin en-suite rooms. 260

Whidborne Manor, Ashill, Bishopsteignton, Devon TQ14 9PY

Tel: 01626 870177
e-mail: nicky.dykes@btinternet.com
Cosy 15th-century thatched cottage, attractively furnished, with many original beams and timbers throughout. Two double rooms. Evening meals by arrangement. 201

Woodlands Hotel, 51 Barnpark Road, Teignmouth, Devon TQ14 8PN

Tel: 01626 773094
Delightful Regency-style hotel retaining a great deal of period elegance. Comfortable guest rooms with many having superb views out to sea. Half- or Full-board available. 221

Food and Drink

Collingwood Hotel, Braddons Hill Road East, Torquay, Devon TQ1 1HB

Tel: 01803 293448 Fax: 01626 400221
e-mail: bookings@collingwood-hotel.co.uk
An elegant Georgian Hotel located a short distance from the sea front. Regular themed breaks. 256

Dartmoor Railway Inn, Station Road, Crediton, Devon EX17 3BX

Tel: 01363 724989
Traditional hostelry offering a warm, friendly welcome to all. Home-cooked food with popular Sunday roast lunches. Three en-suite rooms. 248

The Devon Arms, Kenton, Nr. Exeter, Devon EX6 8LD

Tel: 01626 890213 Fax: 01626 891678
e-mail: devon.arms@ukgateway.net
Next to Powderham Castle, The Exeter Arms is a family-run hostelry serving home-cooked food. Six en-suite rooms available for bed and breakfast. 254

Langstone Cliff Hotel, Dawlish, Devon EX7 0NA

Tel: 01626 868000 Fax: 01626 868006
e-mail: reception@langstone-hotel.co.uk
One of Dorset's premier hotels in superb location overlooking the sea. Excellent facilities including tennis, practice golf and indoor and outdoor pools. Popular restaurant. 237

The Plough Inn, Fore Street, Ipplepen, Devon TQ12 5RP

Tel: 01808 812118 Fax: 01803 814278
website: www.ipplepen.com
An attractive old inn with a great deal of character. Good range of drinks and home-cooked food. 259

The Welcome Stranger, Liverton, Nr. Newton Abbott, Devon TQ12 6JA

Tel: 01626 821224
e-mail: welcomestranger@talk21.com
A friendly, country pub offering a good variety of sensibly priced, home-cooked food. Two twin en-suite rooms. 260

Thurlestone
Golf Club

Thurlestone, Kingsbridge, Devon TQ7 3NZ

Tel: 01548 560405 Fax: 01548 562149

Yet another of those edge-of-cliff courses that Devon seems to specialise in, and yet more of that heady mix - breathtaking coastal views, a saltiness in the air and a downland track littered with what nature intended, and some things she didn't, courtesy of the greenkeepers.

As with all these courses strung out like bunting along the rugged sections of the south coast, the trick is to concentrate on your game rather than the panorama unless, of course, your card starts to read like a horror story, in which case just enjoy the sea air.

Thurlestone is one of numerous Harry S Colt-designed courses in the region, and another which has notched up more than 100 years of golf. There is not much chance to ease your way in here, with the first hole crossing a road and a stream, to a green which is well bunkered, a feature, by the way, of the whole course.

Perhaps the most delightful trio of holes are the ninth, 10th and 11th. The ninth dog-legs gently to a green (yep, more bunkers at the front) with a wall at the back of it and a babbling stream as well. The 10th fairway is lined with stone walls to keep you focused, and is also stroke index one, while the 11th green has the most majestic views you could wish for.

The best is kept until last here, a sweeping 500-yarder taking you all the way downhill back to the clubhouse, a long one offering just enough encouragement that you may finish on a high.

Sec/Manager:	John Scott
Professional:	Peter Laugher
Directions:	4 miles south of Kingsbridge. From A379 Plymouth, Salcombe road take the Thurlestone turning.
Date Founded:	1897
Type of Course:	Clifftop
No of Holes:	18
Length:	6340 yds (5852 mtrs)
Par:	71
SSS:	70
Green Fees:	Weekdays: £30; Weekends/ Bank Holidays: £30
Visitors:	Welcome: Contact Club in Advance. No Restrictions
Societies:	No Societies
Facilities:	Putting Green, Chipping Green, Club Hire, Trolley Hire Bar, Restaurant

Accommodation, Food and Drink

Reference numbers below refer to detailed information provided in section 2

Accommodation

Campbells, 5 Mount Boone, Dartmouth, Devon TQ6 9PB

Tel: 01803 833438 Fax: 01803 833438
Award-winning bed and breakfast enjoying stunning views over the town of Dartmouth. Two elegant, en-suite, double bedrooms. Superb breakfasts with excellent choice. 264

Chuckle Too, Blackawton, Totnes, Devon TQ9 7BG

Tel: 01803 712455
Modern, self-catering cottage offering cosy cottage-style accommodation. Sleeps up to three adults. Very well equipped. 262

The Floating Bridge and Floaters Restaurant, Sandquay, Dartmouth, Devon TQ6 9PQ

Tel: 01803 832354 Fax: 01803 832354
Popular riverside hostelry serving fine refreshment
and award-winning food. Fresh local fish a speciality.
Well worth a detour. 266

The Steam Packet Inn, St. Peter's Quay, Totnes, Devon TQ9 5EN

Tel: 01803 863880 Fax: 01803 862754
Elegant riverside inn with open plan lounge bar and
elegant, conservatory Restaurant. Ten en-suite guest
bedrooms. Private river moorings available. 261

Tides Reach Hotel, South Sands, Salcombe, Devon TQ8 8LJ

Tel: 01548 843466 Fax: 01548 843954
e-mail: enquire@tidesreach.com
website: www.tidesreach.com
Elegant, luxurious hotel with a good reputation for
high standards of service. Superb, south-facing
location and excellent residents' facilities. High
quality restaurant. 234

The White House, Chillington, Nr. Kingsbridge, Devon TQ7 2JX

Tel: 01548 580580 Fax: 01548 581124
A small, high quality hotel and restaurant offering
seven luxuriously furnished bedrooms including two
suites. 203

Yealm Holidays, 8 Whittingham Road, Collaton Park, Yealmpton, Plymouth, Devon PL8 2NF

Tel: 01752 872712 Fax: 01752 873173
e-mail: info@yealm-holidays.co.uk
website: www.yealm-holidays.co.uk
Selection of cottages, houses and flats all situated
around the estuary of the River Yealm, sleeping
between two and nine. Pets welcome in some
properties. 265

Food and Drink

The Laughing Monk Restaurant, Totnes Road, Strete, Nr. Dartmouth, Devon TQ6 0RN

Tel: 01803 770639
Award-winning restaurant, including "Best Restaurant
in the West" Gold Award. Housed within a 160-year
old former church school. Open for dinner
throughout the year. 227

Old Mother Hubbards, 35 Market Street, Yealmpton, Devon PL8 2EA

Tel: 01752 880085
Thought to be the original home of Old Mother
Hubbard, as immortalised in the traditional nursery
rhyme. Now a cosy and intimate restaurant open for a
la carte lunches and evening meals. Ring for opening
details.

The Singing Kettle, 6 Smith Street, Dartmouth, Devon TQ6 9QR

Tel: 01803 832624
Traditional English tea room tucked away on a side
street in the centre of Dartmouth. Open all day for
food and drink, mostly home-made. 263

The Steam Packet Inn, St. Peter's Quay, Totnes, Devon TQ9 5EN

Tel: 01803 863880 Fax: 01803 862754
Elegant riverside inn with open plan lounge bar and
elegant, conservatory Restaurant. Ten en-suite guest
bedrooms. Private river moorings available. 261

Tides Reach Hotel, South Sands, Salcombe, Devon TQ8 8LJ

Tel: 01548 843466 Fax: 01548 843954
e-mail: enquire@tidesreach.com
website: www.tidesreach.com
Elegant, luxurious hotel with a good reputation for
high standards of service. Superb, south-facing
location and excellent residents' facilities. High
quality restaurant. 234

The White House, Chillington, Nr. Kingsbridge, Devon TQ7 2JX

Tel: 01548 580580 Fax: 01548 581124
A small, high quality hotel and restaurant offering
seven luxuriously furnished bedrooms including two
suites. 203

Tiverton Golf Club

Post Hill, Tiverton Devon EX16 4NE
Tel: 01884 252187 Fax: 01884 251607

The house and gardens of Knightshayes Court,
tucked away just off the North Devon Link Road
from the M5, are delightful National Trust treasures only a few minutes away from the golf club.

But what most don't realise is that the former
resident was one of the all-time sporting greats.

That resident was Joyce Wethered, better
known later as Lady Heathcoat-Amory, who holds
a place in golf's Hall of Fame as the woman who
dominated British women's golf in the 1920s.

She literally became a legend in her own life-
time for her outstanding achievements - now
rarely remembered - as she won the Ladies' British Open Amateur Championship three times -
in 1922, 1924 and 1925 - and the English Championship in five consecutive years between 1920
and 1924. She then retired from competition altogether, only to return three years later to take
her fourth British Open title in 1929 and equal
the record of Charlotte Leitch, who had won the
event in 1914, 1920, 1921 and 1926.

To put her talent into perspective, the legendary Bobby Jones, her American contemporary
who quit golf at the age of 28 because he had
won everything there was to win, including a four-
title Grand Slam of British and US Open and
Amateur titles in one year, once described Joyce
as the best golfer - of either sex - he had ever
seen.

With that tribute ringing in her ears, Joyce once
more stepped out of the golfing spotlight, never
to return, at the same age as Jones - a mere 28.
She was president of the Tiverton club, which
rents the course for £1 a year on a 199-year lease,

until her death a few years ago. In tribute to her, the club created a Joyce Wethered Lounge in the clubhouse.

The course itself is renowned for its excellent lush fairways and variety of tree species, and there are plenty of interesting holes to tackle.

Sec/Manager:	Clive Lansdell
Professional:	Mike Hawton
Directions:	2¼ miles east of Tiverton centre. From centre take Blundells Road (B3391) for 2¼ miles. The entrance is on the left hand side.
Date Founded:	1936
Type of Course:	Parkland
No of Holes:	18
Length:	6236 yds (5756 mtrs)
Par:	71
SSS:	71
Green Fees:	Weekdays: £21; Weekends/ Bank Holidays: £31
Visitors:	Welcome: Contact Club in Advance. Handicap Certificates
Societies:	Welcome: Contact Club in Advance. Thursdays only
Facilities:	Putting Green, Chipping Green, Trolley Hire, Bar, Restaurant

Accommodation, Food and Drink

Reference numbers below refer to detailed information provided in section 2

Accommodation

Dartmoor Railway Inn, Station Road, Crediton, Devon EX17 3BX

Tel: 01363 724989
Traditional hostelry offering a warm, friendly welcome to all. Home-cooked food with popular Sunday roast lunches. Three en-suite rooms.   248

'The Oyster', Colebrooke, Devon EX17 5JQ

Tel: 01363 84576
Cosy modern bungalow taking its unusual name from the owner, Pearl. Three bedrooms, each en-suite or with private facilities. Many guests have returned several times - what better recommendation!   245

The Red Lion, Shobrooke, Nr. Crediton, Devon EX17 1AT

Tel: 01363 772340
Friendly country pub run by popular couple. Cosy bars with a separate 50-seater restaurant. Three, double, en-suite rooms.   244

South Farm Holiday Cottages, South Farm, Blackborough, Cullompton, Devon EX15 2JE

Tel: 01823 681078 Fax: 01823 680483
e-mail: chapmans@southfarm.co.uk website: www.southfarm.co.uk
Delightful complex of five cottages in the heart of the Devonshire countryside. Excellent facilities include four coarse fishing lakes, tennis courts, outdoor pool and games barn. Open all year round for short breaks and longer stays.

Turnpike Cottage, Turnpike, Milverton, Somerset TA4 1LF

Tel: 01823 400492
Cosy cottage providing self-contained accommodation, sleeping up to five adults. Very well equipped. Pets welcome.   404

Whidborne Manor, Ashill, Bishopsteignton, Devon TQ14 9PY

Tel: 01626 870177
e-mail: nicky.dykes@btinternet.com
Cosy 15th-century thatched cottage, attractively furnished, with many original beams and timbers throughout. Two double rooms. Evening meals by arrangement.   201

The White Hart Inn, 51-52 East Reach, Taunton, Somerset TA1 3EZ

Tel: 01823 254652
A town centre pub offering a friendly welcome to all. Tea, coffee and home-cooked bar meals and snacks served each day.   401

Food and Drink

The Bird in Hand, Mount Street, Bishops Lydeard, Taunton, Somerset TA4 3LH

Tel: 01823 432090
Traditional country pub dating to the 18th century. Menu offers a selection of meals and snacks while the bar claims to stock the best beer in the area.   437

Dartmoor Railway Inn, Station Road, Crediton, Devon EX17 3BX

Tel: 01363 724989
Traditional hostelry offering a warm, friendly welcome to all. Home-cooked food with popular Sunday roast lunches. Three en-suite rooms.   248

The Red Lion, Shobrooke, Nr. Crediton, Devon EX17 1AT

Tel: 01363 772340
Friendly country pub run by popular couple. Cosy bars with a separate 50-seater restaurant. Three, double, en-suite rooms.   244

The White Hart Inn, 51-52 East Reach, Taunton, Somerset TA1 3EZ

Tel: 01823 254652
A town centre pub offering a friendly welcome to all. Tea, coffee and home-cooked bar meals and snacks served each day.   401

Torquay Golf Club

Petitor Road, St. Marychurch, Torquay,
Devon TQ1 4QF

Tel: 01803 314591 Fax: 01803 316116

To most club players of mid to high handicaps, getting a par on a 500-yarder brings the sort of satisfaction you would normally associate with a birdie on an awkward par four hole. So get down to Torquay!

Thousands upon thousands of holidaying golfers have enjoyed the ups and downs of this course - half of it in a valley, half on a clifftop plateau - and many will have walked away from the 12th green feeling rather smug with themselves. For this 542-yarder, the longest hole on the course plays much shorter, it being downhill and to a green which, if you avoid the fairly recently-added pond on the left, will kindly gather your run-on shot. Mind you, any shot picked up on the 12th may well be lost immediately on the 13th, a little tinker of a hole, 180 yards to a green ringed with bunkers and fronted by that same pond.

Although popular with holidaymakers, this is no summer breeze of a course, and you need to be hitting the straps pretty quickly, as the third is a toughie, 430 yards of uphill fairway which runs left to right, with trees, hedges and bunkers awaiting every slightly miss-hit shot.

The fifth and sixth don't get much easier - still uphill battles - but the climb becomes worthwhile for the fabulous views around the turn, and some splendid holes like the eighth and ninth.

On an historical footnote, this was the first place on the south coast to possess a golf course, in 1882 - a few months before the Royal Isle of Wight club - and the original site of the course on the next headland along can be viewed from the 11th.

Sec/Manager: Barry Long
Professional: Martin Ruth

Directions:	1½ miles north of the centre of Torquay on the A379 Teighmouth Road.
Date Founded:	1910
Type of Course:	Parkland
No of Holes:	18
Length:	6175 yds (5699 mtrs)
Par:	69
SSS:	70
Green Fees:	Weekdays: £25 (Summer) £20 (Winter); Weekends/Bank Holidays: £30 (Summer) £25 (Winter)
Visitors:	Welcome: Contact Club in Advance. No Restrictions Handicap Certificates
Societies:	Welcome: Contact Club in Advance. Unable to play at weekends
Facilities:	Practice Area, Putting Green, Buggy Hire Club Hire, Trolley Hire Bar, Restaurant, Private Rooms

Accommodation, Food and Drink

Reference numbers below refer to detailed information provided in section 2

Accommodation

Alexandra Lodge Holiday Apartments, Grafton Road, Torquay, South Devon TQ1 1QJ

Tel: 01803 213465 Fax: 01803 390933
e-mail: almes@fsbdial.co.uk
website: www.alexandra-lodge.co.uk
Lovely detached Georgian villa in secluded grounds offering seven self-catering apartments sleeping between two and eight people.   249

The Anchorage Guest House, 170 New Road, Brixham, Devon TQ5 8DA

Tel/Fax: 01803 852960
A comfortable, friendly guest house with a fabulous award-winning garden. Seven guest rooms.   257

Babbacombe Hall Hotel, 17 Manor Road, Babbacombe, Torquay, Devon TQ1 3JX

Tel: 01803 325668 Fax: 01803 325668
Victorian seaside hotel with six en-suite rooms. Bar and restaurant open to residents only.   253

Brunswick House, 5 Brunswick Street, Teignmouth, Devon TQ14 8AE

Tel: 01626 774102
e-mail: peterhockings@hotmail.com
Bed and breakfast housed within Victorian terrace just 100 metres from sea front. Spacious accommodation with eight, en-suite guest rooms.   212

Chuckle Too, Blackawton, Totnes, Devon TQ9 7BG

Tel: 01803 712455
Modern, self-catering cottage offering cosy cottage-style accommodation. Sleeps up to three adults. Very well equipped.   262

Collingwood Hotel, Braddons Hill Road East, Torquay, Devon TQ1 1HB

Tel: 01803 293448 Fax: 01626 400221
e-mail: bookings@collingwood-hotel.co.uk
An elegant Georgian Hotel located a short distance from the sea front. Regular themed breaks.   256

Exmouth View Hotel, St. Albans Road, Babbacombe, Torquay, Devon TQ1 3LQ

Tel: 0800 7817817/01803 327307 Fax: 01803 329967
e-mail: relax@exmouth-view.co.uk
website: www.exmouth-view.co.uk
A modern hotel offering comfortable accommodation at an affordable price. Licensed bar and restaurant.250

Langstone Cliff Hotel, Dawlish, Devon EX7 0NA

Tel: 01626 868000 Fax: 01626 868006
e-mail: reception@langstone-hotel.co.uk
One of Dorset's premier hotels in superb location overlooking the sea. Excellent facilities including tennis, practice golf and indoor and outdoor pools. Popular restaurant.   237

The Steam Packet Inn, St. Peter's Quay, Totnes, Devon TQ9 5EN

Tel: 01803 863880 Fax: 01803 862754
Elegant riverside inn with open plan lounge bar and elegant, conservatory Restaurant. Ten en-suite guest bedrooms. Private river moorings available.   261

The Welcome Stranger, Liverton, Nr. Newton Abbott, Devon TQ12 6JA

Tel: 01626 821224
e-mail: welcomestranger@talk21.com
A friendly, country pub offering a good variety of sensibly priced, home-cooked food. Two twin en-suite rooms.   260

Westbury, 51 New Road, Brixham, Devon TQ5 8NL

Tel/Fax: 01803 851684
e-mail: ann.burt@lineone.net
A charming Georgian house offering stylish accommodation with six guest rooms. Private parking.   255

Whidborne Manor, Ashill, Bishopsteignton, Devon TQ14 9PY

Tel: 01626 870177
e-mail: nicky.dykes@btinternet.com
Cosy 15th-century thatched cottage, attractively furnished, with many original beams and timbers throughout. Two double rooms. Evening meals by arrangement.   201

Food and Drink

Collingwood Hotel, Braddons Hill Road East, Torquay, Devon TQ1 1HB

Tel: 01803 293448 Fax: 01626 400221
e-mail: bookings@collingwood-hotel.co.uk
An elegant Georgian Hotel located a short distance from the sea front. Regular themed breaks.   256

The Plough Inn, Fore Street, Ipplepen, Devon TQ12 5RP

Tel: 01808 812118 Fax: 01803 814278
website: www.ipplepen.com
An attractive old inn with a great deal of character. Good range of drinks and home-cooked food.   259

The Steam Packet Inn, St. Peter's Quay, Totnes, Devon TQ9 5EN

Tel: 01803 863880 Fax: 01803 862754
Elegant riverside inn with open plan lounge bar and elegant, conservatory Restaurant. Ten en-suite guest bedrooms. Private river moorings available.   261

The Welcome Stranger, Liverton, Nr. Newton Abbott, Devon TQ12 6JA

Tel: 01626 821224
e-mail: welcomestranger@talk21.com
A friendly, country pub offering a good variety of sensibly priced, home-cooked food. Two twin en-suite rooms.   260

Whidborne Manor, Ashill, Bishopsteignton, Devon TQ14 9PY

Tel: 01626 870177
e-mail: nicky.dykes@btinternet.com
Cosy 15th-century thatched cottage, attractively furnished, with many original beams and timbers throughout. Two double rooms. Evening meals by arrangement.   201

Warren Golf Club

Dawlish Warren, Devon EX7 0NF
Tel: **01626 862255 Fax: 01626 888005**

If, besides golf, you can list your recreational activities as bird watching, train spotting and naturalism (that's the one in which you keep your clothes ON), then a visit to Warren will probably make you think you have died and gone to Heaven.

Not only is this the only true links course in south Devon - it has been referred to, and with some reason, as the "St Andrews of the South" - but is situated on a narrow peninsula, in truth not much more than a wide spit of land, between the sea and the estuary of the River Exe.

The area is an internationally-renowned wildlife conservation area, flat as you might expect, with the usual enemies on a links course, such as narrow fairways, gorse, heather, naturally-occurring bunkers, the odd sandhill, a none-too-friendly wind and the occasional train. This being Dawlish, the coastal railway line is never that far away, although far enough not to disturb the peace, except on the 18th.

This last hole is exceptional in that, from the white markers, the tee is on an island when the tide is in, and players have to cross a little bridge to get to it. It shares a fairway with the first and the green nestles below the Paddington-Penzance West of England main line.

The other hole which will burn itself onto the memory is the seventh, which tempts you to play across a bay on the estuary, but slightly too far right lands you among the bucket-and-spade brigade on the beach.

Sec/Manager:	Tim Aggett
Professional:	Darren Prowse
Directions:	1½ miles northeast of Dawlish centre. From centre take Exeter Road (A379). After ¾ mile turn right into Warren Road. The entrance is on the right, signed, after 1¼ miles.
Date Founded:	1892
Type of Course:	Links
No of Holes:	18
Length:	5965 yds (5506 mtrs)
Par:	69
SSS:	69
Green Fees:	Weekdays: £21.50; Weekends/ Bank Holidays: £24.50
Visitors:	Welcome: Contact Club in Advance. No restrictions. Handicap Certificates

Societies:	Welcome: Contact Club in Advance
Facilities:	Putting Green, Club Hire, Trolley Hire, Bar, Restaurant

Accommodation, Food and Drink

Reference numbers below refer to detailed information provided in section 2

Accommodation

Babbacombe Hall Hotel, 17 Manor Road, Babbacombe, Torquay, Devon TQ1 3JX

Tel: 01803 325668 Fax: 01803 325668
Victorian seaside hotel with six en-suite rooms. Bar and restaurant open to residents only. 253

Brunswick House, 5 Brunswick Street, Teignmouth, Devon TQ14 8AE

Tel: 01626 774102
e-mail: peterhockings@hotmail.com
Bed and breakfast housed within Victorian terrace just 100 metres from sea front. Spacious accommodation with eight, en-suite guest rooms. 212

Chimneys of Starcross, Starcross, Nr. Exeter, Devon EX6 8PA

Tel: 01626 890813
A characterful, detached house situated overlooking the Exe estuary. Built in 1888, many of the original features have been preserved. Seven rooms with five en-suite. 202

Collingwood Hotel, Braddons Hill Road East, Torquay, Devon TQ1 1HB

Tel: 01803 293448 Fax: 01626 400221
e-mail: bookings@collingwood-hotel.co.uk
An elegant Georgian Hotel located a short distance from the sea front. Regular themed breaks. 256

The Devon Arms, Kenton, Nr. Exeter, Devon EX6 8LD

Tel: 01626 890213 Fax: 01626 891678
e-mail: devon.arms@ukgateway.net
Next to Powderham Castle, The Exeter Arms is a family-run hostelry serving home-cooked food. Six en-suite rooms available for bed and breakfast. 254

Exmouth View Hotel, St. Albans Road, Babbacombe, Torquay, Devon TQ1 3LQ

Tel: 0800 7817817/01803 327307 Fax: 01803 329967
e-mail: relax@exmouth-view.co.uk
website: www.exmouth-view.co.uk
A modern hotel offering comfortable accommodation at an affordable price. Licensed bar and restaurant.250

Langstone Cliff Hotel, Dawlish, Devon EX7 0NA

Tel: 01626 868000 Fax: 01626 868006
e-mail: reception@langstone-hotel.co.uk
One of Dorset's premier hotels in superb location overlooking the sea. Excellent facilities including tennis, practice golf and indoor and outdoor pools. Popular restaurant. 237

Shell Cove House, Old Teignmouth Road, Dawlish, Devon EX7 0NJ

Tel: 01626 862523 Fax: 01626 862523
A Georgian house converted into a number of self-contained, self-catering apartments. Also a luxurious cottage available. Excellent facilities on site.   251
Sir Walter Raleigh,

22 High Street, East Budleigh, Devon EX9 7EB

Tel: 01395 442510
A charming, traditional, thatched building serving fine local ales and freshly prepared food. Bed and breakfast accommodation available.   252

The Welcome Stranger, Liverton, Nr. Newton Abbott, Devon TQ12 6JA

Tel: 01626 821224
e-mail: welcomestranger@talk21.com
A friendly, country pub offering a good variety of sensibly priced, home-cooked food. Two twin en-suite rooms.   260

Whidborne Manor, Ashill, Bishopsteignton, Devon TQ14 9PY

Tel: 01626 870177
e-mail: nicky.dykes@btinternet.com
Cosy 15th-century thatched cottage, attractively furnished, with many original beams and timbers throughout. Two double rooms. Evening meals by arrangement.   201

Woodlands Hotel, 51 Barnpark Road, Teignmouth, Devon TQ14 8PN

Tel: 01626 773094
Delightful Regency-style hotel retaining a great deal of period elegance. Comfortable guest rooms with many having superb views out to sea. Half- or Full-board available.   221

Food and Drink

Collingwood Hotel, Braddons Hill Road East, Torquay, Devon TQ1 1HB

Tel: 01803 293448 Fax: 01626 400221
e-mail: bookings@collingwood-hotel.co.uk
An elegant Georgian Hotel located a short distance from the sea front. Regular themed breaks.   256

The Devon Arms, Kenton, Nr. Exeter, Devon EX6 8LD

Tel: 01626 890213 Fax: 01626 891678
e-mail: devon.arms@ukgateway.net
Next to Powderham Castle, The Exeter Arms is a family-run hostelry serving home-cooked food. Six en-suite rooms available for bed and breakfast.   254

Langstone Cliff Hotel, Dawlish, Devon EX7 0NA

Tel: 01626 868000 Fax: 01626 868006
e-mail: reception@langstone-hotel.co.uk
One of Dorset's premier hotels in superb location overlooking the sea. Excellent facilities including tennis, practice golf and indoor and outdoor pools. Popular restaurant.   237

Sir Walter Raleigh, 22 High Street, East Budleigh, Devon EX9 7EB

Tel: 01395 442510
A charming, traditional, thatched building serving fine local ales and freshly prepared food. Bed and breakfast accommodation available.   252

The Welcome Stranger, Liverton, Nr. Newton Abbott, Devon TQ12 6JA

Tel: 01626 821224
e-mail: welcomestranger@talk21.com
A friendly, country pub offering a good variety of sensibly priced, home-cooked food. Two twin en-suite rooms.   260

Woodbury Park Golf Club

Woodbury Castle, Woodbury, Devon EX5 1JJ
Tel: 01395 233382 Fax: 01395 234701

Nigel Mansell provided an exciting finish or two in his heyday as a Formula 1 racing driver, so it is little surprise that the golf course he owns just outside Exeter also provides a spectacular finale.

It is said that if you leave a course's signature hole until the 18th, it ingrains itself on the golfer's memory indelibly, and that's precisely what will happen at Woodbury Park. Although only a par three of about 170 yards off the back tees, the hole - aptly named "The Splash" - has a green almost entirely surrounded by water and is set in a natural amphitheatre slap-bang next to the clubhouse, so everyone can watch you landing in the water, or missing that 'gimme' putt from two feet. Rather surprisingly, this island hole is stroke index 18, which is an indication of what the rest of the course offers.

Once you have finished gawping at the former world champion's Grand Prix cars in the reception area of the clubhouse, you are confronted with a J Hamilton Stutt-designed championship course of 6,300 yards off the yellows, a tree-lined parkland track set in 400 acres of glorious countryside. It's long and it's tough, with plenty of

No of Holes: 9
Length: 2796 yds (2582 mtrs)
Par: 35
SSS: None
Green Fees: Weekdays: £12; Weekends/
Bank Holidays: £14

Accommodation, Food and Drink

Reference numbers below refer to detailed
information provided in section 2

Accommodation

water hazards and dog-legs, but with forgivingly-large greens to try and hit.

Any course whose first two holes measure more than 1,000 yards and which expects your score to still be in single fingers as you stand on the third tee is really throwing down the gauntlet!

Sec/Manager: Phil Holly
Professional: Allan Richard
Directions: 7½ miles southeast of Exeter
City centre. From M5 junction
30 take the A3052 (Sidmouth).
After 5 miles turn right, just
before the Half Way Inn onto
the B3180 (Exmouth). The
entrance is on the right hand
side after 1½ miles.
Visitors: Welcome: Contact club in
advance. No restrictions
Societies: Welcome: Contact club in
advance. No restrictions
Facilities: Putting Green, Chipping
Green, Club Hire, Trolley Hire,
Buggy Hire, Bar, Restaurant,
Driving Range

Oaks Course

Date Founded: 1982
Type of Course: Parkland, Heathland
No of Holes: 18
Length: 6870 yds (6341 mtrs)
Par: 72
SSS: 73
Green Fees: Weekdays: £30; Weekends/
Bank Holidays: £40

Acorns Course

Date Founded: 1982
Type of Course: Parkland, Heathland

**Alexandra Lodge Holiday Apartments,
Grafton Road, Torquay, South Devon TQ1 1QJ**
Tel: 01803 213465 Fax: 01803 390933
e-mail: almes@fsbdial.co.uk
website: www.alexandra-lodge.co.uk
Lovely detached Georgian villa in secluded grounds
offering seven self-catering apartments sleeping
between two and eight people.   249

**The Anchorage Guest House, 170 New Road,
Brixham, Devon TQ5 8DA**
Tel/Fax: 01803 852960
A comfortable, friendly guest house with a fabulous
award-winning garden. Seven guest rooms.   257

**Babbacombe Hall Hotel, 17 Manor Road,
Babbacombe, Torquay, Devon TQ1 3JX**
Tel: 01803 325668 Fax: 01803 325668
Victorian seaside hotel with six en-suite rooms. Bar
and restaurant open to residents only.   253

**Brunswick House, 5 Brunswick Street,
Teignmouth, Devon TQ14 8AE**
Tel: 01626 774102
e-mail: peterhockings@hotmail.com
Bed and breakfast housed within Victorian terrace just
100 metres from sea front. Spacious accommodation
with eight, en-suite guest rooms.   212

**Chuckle Too, Blackawton, Totnes,
Devon TQ9 7BG**
Tel: 01803 712455
Modern, self-catering cottage offering cosy cottage-style accommodation. Sleeps up to three adults. Very
well equipped.   262

**Collingwood Hotel, Braddons Hill Road East,
Torquay, Devon TQ1 1HB**
Tel: 01803 293448 Fax: 01626 400221
e-mail: bookings@collingwood-hotel.co.uk
An elegant Georgian Hotel located a short distance
from the sea front. Regular themed breaks.   256

**The Halfway Inn, Sidmouth Road, Aylesbeare,
Devon EX5 2JP**
Tel: 01395 232273 Fax: 01395 516398
Former coaching inn offering a fine selection of
refreshments with very extensive food menu. Four
guest rooms for bed and breakfast, two en-suite. 243

Hole Mill, Branscombe, Seaton, Devon EX12 3BX

Tel: 01297 680314
website: www.users.globalnet.co.uk/~branscombe/
hole1.htm
Former working watermill, located in pretty valley, converted into a charming house on many levels. Surrounded by colourful gardens. 3 guest rooms. 267

Marlborough Hotel, The Esplanade, Sidmouth, Devon EX10 8AR

Tel: 01395 513320
Super sea front property just a stone's throw from the beach. Popular pub and hotel, offering fine food all day. 18 en-suite rooms. 224

22 High Street, East Budleigh, Devon EX9 7EB

Tel: 01395 442510
A charming, traditional, thatched building serving fine local ales and freshly prepared food. Bed and breakfast accommodation available. 252

The Steam Packet Inn, St. Peter's Quay, Totnes, Devon TQ9 5EN

Tel: 01803 863880 Fax: 01803 862754
Elegant riverside inn with open plan lounge bar and elegant, conservatory Restaurant. Ten en-suite guest bedrooms. Private river moorings available. 261

The Welcome Stranger, Liverton, Nr. Newton Abbott, Devon TQ12 6JA

Tel: 01626 821224
e-mail: welcomestranger@talk21.com
A friendly, country pub offering a good variety of sensibly priced, home-cooked food. Two twin en-suite rooms. 260

Westbury, 51 New Road, Brixham, Devon TQ5 8NL

Tel/Fax: 01803 851684
e-mail: ann.burt@lineone.net
A charming Georgian house offering stylish accommodation with six guest rooms. Private parking. 255

Woodlands Hotel, 51 Barnpark Road, Teignmouth, Devon TQ14 8PN

Tel: 01626 773094
Delightful Regency-style hotel retaining a great deal of period elegance. Comfortable guest rooms with many having superb views out to sea. Half- or Full-board available. 221

Food and Drink

Collingwood Hotel, Braddons Hill Road East, Torquay, Devon TQ1 1HB

Tel: 01803 293448 Fax: 01626 400221
e-mail: bookings@collingwood-hotel.co.uk
An elegant Georgian Hotel located a short distance from the sea front. Regular themed breaks. 256

The Halfway Inn, Sidmouth Road, Aylesbeare, Devon EX5 2JP

Tel: 01395 232273 Fax: 01395 516398
Former coaching inn offering a fine selection of refreshments with very extensive food menu. Four guest rooms for bed and breakfast, two en-suite. 243

Marlborough Hotel, The Esplanade, Sidmouth, Devon EX10 8AR

Tel: 01395 513320
Super sea front property just a stone's throw from the beach. Popular pub and hotel, offering fine food all day. 18 en-suite rooms. 224

The Plough Inn, Fore Street, Ipplepen, Devon TQ12 5RP

Tel: 01808 812118 Fax: 01803 814278
website: www.ipplepen.com
An attractive old inn with a great deal of character. Good range of drinks and home-cooked food. 259

Sir Walter Raleigh, 22 High Street, East Budleigh, Devon EX9 7EB

Tel: 01395 442510
A charming, traditional, thatched building serving fine local ales and freshly prepared food. Bed and breakfast accommodation available. 252

The Steam Packet Inn, St. Peter's Quay, Totnes, Devon TQ9 5EN

Tel: 01803 863880 Fax: 01803 862754
Elegant riverside inn with open plan lounge bar and elegant, conservatory Restaurant. Ten en-suite guest bedrooms. Private river moorings available. 261

The Welcome Stranger, Liverton, Nr. Newton Abbott, Devon TQ12 6JA

Tel: 01626 821224
e-mail: welcomestranger@talk21.com
A friendly, country pub offering a good variety of sensibly priced, home-cooked food. Two twin en-suite rooms. 260

Wrangaton Golf Club

Golf Links Road, Wrangaton, South Brent, Devon TQ10 9HJ

Tel: 01364 73229

If ever there was golfing version of the old saying, 'It was a game of two halves,' then Wrangaton epitomises it. The course lies within the boundaries of the Dartmoor National Park and is highly unusual in that the front nine holes are moorland and the back nine are parkland, so its almost like getting two for the price of one.

Strangely, the club had flourished as a nineholer - the moorland section sat beneath the brooding presence of Ugborough Beacon - for more than 90 years before having the opportunity to buy the 50 acres of parkland that now houses the back nine, and which were designed by Donald Steele in the late 1980s.

You still get those distant sea views and some rugged countryside, but also encounter more natural hazards, these being, in this case, grazing sheep, meandering ponies and the occasional swooping buzzard looking for a tasty tit-bit. For those who like their golf in the raw, Wrangaton's the place to be.

The word unique is often casually tossed around to describe golf courses, but it is perhaps more apt in the case of Wrangaton than most others. There are so many memorable holes, each with something of interest and challenge, that it is almost unfair to pick out any, but the third, with its wall and stream, and the ninth, with its lofty position overlooking the course, are highlights of the front nine. As the club secretary once told me, you really have to play it to see it, and it takes some believing.

Sec/Manager:	Graham Williams
Professional:	Adrian Whitehead
Directions:	3 miles northeast of Ivybridge. From centre take Exeter Road (B3213, Bittaford). After 3½ miles at Wrangaton turn left into Green Lane. At staggered cross roads straight on into Golf Links Road. The entrance is after 300 yds.
Date Founded:	1895
Type of Course:	Moorland, Parkland
No of Holes:	18
Length:	6983 yds (5615 mtrs)
Par:	70
SSS:	69
Green Fees:	Weekdays: £18; Weekends/ Bank Holidays: £18
Visitors:	Welcome: Contact Club in Advance. No Restrictions
Societies:	Welcome: Contact Club in Advance. Unable to play Wednesday
Facilities:	Practice Area, Club Hire, Trolley Hire, Buggy Hire, Bar, Restaurant

Accommodation, Food and Drink

Reference numbers below refer to detailed information provided in section 2

Accommodation

Chuckle Too, Blackawton, Totnes, Devon TQ9 7BG

Tel: 01803 712455
Modern, self-catering cottage offering cosy cottage-style accommodation. Sleeps up to three adults. Very well equipped. 262

The Laurels, Huckworthy Bridge, Yelverton, Devon PL20 6LP

Tel: 01822 853622
Charming old cottage in riverside setting, recently restored and converted into a self-catering cottage and private home, in which bed and breakfast is available. Ideal holiday base. 239

The Steam Packet Inn, St. Peter's Quay, Totnes, Devon TQ9 5EN

Tel: 01803 863880 Fax: 01803 862754
Elegant riverside inn with open plan lounge bar and elegant, conservatory Restaurant. Ten en-suite guest bedrooms. Private river moorings available. 261

The Welcome Stranger, Liverton, Nr. Newton Abbott, Devon TQ12 6JA

Tel: 01626 821224
e-mail: welcomestranger@talk21.com
A friendly, country pub offering a good variety of sensibly priced, home-cooked food. Two twin en-suite rooms. 260

Yealm Holidays, 8 Whittingham Road, Collaton Park, Yealmpton, Plymouth, Devon PL8 2NF

Tel: 01752 872712 Fax: 01752 873173
e-mail: info@yealm-holidays.co.uk
website: www.yealm-holidays.co.uk
Selection of cottages, houses and flats all situated around the estuary of the River Yealm, sleeping between two and nine. Pets welcome in some properties. 265

Food and Drink

Old Mother Hubbards, 35 Market Street, Yealmpton, Devon PL8 2EA

Tel: 01752 880085
Thought to be the original home of Old Mother Hubbard, as immortalised in the traditional nursery rhyme. Now a cosy and intimate restaurant open for a la carte lunches and evening meals. Ring for opening details.

The Steam Packet Inn, St. Peter's Quay, Totnes, Devon TQ9 5EN

Tel: 01803 863880 Fax: 01803 862754
Elegant riverside inn with open plan lounge bar and elegant, conservatory Restaurant. Ten en-suite guest bedrooms. Private river moorings available. 261

The Walkhampton Inn, Walkhampton, Nr. Yelverton, Devon PL20 6JY

Tel: 01822 855556 Fax: 01822 855556
e-mail: info@walkhamptoninn.co.uk
Historic establishment, popular in the area for serving a good range of beer and traditional pub fayre. Two guest rooms both of which are en-suite. 238

The Welcome Stranger, Liverton, Nr. Newton Abbott, Devon TQ12 6JA

Tel: 01626 821224
e-mail: welcomestranger@talk21.com
A friendly, country pub offering a good variety of sensibly priced, home-cooked food. Two twin en-suite rooms. 260

Yelverton Golf Club

Golf Links road, Yelverton, Devon PL20 6BN
Tel: 01822 852824 Fax: 01822 854869

Nestling in the south west corner of Dartmoor is yet another Devonian delight, the home of the South West of England Open Winter Foursomes. It is said that no matter what the weather throws at it, this competition simply goes on, and that speaks volumes for this moorland track sitting 400 feet up and offering far-reaching views across the tors on one side, and away to Cornwall on the other.

But the Foursomes aren't held at Yelverton so that the players can admire the vistas, rather that it tests them with tight fairway lies and fast greens, heather and gorse everywhere waiting to swallow wayward shots, a couple of natural meandering streams - leats, as they're known in these parts - and the occasional sunken mine workings.

The advice here is to take advantage of the relatively gentle front nine, because if you don't make your score there, Heaven help you, because then you face what is generally regarded as one of the toughest back nines in the county.

Standing on the 10th tee, you face a dreaded mile at 10, 11, 12 and 13, and anybody coming out of that lot at par ought to be playing the game for money.

At 10, the stream runs diagonally across the fairway; the par 5 11th has a 195-yard carry over water from the tee; the 12th, a par 3, has a green surrounded by five bunkers; and the 13th, 440 yards of slightly uphill par 4, has a 20ft deep sunken mine shaft in the fairway - with sand in the bottom. Not for the faint-hearted!

Sec/Manager:	S. Barnes
Professional:	T. McSherry
Directions:	8 miles north of Plymouth City the centre. From the Manadon junction on the A38 take the A386 (Yelverton, Tavistock).

After 5¾ miles, but before Yelverton, turn left into Golf Links Road. The entrance is signed.

Date Founded:	1904
Type of Course:	Moorland
No of Holes:	18
Length:	6351 yds (5862 mtrs)
Par:	71
SSS:	71
Green Fees:	Weekdays: £30; Weekends/ Bank Holidays: £40
Visitors:	Welcome: Contact Club in Advance. Handicap Certificates
Societies:	Welcome: Contact Club in Advance
Facilities:	Practice Area, Putting Green, Chipping Green, Driving Range, Club Hire, Trolley Hire, Bar, Restaurant

Accommodation, Food and Drink

Reference numbers below refer to detailed
information provided in section 2

Accommodation

The Bridge Inn, Bridge Street, Hatherleigh, Nr. Okehampton, Devon EX20 3JA

Tel: 01837 810947 Fax: 01837 810614
The Bridge Inn dates from the 16th century and is one of the oldest buildings in the area. Cosy interior with bar and separate restaurant. Six en-suite guest rooms of varying sizes. 231

The Carpenters Arms, Metherell, Nr. Callington, Cornwall PL17 8BJ

Tel: 01579 350242 Fax: 01579 350242
A picturesque Cornish pub with friendly and welcoming service. Wide-ranging menu of home-cooked bar meals and snacks. 117

The Coffee Pot, 14 St. James Street, Okehampton, Devon EX20 1DA

Tel: 01837 52988
Traditional coffee shop, open daily serving early breakfast, coffee, lunches and afternoon teas. Conveniently located close to the town centre. 233

The Halfway House Inn, Grenofen, Tavistock, Devon PL19 9ER

Tel: 01822 612960 Fax: 01822 617697
A large, sprawling black and white 16th-century building with friendly atmosphere. Excellent reputation for high quality food with two restaurants serving an a la carte menu. Four guest rooms. 206

The Laurels, Huckworthy Bridge, Yelverton, Devon PL20 6LP

Tel: 01822 853622

Charming old cottage in riverside setting, recently restored and converted into a self-catering cottage and private home, in which bed and breakfast is available. Ideal holiday base. 239

Lifton Hall Hotel, Lifton, Devon PL16 0DR

Tel: 01566 784863 Fax: 01566 784770
e-mail mail@liftonhall.co.uk
Traditional 250-year old Country House hotel in peaceful village location with ten en-suite rooms. Formal restaurant and a bistro, both specialising in local fish. 240

The Old Coach House, Ottery, Tavistock, Devon PL19 8NS

Tel: 01822 617515 Fax: 01822 617515
e-mail eddie@coachhouseone.supanet.com
Old coach house which was substantially renovated in 1989 to create a delightful hotel and restaurant. Comfortable accommodation and superb a la carte restaurant. 236

Pressland Country House Hotel, Hatherleigh, Nr. Okehampton, Devon EX20 3LW

Tel: 01837 810871 Fax: 01837 810303
e-mail graham@presslandhouse.co.uk
website www.presslandhouse.co.uk
Victorian manor house surrounded by lawns and woodland. Five spacious guest rooms, most with en-suite facilities, and superb residents' restaurant. 230

Tavistock Arms, Fore Street, Gunnislake, Cornwall PL18 9BN

Tel: 01822 832217
Traditional, country pub located directly on the Devon/Cornwall border. Food is served all day. Bed and breakfast accommodation available. 118

The Torrs, Belstone, Okehampton, Devon EX20 1QZ

Tel: 01837 840689
Small, cosy pub, popular with locals and visitors. Refreshing ales and tasty, home-cooked meals. Bed and breakfast accommodation available with three en-suite guest rooms. 232

Food and Drink

The Bridge Inn, Bridge Street, Hatherleigh, Nr. Okehampton, Devon EX20 3JA

Tel: 01837 810947 Fax: 01837 810614
The Bridge Inn dates from the 16th century and is one of the oldest buildings in the area. Cosy interior with bar and separate restaurant. Six en-suite guest rooms of varying sizes. 231

The Carpenters Arms, Metherell, Nr. Callington, Cornwall PL17 8BJ

Tel: 01579 350242 Fax: 01579 350242
A picturesque Cornish pub with friendly and welcoming service. Wide-ranging menu of home-cooked bar meals and snacks. 117

The Halfway House Inn, Grenofen, Tavistock, Devon PL19 9ER

Tel: 01822 612960 Fax: 01822 617697
A large, sprawling black and white 16th-century building with friendly atmosphere. Excellent

reputation for high quality food with two restaurants serving an a la carte menu. Four guest rooms. 206

Lifton Hall Hotel, Lifton, Devon PL16 0DR

Tel: 01566 784863 Fax: 01566 784770
e-mail mail@liftonhall.co.uk
Traditional 250-year old Country House hotel in peaceful village location with ten en-suite rooms. Formal restaurant and a bistro, both specialising in local fish. 240

The Old Coach House, Ottery, Tavistock, Devon PL19 8NS

Tel: 01822 617515 Fax: 01822 617515
e-mail eddie@coachhouse.supanet.com
Old coach house which was substantially renovated in 1989 to create a delightful hotel and restaurant. Comfortable accommodation and superb a la carte restaurant. 236

Old Mother Hubbards, 35 Market Street, Yealmpton, Devon PL8 2EA

Tel: 01752 880085
Thought to be the original home of Old Mother Hubbard, as immortalised in the traditional nursery rhyme. Now a cosy and intimate restaurant open for a la carte lunches and evening meals. Ring for opening details.

Royal Standard Inn, Mary Tavy, Nr. Tavistock, Devon PL19 9QB

Tel: 01822 810289 Fax: 01822 810615
Former coaching inn with an atmosphere of character and charm. The inn claims to serve the best beer in the area while the food comprises a good selection of traditional meals and snacks. 235

Tavistock Arms, Fore Street, Gunnislake, Cornwall PL18 9BN

Tel: 01822 832217
Traditional, country pub located directly on the Devon/Cornwall border. Food is served all day. Bed and breakfast accommodation available. 118

The Torrs, Belstone, Okehampton, Devon EX20 1QZ

Tel: 01837 840689
Small, cosy pub, popular with locals and visitors. Refreshing ales and tasty, home-cooked meals. Bed and breakfast accommodation available with three en-suite guest rooms. 232

Victorian Pantry, Museum Courtyard, West Street, Okehampton, Devon EX20 1HQ

Tel: 01837 53988
Housed within an historic building not far from the Dartmoor Museum. Open daily serving a good selection of drinks, home-cooked cakes and hot meals. 229

The Walkhampton Inn, Walkhampton, Nr. Yelverton, Devon PL20 6JY

Tel: 01822 855556 Fax: 01822 855556
e-mail info@walkhamptoninn.co.uk
Historic establishment, popular in the area for serving a good range of beer and traditional pub fayre. Two guest rooms both of which are en-suite. 238

DORSET

When I first ventured nervously south from the foothills of the Pennines to what seemed then like the Mediterranean climes of Bournemouth, conspiratorial colleagues would continually mutter the phrase, "Dorset smothers ambition," giving me a nudge and a wink for good measure. I did tend to think this a little odd at the time as, histori-

cally, Bournemouth had always been in Hampshire, and the boundary had moved only a couple of years before. Indeed, when I got to know the real locals, they insisted they were "Hampshire Hogs", and their sporting Mecca was Bournemouth's Dean Park cricket ground. While they may remain "Hampshire Hogs" at heart, physically they are now part of Dorset, and their town's metamorphosis from sleepy, genteel seaside resort to vibrant and trendy magnet for the young has both added to and highlighted the diversity of the county. It does, however, soon become clear how true that old saying is once you start getting to know this lovely county.

Bournemouth Beach and Pier

As might be expected, most of the Dorset's golf courses are peppered around the Poole, Bournemouth and Christchurch conurbation, with something like 15 clubs within a half-hour's drive from Bournemouth town centre. Like the resorts themselves, the courses are a mixture of the old and the new, with **Highcliffe Castle** in the east, Bournemouth's **Queens Park** and **Meyrick**, to **Ferndown** north of the town, and Broadstone and Parkstone in the west, in the vanguard for the established. Lining up on the newcomers' side, there is the big and modern **Canford Magna** complex, **Crane Valley**, **Dudsbury**, **Bulbury Woods** and **Ferndown Forest**, all of which have sprung up in the past 10 years or so as the 1990s golfing boom reached its peak. Holidaying golfers will find that most of these clubs welcome visitors and, although the out-of-town courses might be quieter, the two on the fringes of Bournemouth town centre - **Meyrick Park** and **Queen's Park** - offer excellent golf at about half the price, reflecting their municipal history.

As befits a resort which has been variously described as "the next coolest city on the planet" - by Harpers & Queen, no less - and "Britain's Baywatch" because of its miles of glorious beach and the female lifeguards that patrol it, Bournemouth has plenty of apres-golf entertainment, and probably the largest collection of ethnic restaurants in the country, outside the capital. On its western flank, the much older port of Poole has very nearly as much to offer, not least of its

attractions being its vast harbour, reputed to be the second biggest natural harbour in the world, which in turn houses the National Trust's Brownsea Island, made famous by Baden-Powell, who launched the Scout movement there, and now one of the few remaining sanctuaries of Britain's red squirrel population. Talking of squirrels, there are huge numbers of the grey variety living in the area's array of pines, so it might well be worth checking on any local rules referring to golf balls squirrelled away!

Brownsea Island

To the east, nestling gently between the bustle of town and the peace of the New Forest, is the charming little town of Christchurch where, even today, it is possible to find life lived at a slightly less hectic pace.

This is where the Rivers Avon and Stour meet, and there is also the splendid Priory to investigate. Seafood lovers might also meander along to Mudeford quay, where fishing boats still land their catches, and where you can taste crab as fresh as it comes. Away from this large conurbation, a different Dorset emerges, a Dorset redolent with easily-conjured-up images of Thomas Hardy novels. This is hardly surprising, as Hardy, rural Dorset born and bred, drew extensively not only on the characteristics of the rustic population of the 1800s, but also on the towns and villages of the county. His "Casterbridge" is, of course, Dorchester as it was, and great swathes of Dorset, from Blandford through to Weymouth, are now ingrained in the county's heritage as Hardy Country. How appropriate it seems that, as Hardy's life was drawing to a close in the 1920s, Dorchester's golf club - **Came Down** - was at the centre of the embryonic moves to get Britain and the USA to play each other in a golf tournament, thanks to the efforts of one Samuel Ryder. History and the county town seem to go hand in hand.

But then, history springs out at you around almost every bend in the country roads that criss-cross the rolling fields, be it from the old hill top town of Shaftesbury - home of Gold Hill, made

famous as the steep, cobbled street in the Hovis TV advertisements of yesteryear - to the ancient and historic town of Sherborne, with its Abbey dating back almost 1,300 years, which was once the Mother Cathedral for the whole of the south west; and Sherborne New Castle, a pretty unappealing sight from the outside, thanks to Sir Walter Raleigh, who had it built, but somewhat more splendid inside. You want more history? How about Tolpuddle, home of the famous martyrs; the stunning ruins of Corfe Castle; or Cloud's Hill, the final home of one TE Lawrence (of Arabia), at Moreton, who was buried in the village graveyard after his fatal motorbike crash in the 1930s.

Gold Hill, Shaftesbury

Away from the main centres of population, golf courses are a bit thin on the ground, but there are those such as **Ashley Wood**, east of Blandford; **Dorset Heights**, north west of the same town at Belchalwell; the developing **Rushmore Park** at the delightfully-named Tollard Royal, set on Cranborne Chase south east of Shaftesbury; and **Chedington Court**, tucked up near the Somerset border north of Beaminster, which are all worth a visit, as well as the better-known ones such as **Wareham**, **Weymouth**, and **Bridport & West Dorset**.

If the resorts to the east end of the county have the beaches, the rest of the coastline has the dramatic views and breathtaking scenery. From the Purbeck Hills rising above Swanage, along to the Devon border, there are wild and spectacular cliffscapes, broken only briefly by the golden sweep of sand at Weymouth, and you can walk the whole way, should you so desire, along the South West Coastal Path. If that sounds a bit too energetic, then select the steepish trek out of Lulworth Cove over to the spectacular Durdle Door as one not to be shirked. West of the traditional seaside delights of Weymouth - first made fashionable as a resort by the royal patronage of George III - are the wildlife treasures of Chesil Bank and the swannery at Abbotsbury, home to hundreds upon hundreds of the majestic birds, and a particular must if you are thereabouts in early June - the hatching season.

Any visit to Dorset would not be complete without a trip to Lyme Regis. As mentioned elsewhere in this guide, it is worth playing the town's golf course, not only for its views but also because large lumps of it may not be there much longer! Fossil hunting at the base of the

Corfe Castle

cliffs has also been enjoyed here for generations - you are almost guaranteed to find something - but take note of any restrictions. The soft cliff face has become fairly unstable, and some stretches of the coastline may be strictly out of bounds.

Location of Golf Courses

© MAPS IN MINUTES ™ 2001   © Crown Copyright, Ordnance Survey 2001

Ashley Wood Golf Club

Wimbourne Road, Blandford, Forum,
Dorset DT11 9HN

Tel: 01258 452253 Fax: 01258 450590

Sec/Manager:	Nigel Stone
Professional:	John Simmonds
Directions:	1¼ miles east of Blandford Forum. From centre take Damory St then Wimborne Rd (A3082, Wimborne). The entrance is on the left hand side after 1¼ mile.
Date Founded:	1896
Type of Course:	Downland
No of Holes:	18
Length:	6236 yds (5759 mtrs)
Par:	70
SSS:	70
Green Fees:	Weekdays: £26 (day); Weekends/Bank Holidays: £28.50
Visitors:	Welcome: Contact Club in Advance. Before 11.00 am at weekends Handicap Certificates
Societies:	Welcome: Contact Club in Advance
Facilities:	Putting Green, Chipping Green, Trolley Hire, Buggy Hire, Bar, Restaurant

Accommodation, Food and Drink

Reference numbers below refer to detailed information provided in section 2

Accommodation

Cleff House, Brookmans Valley, Iwerne Minster, Blandford Forum, Dorset D11 8NG

Tel: 01747 811129 Fax: 01747 811112
Somewhere special, a unique house offering style, comfort, good food, superb views. Set in nine acres of a beautiful valley, yet within the bounds of the picturesque village. Ideal for a truly relaxing break.

The Greyhound, North Street, Winterbourne Kingston, Blandford Forum, Dorset D11 9AZ

Tel: 01929 471332 Fax: 01929 427610
website: www.greyhoundinnwk.co.uk
Traditional, country inn with spacious, comfortable interior. Selection of real ales and tasty home-cooked food. Four en-suite rooms. 304

The Sheaf of Arrows, 4 The Square, Cranborne, Dorset BH21 5PR

Tel: 01725 517456
Traditional village hostelry popular with locals and visitors to the area. Choice of real ales and a good selection of sensibly priced meals. Five en-suite rooms. 310

Food and Drink

The Greyhound, North Street, Winterbourne Kingston, Blandford Forum, Dorset D11 9AZ

Tel: 01929 471332 Fax: 01929 427610
website: www.greyhoundinnwk.co.uk
Traditional, country inn with spacious, comfortable interior. Selection of real ales and tasty home-cooked food. Four en-suite rooms. 304

The Mount, 49 Blandford Road, Corfe Mullen, Wimborne, Dorset BH21 3HD

Tel: 01202 693908
With a comfortable, relaxed atmosphere, this pub is popular for its fine ales and tasty meals and snacks. Regular karaoke, live music and pub quizzes. Large rear gardens. 318

The Sheaf of Arrows, 4 The Square, Cranborne, Dorset BH21 5PR

Tel: 01725 517456
Traditional village hostelry popular with locals and visitors to the area. Choice of real ales and a good selection of sensibly priced meals. Five en-suite rooms. 310

The White Hart, Bishops Caundle, Sherborne, Dorset DT9 5ND

Tel: 01963 23301 Fax: 01963 23301
Popular inn serving a full range of traditional meals ranging from bar snacks to a la carte. The bar stocks range of locally brewed real ales.

Winstons Restaurant and Bar, 45 High Street, Sturminster Marshall, Dorset BH21 4AS

Tel: 01258 857211 Fax: 01258 858225
Winstons is a self-contained restaurant and bar adjoining The Churchill Arms pub. Serving a good selection of good quality home-cooked dishes from an a la carte menu, it is open for lunch and dinner, from Wednesday to Saturday, and for Sunday lunch.

Bournemouth and Meyrick Park Golf Club

Central Drive, Meyrick Park, Bournemouth, Dorset BH2 6LH

Tel: 01202 290307, 290862 Fax: 01202 290233

This is a picturesque and undulating municipal parkland course founded in the 1890s, the first munipal course in England. It is centrally located in the resort, not far from the town hall and set in Meyrick Park, part of the former Meyrick Estate.

Mature trees, many of them Bournemouth's famous pines, line the fairways and their dropped needles give many of the fairway edges a softish touch to help you get out of trouble.

Don't be lulled into a false sense of security just because the card shows the opening hole is a par three. It's one of several short-ish testers - 244 yards - and involves driving over a valley to try and hit a pocket-handkerchief green cut into the hillside behind. And how about this for a testimonial: "There is no finer golf hole than the 14th at Meyrick Park." Not my words, but those of Henry Cotton. With that in mind, you can't turn your nose up at this course, owned by the local council but leased by Clubhaus.

The 14th captured Cotton's heart as much for its scenic value as for its test of golf. A par five, but not overlong at 500 yards off the back tees, it dog-legs gently through the trees. Bear in mind before you start that this is not a course where you can smack a tee shot 300 yards and get away with it - it is designed for a far more subtle approach.

Sec/Manager:	Diane Ward
Professional:	David Miles
Directions:	¾ mile north of Bournemouth pier. From the A347 (Wimborne to Christchurch road) turn south into Meyrick Park Crescent, which is 250 yds west of Winton roundabout, then follow into Central Drive. The entrance is on the right hand side after ¾ mile.
Date Founded:	1890

Type of Course: Parkland

No of Holes:	18
Length:	5757 yds (5314 mtrs)
Par:	69
SSS:	68
Green Fees:	Weekdays: £15; Weekends/ Bank Holidays: £16.50
Visitors:	Welcome: Contact Club in Advance. No restrictions
Societies:	Welcome: Contact Club in Advance
Facilities:	Practice Area, Putting Green, Club Hire, Trolley Hire, Restaurant, Hotel and Leisure the centre

Accommodation, Food and Drink

Reference numbers below refer to detailed information provided in section 2

Accommodation

The Anglebury House and Restaurant, 15-17 North Street, Wareham, Dorset BH20 4AB

Tel: 01929 552988 Fax: 01929 554665
e-mail: anglebury@btconnect.com
Guest house accommodation with seven letting rooms, all but one with en-suite facilities. Long-established coffee shop, at one time frequented by Thomas Hardy and T.E. Lawrence (Lawrence of Arabia). Restaurant offers a la carte and fixed price menus.   302

Belvedere Hotel, 14 Bath Road, Bournemouth, Dorset BH1 2EU

Tel: 01202 293336 Fax: 01202 294699
e-mail: enquiries@belvedere-hotel.co.uk
website: www.belvedere-hotel.co.uk
Comfortable, stylish accommodation with a total of 60 en-suite rooms of varying sizes. The restaurant provides elegant dining with a superb a la carte menu. Two bars.   314

Bourne Dene Hotel, 12 Manor Road, Bournemouth, Dorset BH1 3HU

Tel: 01202 553127
e-mail: enquiries@bournedene.co.uk
website: www. bournedene.co.uk
Deceptively large country house hotel, surrounded by landscaped gardens, with fine reputation for comfort and excellent cuisine. 21 en-suite bedrooms.   303

Cobbs Holiday Park, 32 Gordon Road, Highcliffe on Sea, Christchurch, Dorset BH23 5HN

Tel: 01425 273301/275313 Fax: 01425 276090
Long established family-run holiday park in fine location not far from the sea. Selection of nine, mostly six berth, chalets and caravans on an attractive site. Licensed social club, shop, laundrette and children's play area.   312

Manor Farm Caravan Park, East Stoke, Wareham, Dorset BH20 6AW

Tel: 01929 462870 Fax: 01929 462870
Quiet, clean caravan park situated between Wareham and Wool in an area of outstanding natural beauty. Suitable for mobile homes and caravans with seasonal pitches and storage.

San Simeon Hotel, 52 Wimborne Road, Bournemouth, Dorset BH3 7AE

Tel: 01202 551935 Fax: 01202 551935
Small, privately-run bed and breakfast establishment. Eleven en-suite guest rooms, two singles and nine doubles. Licensed bar and restaurant available to guests.

Sunnydene Hotel, 11 Spencer Road, Bournemouth, Dorset BH1 3TE

Tel: 01202 552281
Good-sized, family-run establishment offering comfortable bed and breakfast accommodation in ten guest rooms, mostly en-suite. Evening meals available on request.   316

Food and Drink

The Anglebury House and Restaurant, 15-17 North Street, Wareham, Dorset BH20 4AB

Tel: 01929 552988 Fax: 01929 554665
e-mail: anglebury@btconnect.com
Guest house accommodation with seven letting rooms, all but one with en-suite facilities. Long-established coffee shop, at one time frequented by Thomas Hardy and T.E. Lawrence (Lawrence of Arabia). Restaurant offers a la carte and fixed price menus.   302

Belvedere Hotel, 14 Bath Road, Bournemouth, Dorset BH1 2EU

Tel: 01202 293336 Fax: 01202 294699
e-mail: enquiries@belvedere-hotel.co.uk
website: www.belvedere-hotel.co.uk
Comfortable, stylish accommodation with a total of 60 en-suite rooms of varying sizes. The restaurant provides elegant dining with a superb a la carte menu. Two bars.   314

La Mamma, 51-53 Bridge Street, Christchurch, Dorset BH23 1DY

Tel: 01202 471608 Fax: 01202 471608
website: www.lamamma.co.uk
Popular pizzeria and trattoria offering an Italian experience for all the family. Opened in 1974 by Giuseppe and John Mirco, La Mamma has established a far reaching reputation for serving freshly prepared, authentic dishes. Open lunch time and evening (closed Monday in Winter).

Bridport and West Dorset Golf Club

East Cliff, West Bay, Bridport, Dorset DT6 4EP
Tel: 01308 421095, 422597 Fax: 01308 421095

Sec/Manager:	Peter Riddler
Professional:	David Parsons
Directions:	1¾ miles south of Bridport. At Bothenhampton roundabout on the A35 immediately south of Bridport take Burton Road (B3157, Burton Bradstock). After 1 mile turn right signed West Bay. The entrance is on left hand side after ½ mile.
Date Founded:	1891
Type of Course:	Clifftop, Links
No of Holes:	18
Length:	6028 yds (5564 mtrs)
Par:	73
SSS:	69
Green Fees:	Weekdays: £22; Weekends/ Bank Holidays: £22
Visitors:	Welcome: Contact Club in Advance. No Restrictions
Societies:	Welcome: Contact Club in Advance. Unable to play Mon, Tues, Thurs.
Facilities:	Putting Green, Trolley Hire, Bar, Restaurant

Accommodation, Food and Drink

Reference numbers below refer to detailed information provided in section 2

Accommodation

Chideock House Hotel, Main Street, Chideock, Dorset DT6 6JN

Tel: 01297 489242 Fax: 01297 489184
website: www.chideockhousehotel.com
Picturesque 15th-century house which has been converted into a comfortable, stylish hotel and restaurant. Nine double, en-suite rooms.   309

Coverdale Guest House, Woodmead Road, Lyme Regis, Dorset DT7 3AB

Tel: 01297 442882 Fax: 01297 444673
e-mail: coverdale@tinyworld.co.uk
Spacious non-smoking accommodation enjoying spectacular views to the coast and overlooking woodland. Eight comfortable bedrooms.   306

George Hotel, 65 Dorchester Road, Weymouth, Dorset D4 7TY

Tel: 01305 786170 Fax: 01305 786170
Family-run hotel in prominent location on through road. Eight guest rooms, two singles and six doubles. Evenings meals available. Large car park.

Gorwell Farm Cottages, Abbotsbury, Weymouth, Dorset D3 4JX

Tel: 01305 871401 Fax: 01305 871441
e-mail: mary@gorwellfarm.co.uk

website: www.gorwellfarm.co.uk
Small collection of self-contained cottage-style apartments. Available for week-long holidays or short breaks. 301

Kent House Hotel, Silver Street, Lyme Regis, Dorset DT7 3HT

Tel: 01297 443442 Fax: 01297 444626
e-mail: thekenthouse@talk21.com
Large Victorian property providing bright, airy and well-appointed accommodation. Nine rooms, varying sizes, most en-suite. Restaurant specialises in seafood dishes. 305

Mariners Hotel, Silver Street, Lyme Regis, Dorset DT7 3HS

Tel: 01297 442753 Fax: 01297 442431
e-mail: mariners@ukgateway.net
This former 17th-century coaching inn retains much of its original character, while offering a comfortable and stylish place to stay. 12 en-suite bedrooms, relaxing lounge and cosy restaurant.

Mermaid House, 32 Coombe Street, Lyme Regis, Dorset DT7 3PP

Tel: 01297 445351
website: www.smoothhound.co.uk/hotels/mermaid
Charming, relaxing house in old part of Lyme Regis, three minutes walk from the sea. Superb breakfast using free range produce. Free parking nearby.

Quiet Woman House, Halstock, Dorset BA22 9RX

Tel: 01935 891218
e-mail: quietwomanhouse@ukonline.com
Newly converted bed and breakfast offering high quality accommodation in traditional surroundings. Three guest rooms of varying sizes and two self-catering cottages. Evening meals on request. 315

Springfield House, Woodmead Road, Lyme Regis, Dorset DT7 3LJ

Tel: 01297 443409 Fax: 01297 443685
e-mail: springfield@lymeregis.com
website: www.lymeregis.com/springfield
An elegant Georgian town house, tastefully converted to provide guest house accommodation with five en-suite rooms of varying sizes, all with sea views. Residents benefit from reduced fees at Lyme Regis Golf Club.

Food and Drink

Chideock House Hotel, Main Street, Chideock, Dorset DT6 6JN

Tel: 01297 489242 Fax: 01297 489184
website: www.chideockhousehotel.com
Picturesque 15th-century house which has been converted into a comfortable, stylish hotel and restaurant. Nine double, en-suite rooms. 309

The Crown Inn, 59 West Bay Road, Bridport, Dorset DT6 4AX

Tel: 01308 422037 Fax: 01308 458875
e-mail: enquiries@thecrowninn.org.uk
website: www.thecrowninn.org.uk

Situated midway between Bridport and West Bay, The Crown Inn offers classic Irish hospitality in a traditional English setting. A full menu is always available, and parties can be catered for. Children are welcomed and there is a special children's menu.

Kent House Hotel, Silver Street, Lyme Regis, Dorset DT7 3HT

Tel: 01297 443442 Fax: 01297 444626
e-mail: thekenthouse@talk21.com
Large Victorian property providing bright, airy and well-appointed accommodation. Nine rooms, varying sizes, most en-suite. Restaurant specialises in seafood dishes. 305

Mariners Hotel, Silver Street, Lyme Regis, Dorset DT7 3HS

Tel: 01297 442753 Fax: 01297 442431
e-mail: mariners@ukgateway.net
This former 17th-century coaching inn retains much of its original character, while offering a comfortable and stylish place to stay. 12 en-suite bedrooms, relaxing lounge and cosy restaurant.

The Volunteer Inn, Broad Street, Lyme Regis, Dorset DT7 3QS

Tel: 01297 442214
Historic, town centre free house serving a good selection of real ales, including draught Guinness. Also offers a full range of freshly cooked meals with seafood being a speciality.

Broadstone Golf Club

Wentworth Drive, Broadstone, Dorset BH18 8DQ

Tel: 01202 692595 Fax: 01202 692595

Another undulating and extremely demanding course sat on Dorset's heathland north of Poole, and one which has, in the past, been a haunt of Prime Ministers.

The course was initially designed by George Dunn in 1898 and remoulded by HS Colt 27 years later. The inaugural match was a pretty high-powered affair, featuring Prime Minister AJ Balfour and JH Taylor, who already had two Open titles under his belt, against MP John Penn and James Braid, who was to win the first of his five Open championships three years later. Several photoprints adorn the clubhouse to commemorate the event.

Other Prime Ministers who have enjoyed the panoramic views across 30 miles of countryside that parts of the course afford include Bonar Law, Ramsay McDonald and Sir Winston Churchill.

The spacious fairways are under the control and protection of the Nature Conservancy Council and feature rare heathers and rare species of wildlife. Of further interest are the high tee at the seventh hole and the tumulus on the right of the ninth fairway; both believed to be ancient burial grounds!

To help modern-day golfers to survive, there is a natural freshwater spring - known locally as the "Oakley Arms" - by the 10th fairway, which can provide a refreshing drink in summer. On top of that little lot, there is some excellent golf to be had. Even the best may well be found wanting with challenges presented by the second, seventh, 13th and 16th holes, all 400-yards-plus par fours.

Anyone trying to hit the 415-yard seventh green in regulation will have to make sure they clear a battery of protective bunkers guarding the approach. The 13th, at 440 yards, should be given due respect, and brains rather than brawn might be the percentage approach.

Sec/Manager:	Colin Robinson
Professional:	Nigel Tokeley
Directions:	3¾ miles north of Poole seafront. From seafront take A350 then A3049 leading to A349 (Wimborne). At roundabout in Broadstone turn left onto B3074 (Corfe Mullen). At roundabout after 1 mile turn right into Station Road leading to Wentworth Road. The entrance is after 400 yds.

Date Founded:	1898
Type of Course:	Heathland
No of Holes:	18
Length:	6315 yds (5829 mtrs)
Par:	70
SSS:	70
Green Fees:	Weekdays: £35; Weekends/ Bank Holidays: £45
Visitors:	Welcome: Contact Club in Advance. Handicap Certificates
Societies:	Welcome: Contact Club in

	Advance. Unable to play at weekends
Facilities:	Putting Green, Chipping Green, Driving Range, Club Hire, Trolley Hire, Bar, Restaurant

Accommodation, Food and Drink

Reference numbers below refer to detailed information provided in section 2

Accommodation

Belvedere Hotel, 14 Bath Road, Bournemouth, Dorset BH1 2EU

Tel: 01202 293336 Fax: 01202 294699
e-mail: enquiries@belvedere-hotel.co.uk
website: www.belvedere-hotel.co.uk
Comfortable, stylish accommodation with a total of 60 en-suite rooms of varying sizes. The restaurant provides elegant dining with a superb a la carte menu. Two bars.   314

Bourne Dene Hotel, 12 Manor Road, Bournemouth, Dorset BH1 3HU

Tel: 01202 553127
e-mail: enquiries@bournedene.co.uk
website: www. bournedene.co.uk
Deceptively large country house hotel, surrounded by landscaped gardens, with fine reputation for comfort and excellent cuisine. 21 en-suite bedrooms.   303

Cobbs Holiday Park, 32 Gordon Road, Highcliffe on Sea, Christchurch, Dorset BH23 5HN

Tel: 01425 273301/275313 Fax: 01425 276090
Long established family-run holiday park in fine location not far from the sea. Selection of nine, mostly six berth, chalets and caravans on an attractive site. Licensed social club, shop, laundrette and children's play area.   312

Pear Tree Cottage, 248 Wimborne Road West, Stapehill, Wimborne, Dorset BH21 2DZ

Tel: 01202 890174
An exceptionally pretty, picture-postcard cottage with comfortable bed and breakfast accommodation in three cosy rooms. Superb gardens.   317

San Simeon Hotel, 52 Wimborne Road, Bournemouth, Dorset BH3 7AE

Tel: 01202 551935 Fax: 01202 551935
Small, privately-run bed and breakfast establishment. Eleven en-suite guest rooms, two singles and nine doubles. Licensed bar and restaurant available to guests.

The Sheaf of Arrows, 4 The Square, Cranborne, Dorset BH21 5PR

Tel: 01725 517456
Traditional village hostelry popular with locals and visitors to the area. Choice of real ales and a good selection of sensibly priced meals. Five en-suite rooms.   310

**Sunnydene Hotel, 11 Spencer Road,
Bournemouth, Dorset BH1 3TE**

Tel: 01202 552281
Good-sized, family-run establishment offering
comfortable bed and breakfast accommodation in ten
guest rooms, mostly en-suite. Evening meals available
on request.   316

Food and Drink

**Belvedere Hotel, 14 Bath Road, Bournemouth,
Dorset BH1 2EU**

Tel: 01202 293336 Fax: 01202 294699
e-mail: enquiries@belvedere-hotel.co.uk
website: www.belvedere-hotel.co.uk
Comfortable, stylish accommodation with a total of
60 en-suite rooms of varying sizes. The restaurant
provides elegant dining with a superb a la carte menu.
Two bars.   314

**La Mamma, 51-53 Bridge Street, Christchurch,
Dorset BH23 1DY**

Tel: 01202 471608 Fax: 01202 471608
website: www.lamamma.co.uk
Popular pizzeria and trattoria offering an Italian
experience for all the family. Opened in 1974 by
Giuseppe and John Mirco, La Mamma has established
a far reaching reputation for serving freshly prepared,
authentic dishes. Open lunch time and evening
(closed Monday in Winter).

**The Mount, 49 Blandford Road, Corfe Mullen,
Wimborne, Dorset BH21 3HD**

Tel: 01202 693908
With a comfortable, relaxed atmosphere, this pub is
popular for its fine ales and tasty meals and snacks.
Regular karaoke, live music and pub quizzes. Large
rear gardens.   318

**The Sheaf of Arrows, 4 The Square, Cranborne,
Dorset BH21 5PR**

Tel: 01725 517456
Traditional village hostelry popular with locals and
visitors to the area. Choice of real ales and a good
selection of sensibly priced meals. Five en-suite
rooms.   310

**Winstons Restaurant and Bar, 45 High Street,
Sturminster Marshall, Dorset BH21 4AS**

Tel: 01258 857211 Fax: 01258 858225
Winstons is a self-contained restaurant and bar
adjoining The Churchill Arms pub. Serving a good
selection of good quality home-cooked dishes from
an a la carte menu, it is open for lunch and dinner,
from Wednesday to Saturday, and for Sunday lunch.

Professional:	None
Directions:	6 miles west of Poole. Take A35 from Poole towards Bere Regis. Turn right at Slope.
Date Founded:	1991
Type of Course:	Parkland
No of Holes:	18
Length:	6078 yds (5700 mtrs)
Par:	71
SSS:	72
Green Fees:	Weekdays: £24; Weekends/ Bank Holidays: £28
Visitors:	Welcome: Contact Club in Advance. No Restrictions
Societies:	Welcome: Contact Club in Advance
Facilities:	Putting Green, Chipping Green, Buggy Hire, Trolley Hire Bar, Restaurant, Private Rooms

Bulbury Golf Club

**Bulbury Lane, Lytchett, Matravers, Poole,
Dorset BH16 6EP**

Tel: 01929 459574 Fax: 01929 459000

Sec/Manager: Ian Brooks

Accommodation, Food and Drink

Reference numbers below refer to detailed
information provided in section 2

Accommodation

**The Anglebury House and Restaurant,
15-17 North Street, Wareham, Dorset BH20 4AB**

Tel: 01929 552988 Fax: 01929 554665
e-mail: anglebury@btconnect.com
Guest house accommodation with seven letting
rooms, all but one with en-suite facilities. Long-
established coffee shop, at one time frequented by
Thomas Hardy and T.E. Lawrence (Lawrence of
Arabia). Restaurant offers a la carte and fixed price
menus.   302

**Cleff House, Brookmans Valley, Iwerne Minster,
Blandford Forum, Dorset D11 8NG**

Tel: 01747 811129 Fax: 01747 811112
Somewhere special, a unique house offering style,
comfort, good food, superb views. Set in nine acres of
a beautiful valley, yet within the bounds of the
picturesque village. Ideal for a truly relaxing break.

**The Greyhound, North Street, Winterbourne
Kingston, Blandford Forum, Dorset D11 9AZ**

Tel: 01929 471332 Fax: 01929 427610
website: www.greyhoundinnwk.co.uk
Traditional, country inn with spacious, comfortable
interior. Selection of real ales and tasty home-cooked
food. Four en-suite rooms.   304

**High Tor, Worgret Hill, Wareham,
Dorset BH20 6AD**

Tel: 01929 556869 Fax: 01929 555068
e-mail jeannie@innerpower.freeserve.co.uk
Holistic health centre which calls itself 'a new
concept in complementary medicine' offering sixteen
natural therapies. Also one room, sleeping four, for
bed and breakfast.   319

**Manor Farm Caravan Park, East Stoke,
Wareham, Dorset BH20 6AW**

Tel: 01929 462870 Fax: 01929 462870
Quiet, clean caravan park situated between Wareham
and Wool in an area of outstanding natural beauty.
Suitable for mobile homes and caravans with seasonal
pitches and storage.

**The Old Granary, West Holme Farm, Wareham,
Dorset BH20 6AQ**

Tel: 01929 552972 Fax: 01929 551616
Charming conversion of former granary in which
comfortable en-suite bed and breakfast
accommodation is available. One downstairs room is
equipped for category 3 disabled visitors. Evening
meals by prior arrangement.   320

**The Sheaf of Arrows, 4 The Square, Cranborne,
Dorset BH21 5PR**

Tel: 01725 517456
Traditional village hostelry popular with locals and
visitors to the area. Choice of real ales and a good
selection of sensibly priced meals. Five en-suite
rooms.   310

Food and Drink

**The Anglebury House and Restaurant,
15-17 North Street, Wareham, Dorset BH20 4AB**

Tel: 01929 552988 Fax: 01929 554665
e-mail: anglebury@btconnect.com
Guest house accommodation with seven letting
rooms, all but one with en-suite facilities. Long-
established coffee shop, at one time frequented by
Thomas Hardy and T.E. Lawrence (Lawrence of
Arabia). Restaurant offers a la carte and fixed price
menus.   302

**The Greyhound, North Street, Winterbourne
Kingston, Blandford Forum, Dorset D11 9AZ**

Tel: 01929 471332 Fax: 01929 427610
website: www.greyhoundinnwk.co.uk
Traditional, country inn with spacious, comfortable
interior. Selection of real ales and tasty home-cooked
food. Four en-suite rooms.   304

**The Mount, 49 Blandford Road, Corfe Mullen,
Wimborne, Dorset BH21 3HD**

Tel: 01202 693908
With a comfortable, relaxed atmosphere, this pub is
popular for its fine ales and tasty meals and snacks.
Regular karaoke, live music and pub quizzes. Large
rear gardens.   318

**The Sheaf of Arrows, 4 The Square, Cranborne,
Dorset BH21 5PR**

Tel: 01725 517456
Traditional village hostelry popular with locals and
visitors to the area. Choice of real ales and a good
selection of sensibly priced meals. Five en-suite
rooms.   310

**The White Hart, Bishops Caundle, Sherborne,
Dorset DT9 5ND**

Tel: 01963 23301 Fax: 01963 23301
Popular inn serving a full range of traditional meals
ranging from bar snacks to a la carte. The bar stocks
range of locally brewed ales.

**Winstons Restaurant and Bar, 45 High Street,
Sturminster Marshall, Dorset BH21 4AS**

Tel: 01258 857211 Fax: 01258 858225
Winstons is a self-contained restaurant and bar
adjoining The Churchill Arms pub. Serving a good
selection of good quality home-cooked dishes from
an a la carte menu, it is open for lunch and dinner,
from Wednesday to Saturday, and for Sunday lunch.

Came Down
Golf Club

Came Down, Dorchester, Dorset DT2 8NR

Tel: 01305 813494

Not the most famous course, as far as the average
golfer may be concerned, but one which is steeped
in history. For it was here that a certain Samuel

Ryder came up with the notion of Britain's best golfers playing the cream of the crop from the United States, donated a trophy for the teams to play for, and thus engraved his name indelibly into the history of the game.

Ryder would spend his holidays away from his St Alban's base at Weymouth, and take the short drive to Came Down to play.

It was here that he encountered the Whitcombe brothers - Charles, Ernest and Reg - who were also to etch their names across the game for decades. Ernest, the club pro at the time, was asked by Ryder if he ever played against the top Americans in important events, and Ernest's reply was that he simply couldn't afford time off to play. From that moment, first with sponsorship and later with prize money, the format and idea for the Ryder Cup gradually took shape.

As for the Whitcombes, all played Ryder Cup golf, Charles in the first six tournaments - three times as playing captain - and all three brothers played in 1935. And a Whitcombe finished in the top 20 of every British Open except three played between 1922 and 1950, Reg finishing second behind Henry Cotton in 1937 and winning it the year after. Here endeth the history lesson.

The course itself has hosted the West of England Championship numerous times, and lies high above the Thomas Hardy Dorset countryside, affording views as far as Portland Harbour from the highest point.

The rolling downland fairways give a springy feel underfoot, and the course is peppered with the humps of ancient burial mounds which often do not help with your lie, particularly on the par fives.

Sec/Manager:	R. Kelly
Professional:	Nick Rogers
Directions:	2 miles south of Dorchester. From A35 ring road at the junction of the B3147 (Dorchester) and the A354 (Weymouth) proceed 400 yds east and turn right (south) signed Preston. The entrance is on left hand side after 1¼ miles.
Date Founded:	1896
Type of Course:	Undulating Downland
No of Holes:	18
Length:	6800 yds (6274 mtrs)
Par:	70
SSS:	70
Green Fees:	Weekdays £24:; Weekends/ Bank Holidays: £30

Visitors:	Welcome: Contact Club in Advance
Societies:	Welcome: Play on Wednesdays. Small Societies can be fitted in as and when.
Facilities:	Practice Area, Putting Green, Chipping Green, Trolley Hire, Bar, Restaurant

Accommodation, Food and Drink

Reference numbers below refer to detailed information provided in section 2

Accommodation

The Beach House, Brunswick Terrace, Weymouth, Dorset D4 7RW

Tel: 01305 789353
Prime location just ten metres from the sea front with many guest rooms, some en-suite, enjoying superb views. Cooked English breakfasts and licensed bar. 311

Chideock House Hotel, Main Street, Chideock, Dorset DT6 6JN

Tel: 01297 489242 Fax: 01297 489184
website: www.chideockhousehotel.com
Picturesque 15th-century house which has been converted to a comfortable, stylish hotel and restaurant. Nine double, en-suite rooms. 309

George Hotel, 65 Dorchester Road, Weymouth, Dorset D4 7TY

Tel: 01305 786170 Fax: 01305 786170
Family-run hotel in prominent location on through road. Eight guest rooms, two singles and six doubles. Evenings meals available. Large car park.

Gorwell Farm Cottages, Abbotsbury, Weymouth, Dorset D3 4JX

Tel: 01305 871401 Fax: 01305 871441
e-mail: mary@gorwellfarm.co.uk
website: www.gorwellfarm.co.uk
Small collection of self-contained cottage-style apartments. Available for week-long holidays or short breaks. 301

The Greyhound, North Street, Winterbourne Kingston, Blandford Forum, Dorset D11 9AZ

Tel: 01929 471332 Fax: 01929 427610
website: www.greyhoundinnwk.co.uk
Traditional, country inn with spacious, comfortable interior. Selection of real ales and tasty home-cooked food. Four en-suite rooms. 304

High Tor, Worgret Hill, Wareham, Dorset BH20 6AD

Tel: 01929 556869 Fax: 01929 555068
e-mail jeannie@innerpower.freeserve.co.uk
Holistic health centre which calls itself 'a new concept in complementary medicine' offering sixteen natural therapies. Also one room, sleeping four, for bed and breakfast. 319

Food and Drink

Chideock House Hotel, Main Street, Chideock, Dorset DT6 6JN

Tel: 01297 489242 Fax: 01297 489184
website: www.chideockhousehotel.com
Picturesque 15th-century house which has been converted into a comfortable, stylish hotel and restaurant. Nine double, en-suite rooms.   309

The Crown Inn, 59 West Bay Road, Bridport, Dorset DT6 4AX

Tel: 01308 422037 Fax: 01308 458875
e-mail: enquiries@thecrowninn.org.uk
website: www.thecrowninn.org.uk
Situated midway between Bridport and West Bay, The Crown Inn offers classic Irish hospitality in a traditional English setting. A full menu is always available, and parties can be catered for. Children are welcomed and there is a special children's menu.

The Greyhound, North Street, Winterbourne Kingston, Blandford Forum, Dorset D11 9AZ

Tel: 01929 471332 Fax: 01929 427610
website: www.greyhoundinnwk.co.uk
Traditional, country inn with spacious, comfortable interior. Selection of real ales and tasty home-cooked food. Four en-suite rooms.   304

Swanson's Restaurant, Lakeside Walk, Weymouth, Dorset D4 7AW

Tel: 01305 776740 Fax: 01305 776740
Located on the edge of a small lake, built over the water, with an open, conservatory feel. High quality menu specialising in seafood.   313

The White Hart, Bishops Caundle, Sherborne, Dorset DT9 5ND

Tel: 01963 23301 Fax: 01963 23301
Popular inn serving a full range of traditional meals ranging from bar snacks to a la carte. The bar stocks range of locally brewed real ales.

Canford Magna Golf Club

Knighton Lane, Wimborne, Dorset BH21 3AS
Tel: 01202 592505/582606 Fax: 01202 592550

It is rather difficult to believe that a decade ago this thriving golf complex didn't even exist. It was merely a twinkle in the eye of joint owners Bill Riddle and Richard Harding, who saw hundreds of acres of lush Dorset countryside almost begging to become a haven for the county's golfers. How things have changed - and how quickly, too.

Their vision was turned into reality by course architect Howard Swan and Trevor Smith, who gently set about transforming 350 acres along the banks of the River Stour. Now the land is home to one of the biggest golf complexes in the region, with 51 holes in total - two 18-hole courses, a challenging nine-holer with some tiered greens to test your short game to the full, and even a six-hole academy course to warm you up for the harder stuff ahead.

The Parkland course is, at 6,496 yards, marginally the longer of the two 18-holers, covering undulating grassland and with a good mix of challenges. One of the most testing is the 440-yard par four ninth, a dog-leg which hugs water down the left hand side all the way from tee to two-tier green. You will probably see more birdies than you will card, the area being a popular wildfowl habitat.

The Riverside course is no less a test, at 6,231 yards, with the Stour winding through numerous ponds and water features to provide some extremely tricky approaches that require more brain than brawn. There's no easy start on this one, the first hole being the second longest, a par five of 534 yards off the whites. Things can only get better. At least until you get to the 12th, where virtually all 195 yards are carry over more of the wet stuff.

Sec/Manager:	Clare Regan
Professional:	Roger Tuddenham
Directions:	1 mile southeast of Wimborne Minster. From the centre of Wimborne follow road south over the river bridge. Turn left after the bridge and follow signs to Canford Magna. Immediately before Willet Arms turn left and follow road for 1½ miles. Turn left into Magna Road and follow signs to course.
Visitors:	Welcome: Contact Club in Advance. No Restrictions
Societies:	Welcome: Contact Club in Advance
Facilities:	Putting Green, Chipping

Green, Club Hire, Trolley Hire, Buggy Hire, Bar, Restaurant, Driving Range

Parkland

Date Founded:	1990
Type of Course:	Parkland
No of Holes:	18
Length:	6495 yds (5995 mtrs)
Par:	71
SSS:	71
Green Fees:	Weekdays: £21; Weekends/ Bank Holidays: £25

Riverside

Date Founded:	1990
Type of Course:	Parkland
No of Holes:	18
Length:	6214 yds (5735 mtrs)
Par:	70
SSS:	70
Green Fees:	Weekdays: £17; Weekends/ Bank Holidays: £20

Knighton

Date Founded:	1999
Type of Course:	Parkland
No of Holes:	9 (Par 3)
Length:	None
Par:	27
SSS:	None
Green Fees:	Weekdays: £10; Weekends/ Bank Holidays: £13

Accommodation, Food and Drink

Reference numbers below refer to detailed information provided in section 2

Accommodation

Belvedere Hotel, 14 Bath Road, Bournemouth, Dorset BH1 2EU

Tel: 01202 293336 Fax: 01202 294699
e-mail: enquiries@belvedere-hotel.co.uk
website: www.belvedere-hotel.co.uk
Comfortable, stylish accommodation with a total of 60 en-suite rooms of varying sizes. The restaurant provides elegant dining with a superb a la carte menu. Two bars.   314

Bourne Dene Hotel, 12 Manor Road, Bournemouth, Dorset BH1 3HU

Tel: 01202 553127

e-mail: enquiries@bournedene.co.uk
website: www. bournedene.co.uk
Deceptively large country house hotel, surrounded by landscaped gardens, with fine reputation for comfort and excellent cuisine. 21 en-suite bedrooms.   303

Cobbs Holiday Park, 32 Gordon Road, Highcliffe on Sea, Christchurch, Dorset BH23 5HN

Tel: 01425 273301/275313 Fax: 01425 276090
Long established family-run holiday park in fine location not far from the sea. Selection of nine, mostly six berth, chalets and caravans on an attractive site. Licensed social club, shop, laundrette and children's play area.   312

Pear Tree Cottage, 248 Wimborne Road West, Stapehill, Wimborne, Dorset BH21 2DZ

Tel: 01202 890174
An exceptionally pretty, picture-postcard cottage with comfortable bed and breakfast accommodation in three cosy rooms. Superb gardens.   317

San Simeon Hotel, 52 Wimborne Road, Bournemouth, Dorset BH3 7AE

Tel: 01202 551935 Fax: 01202 551935
Small, privately-run bed and breakfast establishment. Eleven en-suite guest rooms, two singles and nine doubles. Licensed bar and restaurant available to guests.

The Sheaf of Arrows, 4 The Square, Cranborne, Dorset BH21 5PR

Tel: 01725 517456
Traditional village hostelry popular with locals and visitors to the area. Choice of real ales and a good selection of sensibly priced meals. Five en-suite rooms.   310

Sunnydene Hotel, 11 Spencer Road, Bournemouth, Dorset BH1 3TE

Tel: 01202 552281
Good-sized, family-run establishment offering comfortable bed and breakfast accommodation in ten guest rooms, mostly en-suite. Evening meals available on request.   316

Food and Drink

Belvedere Hotel, 14 Bath Road, Bournemouth, Dorset BH1 2EU

Tel: 01202 293336 Fax: 01202 294699
e-mail: enquiries@belvedere-hotel.co.uk
website: www.belvedere-hotel.co.uk
Comfortable, stylish accommodation with a total of 60 en-suite rooms of varying sizes. The restaurant provides elegant dining with a superb a la carte menu. Two bars.   314

La Mamma, 51-53 Bridge Street, Christchurch, Dorset BH23 1DY

Tel: 01202 471608 Fax: 01202 471608
website: www.lamamma.co.uk
Popular pizzeria and trattoria offering an Italian experience for all the family. Opened in 1974 by Giuseppe and John Mirco, La Mamma has established a far reaching reputation for serving freshly prepared,

authentic dishes. Open lunch time and evening (closed Monday in Winter).

The Mount, 49 Blandford Road, Corfe Mullen, Wimborne, Dorset BH21 3HD

Tel: 01202 693908
With a comfortable, relaxed atmosphere, this pub is popular for its fine ales and tasty meals and snacks. Regular karaoke, live music and pub quizzes. Large rear gardens. 318

The Sheaf of Arrows, 4 The Square, Cranborne, Dorset BH21 5PR

Tel: 01725 517456
Traditional village hostelry popular with locals and visitors to the area. Choice of real ales and a good selection of sensibly priced meals. Five en-suite rooms. 310

Winstons Restaurant and Bar, 45 High Street, Sturminster Marshall, Dorset BH21 4AS

Tel: 01258 857211 Fax: 01258 858225
Winstons is a self-contained restaurant and bar adjoining The Churchill Arms pub. Serving a good selection of good quality home-cooked dishes from an a la carte menu, it is open for lunch and dinner, from Wednesday to Saturday, and for Sunday lunch.

Chedington Court Golf Club

South Perrott, Beaminster, Dorset DT8 3HU
Tel: 01935 891413 Fax: 01935 891217

Sec/Manager:	David Astill
Professional:	None
Directions:	½ mile east from the centre of South Perrott on the A356 Crewkerne, Dorchester Road
Date Founded:	1991
Type of Course:	Parkland
No of Holes:	18
Length:	5924 yds (5468 mtrs)
Par:	71
SSS:	71
Green Fees:	Weekdays: £16; Weekends/Bank Holidays: £20
Visitors:	Welcome: Contact Club in Advance. No Restrictions
Societies:	Welcome: Contact Club in Advance
Facilities:	Putting Green, Club Hire, Trolley Hire, Bar, Restaurant

Accommodation, Food and Drink

Reference numbers below refer to detailed information provided in section 2

Accommodation

Chideock House Hotel, Main Street, Chideock, Dorset DT6 6JN

Tel: 01297 489242 Fax: 01297 489184
website: www.chideockhousehotel.com
Picturesque 15th-century house which has been converted into a comfortable, stylish hotel and restaurant. Nine double, en-suite rooms. 309

Mermaid House, 32 Coombe Street, Lyme Regis, Dorset DT7 3PP

Tel: 01297 445351
website: www.smoothhound.co.uk/hotels/mermaid
Charming, relaxing house in old part of Lyme Regis, three minutes walk from the sea. Superb breakfast using free range produce. Free parking nearby.

The Portman Arms, High Street, East Chinnock, Yeovil, Somerset BA22 9DP

Tel: 01935 862227 Fax: 01935 862227
An imposing building dating from the early 1800s providing a spacious eating and drinking area. Menu. Five, newly-refurbished, en-suite guest rooms. Caravan pitches also available. 429

Quiet Woman House, Halstock, Dorset BA22 9RX

Tel: 01935 891218
e-mail: quietwomanhouse@ukonline.com
Newly converted bed and breakfast offering high quality accommodation in traditional surroundings. Three guest rooms of varying sizes and two self-catering cottages. Evening meals on request. 315

The Royal George, West Coker, Yeovil, Somerset BA22 9AN

Tel: 01935 862334 Fax: 01935 864499
18th-century hostelry with a cosy, traditional interior. Menu offers a good selection of dishes. Occasional live music and a regular quiz night. Two en-suite guest rooms. 428

Weston House Cottages, East Chinnock, Nr. Yeovil, Somerset BA22 9EL

Tel: 01935 863712/863394 Mobile: 07884 214768
e-mail: westonhouseuk@netscapeonline.co.uk
Two cottages converted from former barns located within a working farm. High quality well-equipped accommodation. One cottage sleeps four, the other sleeps five. Dogs welcome. 430

The Yew Tree Inn, Forest Hill, Yeovil, Somerset BA20 2PG

Tel: 01935 476808 Fax: 01935 476808
Former gentleman's residence which was converted into a pub only 30 years ago. Cosy, friendly atmosphere. Excellent food with a menu of traditional pub food. Four guest rooms of varying sizes. 432

Food and Drink

The Chetnole Inn, Chetnole, Nr. Sherborne, Dorset DT9 6NU

Tel: 01935 872337
Popular local's inn, well-liked for top-quality real ales, fine food and its fabulous atmosphere. Cosy music-free lounge bar, spacious restaurant and friendly public bar.   308

Chideock House Hotel, Main Street, Chideock, Dorset DT6 6JN

Tel: 01297 489242 Fax: 01297 489184
website: www.chideockhousehotel.com
Picturesque 15th-century house which has been converted into a comfortable, stylish hotel and restaurant. Nine double, en-suite rooms.   309

The Portman Arms, High Street, East Chinnock, Yeovil, Somerset BA22 9DP

Tel: 01935 862227 Fax: 01935 862227
An imposing building dating from the early 1800s providing a spacious eating and drinking area. Good menu. Five, newly-refurbished, en-suite guest rooms. Caravan pitches also available.   429

The Royal George, West Coker, Yeovil, Somerset BA22 9AN

Tel: 01935 862334 Fax: 01935 864499
18th-century hostelry with a cosy, traditional interior. Menu offers a good selection of dishes. Occasional live music and a regular quiz night. Two en-suite guest rooms.   428

The Royal Oak, Stoford, Yeovil, Somerset BA22 9UD

Tel: 01935 475071
Quiet village location just a couple of miles from the centre of Yeovil. Cosy interior with separate restaurant. Well-priced menu of traditional dishes. Occasional quiz and theme nights.   427

The Yew Tree Inn, Forest Hill, Yeovil, Somerset BA20 2PG

Tel: 01935 476808 Fax: 01935 476808
Former gentleman's residence which was converted into a pub only 30 years ago. Cosy, friendly atmosphere. Excellent food with a menu of traditional pub food. Four guest rooms of varying sizes.   432

Crane Valley Golf Club

The Clubhouse, Verwood, Dorset BH31 7LE
Tel: 01202 814088 Fax: 01202 813407

Sec/Manager:	Andrew Blackwell
Professional:	Darrel Ranson
Directions:	6½ miles northwest of Ringwood. From the A31 dual

carriageway 1 mile west of Ringwood take the B3081 (Verwood). Pass through Verwood and the entrance is on the left hand side ¼ mile after crossing River Moors.

Visitors:	Welcome: contact club in advance. No restrictions
Societies:	Welcome: contact club in advance. Unable to play weekends.
Facilities:	Putting Green, Chipping Green, Club Hire, Trolley Hire, Buggy Hire, Bar, Restaurant, Driving Range

Valley Course

Date Founded:	1991
Type of Course:	Parkland
No of Holes:	18
Length:	6500 yds (5999 mtrs)

Par:	72
SSS:	71
Green Fees:	Weekdays: £25; Weekends/ Bank Holidays: £32.50

Woodland Course

Date Founded:	1991
Type of Course:	Parkland
No of Holes:	9
Length:	2020 yds (1864 mtrs)
Par:	33
SSS:	30
Green Fees:	Weekdays: £5.50; Weekends/ Bank Holidays: £6.50

Accommodation, Food and Drink

Reference numbers below refer to detailed information provided in section 2

Accommodation

Belvedere Hotel, 14 Bath Road, Bournemouth, Dorset BH1 2EU

Tel: 01202 293336 Fax: 01202 294699
e-mail: enquiries@belvedere-hotel.co.uk
website: www.belvedere-hotel.co.uk
Comfortable, stylish accommodation with a total of 60 en-suite rooms of varying sizes. The restaurant provides elegant dining with a superb a la carte menu. Two bars. 314

Bourne Dene Hotel, 12 Manor Road, Bournemouth, Dorset BH1 3HU

Tel: 01202 553127
e-mail: enquiries@bournedene.co.uk
website: www. bournedene.co.uk
Deceptively large country house hotel, surrounded by landscaped gardens, with fine reputation for comfort and excellent cuisine. 21 en-suite bedrooms. 303

Cleff House, Brookmans Valley, Iwerne Minster, Blandford Forum, Dorset D11 8NG

Tel: 01747 811129 Fax: 01747 811112
Somewhere special, a unique house offering style, comfort, good food, superb views. Set in nine acres of a beautiful valley, yet within the bounds of the picturesque village. Ideal for a truly relaxing break.

Cobbs Holiday Park, 32 Gordon Road, Highcliffe on Sea, Christchurch, Dorset BH23 5HN

Tel: 01425 273301/275313 Fax: 01425 276090
Long established family-run holiday park in fine location not far from the sea. Selection of nine, mostly six berth, chalets and caravans on an attractive site. Licensed social club, shop, laundrette and children's play area. 312

Pear Tree Cottage, 248 Wimborne Road West, Stapehill, Wimborne, Dorset BH21 2DZ

Tel: 01202 890174

An exceptionally pretty, picture-postcard cottage with comfortable bed and breakfast accommodation in three cosy rooms. Superb gardens. 317

San Simeon Hotel, 52 Wimborne Road, Bournemouth, Dorset BH3 7AE

Tel: 01202 551935 Fax: 01202 551935
Small, privately-run bed and breakfast establishment. Eleven en-suite guest rooms, two singles and nine doubles. Licensed bar and restaurant available to guests.

The Sheaf of Arrows, 4 The Square, Cranborne, Dorset BH21 5PR

Tel: 01725 517456
Traditional village hostelry popular with locals and visitors to the area. Choice of real ales and a good selection of sensibly priced meals. Five en-suite rooms. 310

Sunnydene Hotel, 11 Spencer Road, Bournemouth, Dorset BH1 3TE

Tel: 01202 552281
Good-sized, family-run establishment offering comfortable bed and breakfast accommodation in ten guest rooms, mostly en-suite. Evening meals available on request. 316

Food and Drink

Belvedere Hotel, 14 Bath Road, Bournemouth, Dorset BH1 2EU

Tel: 01202 293336 Fax: 01202 294699
e-mail: enquiries@belvedere-hotel.co.uk
website: www.belvedere-hotel.co.uk
Comfortable, stylish accommodation with a total of 60 en-suite rooms of varying sizes. The restaurant provides elegant dining with a superb a la carte menu. Two bars. 314

La Mamma, 51-53 Bridge Street, Christchurch, Dorset BH23 1DY

Tel: 01202 471608 Fax: 01202 471608
website: www.lamamma.co.uk
Popular pizzeria and trattoria offering an Italian experience for all the family. Owned by Giuseppe and John Mirco, La Mamma has established a far reaching reputation for serving freshly prepared, authentic dishes. Open lunch time and evening (closed Monday in Winter).

The Mount, 49 Blandford Road, Corfe Mullen, Wimborne, Dorset BH21 3HD

Tel: 01202 693908
With a comfortable, relaxed atmosphere, this pub is popular for its fine ales and tasty meals and snacks. Regular karaoke, live music and pub quizzes. Large rear gardens. 318

The Sheaf of Arrows, 4 The Square, Cranborne, Dorset BH21 5PR

Tel: 01725 517456
Traditional village hostelry popular with locals and visitors to the area. Choice of real ales and a good selection of sensibly priced meals. Five en-suite rooms. 310

The Sheaf of Arrows, 4 The Square, Cranborne, Dorset BH21 5PR

Tel: 01725 517456
Traditional village hostelry popular with locals and visitors to the area. Choice of real ales and a good selection of sensibly priced meals. Five en-suite rooms.   310

Winstons Restaurant and Bar, 45 High Street, Sturminster Marshall, Dorset BH21 4AS

Tel: 01258 857211 Fax: 01258 858225
Winstons is a self-contained restaurant and bar adjoining The Churchill Arms pub. Serving a good selection of good quality home-cooked dishes from an a la carte menu, it is open for lunch and dinner, from Wednesday to Saturday, and for Sunday lunch.

Dudsbury Golf Club

64 Christchurch Road, Ferndown,
Dorset BH22 8ST

Tel: **01202 593499** Fax: **01202 594555**

This delightful golf course is a fairly recent addition to the venues around Bournemouth, established only 10 years ago and designed by Donald Steel.

Despite its freshness, Dudsbury is maturing into a very good - and pretty long - test of golf, set in 150 acres of parkland which rolls gently down to the banks of the River Stour.

Just to add a bit more interest, water comes into play on 14 holes, with numerous little streams, crossed by picturesque Purbeck stone bridges, linking nine lakes around the course.

One of the pleasures of Dudsbury is that you can make it as much of a challenge as your own game demands by choosing from three sets of tees - yellow, white and blue. Off the yellows, the course is a pleasant 6,000 yards with no fearsome carries, but add nearly an extra 1,000 yards off the blues and it becomes just a tad tougher.

Besides boasting what must be one of the longest par-four holes in the country - at 490 yards, only 30 feet off being a five - it has a signature hole which is both beauty and beast. The par-four, 400-yard 16th looks a joy from the elevated tee, but it is certainly a risk-and-reward hole. Playing over the biggest lake on the course, you can opt for a shortish carry across the corner of the water, leaving yourself a longish second to clear another pond, or risk the longer carry for an easier second.

As a pointer to its quality, the course has begun to attract county and regional championships and this year (2001) will host a Euro Pro Tour tournament.

Sec/Manager:	Giles Legg
Professional:	Mark Thomas
Directions:	4½ miles north of Bournemouth seafront. From the A338 Ringwood to Bournemouth road join the B3073 (Hurn, Parley Cross, Dudsbury). At Parley Cross keep on the same road and the entrance is on the left hand side after 1 mile.
Date Founded:	1990
Type of Course:	Parkland
No of Holes:	18
Length:	6606 yds (6097 mtrs)
Par:	71
SSS:	72
Green Fees:	Weekdays: £32; Weekends/ Bank Holidays: £37
Visitors:	Welcome: Contact Club in Advance. No Restrictions
Societies:	Welcome: Contact Club in Advance
Facilities:	Putting Green, Chipping Green, Driving Range, Trolley Hire, Buggy Hire, Bar, Restaurant

Accommodation, Food and Drink

Reference numbers below refer to detailed information provided in section 2

Accommodation

Belvedere Hotel, 14 Bath Road, Bournemouth, Dorset BH1 2EU

Tel: 01202 293336 Fax: 01202 294699
e-mail: enquiries@belvedere-hotel.co.uk
website: www.belvedere-hotel.co.uk
Comfortable, stylish accommodation with a total of 60 en-suite rooms of varying sizes. The restaurant provides elegant dining with a superb a la carte menu. Two bars.   314

Bourne Dene Hotel, 12 Manor Road, Bournemouth, Dorset BH1 3HU

Tel: 01202 553127
e-mail: enquiries@bournedene.co.uk
website: www. bournedene.co.uk
Deceptively large country house hotel, surrounded by landscaped gardens, with fine reputation for comfort and excellent cuisine. 21 en-suite bedrooms.   303

Cobbs Holiday Park, 32 Gordon Road, Highcliffe on Sea, Christchurch, Dorset BH23 5HN

Tel: 01425 273301/275313 Fax: 01425 276090
Long established family-run holiday park in fine location not far from the sea. Selection of nine,

mostly six berth, chalets and caravans on an attractive site. Licensed social club, shop, laundrette and children's play area. 312

Pear Tree Cottage, 248 Wimborne Road West, Stapehill, Wimborne, Dorset BH21 2DZ

Tel: 01202 890174
An exceptionally pretty, picture-postcard cottage with comfortable bed and breakfast accommodation in three cosy rooms. Superb gardens. 317

San Simeon Hotel, 52 Wimborne Road, Bournemouth, Dorset BH3 7AE

Tel: 01202 551935 Fax: 01202 551935
Small, privately-run bed and breakfast establishment. Eleven en-suite guest rooms, two singles and nine doubles. Licensed bar and restaurant available to guests.

The Sheaf of Arrows, 4 The Square, Cranborne, Dorset BH21 5PR

Tel: 01725 517456
Traditional village hostelry popular with locals and visitors to the area. Choice of real ales and a good selection of sensibly priced meals. Five en-suite rooms. 310

Sunnydene Hotel, 11 Spencer Road, Bournemouth, Dorset BH1 3TE

Tel: 01202 552281
Good-sized, family-run establishment offering comfortable bed and breakfast accommodation in ten guest rooms, mostly en-suite. Evening meals available on request. 316

Food and Drink

Belvedere Hotel, 14 Bath Road, Bournemouth, Dorset BH1 2EU

Tel: 01202 293336 Fax: 01202 294699
e-mail: enquiries@belvedere-hotel.co.uk
website: www.belvedere-hotel.co.uk
Comfortable, stylish accommodation with a total of 60 en-suite rooms of varying sizes. The restaurant provides elegant dining with a superb a la carte menu. Two bars. 314

La Mamma, 51-53 Bridge Street, Christchurch, Dorset BH23 1DY

Tel: 01202 471608 Fax: 01202 471608
website: www.lamamma.co.uk
Popular pizzeria and trattoria offering an Italian experience for all the family. Opened in 1974 by Giuseppe and John Mirco, La Mamma has established a far reaching reputation for serving freshly prepared, authentic dishes. Open lunch time and evening (closed Monday in Winter).

The Mount, 49 Blandford Road, Corfe Mullen, Wimborne, Dorset BH21 3HD

Tel: 01202 693908
With a comfortable, relaxed atmosphere, this pub is popular for its fine ales and tasty meals and snacks. Regular karaoke, live music and pub quizzes. Large rear gardens. 318

The Sheaf of Arrows, 4 The Square, Cranborne, Dorset BH21 5PR

Tel: 01725 517456
Traditional village hostelry popular with locals and visitors to the area. Choice of real ales and a good selection of sensibly priced meals. Five en-suite rooms. 310

The Sheaf of Arrows, 4 The Square, Cranborne, Dorset BH21 5PR

Tel: 01725 517456
Traditional village hostelry popular with locals and visitors to the area. Choice of real ales and a good selection of sensibly priced meals. Five en-suite rooms. 310

Winstons Restaurant and Bar, 45 High Street, Sturminster Marshall, Dorset BH21 4AS

Tel: 01258 857211 Fax: 01258 858225
Winstons is a self-contained restaurant and bar adjoining The Churchill Arms pub. Serving a good selection of good quality home-cooked dishes from an a la carte menu, it is open for lunch and dinner, from Wednesday to Saturday, and for Sunday lunch.

East Dorset Golf Club

Bere Regis, Wareham, Dorset BH20 7NT
Tel: 01929 472244 Fax: 01929 471294

Sometimes you discover a golf course which you want to keep to yourself. It could be the scenery, maybe the history, or simply the course itself in all its testing glory. Well, here's one to keep to yourself.

East Dorset is rapidly gaining the reputation as Dorset's finest course. Pro Derwynne Honan, who obviously might be ever so slightly biased, says of it: "It is probably the best laid-out course

in the county, and a very, very good test of golf indeed."

So what's so special? To start with, it is pretty much in the middle of nowhere, away from Dorset's busy holiday resorts and on the slopes of the Purbeck Hills. Secondly, it is owned by the Danish Count and Countess Lerche. And thirdly, it is a few feet over the 7,000-yard mark off the championship tees, with an SSS of 76 and a total of 72 cleverly-placed bunkers! Oh, and the delightfully-named River Piddle meanders nearby.

The course started life as a nine-holer known as Lakey Hill in the late 1970s, but that original nine is now the separate and interestingly varied Woodland Course.

What you want to head for is the Lakeland, a parkland par 72 with numerous natural water features. Don't get too carried away with your winner's speech if the front nine goes like a dream, for there are some nasties awaiting after the turn, with four rather demanding consecutive holes, starting with the 12th. You can thank designer Martin Hawtree for spoiling your day.

Sec/Manager:	Graham Packer, Brian Lee
Professional:	Derwynne Honan
Directions:	3½ miles northwest of Wareham. From centre take the B3070 and join the A352 (Wool, Dorchester). ½ mile from the roundabout turn right into Puddletown Rd, then after 3½ miles take first right. The

entrance is on the right hand side after ¾ mile.

Visitors:	Welcome: contact club in advance. Unable to play before 11:30am on weekends
Societies:	Welcome: contact club in advance. No restrictions
Facilities:	Putting Green, Chipping Green, Club Hire, Trolley Hire, Buggy Hire, Bar, Restaurant, Driving Range

Lakeland Course

Date Founded:	1978
Type of Course:	Parkland
No of Holes:	18
Length:	6580 yds (6073 mtrs)
Par:	72
SSS:	72
Green Fees:	Weekdays: £30; Weekends/ Bank Holidays: £35

Woodland Course

Date Founded:	1978
Type of Course:	Treelined Parkland
No of Holes:	9
Length:	5032 yds (4644 mtrs)
Par:	66
SSS:	64
Green Fees:	Weekdays: £21; Weekends/ Bank Holidays: £23

Accommodation, Food and Drink

Reference numbers below refer to detailed information provided in section 2

Accommodation

The Anglebury House and Restaurant, 15-17 North Street, Wareham, Dorset BH20 4AB

Tel: 01929 552988 Fax: 01929 554665
e-mail: anglebury@btconnect.com
Guest house accommodation with seven letting

rooms, all but one with en-suite facilities. Long-established coffee shop, at one time frequented by Thomas Hardy and T.E. Lawrence (Lawrence of Arabia). Restaurant offers a la carte and fixed price menus. 302

The Beach House, Brunswick Terrace, Weymouth, Dorset D4 7RW

Tel: 01305 789353
Prime location just ten metres from the sea front with many guest rooms, some en-suite, enjoying superb views. Cooked English breakfasts and licensed bar. 311

The Greyhound, North Street, Winterbourne Kingston, Blandford Forum, Dorset D11 9AZ

Tel: 01929 471332 Fax: 01929 427610
website: www.greyhoundinnwk.co.uk
Traditional, country inn with spacious, comfortable interior. Selection of real ales and tasty home-cooked food. Four en-suite rooms. 304

High Tor, Worgret Hill, Wareham, Dorset BH20 6AD

Tel: 01929 556869 Fax: 01929 555068
e-mail jeannie@innerpower.freeserve.co.uk
Holistic health centre which calls itself 'a new concept in complementary medicine' offering sixteen natural therapies. Also one room, sleeping four, for bed and breakfast. 319

Manor Farm Caravan Park, East Stoke, Wareham, Dorset BH20 6AW

Tel: 01929 462870 Fax: 01929 462870
Quiet, clean caravan park situated between Wareham and Wool in an area of outstanding natural beauty. Suitable for mobile homes and caravans with seasonal pitches and storage.

The Old Granary, West Holme Farm, Wareham, Dorset BH20 6AQ

Tel: 01929 552972 Fax: 01929 551616
Charming conversion of former granary in which comfortable en-suite bed and breakfast accommodation is available. One downstairs room is equipped for category 3 disabled visitors. Evening meals by prior arrangement. 320

Food and Drink

The Anglebury House and Restaurant, 15-17 North Street, Wareham, Dorset BH20 4AB

Tel: 01929 552988 Fax: 01929 554665
e-mail: anglebury@btconnect.com
Guest house accommodation with seven letting rooms, all but one with en-suite facilities. Long-established coffee shop, at one time frequented by Thomas Hardy and T.E. Lawrence (Lawrence of Arabia). Restaurant offers a la carte and fixed price menus. 302

The Greyhound, North Street, Winterbourne Kingston, Blandford Forum, Dorset D11 9AZ

Tel: 01929 471332 Fax: 01929 427610
website: www.greyhoundinnwk.co.uk
Traditional, country inn with spacious, comfortable interior. Selection of real ales and tasty home-cooked food. Four en-suite rooms. 304

The Mount, 49 Blandford Road, Corfe Mullen, Wimborne, Dorset BH21 3HD

Tel: 01202 693908
With a comfortable, relaxed atmosphere, this pub is popular for its fine ales and tasty meals and snacks. Regular karaoke, live music and pub quizzes. Large rear gardens. 318

Swanson's Restaurant, Lakeside Walk, Weymouth, Dorset D4 7AW

Tel: 01305 776740 Fax: 01305 776740
Located on the edge of a small lake, built over the water, with an open, conservatory feel. High quality menu specialising in seafood. 313

Winstons Restaurant and Bar, 45 High Street, Sturminster Marshall, Dorset BH21 4AS

Tel: 01258 857211 Fax: 01258 858225
Winstons is a self-contained restaurant and bar adjoining The Churchill Arms pub. Serving a good selection of good quality home-cooked dishes from an a la carte menu, it is open for lunch and dinner, from Wednesday to Saturday, and for Sunday lunch.

Ferndown Golf Club

119 Golf Links Road, Ferndown, Dorset BH22 8BU

Tel: 01202 874602 Fax: 01202 873926

Most watchers of golf on television will no doubt have heard the inimitable Peter Alliss mention Ferndown at some point in one of his wandering commentaries about yesteryear, and that mention will almost certainly have included the phrase "...my old dad used to say ..."

For it was at Ferndown that Peter's 'old dad', Percy Alliss, became pro in 1937, and stayed on until 1969. It was also at Ferndown that young Peter joined him as assistant and began his career on tour, even playing in the Ryder Cup while still attached to the club.

The Alliss connection is still strong, and Peter runs a big celebrity charity pro-am at the club each year to raise money to buy state-of-the-art

electric wheelchairs for disabled children. The championship course is also on the European Seniors' Tour and hosts the De Vere Seniors' Classic on its natural heathland fairways fringed with heather and the almost-inevitable pine trees.

Despite its spacious and open feel, anything wayward will be punished and, as you would imagine, there are some pretty mean holes, none more so than the long, uphill par-four sixth, usually played into the prevailing wind. Throw in a few dog-legs, and a multi-level green to test anyone's putting and patience on the 16th – "Hilton's", named after course architect Harold Hilton - and you know you are getting your money's worth.

If all that sounds just a bit too much, there is always the adjacent President's course which, at 5,604 yards, with nine holes and 18 tees, is half a mile shorter, if not much easier.

Sec/Manager:	Terry Pond
Professional:	Iain Parker
Directions:	5½ miles southwest of Ringwood. From centre take A31 (Ashley Heath, Ferndown). After 5 miles turn left at roundabout onto A348 (Bearwood). After 300 yds turn left into Golf Links Road The entrance is on the left hand side after ¾ mile.
Visitors:	Welcome: Contact Club in Advance. Limited at weekends
Societies:	Welcome: Contact Club in Advance. Unable to play Mon, Wed, Thurs and weekends
Facilities:	Practice Area, Putting Green, Chipping Green, Club Hire, Trolley Hire, Buggy Hire, Bar, Restaurant, Private Rooms

Championship Course

Date Founded:	1913
Type of Course:	Heathland
No of Holes:	18
Length:	6452 yds (5955 mtrs)
Par:	71
SSS:	71
Green Fees:	Weekdays: £42; Weekends/ Bank Holidays: £50

President Course

Date Founded:	1913
Type of Course:	Heathland
No of Holes:	9
Length:	5604 yds (5172 mtrs)
Par:	70
SSS:	68
Green Fees:	Weekdays: £15; Weekends/ Bank Holidays: £20

Accommodation, Food and Drink

Reference numbers below refer to detailed information provided in section 2

Accommodation

Belvedere Hotel, 14 Bath Road, Bournemouth, Dorset BH1 2EU

Tel: 01202 293336 Fax: 01202 294699
e-mail: enquiries@belvedere-hotel.co.uk
website: www.belvedere-hotel.co.uk
Comfortable, stylish accommodation with a total of 60 en-suite rooms of varying sizes. The restaurant provides elegant dining with a superb a la carte menu. Two bars.   314

Bourne Dene Hotel, 12 Manor Road, Bournemouth, Dorset BH1 3HU

Tel: 01202 553127
e-mail: enquiries@bournedene.co.uk
website: www. bournedene.co.uk
Deceptively large country house hotel, surrounded by landscaped gardens, with fine reputation for comfort and excellent cuisine. 21 en-suite bedrooms.   303

Cobbs Holiday Park, 32 Gordon Road, Highcliffe on Sea, Christchurch, Dorset BH23 5HN

Tel: 01425 273301/275313 Fax: 01425 276090
Long established family-run holiday park in fine location not far from the sea. Selection of nine, mostly six berth, chalets and caravans on an attractive site. Licensed social club, shop, laundrette and children's play area.   312

Pear Tree Cottage, 248 Wimborne Road West, Stapehill, Wimborne, Dorset BH21 2DZ

Tel: 01202 890174
An exceptionally pretty, picture-postcard cottage with comfortable bed and breakfast accommodation in three cosy rooms. Superb gardens.   317

San Simeon Hotel, 52 Wimborne Road, Bournemouth, Dorset BH3 7AE

Tel: 01202 551935 Fax: 01202 551935
Small, privately-run bed and breakfast establishment. Eleven en-suite guest rooms, two singles and nine doubles. Licensed bar and restaurant available to guests.

The Sheaf of Arrows, 4 The Square, Cranborne, Dorset BH21 5PR

Tel: 01725 517456
Traditional village hostelry popular with locals and visitors to the area. Choice of real ales and a good selection of sensibly priced meals. Five en-suite rooms. 310

Sunnydene Hotel, 11 Spencer Road, Bournemouth, Dorset BH1 3TE

Tel: 01202 552281
Good-sized, family-run establishment offering comfortable bed and breakfast accommodation in ten guest rooms, mostly en-suite. Evening meals available on request. 316

Food and Drink

Belvedere Hotel, 14 Bath Road, Bournemouth, Dorset BH1 2EU

Tel: 01202 293336 Fax: 01202 294699
e-mail: enquiries@belvedere-hotel.co.uk
website: www.belvedere-hotel.co.uk
Comfortable, stylish accommodation with a total of 60 en-suite rooms of varying sizes. The restaurant provides elegant dining with a superb a la carte menu. Two bars. 314

La Mamma, 51-53 Bridge Street, Christchurch, Dorset BH23 1DY

Tel: 01202 471608 Fax: 01202 471608
website: www.lamamma.co.uk
Popular pizzeria and trattoria offering an Italian experience for all the family. Opened in 1974 by Giuseppe and John Mirco, La Mamma has established a far reaching reputation for serving freshly prepared, authentic dishes. Open lunch time and evening (closed Monday in Winter).

The Mount, 49 Blandford Road, Corfe Mullen, Wimborne, Dorset BH21 3HD

Tel: 01202 693908
With a comfortable, relaxed atmosphere, this pub is popular for its fine ales and tasty meals and snacks. Regular karaoke, live music and pub quizzes. Large rear gardens. 318

The Sheaf of Arrows, 4 The Square, Cranborne, Dorset BH21 5PR

Tel: 01725 517456
Traditional village hostelry popular with locals and visitors to the area. Choice of real ales and a good selection of sensibly priced meals. Five en-suite rooms. 310

Winstons Restaurant and Bar, 45 High Street, Sturminster Marshall, Dorset BH21 4AS

Tel: 01258 857211 Fax: 01258 858225
Winstons is a self-contained restaurant and bar adjoining The Churchill Arms pub. Serving a good selection of good quality home-cooked dishes from an a la carte menu, it is open for lunch and dinner, from Wednesday to Saturday, and for Sunday lunch.

Ferndown Forest Golf Club

Forest Links Road, Ferndown, Dorset BH22 9QE

Tel: 01202 876096 Fax: 01202 894095

Sec/Manager:	Mike Dodd
Professional:	Mike Dodd
Directions:	6 miles southwest of Ringwood. From centre take A31 (Ferndown, Wimborne). After 6¾ miles at roundabout turn right into Ameysford Rd that doubles back towards Ferndown. The entrance is on the left hand side after ½ mile.
Date Founded:	1993
Type of Course:	Parkland
No of Holes:	18
Length:	5094 yds (4702 mtrs)
Par:	68
SSS:	65

Green Fees:	Weekdays: £11; Weekends/Bank Holidays: £13
Visitors:	Welcome: Contact Club in Advance. Tee times bookable at weekends
Societies:	Welcome: Contact Club in Advance
Facilities:	Putting Green, Driving Range, Club Hire, Trolley Hire, Bar, Restaurant, Private Rooms

Accommodation, Food and Drink

Reference numbers below refer to detailed information provided in section 2

Accommodation

The Anglebury House and Restaurant, 15-17 North Street, Wareham, Dorset BH20 4AB

Tel: 01929 552988 Fax: 01929 554665
e-mail: anglebury@btconnect.com
Guest house accommodation with seven letting rooms, all but one with en-suite facilities. Long-established coffee shop, at one time frequented by Thomas Hardy and T.E. Lawrence (Lawrence of Arabia). Restaurant offers a la carte and fixed price menus.   302

Belvedere Hotel, 14 Bath Road, Bournemouth, Dorset BH1 2EU

Tel: 01202 293336 Fax: 01202 294699
e-mail: enquiries@belvedere-hotel.co.uk
website: www.belvedere-hotel.co.uk
Comfortable, stylish accommodation with a total of 60 en-suite rooms of varying sizes. The restaurant provides elegant dining with a superb a la carte menu. Two bars.   314

Bourne Dene Hotel, 12 Manor Road, Bournemouth, Dorset BH1 3HU

Tel: 01202 553127
e-mail: enquiries@bournedene.co.uk
website: www. bournedene.co.uk
Deceptively large country house hotel, surrounded by landscaped gardens, with fine reputation for comfort and excellent cuisine. 21 en-suite bedrooms.   303

Cobbs Holiday Park, 32 Gordon Road, Highcliffe on Sea, Christchurch, Dorset BH23 5HN

Tel: 01425 273301/275313 Fax: 01425 276090
Long established family-run holiday park in fine location not far from the sea. Selection of nine, mostly six berth, chalets and caravans on an attractive site. Licensed social club, shop, laundrette and children's play area.   312

Pear Tree Cottage, 248 Wimborne Road West, Stapehill, Wimborne, Dorset BH21 2DZ

Tel: 01202 890174
An exceptionally pretty, picture-postcard cottage with comfortable bed and breakfast accommodation in three cosy rooms. Superb gardens.   317

San Simeon Hotel, 52 Wimborne Road, Bournemouth, Dorset BH3 7AE

Tel: 01202 551935 Fax: 01202 551935
Small, privately-run bed and breakfast establishment. Eleven en-suite guest rooms, two singles and nine doubles. Licensed bar and restaurant available to guests.

The Sheaf of Arrows, 4 The Square, Cranborne, Dorset BH21 5PR

Tel: 01725 517456
Traditional village hostelry popular with locals and visitors to the area. Choice of real ales and a good selection of sensibly priced meals. Five en-suite rooms.   310

Sunnydene Hotel, 11 Spencer Road, Bournemouth, Dorset BH1 3TE

Tel: 01202 552281
Good-sized, family-run establishment offering comfortable bed and breakfast accommodation in ten guest rooms, mostly en-suite. Evening meals available on request.   316

Food and Drink

The Anglebury House and Restaurant, 15-17 North Street, Wareham, Dorset BH20 4AB

Tel: 01929 552988 Fax: 01929 554665
e-mail: anglebury@btconnect.com
Guest house accommodation with seven letting rooms, all but one with en-suite facilities. Long-established coffee shop, at one time frequented by Thomas Hardy and T.E. Lawrence (Lawrence of Arabia). Restaurant offers a la carte and fixed price menus.   302

Belvedere Hotel, 14 Bath Road, Bournemouth, Dorset BH1 2EU

Tel: 01202 293336 Fax: 01202 294699
e-mail: enquiries@belvedere-hotel.co.uk
website: www.belvedere-hotel.co.uk
Comfortable, stylish accommodation with a total of 60 en-suite rooms of varying sizes. The restaurant provides elegant dining with a superb a la carte menu. Two bars.   314

La Mamma, 51-53 Bridge Street, Christchurch, Dorset BH23 1DY

Tel: 01202 471608 Fax: 01202 471608

website: www.lamamma.co.uk
Popular pizzeria and trattoria offering an Italian experience for all the family. Opened in 1974 by Giuseppe and John Mirco, La Mamma has established a far reaching reputation for serving freshly prepared, authentic dishes. Open lunch time and evening (closed Monday in Winter).

The Mount, 49 Blandford Road, Corfe Mullen, Wimborne, Dorset BH21 3HD

Tel: 01202 693908
With a comfortable, relaxed atmosphere, this pub is popular for its fine ales and tasty meals and snacks. Regular karaoke, live music and pub quizzes. Large rear gardens.   318

The Sheaf of Arrows, 4 The Square, Cranborne, Dorset BH21 5PR

Tel: 01725 517456
Traditional village hostelry popular with locals and visitors to the area. Choice of real ales and a good selection of sensibly priced meals. Five en-suite rooms.   310

Winstons Restaurant and Bar, 45 High Street, Sturminster Marshall, Dorset BH21 4AS

Tel: 01258 857211 Fax: 01258 858225
Winstons is a self-contained restaurant and bar adjoining The Churchill Arms pub. Serving a good selection of good quality home-cooked dishes from an a la carte menu, it is open for lunch and dinner, from Wednesday to Saturday, and for Sunday lunch.

Halstock Golf Club

Common Lane, Halstock, Dorset BA22 9SF

Tel: 01935 891689 Fax: 01935 891839

Sec/Manager:	L.R. Church
Professional:	Adrian Thomson
Directions:	6 miles south of Yeovil. From Halstock village turn right at the Green and the course is 50 yds on the left hand side.
Date Founded:	1987
Type of Course:	Parkland
No of Holes:	18
Length:	4481 yds (4136 mtrs)
Par:	66
SSS:	63
Green Fees:	Weekdays: £11; Weekends/ Bank Holidays: £13
Visitors:	Welcome: Contact Club in Advance. Unable to play between 8.00-10.00 am Sundays
Societies:	Welcome: Contact Club in Advance

Facilities:	Driving Range, Putting Green, Club Hire, Trolley Hire, Bar

Accommodation, Food and Drink

Reference numbers below refer to detailed information provided in section 2

Accommodation

Chideock House Hotel, Main Street, Chideock, Dorset DT6 6JN

Tel: 01297 489242 Fax: 01297 489184
website: www.chideockhousehotel.com
Picturesque 15th-century house which has been converted into a comfortable, stylish hotel and restaurant. Nine double, en-suite rooms.   309

Mermaid House, 32 Coombe Street, Lyme Regis, Dorset DT7 3PP

Tel: 01297 445351
website: www.smoothhound.co.uk/hotels/mermaid
Charming, relaxing house in old part of Lyme Regis, three minutes walk from the sea. Superb breakfast using free range produce. Free parking nearby.

The Portman Arms, High Street, East Chinnock, Yeovil, Somerset BA22 9DP

Tel: 01935 862227 Fax: 01935 862227
An imposing building dating from the early 1800s providing a spacious eating and drinking area. Good menu. Five, newly-refurbished, en-suite guest rooms. Caravan pitches also available.   429

Quiet Woman House, Halstock, Dorset BA22 9RX

Tel: 01935 891218
e-mail: quietwomanhouse@ukonline.com
Newly converted bed and breakfast offering high quality accommodation in traditional surroundings. Three guest rooms of varying sizes and two self-catering cottages. Evening meals on request.   315

The Royal George, West Coker, Yeovil, Somerset BA22 9AN

Tel: 01935 862334 Fax: 01935 864499
18th-century hostelry with a cosy, traditional interior. Menu offers a good selection of dishes. Occasional live music and a regular quiz night. Two en-suite guest rooms.   428

Weston House Cottages, East Chinnock, Nr. Yeovil, Somerset BA22 9EL

Tel: 01935 863712/863394 Mobile: 07884 214768
e-mail: westonhouseuk@netscapeonline.com
Two cottages converted from former barns located within a working farm. High quality well-equipped accommodation. One cottage sleeps four, the other sleeps five. Dogs welcome.   430

The Yew Tree Inn, Forest Hill, Yeovil, Somerset BA20 2PG

Tel: 01935 476808 Fax: 01935 476808
Former gentleman's residence which was converted into a pub only 30 years ago. Cosy, friendly atmosphere. Excellent food with a menu of

traditional pub food. Four guest rooms of varying sizes. 432

Food and Drink

The Chetnole Inn, Chetnole, Nr. Sherborne, Dorset DT9 6NU

Tel: 01935 872337
Popular local's inn, well-liked for top-quality real ales, fine food and its fabulous atmosphere. Cosy music-free lounge bar, spacious restaurant and friendly public bar. 308

Chideock House Hotel, Main Street, Chideock, Dorset DT6 6JN

Tel: 01297 489242 Fax: 01297 489184
website: www.chideockhousehotel.com
Picturesque 15th-century house which has been converted into a comfortable, stylish hotel and restaurant. Nine double, en-suite rooms. 309

The Crown Inn, 59 West Bay Road, Bridport, Dorset DT6 4AX

Tel: 01308 422037 Fax: 01308 458875
e-mail: enquiries@thecrowninn.org.uk
website: www.thecrowninn.org.uk
Situated midway between Bridport and West Bay, The Crown Inn offers classic Irish hospitality in a traditional English setting. A full menu is always available, and parties can be catered for. Children are welcomed and there is a special children's menu.

The Portman Arms, High Street, East Chinnock, Yeovil, Somerset BA22 9DP

Tel: 01935 862227 Fax: 01935 862227
An imposing building dating from the early 1800s providing a spacious eating and drinking area. Good menu. Five, newly-refurbished, en-suite guest rooms. Caravan pitches also available. 429

The Royal George, West Coker, Yeovil, Somerset BA22 9AN

Tel: 01935 862334 Fax: 01935 864499
18th-century hostelry with a cosy, traditional interior. Menu offers a good selection of dishes. Occasional live music and a regular quiz night. Two en-suite guest rooms. 428

The Royal Oak, Stoford, Yeovil, Somerset BA22 9UD

Tel: 01935 475071
Quiet village location just a couple of miles from the centre of Yeovil. Cosy interior with separate restaurant. Well-priced menu of traditional dishes. Occasional quiz and theme nights. 427

The Yew Tree Inn, Forest Hill, Yeovil, Somerset BA20 2PG

Tel: 01935 476808 Fax: 01935 476808
Former gentleman's residence which was converted into a pub only 30 years ago. Cosy, friendly atmosphere. Excellent food with a menu of traditional pub food. Four guest rooms of varying sizes. 432

Highcliffe Castle Golf Club

107 Lymington Road, Highcliffe-on-Sea, Christchurch, Dorset BH23 4LA

Tel: 01425 272953 Fax: 01425 272210

Sec/Manager:	Brian Savery
Professional:	None
Directions:	2 miles east of Christchurch off the A337 at Highcliffe
Date Founded:	1913
Type of Course:	Parkland
No of Holes:	18
Length:	4778 yds (4410 mtrs)
Par:	64
SSS:	63
Green Fees:	Weekdays: £25.50; Weekends/ Bank Holidays: £35.50
Visitors:	Welcome: Contact Club in Advance. Handicap Certificates
Societies:	Welcome: Contact Club in Advance
Facilities:	Putting Green, Chipping Green, Trolley Hire Bar, Restaurant

Accommodation, Food and Drink

Reference numbers below refer to detailed information provided in section 2

Accommodation

Belvedere Hotel, 14 Bath Road, Bournemouth, Dorset BH1 2EU

Tel: 01202 293336 Fax: 01202 294699
e-mail: enquiries@belvedere-hotel.co.uk
website: www.belvedere-hotel.co.uk
Comfortable, stylish accommodation with a total of 60 en-suite rooms of varying sizes. The restaurant provides elegant dining with a superb a la carte menu. Two bars. 314

Bourne Dene Hotel, 12 Manor Road, Bournemouth, Dorset BH1 3HU

Tel: 01202 553127
e-mail: enquiries@bournedene.co.uk
website: www. bournedene.co.uk
Deceptively large country house hotel, surrounded by landscaped gardens, with fine reputation for comfort and excellent cuisine. 21 en-suite bedrooms. 303

Cobbs Holiday Park, 32 Gordon Road, Highcliffe on Sea, Christchurch, Dorset BH23 5HN

Tel: 01425 273301/275313 Fax: 01425 276090
Long established family-run holiday park in fine
location not far from the sea. Selection of nine,
mostly six berth, chalets and caravans on an attractive
site. Licensed social club, shop, laundrette and
children's play area.   312

**Pear Tree Cottage, 248 Wimborne Road West,
Stapehill, Wimborne, Dorset BH21 2DZ**

Tel: 01202 890174
An exceptionally pretty, picture-postcard cottage with
comfortable bed and breakfast accommodation in
three cosy rooms. Superb gardens.   317

**San Simeon Hotel, 52 Wimborne Road,
Bournemouth, Dorset BH3 7AE**

Tel: 01202 551935 Fax: 01202 551935
Small, privately-run bed and breakfast establishment.
Eleven en-suite guest rooms, two singles and nine
doubles. Licensed bar and restaurant available to
guests.

**Sunnydene Hotel, 11 Spencer Road,
Bournemouth, Dorset BH1 3TE**

Tel: 01202 552281
Good-sized, family-run establishment offering
comfortable bed and breakfast accommodation in ten
guest rooms, mostly en-suite. Evening meals available
on request.   316

Food and Drink

**Belvedere Hotel, 14 Bath Road, Bournemouth,
Dorset BH1 2EU**

Tel: 01202 293336 Fax: 01202 294699
e-mail: enquiries@belvedere-hotel.co.uk
website: www.belvedere-hotel.co.uk
Comfortable, stylish accommodation with a total of
60 en-suite rooms of varying sizes. The restaurant
provides elegant dining with a superb a la carte menu.
Two bars.   314

**La Mamma, 51-53 Bridge Street, Christchurch,
Dorset BH23 1DY**

Tel: 01202 471608 Fax: 01202 471608
website: www.lamamma.co.uk
Popular pizzeria and trattoria offering an Italian
experience for all the family. Opened in 1974 by
Giuseppe and John Mirco, La Mamma has established
a far reaching reputation for serving freshly prepared,
authentic dishes. Open lunch time and evening
(closed Monday in Winter).

**The Mount, 49 Blandford Road, Corfe Mullen,
Wimborne, Dorset BH21 3HD**

Tel: 01202 693908
With a comfortable, relaxed atmosphere, this pub is
popular for its fine ales and tasty meals and snacks.
Regular karaoke, live music and pub quizzes. Large
rear gardens.   318

**Winstons Restaurant and Bar, 45 High Street,
Sturminster Marshall, Dorset BH21 4AS**

Tel: 01258 857211 Fax: 01258 858225
Winstons is a self-contained restaurant and bar
adjoining The Churchill Arms pub. Serving a good

selection of good quality home-cooked dishes from
an a la carte menu, it is open for lunch and dinner,
from Wednesday to Saturday, and for Sunday lunch.

Isle of Purbeck
Golf Club

Studland, Dorset BH19 3AB

Tel: 01929 450361 Fax: 01929 450501

Here's one for the next clubhouse quiz on those
long winter evenings: Which famous writer once
owned the Isle of Purbeck golf course? Now remember, you are in deepest Dorset. Thomas
Hardy, perhaps? Or maybe one of the literary
Durrells? Nope. Did someone say Enid Blyton?
Good shout!

History doesn't tell whether her Famous Five
books were the inspiration behind the course's
famous fifth hole (or vice versa), but this excellent course is definitely not one for Noddies.

HS Colt designed this superb course - it regularly features in just about everybody's top 100
courses in the UK - but, given the landscape he
had to work with, it would have been somewhat
remiss of him if he had failed to produce the
goods.

Set on the Purbeck Hills, with views as far as
the Isle of Wight, this rugged heathland course
populated by unforgiving gorse and heather offers 6,000 yards of testing, almost links-like golf.

No two holes are the same, each making you
think twice, or even three times, about every shot.

The pick is that glorious fifth, "Agglestone",
with its tee elevated on a Saxon burial mound
and its small green 404 yards distant, down what
appears to be a peninsula out into the vast ex-
panse of Poole Harbour. Anybody distracted by
the view could, indeed, be spoiling a good walk.

As if to emphasise the diversity of the course,
the following hole is a long par five played back
up a valley, while Purbeck's version of "Amen
Corner" comes at 11, 12 and 13.

The clubhouse, built of local stone, is also full of old fossils - no, no, real ones from local beaches used as a touch of interior decor!

Sec/Manager:	Mrs. J. Robinson
Professional:	Ian Braile
Directions:	7¼ miles southeast of Wareham. From centre take A351 (Swanage). After 4¼ miles turn left onto B3351 (Studland). After another 4¼ miles turn sharp right signed Ulwell. The entrance is on the left hand side after 250 yds.
Visitors:	Welcome: Contact club in advance
Societies:	Welcome: Contact club in advance
Facilities:	Putting Green, Club Hire, Trolley Hire, Buggy Hire, Bar, Restaurant

Purbeck

Date Founded:	1892
Type of Course:	Heathland
No of Holes:	18
Length:	6295 yds (5810 mtrs)
Par:	70
SSS:	70
Green Fees:	Weekdays: £35 (round) £45 (day); Weekends/Bank Holidays: £40 (round) £47.50 (day)

Dean

Date Founded:	1892
Type of Course:	Heathland
No of Holes:	9
Length:	2007 yds (1853 mtrs)
Par:	30
SSS:	30
Green Fees:	Weekdays: £13; Weekends/Bank Holidays: £13

Accommodation, Food and Drink

Reference numbers below refer to detailed information provided in section 2

Accommodation

Belvedere Hotel, 14 Bath Road, Bournemouth, Dorset BH1 2EU

Tel: 01202 293336 Fax: 01202 294699
e-mail: enquiries@belvedere-hotel.co.uk
website: www.belvedere-hotel.co.uk
Comfortable, stylish accommodation with a total of 60 en-suite rooms of varying sizes. The restaurant provides elegant dining with a superb a la carte menu. Two bars. 314

Eastbury Hotel, Long Street, Sherborne, Dorset DT9 3BY

Tel: 01935 813131 Fax: 01935 817296
e-mail: eastbury.sherborne@virgin.net
An elegant Georgian hotel surrounded by fine gardens. Award-winning Conservatory Restaurant enjoys a fine reputation serving mainly English cuisine. 15 en-suite bedrooms. 307

High Tor, Worgret Hill, Wareham, Dorset BH20 6AD

Tel: 01929 556869 Fax: 01929 555068
e-mail jeannie@innerpower.freeserve.co.uk
Holistic health centre which calls itself 'a new concept in complementary medicine' offering sixteen natural therapies. Also one room, sleeping four, for bed and breakfast. 319

Manor Farm Caravan Park, East Stoke, Wareham, Dorset BH20 6AW

Tel: 01929 462870 Fax: 01929 462870
Quiet, clean caravan park situated between Wareham and Wool in an area of outstanding natural beauty. Suitable for mobile homes and caravans with seasonal pitches and storage.

The Old Granary, West Holme Farm, Wareham, Dorset BH20 6AQ

Tel: 01929 552972 Fax: 01929 551616
Charming conversion of former granary in which comfortable en-suite bed and breakfast accommodation is available. One downstairs room is equipped for category 3 disabled visitors. Evening meals by prior arrangement. 320

San Simeon Hotel, 52 Wimborne Road, Bournemouth, Dorset BH3 7AE

Tel: 01202 551935 Fax: 01202 551935
Small, privately-run bed and breakfast establishment. Eleven en-suite guest rooms, two singles and nine doubles. Licensed bar and restaurant available to guests.

Food and Drink

Belvedere Hotel, 14 Bath Road, Bournemouth, Dorset BH1 2EU

Tel: 01202 293336 Fax: 01202 294699
e-mail: enquiries@belvedere-hotel.co.uk
website: www.belvedere-hotel.co.uk
Comfortable, stylish accommodation with a total of 60 en-suite rooms of varying sizes. The restaurant provides elegant dining with a superb a la carte menu. Two bars. 314

Eastbury Hotel, Long Street, Sherborne, Dorset DT9 3BY

Tel: 01935 813131 Fax: 01935 817296
e-mail: eastbury.sherborne@virgin.net
An elegant Georgian hotel surrounded by fine

gardens. Award-winning Conservatory Restaurant enjoys a fine reputation serving mainly English cuisine. 15 en-suite bedrooms.   307

La Mamma, 51-53 Bridge Street, Christchurch, Dorset BH23 1DY

Tel: 01202 471608 Fax: 01202 471608
website: www.lamamma.co.uk
Popular pizzeria and trattoria offering an Italian experience for all the family. Opened in 1974 by Giuseppe and John Mirco, La Mamma has established a far reaching reputation for serving freshly prepared, authentic dishes. Open lunch time and evening (closed Monday in Winter).

The Mount, 49 Blandford Road, Corfe Mullen, Wimborne, Dorset BH21 3HD

Tel: 01202 693908
With a comfortable, relaxed atmosphere, this pub is popular for its fine ales and tasty meals and snacks. Regular karaoke, live music and pub quizzes. Large rear gardens.   318

Winstons Restaurant and Bar, 45 High Street, Sturminster Marshall, Dorset BH21 4AS

Tel: 01258 857211 Fax: 01258 858225
Winstons is a self-contained restaurant and bar adjoining The Churchill Arms pub. Serving a good selection of good quality home-cooked dishes from an a la carte menu, it is open for lunch and dinner, from Wednesday to Saturday, and for Sunday lunch.

Knighton Heath Golf Club

Francis Avenue, West Howe, Bournemouth, Dorset BH11 8NX

Tel: 01202 572633 Fax: 01202 590774

Sec/Manager:	R. Bestwick
Professional:	None
Directions:	4¼ miles northwest of Bournemouth pier. From Horseshoe Common near centre take A347 leading to A3049 (West Howe, Broadstone). At roundabout with A348 (Ferndown) go straight on into Francis Av. The entrance is on the right hand side after 200 yds.
Date Founded:	1930
Type of Course:	Heathland
No of Holes:	18
Length:	6094 yds (5625 mtrs)
Par:	70
SSS:	69
Green Fees:	Weekdays: £25 (round) £30

(day); Weekends/Bank Holidays: £25 (round) £30 (day)

Visitors:	Welcome: Contact Club in Advance. Unable to play at weekends
Societies:	Welcome: Contact Club in Advance. Unable to play at weekends
Facilities:	Practice Area, Putting Green, Chipping Green, Trolley Hire, Buggy Hire, Bar, Restaurant

Accommodation, Food and Drink

Reference numbers below refer to detailed information provided in section 2

Accommodation

Belvedere Hotel, 14 Bath Road, Bournemouth, Dorset BH1 2EU

Tel: 01202 293336 Fax: 01202 294699
e-mail: enquiries@belvedere-hotel.co.uk
website: www.belvedere-hotel.co.uk
Comfortable, stylish accommodation with a total of 60 en-suite rooms of varying sizes. The restaurant provides elegant dining with a superb a la carte menu. Two bars.   314

Bourne Dene Hotel, 12 Manor Road, Bournemouth, Dorset BH1 3HU

Tel: 01202 553127
e-mail: enquiries@bournedene.co.uk
website: www. bournedene.co.uk
Deceptively large country house hotel, surrounded by landscaped gardens, with fine reputation for comfort and excellent cuisine. 21 en-suite bedrooms.   303

Cobbs Holiday Park, 32 Gordon Road, Highcliffe on Sea, Christchurch, Dorset BH23 5HN

Tel: 01425 273301/275313 Fax: 01425 276090
Long established family-run holiday park in fine location not far from the sea. Selection of nine, mostly six berth, chalets and caravans on an attractive site. Licensed social club, shop, laundrette and children's play area.   312

Pear Tree Cottage, 248 Wimborne Road West, Stapehill, Wimborne, Dorset BH21 2DZ

Tel: 01202 890174
An exceptionally pretty, picture-postcard cottage with comfortable bed and breakfast accommodation in three cosy rooms. Superb gardens.   317

San Simeon Hotel, 52 Wimborne Road, Bournemouth, Dorset BH3 7AE

Tel: 01202 551935 Fax: 01202 551935
Small, privately-run bed and breakfast establishment. Eleven en-suite guest rooms, two singles and nine doubles. Licensed bar and restaurant available to guests.

The Sheaf of Arrows, 4 The Square, Cranborne, Dorset BH21 5PR

Tel: 01725 517456
Traditional village hostelry popular with locals and visitors to the area. Choice of real ales and a good selection of sensibly priced meals. Five en-suite rooms.   310

Sunnydene Hotel, 11 Spencer Road, Bournemouth, Dorset BH1 3TE

Tel: 01202 552281
Good-sized, family-run establishment offering comfortable bed and breakfast accommodation in ten guest rooms, mostly en-suite. Evening meals available on request.   316

Food and Drink

Belvedere Hotel, 14 Bath Road, Bournemouth, Dorset BH1 2EU

Tel: 01202 293336 Fax: 01202 294699
e-mail: enquiries@belvedere-hotel.co.uk
website: www.belvedere-hotel.co.uk
Comfortable, stylish accommodation with a total of 60 en-suite rooms of varying sizes. The restaurant provides elegant dining with a superb a la carte menu. Two bars.   314

La Mamma, 51-53 Bridge Street, Christchurch, Dorset BH23 1DY

Tel: 01202 471608 Fax: 01202 471608
website: www.lamamma.co.uk
Popular pizzeria and trattoria offering an Italian experience for all the family. Opened in 1974 by Giuseppe and John Mirco, La Mamma has established a far reaching reputation for serving freshly prepared, authentic dishes. Open lunch time and evening (closed Monday in Winter).

The Mount, 49 Blandford Road, Corfe Mullen, Wimborne, Dorset BH21 3HD

Tel: 01202 693908
With a comfortable, relaxed atmosphere, this pub is popular for its fine ales and tasty meals and snacks. Regular karaoke, live music and pub quizzes. Large rear gardens.   318

The Sheaf of Arrows, 4 The Square, Cranborne, Dorset BH21 5PR

Tel: 01725 517456
Traditional village hostelry popular with locals and visitors to the area. Choice of real ales and a good selection of sensibly priced meals. Five en-suite rooms.   310

Winstons Restaurant and Bar, 45 High Street, Sturminster Marshall, Dorset BH21 4AS

Tel: 01258 857211 Fax: 01258 858225
Winstons is a self-contained restaurant and bar adjoining The Churchill Arms pub. Serving a good selection of good quality home-cooked dishes from an a la carte menu, it is open for lunch and dinner, from Wednesday to Saturday, and for Sunday lunch.

Lyme Regis Golf Club

Timber Hill, Lyme Regis, Dorset DT7 3HQ

Tel: 01297 442 963

Building a golf course atop cliffs which form part of the largest coastal mud slide region in Europe could be said to be foolhardy at best. Nonetheless, that is precisely what you have at Lyme Regis, where large chunks of green and fairway have been known to suddenly and dramatically disappear hundreds of feet down to the fossil hunters' goldmine below.

Those of a rather nervous disposition, or those who started off with only half-a-dozen balls in their bag, may well decide to settle for a 15-hole round rather than risk holes 14, 15 and 16.

Much braver souls will plough on, safe in the knowledge that the last time the course was threatened in a big way was back in 1986, when the 15th fairway became a tad narrower. Before that it was 1959, when early starters pitched up at the 16th tee - and found it wasn't there any more.

The Whitcombes of Came Down also feature in Lyme's history, Ernie advising on the placing of bunkers back in the 1920s, and Reg playing an exhibition match to officially open the new 18-hole course in 1931.

The course itself is a mature delight, as befits one of the oldest in Dorset, and, although there are some stern challenges on the front nine, it is the back nine where lurk the real gremlins.

Real trouble begins on the short 14th, where a gusting sea breeze, known as "The Devil's Bellows", will quite easily deposit your well-intentioned tee shot down on the beach. The 15th gives spectacular views of the town and The Cobb - remember The French Lieutenant's Woman? - 600ft below, and every chance of a par at 294 yards, unless your hook produces a distant yelp from the fossil fiends at the foot of the cliffs. And then there's the 16th, if the tee is still there!

Sec/Manager:	Brian Wheeler
Professional:	Andrew Black
Directions:	1 mile east of Lyme Regis off the A3052 road to Charmouth
Date Founded:	1900
Type of Course:	Clifftop
No of Holes:	18
Length:	6264 yds (5782 mtrs)

Par:	71
SSS:	70
Green Fees:	Weekdays: £23 (£20 after 2.00 pm) £27 (day); Weekends/ Bank Holidays: £23 (£20 after 2.00 pm) £27 (day)
Visitors:	Welcome: Contact Club in Advance. Unable to play Thurs & Sun mornings.
Societies:	Welcome: Contact Club in Advance. Unable to play Thurs & Sun mornings.
Facilities:	Putting Green, Club Hire, Trolley Hire Bar, Restaurant

Accommodation, Food and Drink

Reference numbers below refer to detailed information provided in section 2

Accommodation

Chideock House Hotel, Main Street, Chideock, Dorset DT6 6JN

Tel: 01297 489242 Fax: 01297 489184
website: www.chideockhousehotel.com
Picturesque 15th-century house which has been converted into a comfortable, stylish hotel and restaurant. Nine double, en-suite rooms.　309

Coverdale Guest House, Woodmead Road, Lyme Regis, Dorset DT7 3AB

Tel: 01297 442882 Fax: 01297 444673
e-mail: coverdale@tinyworld.co.uk
Spacious non-smoking accommodation enjoying spectacular views to the coast and overlooking woodland. Eight comfortable bedrooms.　306

Eastbury Hotel, Long Street, Sherborne, Dorset DT9 3BY

Tel: 01935 813131 Fax: 01935 817296
e-mail: eastbury.sherborne@virgin.net
An elegant Georgian hotel surrounded by fine gardens. Award-winning Conservatory Restaurant enjoys a fine reputation serving mainly English cuisine. 15 en-suite bedrooms.　307

Kent House Hotel, Silver Street, Lyme Regis, Dorset DT7 3HT

Tel: 01297 443442 Fax: 01297 444626
e-mail: thekenthouse@talk21.com
Large Victorian property providing bright, airy and well-appointed accommodation. Nine rooms, varying sizes, most en-suite. Restaurant specialises in seafood dishes.　305

Kersbrook Hotel, Pound Road, Lyme Regis, Dorset DT7 3HX

Tel: 01297 442596 Fax: 01297 442596
A family-run bed and breakfast establishment housed within an historic, listed building. Ten en-suite guest bedrooms with many enjoying fine views.

Mariners Hotel, Silver Street, Lyme Regis, Dorset DT7 3HS

Tel: 01297 442753 Fax: 01297 442431
e-mail: mariners@ukgateway.net
This former 17th-century coaching inn retains much of its original character, while offering a comfortable and stylish place to stay. 12 en-suite bedrooms, relaxing lounge and cosy restaurant.

Mermaid House, 32 Coombe Street, Lyme Regis, Dorset DT7 3PP

Tel: 01297 445351
website: www.smoothhound.co.uk/hotels/mermaid
Charming, relaxing house in old part of Lyme Regis, three minutes walk from the sea. Superb breakfast using free range produce. Free parking nearby.

Springfield House, Woodmead Road, Lyme Regis, Dorset DT7 3LJ

Tel: 01297 443409 Fax: 01297 443685
e-mail: springfield@lymeregis.com
website: www.lymeregis.com/springfield
An elegant Georgian town house, tastefully converted to provide guest house accommodation with five en-suite rooms of varying sizes, all with sea views. Residents benefit from reduced fees at Lyme Regis Golf Club.

Food and Drink

Chideock House Hotel, Main Street, Chideock, Dorset DT6 6JN

Tel: 01297 489242 Fax: 01297 489184
website: www.chideockhousehotel.com
Picturesque 15th-century house which has been converted into a comfortable, stylish hotel and restaurant. Nine double, en-suite rooms.　309

The Crown Inn, 59 West Bay Road, Bridport, Dorset DT6 4AX

Tel: 01308 422037 Fax: 01308 458875
e-mail: enquiries@thecrowninn.org.uk
website: www.thecrowninn.org.uk
Situated midway between Bridport and West Bay, The Crown Inn offers classic Irish hospitality in a traditional English setting. A full menu is always available, and parties can be catered for. Children are welcomed and there is a special children's menu.

Eastbury Hotel, Long Street, Sherborne, Dorset DT9 3BY

Tel: 01935 813131 Fax: 01935 817296
e-mail: eastbury.sherborne@virgin.net
An elegant Georgian hotel surrounded by fine gardens. Award-winning Conservatory Restaurant enjoys a fine reputation serving mainly English cuisine. 15 en-suite bedrooms.　307

Kent House Hotel, Silver Street, Lyme Regis, Dorset DT7 3HT

Tel: 01297 443442 Fax: 01297 444626
e-mail: thekenthouse@talk21.com
Large Victorian property providing bright, airy and well-appointed accommodation. Nine rooms, varying sizes, most en-suite. Restaurant specialises in seafood dishes.　305

Mariners Hotel, Silver Street, Lyme Regis, Dorset DT7 3HS

Tel: 01297 442753 Fax: 01297 442431
e-mail: mariners@ukgateway.net
This former 17th-century coaching inn retains much of its original character, while offering a comfortable and stylish place to stay. 12 en-suite bedrooms, relaxing lounge and cosy restaurant.

The Volunteer Inn, Broad Street, Lyme Regis, Dorset DT7 3QS

Tel: 01297 442214
Historic, town centre free house serving a good selection of real ales, including draught Guinness. Also offers a full range of freshly cooked meals with seafood being a speciality.

Moors Valley Golf Club

Horton Road, Ringwood, Dorset BH24 2ET

Tel: 01425 479776 Fax: 01425 472057

Sec/Manager:	None
Professional:	Michael Torrens
Directions:	3 miles northwest of Ringwood. From Ringwood take A31 towards Wimborne and at the roundabout turn right following signs to Moors Valley Country Park.
Date Founded:	1988
Type of Course:	Parkland
No of Holes:	18

Length:	6200 yds (5723 mtrs)
Par:	72
SSS:	70
Green Fees:	Weekdays: £12.50; Weekends/ Bank Holidays: £15
Visitors:	Welcome: Contact Club in Advance. No Restrictions
Societies:	Welcome: Contact Club in Advance
Facilities:	Putting Green, Club Hire, Trolley Hire, Bar

Accommodation, Food and Drink

Reference numbers below refer to detailed information provided in section 2

Accommodation

Belvedere Hotel, 14 Bath Road, Bournemouth, Dorset BH1 2EU

Tel: 01202 293336 Fax: 01202 294699
e-mail: enquiries@belvedere-hotel.co.uk
website: www.belvedere-hotel.co.uk
Comfortable, stylish accommodation with a total of 60 en-suite rooms of varying sizes. The restaurant provides elegant dining with a superb a la carte menu. Two bars.   314

Bourne Dene Hotel, 12 Manor Road, Bournemouth, Dorset BH1 3HU

Tel: 01202 553127
e-mail: enquiries@bournedene.co.uk
website: www. bournedene.co.uk
Deceptively large country house hotel, surrounded by landscaped gardens, with fine reputation for comfort and excellent cuisine. 21 en-suite bedrooms.   303

Cleff House, Brookmans Valley, Iwerne Minster, Blandford Forum, Dorset D11 8NG

Tel: 01747 811129 Fax: 01747 811112
Somewhere special, a unique house offering style, comfort, good food, superb views. Set in nine acres of a beautiful valley, yet within the bounds of the picturesque village. Ideal for a truly relaxing break.

Cobbs Holiday Park, 32 Gordon Road, Highcliffe on Sea, Christchurch, Dorset BH23 5HN

Tel: 01425 273301/275313 Fax: 01425 276090
Long established family-run holiday park in fine location not far from the sea. Selection of nine, mostly six berth, chalets and caravans on an attractive site. Licensed social club, shop, laundrette and children's play area.   312

Pear Tree Cottage, 248 Wimborne Road West, Stapehill, Wimborne, Dorset BH21 2DZ

Tel: 01202 890174
An exceptionally pretty, picture-postcard cottage with comfortable bed and breakfast accommodation in three cosy rooms. Superb gardens.   317

San Simeon Hotel, 52 Wimborne Road, Bournemouth, Dorset BH3 7AE

Tel: 01202 551935 Fax: 01202 551935
Small, privately-run bed and breakfast establishment. Eleven en-suite guest rooms, two singles and nine doubles. Licensed bar and restaurant available to guests.

The Sheaf of Arrows, 4 The Square, Cranborne, Dorset BH21 5PR

Tel: 01725 517456
Traditional village hostelry popular with locals and visitors to the area. Choice of real ales and a good selection of sensibly priced meals. Five en-suite rooms.   310

Sunnydene Hotel, 11 Spencer Road, Bournemouth, Dorset BH1 3TE

Tel: 01202 552281
Good-sized, family-run establishment offering comfortable bed and breakfast accommodation in ten guest rooms, mostly en-suite. Evening meals available on request.   316

Food and Drink

Belvedere Hotel, 14 Bath Road, Bournemouth, Dorset BH1 2EU

Tel: 01202 293336 Fax: 01202 294699
e-mail: enquiries@belvedere-hotel.co.uk
website: www.belvedere-hotel.co.uk
Comfortable, stylish accommodation with a total of 60 en-suite rooms of varying sizes. The restaurant provides elegant dining with a superb a la carte menu. Two bars.   314

La Mamma, 51-53 Bridge Street, Christchurch, Dorset BH23 1DY

Tel: 01202 471608 Fax: 01202 471608
website: www.lamamma.co.uk
Popular pizzeria and trattoria offering an Italian experience for all the family. Opened in 1974 by Giuseppe and John Mirco, La Mamma has established a far reaching reputation for serving freshly prepared, authentic dishes. Open lunch time and evening (closed Monday in Winter).

The Mount, 49 Blandford Road, Corfe Mullen, Wimborne, Dorset BH21 3HD

Tel: 01202 693908
With a comfortable, relaxed atmosphere, this pub is popular for its fine ales and tasty meals and snacks. Regular karaoke, live music and pub quizzes. Large rear gardens.   318

The Sheaf of Arrows, 4 The Square, Cranborne, Dorset BH21 5PR

Tel: 01725 517456
Traditional village hostelry popular with locals and visitors to the area. Choice of real ales and a good selection of sensibly priced meals. Five en-suite rooms.   310

The Sheaf of Arrows, 4 The Square, Cranborne, Dorset BH21 5PR

Tel: 01725 517456
Traditional village hostelry popular with locals and visitors to the area. Choice of real ales and a good selection of sensibly priced meals. Five en-suite rooms.   310

Winstons Restaurant and Bar, 45 High Street, Sturminster Marshall, Dorset BH21 4AS

Tel: 01258 857211 Fax: 01258 858225
Winstons is a self-contained restaurant and bar adjoining The Churchill Arms pub. Serving a good selection of good quality home-cooked dishes from an a la carte menu, it is open for lunch and dinner, from Wednesday to Saturday, and for Sunday lunch.

Parkstone Golf Club

Links Road, Parkstone, Poole, Dorset BH14 9QS
Tel: 01202 707138 Fax: 01202 706027

Sec/Manager:	J. Harper
Professional:	Martin Thompson
Directions:	2½ miles west of Bournemouth pier. From centre take A338 then A35 (Poole). After 1¾ miles at Branksome turn left just after roundabout into Archway Rd leading to Canford Cliffs Road. 1 mile from the A35 turn right into Links Road. The entrance is on the left hand side after ¼ mile.

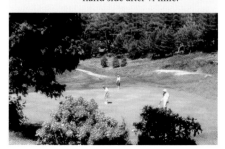

Date Founded: 1909
Type of Course: Heathland
No of Holes: 18
Length: 6263 yds (5781 mtrs)
Par: 72
SSS: 70
Green Fees: Weekdays: £35 (round) £50 (day); Weekends/Bank Holidays: £35 (round) £50 (day)
Visitors: Welcome: Contact Club in Advance. Restrictions at weekends
Societies: Welcome: Contact Club in Advance
Facilities: Putting Green, Trolley Hire, Bar, Restaurant

Accommodation, Food and Drink

Reference numbers below refer to detailed information provided in section 2

Accommodation

Belvedere Hotel, 14 Bath Road, Bournemouth, Dorset BH1 2EU

Tel: 01202 293336 Fax: 01202 294699
e-mail: enquiries@belvedere-hotel.co.uk
website: www.belvedere-hotel.co.uk
Comfortable, stylish accommodation with a total of 60 en-suite rooms of varying sizes. The restaurant provides elegant dining with a superb a la carte menu. Two bars. 314

Bourne Dene Hotel, 12 Manor Road, Bournemouth, Dorset BH1 3HU

Tel: 01202 553127
e-mail: enquiries@bournedene.co.uk
website: www. bournedene.co.uk
Deceptively large country house hotel, surrounded by landscaped gardens, with fine reputation for comfort and excellent cuisine. 21 en-suite bedrooms. 303

Eastbury Hotel, Long Street, Sherborne, Dorset DT9 3BY

Tel: 01935 813131 Fax: 01935 817296
e-mail: eastbury.sherborne@virgin.net
An elegant Georgian hotel surrounded by fine gardens. Award-winning Conservatory Restaurant enjoys a fine reputation serving mainly English cuisine. 15 en-suite bedrooms. 307

High Tor, Worgret Hill, Wareham, Dorset BH20 6AD

Tel: 01929 556869 Fax: 01929 555068
e-mail jeannie@innerpower.freeserve.co.uk
Holistic health centre which calls itself 'a new concept in complementary medicine' offering sixteen natural therapies. Also one room, sleeping four, for bed and breakfast. 319

Manor Farm Caravan Park, East Stoke, Wareham, Dorset BH20 6AW

Tel: 01929 462870 Fax: 01929 462870
Quiet, clean caravan park situated between Wareham and Wool in an area of outstanding natural beauty. Suitable for mobile homes and caravans with seasonal pitches and storage.

The Old Granary, West Holme Farm, Wareham, Dorset BH20 6AQ

Tel: 01929 552972 Fax: 01929 551616
Charming conversion of former granary in which comfortable en-suite bed and breakfast accommodation is available. One downstairs room is equipped for category 3 disabled visitors. Evening meals by prior arrangement. 320

San Simeon Hotel, 52 Wimborne Road, Bournemouth, Dorset BH3 7AE

Tel: 01202 551935 Fax: 01202 551935
Small, privately-run bed and breakfast establishment. Eleven en-suite guest rooms, two singles and nine doubles. Licensed bar and restaurant available to guests.

Food and Drink

Belvedere Hotel, 14 Bath Road, Bournemouth, Dorset BH1 2EU

Tel: 01202 293336 Fax: 01202 294699
e-mail: enquiries@belvedere-hotel.co.uk
website: www.belvedere-hotel.co.uk
Comfortable, stylish accommodation with a total of 60 en-suite rooms of varying sizes. The restaurant provides elegant dining with a superb a la carte menu. Two bars. 314

Eastbury Hotel, Long Street, Sherborne, Dorset DT9 3BY

Tel: 01935 813131 Fax: 01935 817296
e-mail: eastbury.sherborne@virgin.net
An elegant Georgian hotel surrounded by fine
gardens. Award-winning Conservatory Restaurant
enjoys a fine reputation serving mainly English
cuisine. 15 en-suite bedrooms.   307

La Mamma, 51-53 Bridge Street, Christchurch, Dorset BH23 1DY

Tel: 01202 471608 Fax: 01202 471608
website: www.lamamma.co.uk
Popular pizzeria and trattoria offering an Italian
experience for all the family. Opened in 1974 by
Giuseppe and John Mirco, La Mamma has established
a far reaching reputation for serving freshly prepared,
authentic dishes. Open lunch time and evening
(closed Monday in Winter).

The Mount, 49 Blandford Road, Corfe Mullen, Wimborne, Dorset BH21 3HD

Tel: 01202 693908
With a comfortable, relaxed atmosphere, this pub is
popular for its fine ales and tasty meals and snacks.
Regular karaoke, live music and pub quizzes. Large
rear gardens.   318

Winstons Restaurant and Bar, 45 High Street, Sturminster Marshall, Dorset BH21 4AS

Tel: 01258 857211 Fax: 01258 858225
Winstons is a self-contained restaurant and bar
adjoining The Churchill Arms pub. Serving a good
selection of good quality home-cooked dishes from
an a la carte menu, it is open for lunch and dinner,
from Wednesday to Saturday, and for Sunday lunch.

Queens Park Golf Club

Queens Park West Drive, Queens Park,
Bournemouth, Dorset BH8 9BY

Tel: 01202 302611 Fax: 01202 396817

It is strange that a seaside resort like Bournemouth, which came of age around the turn of
the century, much as golf did among the chatter-
ing classes, doesn't actually boast more golf clubs
than Queen's, Meyrick and Knighton Heath
(which is almost as much in the neighbouring
borough of Poole as it is in Bournemouth). And
strange, also, that the resort's two central courses
are both owned by the local council, are only a
couple of miles apart, and yet are so different.

One of the great assets of Queen's is the seeming novelty value of every hole. No two holes
appear to be similar, and that individuality means
players should never get bored. About the only
similarity between Queen's and Meyrick is the
aroma of the pines which line the fairways, fairways which are somewhat more generous here.

Interest is captured early on, with the second
hole being a short, downhill play which isn't quite

as easy at it may first appear, and catches out
many an unwary and over-confident golfer. And
the 13th - stroke index 1 - is also a bit of a beast
with a dog-leg left.

But a personal favourite is the 12th - if favourite is the right word for one which caused a broken
heart. Not only is it a par five, but the tees and
the green are on opposite sides of a valley, and
the average club handicappers will invariably find
themselves playing from the valley floor to a green
out of view and way, way above. Quite possibly
more than once, if experience is anything to go
by.

Remember, it's only a game!

Sec/Manager:	Diane Gibb
Professional:	Richard Hill
Directions:	1½ miles northeast of Bournemouth town the centre off the A338
Date Founded:	1900
Type of Course:	Parkland
No of Holes:	18
Length:	6300 yds (5815 mtrs)
Par:	72
SSS:	70
Green Fees:	Weekdays: £15 (round) £22 (day); Weekends/Bank Holidays: £16.50 (round) £30 (day)
Visitors:	Welcome: Contact Club in Advance. Unable to play Thurs. 10.00-12.00
Societies:	Welcome: Contact Club in Advance
Facilities:	Putting Green, Club Hire, Buggy Hire, Trolley Hire Bar, Restaurant

Accommodation, Food and Drink

Reference numbers below refer to detailed
information provided in section 2

Accommodation

Belvedere Hotel, 14 Bath Road, Bournemouth, Dorset BH1 2EU

Tel: 01202 293336 Fax: 01202 294699
e-mail: enquiries@belvedere-hotel.co.uk
website: www.belvedere-hotel.co.uk
Comfortable, stylish accommodation with a total of
60 en-suite rooms of varying sizes. The restaurant
provides elegant dining with a superb a la carte menu.
Two bars.   314

Bourne Dene Hotel, 12 Manor Road, Bournemouth, Dorset BH1 3HU

Tel: 01202 553127
e-mail: enquiries@bournedene.co.uk
website: www. bournedene.co.uk
Deceptively large country house hotel, surrounded by landscaped gardens, with fine reputation for comfort and excellent cuisine. 21 en-suite bedrooms.   303

Cobbs Holiday Park, 32 Gordon Road, Highcliffe on Sea, Christchurch, Dorset BH23 5HN

Tel: 01425 273301/275313 Fax: 01425 276090
Long established family-run holiday park in fine location not far from the sea. Selection of nine, mostly six berth, chalets and caravans on an attractive site. Licensed social club, shop, laundrette and children's play area.   312

Eastbury Hotel, Long Street, Sherborne, Dorset DT9 3BY

Tel: 01935 813131 Fax: 01935 817296
e-mail: eastbury.sherborne@virgin.net
An elegant Georgian hotel surrounded by fine gardens. Award-winning Conservatory Restaurant enjoys a fine reputation serving mainly English cuisine. 15 en-suite bedrooms.   307

High Tor, Worgret Hill, Wareham, Dorset BH20 6AD

Tel: 01929 556869 Fax: 01929 555068
e-mail jeannie@innerpower.freeserve.co.uk
Holistic health centre which calls itself 'a new concept in complementary medicine' offering sixteen natural therapies. Also one room, sleeping four, for bed and breakfast.   319

Manor Farm Caravan Park, East Stoke, Wareham, Dorset BH20 6AW

Tel: 01929 462870 Fax: 01929 462870
Quiet, clean caravan park situated between Wareham and Wool in an area of outstanding natural beauty. Suitable for mobile homes and caravans with seasonal pitches and storage.

The Old Granary, West Holme Farm, Wareham, Dorset BH20 6AQ

Tel: 01929 552972 Fax: 01929 551616
Charming conversion of former granary in which comfortable en-suite bed and breakfast accommodation is available. One downstairs room is equipped for category 3 disabled visitors. Evening meals by prior arrangement.   320

San Simeon Hotel, 52 Wimborne Road, Bournemouth, Dorset BH3 7AE

Tel: 01202 551935 Fax: 01202 551935
Small, privately-run bed and breakfast establishment. Eleven en-suite guest rooms, two singles and nine doubles. Licensed bar and restaurant available to guests.

Sunnydene Hotel, 11 Spencer Road, Bournemouth, Dorset BH1 3TE

Tel: 01202 552281
Good-sized, family-run establishment offering comfortable bed and breakfast accommodation in ten guest rooms, mostly en-suite. Evening meals available on request.   316

Food and Drink

Belvedere Hotel, 14 Bath Road, Bournemouth, Dorset BH1 2EU

Tel: 01202 293336 Fax: 01202 294699
e-mail: enquiries@belvedere-hotel.co.uk
website: www.belvedere-hotel.co.uk
Comfortable, stylish accommodation with a total of 60 en-suite rooms of varying sizes. The restaurant provides elegant dining with a superb a la carte menu. Two bars.   314

Eastbury Hotel, Long Street, Sherborne, Dorset DT9 3BY

Tel: 01935 813131 Fax: 01935 817296
e-mail: eastbury.sherborne@virgin.net
An elegant Georgian hotel surrounded by fine gardens. Award-winning Conservatory Restaurant enjoys a fine reputation serving mainly English cuisine. 15 en-suite bedrooms.   307

La Mamma, 51-53 Bridge Street, Christchurch, Dorset BH23 1DY

Tel: 01202 471608 Fax: 01202 471608
website: www.lamamma.co.uk
Popular pizzeria and trattoria offering an Italian experience for all the family. Opened in 1974 by Giuseppe and John Mirco, La Mamma has established a far reaching reputation for serving freshly prepared, authentic dishes. Open lunch time and evening (closed Monday in Winter).

The Mount, 49 Blandford Road, Corfe Mullen, Wimborne, Dorset BH21 3HD

Tel: 01202 693908
With a comfortable, relaxed atmosphere, this pub is popular for its fine ales and tasty meals and snacks. Regular karaoke, live music and pub quizzes. Large rear gardens.   318

Winstons Restaurant and Bar, 45 High Street, Sturminster Marshall, Dorset BH21 4AS

Tel: 01258 857211 Fax: 01258 858225
Winstons is a self-contained restaurant and bar adjoining The Churchill Arms pub. Serving a good selection of good quality home-cooked dishes from an a la carte menu, it is open for lunch and dinner, from Wednesday to Saturday, and for Sunday lunch.

Sherborne Golf Club

Higher Clatcombe, Sherborne,
Dorset DT9 4RN
Tel: 01935 812475 Fax: 01935 814218

Here's a message for anyone who may have a course guide for this hilltop course - rip it up and throw it in the bin. It will be completely useless to you now following enormous changes which have basically resulted in an entirely different track.

The major reconstruction work has been going on for a couple of years, but the new-look course is due to be finished and opened for the 2002 season, so it will be equally fascinating both for first-timers to this tranquil corner of Dorset and to previous visitors.

The old James Braid-designed track has been revamped by Howard Swan - also responsible for the Canford Magna complex - and an extra 500 yards have been added to the original, taking it up towards 6,500 yards.

In all, seven holes have been affected and improved, with the old ninth and 10th holes becoming one long par five to add a bit of stiffness around the turn, and those who have played here before will notice that two or three other holes have disappeared in the makeover.

Happily, the best hole on the course, the 194-yard par-three seventh, has survived the shake-up, although in future it will be the ninth. It will also be a lot more awkward, with two new pot bunkers added to the right of the green and another on the left.

Another lovely hole, the par-three 15th, played over a valley, also remains, as do the excellent fairways and terrific views, mainly from the front nine, across the Vale of Sparkford and Blackmore Vale.

Sec/Manager:	M Betteridge
Professional:	G Howell
Directions:	1 miles north of Sherborne center off the B 3145 on the left hand side.
Date Founded:	1894
Type of Course:	Parkland
No of Holes:	18
Length:	5882 yds (5429 mtrs)
Par:	70
SSS:	68
Green Fees:	Weekdays: £20-£30; Weekends/Bank Holidays: £20-£30
Visitors:	Welcome: Contact Club in Advance. Restrictions
Societies:	Welcome: Contact Club in Advance. Restrictions
Facilities:	Practice area, Club Hire, Trolley Hire, Bar, Restaurant

Accommodation, Food and Drink

Reference numbers below refer to detailed information provided in section 2

Accommodation

Ash House Country House Hotel and Restaurant, Main Street, Ash, Nr. Martock, Somerset TA12 6PB

Tel: 01935 822036 Fax: 01935 822992
e-mail: reception@ashhousehotel.freeserve.co.uk
website: www.ashhousecountryhotel.co.uk
Small, privately-owned Georgian Country house hotel surrounded by attractive gardens. Popular a la carte restaurant with high standard of cuisine. Eight delightful en-suite rooms.   424

Eastbury Hotel, Long Street, Sherborne, Dorset DT9 3BY

Tel: 01935 813131 Fax: 01935 817296
e-mail: eastbury.sherborne@virgin.net
An elegant Georgian hotel surrounded by fine gardens. Award-winning Conservatory Restaurant enjoys a fine reputation serving mainly English cuisine. 15 en-suite bedrooms.   307

The Ilchester Arms, The Square, Ilchester, Nr. Yeovil, Somerset BA22 8LN

Tel: 01935 840220 Fax: 01935 841353
Impressive Georgian building, dominating the main street, offering comfortable en-suite accommodation. High quality restaurant with wide-ranging menu. 434

Northover Manor Hotel, Northover, Ilchester, Somerset BA22 8LD

Tel: 01935 840447 Fax: 01935 840006
e-mail: melhaddigan@compuserve.com
A rambling, 15th-century, former manor house offering comfortable, stylish accommodation in 13 en-suite rooms. Formal restaurant and more casual Village Bar which are both open to non-residents.406

The Portman Arms, High Street, East Chinnock, Yeovil, Somerset BA22 9DP

Tel: 01935 862227 Fax: 01935 862227
An imposing building dating from the early 1800s providing a spacious eating and drinking area. Good menu. Five, newly-refurbished, en-suite guest rooms. Caravan pitches also available.   429

Quiet Woman House, Halstock, Dorset BA22 9RX

Tel: 01935 891218
e-mail: quietwomanhouse@ukonline.com
Newly converted bed and breakfast offering high quality accommodation in traditional surroundings. Three guest rooms of varying sizes and two self-catering cottages. Evening meals on request.   315

Richmond House Holiday Accommodation, Barrow Farm, North Barrow, Yeovil, Somerset BA22 7LZ

Tel: 01963 240543 Fax: 01963 240543
e-mail: rhholidays@netscapeonline.co.uk
website: www.rhholidays.co.uk
Eight cottages of varying sizes situated on two sites just 50 metres apart and surrounded by 600 acres of grazing land. Well-maintained and well-equipped.431

The Royal George, West Coker, Yeovil, Somerset BA22 9AN

Tel: 01935 862334 Fax: 01935 864499
18th-century hostelry with a cosy, traditional interior. Menu offers a good selection of dishes. Occasional live music and a regular quiz night. Two en-suite guest rooms.   428

The Walnut Tree, West Camel, Nr. Yeovil, Somerset BA22 7QW

Tel: 01935 851292 Fax: 01935 851292
website: www.thewalnuttreehotel.com
Charming family-run hotel, restaurant and inn. Fine menu of imaginative dishes served both in the bar and restaurant, with fish being a speciality. Thirteen en-suite guest rooms. 426

Weston House Cottages, East Chinnock, Nr. Yeovil, Somerset BA22 9EL

Tel: 01935 863712/863394 Mobile: 07884 214768
e-mail: westonhouseuk@netscapeonline.co.uk
Two cottages converted from former barns located within a working farm. High quality well-equipped accommodation. One cottage sleeps four, the other sleeps five. Dogs welcome. 430

The Yew Tree Inn, Forest Hill, Yeovil, Somerset BA20 2PG

Tel: 01935 476808 Fax: 01935 476808
Former gentleman's residence which was converted into a pub only 30 years ago. Cosy, friendly atmosphere. Excellent food with a menu of traditional pub food. Four guest rooms of varying sizes. 432

Food and Drink

Ash House Country House Hotel and Restaurant, Main Street, Ash, Nr. Martock, Somerset TA12 6PB

Tel: 01935 822036 Fax: 01935 822992
e-mail: reception@ashhousehotel.freeserve.co.uk
website: www.ashhousecountryhotel.co.uk
Small, privately-owned Georgian Country house hotel surrounded by attractive gardens. Popular a la carte restaurant with high standard of cuisine. Eight delightful en-suite rooms. 424

The Chetnole Inn, Chetnole, Nr. Sherborne, Dorset DT9 6NU

Tel: 01935 872337
Popular local's inn, well-liked for top-quality real ales, fine food and its fabulous atmosphere. Cosy music-free lounge bar, spacious restaurant and friendly public bar. 308

Eastbury Hotel, Long Street, Sherborne, Dorset DT9 3BY

Tel: 01935 813131 Fax: 01935 817296
e-mail: eastbury.sherborne@virgin.net
An elegant Georgian hotel surrounded by fine gardens. Award-winning Conservatory Restaurant enjoys a fine reputation serving mainly English cuisine. 15 en-suite bedrooms. 307

The Fox and Hounds, Broadway Road, Charlton Adam, Somerset TA11 7AU

Tel: 01458 223466
Small village pub serving traditional, wholesome food and specialising in home-made pies. Real ales served, including local Butcombe Ales. Pool table, function room and can accommodate up to five caravans or motor homes on an adjoining field.

The Ilchester Arms, The Square, Ilchester, Nr. Yeovil, Somerset BA22 8LN

Tel: 01935 840220 Fax: 01935 841353
Impressive Georgian building, dominating the main street, offering comfortable en-suite accommodation. High quality restaurant with wide-ranging menu. 434

The Lamb and Lark, Limington, Nr. Yeovil, Somerset

Tel: 01935 840368
e-mail: thelambandlark@cs.com
Pub housed within a 15th-century building that has been carefully restored. Inside there is a piano bar and lounge. Good selection of freshly-prepared food. 433

Northover Manor Hotel, Northover, Ilchester, Somerset BA22 8LD

Tel: 01935 840447 Fax: 01935 840006
e-mail: melhaddigan@compuserve.com
A rambling, 15th-century, former manor house offering comfortable, stylish accommodation in 13 en-suite rooms. Formal restaurant and more casual Village Bar which are both open to non-residents.406

The Portman Arms, High Street, East Chinnock, Yeovil, Somerset BA22 9DP

Tel: 01935 862227 Fax: 01935 862227
An imposing building dating from the early 1800s providing a spacious eating and drinking area. Good menu. Five, newly-refurbished, en-suite guest rooms. Caravan pitches also available. 429

The Royal George, West Coker, Yeovil, Somerset BA22 9AN

Tel: 01935 862334 Fax: 01935 864499
18th-century hostelry with a cosy, traditional interior. Menu offers a good selection of dishes. Occasional live music and a regular quiz night. Two en-suite guest rooms. 428

The Royal Marine, St. Weston Terrace, Yeovil, Somerset BA21 5AA

Tel: 01935 474350 Fax: 01935 474350
Popular inn just a short walk from the centre of Yeovil. Sensibly priced menu of meals and snacks and a selection of real ales on tap. 435

The Royal Oak, Stoford, Yeovil, Somerset BA22 9UD

Tel: 01935 475071
Quiet village location just a couple of miles from the centre of Yeovil. Cosy interior with separate restaurant. Well-priced menu of traditional dishes. Occasional quiz and theme nights. 427

Rusty Axe, Stembridge, Somerset

Tel: 01460 240109
Friendly, cosy country pub. Popular for food with a wide ranging menu offering excellent choice. Live music on Saturday evenings. 423

The Walnut Tree, West Camel, Nr. Yeovil, Somerset BA22 7QW

Tel: 01935 851292 Fax: 01935 851292
website: www.thewalnuttreehotel.com
Charming family-run hotel, restaurant and inn. Fine

menu of imaginative dishes served both in the bar and restaurant, with fish being a speciality. Thirteen en-suite guest rooms. 426

The White Hart, Bishops Caundle, Sherborne, Dorset DT9 5ND

Tel: 01963 23301 Fax: 01963 23301
Popular inn serving a full range of traditional meals ranging from bar snacks to a la carte. The bar stocks range of locally brewed real ales.

The Yew Tree Inn, Forest Hill, Yeovil, Somerset BA20 2PG

Tel: 01935 476808 Fax: 01935 476808
Former gentleman's residence which was converted into a pub only 30 years ago. Cosy, friendly atmosphere. Excellent food with a menu of traditional pub food. Four guest rooms of varying sizes. 432

Wareham Golf Club

Sandford Road, Wareham, Dorset BH20 4DH

Tel: 01929 554147/554156 Fax: 01929 557993

Sec/Manager:	Gary Prince
Professional:	None
Directions:	½ mile north of Wareham off the A351 close to Wareham Railway Station
Date Founded:	1908
Type of Course:	Parkland, Heathland
No of Holes:	18
Length:	5432 yds (5014 mtrs)
Par:	69
SSS:	67
Green Fees:	Weekdays: £22 (round) £28 (day); Weekends: £25
Visitors:	Welcome: Contact Club in Advance. Unable to play Sat. morning and Bank Holidays. Handicap Certificates
Societies:	Welcome: Contact Club in Advance

Facilities: Practice Green, Chipping Green, Putting Green, Trolley Hire, Bar, Restaurant

Accommodation, Food and Drink

Reference numbers below refer to detailed information provided in section 2

Accommodation

The Anglebury House and Restaurant, 15-17 North Street, Wareham, Dorset BH20 4AB

Tel: 01929 552988 Fax: 01929 554665
e-mail: anglebury@btconnect.com
Guest house accommodation with seven letting rooms, all but one with en-suite facilities. Long-established coffee shop, at one time frequented by Thomas Hardy and T.E. Lawrence (Lawrence of Arabia). Restaurant offers a la carte and fixed price menus. 302

Cleff House, Brookmans Valley, Iwerne Minster, Blandford Forum, Dorset D11 8NG

Tel: 01747 811129 Fax: 01747 811112
Somewhere special, a unique house offering style, comfort, good food, superb views. Set in nine acres of a beautiful valley, yet within the bounds of the picturesque village. Ideal for a truly relaxing break.

The Greyhound, North Street, Winterbourne Kingston, Blandford Forum, Dorset D11 9AZ

Tel: 01929 471332 Fax: 01929 427610
website: www.greyhoundinnwk.co.uk
Traditional, country inn with spacious, comfortable interior. Selection of real ales and tasty home-cooked food. Four en-suite rooms. 304

High Tor, Worgret Hill, Wareham, Dorset BH20 6AD

Tel: 01929 556869 Fax: 01929 555068
e-mail jeannie@innerpower.freeserve.co.uk
Holistic health centre which calls itself 'a new concept in complementary medicine' offering sixteen natural therapies. Also one room, sleeping four, for bed and breakfast. 319

Manor Farm Caravan Park, East Stoke, Wareham, Dorset BH20 6AW

Tel: 01929 462870 Fax: 01929 462870
Quiet, clean caravan park situated between Wareham and Wool in an area of outstanding natural beauty. Suitable for mobile homes and caravans with seasonal pitches and storage.

The Old Granary, West Holme Farm, Wareham, Dorset BH20 6AQ

Tel: 01929 552972 Fax: 01929 551616
Charming conversion of former granary in which comfortable en-suite bed and breakfast accommodation is available. One downstairs room is equipped for category 3 disabled visitors. Evening meals by prior arrangement. 320

The Sheaf of Arrows, 4 The Square, Cranborne, Dorset BH21 5PR

Tel: 01725 517456
Traditional village hostelry popular with locals and
visitors to the area. Choice of real ales and a good
selection of sensibly priced meals. Five en-suite
rooms.   310

Food and Drink

**The Anglebury House and Restaurant,
15-17 North Street, Wareham, Dorset BH20 4AB**

Tel: 01929 552988 Fax: 01929 554665
e-mail: anglebury@btconnect.com
Guest house accommodation with seven letting
rooms, all but one with en-suite facilities. Long-
established coffee shop, at one time frequented by
Thomas Hardy and T.E. Lawrence (Lawrence of
Arabia). Restaurant offers a la carte and fixed price
menus.   302

**The Greyhound, North Street, Winterbourne
Kingston, Blandford Forum, Dorset D11 9AZ**

Tel: 01929 471332 Fax: 01929 427610
website: www.greyhoundinnwk.co.uk
Traditional, country inn with spacious, comfortable
interior. Selection of real ales and tasty home-cooked
food. Four en-suite rooms.   304

**The Mount, 49 Blandford Road, Corfe Mullen,
Wimborne, Dorset BH21 3HD**

Tel: 01202 693908
With a comfortable, relaxed atmosphere, this pub is
popular for its fine ales and tasty meals and snacks.
Regular karaoke, live music and pub quizzes. Large
rear gardens.   318

**The Sheaf of Arrows, 4 The Square, Cranborne,
Dorset BH21 5PR**

Tel: 01725 517456
Traditional village hostelry popular with locals and
visitors to the area. Choice of real ales and a good
selection of sensibly priced meals. Five en-suite
rooms.   310

**The White Hart, Bishops Caundle, Sherborne,
Dorset DT9 5ND**

Tel: 01963 23301 Fax: 01963 23301
Popular inn serving a full range of traditional meals
ranging from bar snacks to a la carte. The bar stocks
range of locally brewed real ales.

**Winstons Restaurant and Bar, 45 High Street,
Sturminster Marshall, Dorset BH21 4AS**

Tel: 01258 857211 Fax: 01258 858225
Winstons is a self-contained restaurant and bar
adjoining The Churchill Arms pub. Serving a good
selection of good quality home-cooked dishes from
an a la carte menu, it is open for lunch and dinner,
from Wednesday to Saturday, and for Sunday lunch.

Sec/Manager:	Brian Chatham
Professional:	Des Lochrie
Directions:	1 mile north of Weymouth town centre. Take A354 towards Dorchester and turn left on B3157 towards Chickerell. The course is signposted after ½ mile
Date Founded:	1910
Type of Course:	Links/Parkland
No of Holes:	18
Length:	5981 yds (5520 mtrs)
Par:	70
SSS:	69
Green Fees:	Weekdays: £24; Weekends/ Bank Holidays: £30
Visitors:	Welcome: Contact Club in Advance. Unable to play at weekends
Societies:	Welcome: Contact Club in Advance. Unable to play at weekends
Facilities:	Practice Area, Putting Green, Trolley Hire Bar, Restaurant

Weymouth Golf Club

Links Road, Weymouth, Dorset DT4 OPF
Tel: 01305 773981 Fax: 01305 788029

Accommodation, Food and Drink

Reference numbers below refer to detailed information provided in section 2

Accommodation

The Beach House, Brunswick Terrace, Weymouth, Dorset D4 7RW

Tel: 01305 789353
Prime location just ten metres from the sea front with many guest rooms, some en-suite, enjoying superb views. Cooked English breakfasts and licensed bar. 311

Chideock House Hotel, Main Street, Chideock, Dorset DT6 6JN

Tel: 01297 489242 Fax: 01297 489184
website: www.chideockhousehotel.com
Picturesque 15th-century house which has been converted into a comfortable, stylish hotel and restaurant. Nine double, en-suite rooms. 309

George Hotel, 65 Dorchester Road, Weymouth, Dorset D4 7TY

Tel: 01305 786170 Fax: 01305 786170
Family-run hotel in prominent location on through road. Eight guest rooms, two singles and six doubles. Evenings meals available. Large car park.

Gorwell Farm Cottages, Abbotsbury, Weymouth, Dorset D3 4JX

Tel: 01305 871401 Fax: 01305 871441
e-mail: mary@gorwellfarm.co.uk
website: www.gorwellfarm.co.uk
Small collection of self-contained cottage-style apartments. Available for week-long holidays or short breaks. 301

The Greyhound, North Street, Winterbourne Kingston, Blandford Forum, Dorset D11 9AZ

Tel: 01929 471332 Fax: 01929 427610
website: www.greyhoundinnwk.co.uk
Traditional, country inn with spacious, comfortable interior. Selection of real ales and tasty home-cooked food. Four en-suite rooms. 304

High Tor, Worgret Hill, Wareham, Dorset BH20 6AD

Tel: 01929 556869 Fax: 01929 555068
e-mail jeannie@innerpower.freeserve.co.uk
Holistic health centre which calls itself 'a new concept in complementary medicine' offering sixteen natural therapies. Also one room, sleeping four, for bed and breakfast. 319

Food and Drink

Chideock House Hotel, Main Street, Chideock, Dorset DT6 6JN

Tel: 01297 489242 Fax: 01297 489184
website: www.chideockhousehotel.com
Picturesque 15th-century house which has been converted into a comfortable, stylish hotel and restaurant. Nine double, en-suite rooms. 309

The Crown Inn, 59 West Bay Road, Bridport, Dorset DT6 4AX

Tel: 01308 422037 Fax: 01308 458875
e-mail: enquiries@thecrowninn.org.uk
website: www.thecrowninn.org.uk
Situated midway between Bridport and West Bay, The Crown Inn offers classic Irish hospitality in a traditional English setting. A full menu is always available, and parties can be catered for. Children are welcomed and there is a special children's menu.

The Greyhound, North Street, Winterbourne Kingston, Blandford Forum, Dorset D11 9AZ

Tel: 01929 471332 Fax: 01929 427610
website: www.greyhoundinnwk.co.uk
Traditional, country inn with spacious, comfortable interior. Selection of real ales and tasty home-cooked food. Four en-suite rooms. 304

Swanson's Restaurant, Lakeside Walk, Weymouth, Dorset D4 7AW

Tel: 01305 776740 Fax: 01305 776740
Located on the edge of a small lake, built over the water, with an open, conservatory feel. High quality menu specialising in seafood. 313

The White Hart, Bishops Caundle, Sherborne, Dorset DT9 5ND

Tel: 01963 23301 Fax: 01963 23301
Popular inn serving a full range of traditional meals ranging from bar snacks to a la carte. The bar stocks range of locally brewed real ales.

SOMERSET

'Here be dragons' might well have been the annotation found on any ancient map of Somerset. And there is at least one - or rather a *wyvern* - which still survives as the county's emblem. Delve into Somerset's history - if you are visiting the county at leisure you are hard-pressed to avoid doing so - and you uncover a land of lore and legend, myth and mystery that belies the popular image of apple-cheeked, smock-wearing farmers full of bonhomie and home-brewed cider.

From Joseph of Arimathea to Roman legions, Arthurian tales to Cromwellian battles, the name of Somerset crops up time and again, so it is perhaps little wonder that the county's golf courses often have connections with such events. The story of Joseph of Arimathea's landing on the shores of Somerset, although apocryphal, is still celebrated in some religious circles, and a plaque in Burnham-on-Sea tells of the event, although it doesn't mention that had he arrived a few centuries later he would have had to cross several fairways at the Burnham & Berrow club!

Yet despite dangling its feet in the deep waters of the past, Somerset has led the regional boom in golf, almost doubling its number of courses in the past 10 years as entrepreneurs and course architects have flocked to mould the natural landscapes into varying tests of skill. Perhaps supply has even outstripped demand at times, with one or two of the newer

Glastonbury Abbey

clubs finding it tough going financially, but all have so far managed to survive. These courses have also introduced thousands of newcomers to the game, people who, previously, would have found it difficult to get membership at the established, and generally over-subscribed, clubs. The beauty of such an old-new split is reflected in the diversity of courses now available the length and breadth of the county, from the truest of true links at the aforementioned **Burnham & Berrow** to the more American-style lakeland-type course a couple of junctions down the M5 at **Oake Manor**, and from the majesty of **Sham Castle** on the hills above Bath to the rolling splendour of the new track at **Orchardleigh** set amid ancient countryside, as if it had been there since the game was invented.

The delightful Roman-cum-Georgian city of Bath is an obvious epicentre for the north of the county, and has several excellent courses within easy striking distance. Not least are **Tracy Park**, built on the site of the Battle of Lansdown and dominated by the great mansion house, and the **Lansdown** course itself, next to Bath racecourse and offering a fairly flat parkland landscape, despite being about 800 feet above sea level. The city itself is small enough to walk around, and its centrepiece is older even than the Roman influence, which started in 43AD. That centrepiece is

the spa, and nobody really knows exactly when the hot water springs first bubbled to the surface and later gave the city its name. It was the Romans who first harnessed the waters as a tourist attraction, mainly for their own high-ranking soldiers, and now, after many years of being closed to the public for bathing, the spa is undergoing a huge and expensive refurbishment which should soon see the public wallowing in the warmth once more. Add to this the resplendent Bath Abbey, more museums than you can shake a stick at, glorious stone architecture and a burgeoning cafe culture, and you may find it difficult to drag yourself off to play golf.

England's smallest cathedral city, Wells, is another good

Hestercombe Gardens

base for a variety of golf and history. **The Wells** club, besides having a lovely wooded course, also has terrific views over the Cathedral and to distant Glastonbury Tor. An equally breathtaking view of the landmark tor can be had from some 10 miles away on the other side of the city, where the viewing platform also doubles as the 11th green at the **Isle of Wedmore**, a club that has King Alfred on its crest - there's more of that history again! It was at Wedmore, the ancient capital of Wessex, that Alfred and the Danish King Guthrum signed the Peace of Wedmore in 878AD, a treaty that left Alfred in charge of Wessex and the Danes with East Anglia, East Mercia and York. If you loi-

Gaulden Manor

ter around Wedmore, it is also well worth turning right as you leave the club, and heading for Chapel Allerton, where you will come across the only windmill left in Somerset. The area is also an ideal launch pad for courses at **Weston-super-Mare, Clevedon, Mendip, Mendip Spring, Brean,** and **Enmore Park**, just south of Bridgwater in the foothills of the Quantocks.

Bridgwater and the nearby county town of Taunton were the centre of the "Pitchfork Rebellion", and it was at Taunton Castle that Judge Jeffreys' Bloody Assizes sentenced to death 150 followers of the Duke of Monmouth, hence the plethora of inns and pubs in the area with names such as the "Rebels' Retreat" and "Monmouth Arms" - they remember well their roots in these parts and enjoy the notoriety of their ancestors. A special footnote in British history goes to the splendidly-named village of Westonzoyland, just to the east of Bridgwater where, in an innocuous-looking field, stands a simple memorial to mark the site of the last pitched battle ever to be fought on English soil. It was here that Monmouth's uprising was finally crushed, and where 700 of his men lay dead at the end of the day. Apart from **Oake Manor**, a couple of miles away, Taunton has three courses to offer on its doorstep. You can choose from the downland **Taunton & Pickeridge** with its extensive views; the rolling parkland of **Taunton Vale**; or the municipally-owned town centre venue of **Vivary Park**, with its tight and narrow fairways and ponds.

If, by this time, you have overloaded on history, you can allow the scenic charms of the county to take over, with the Quantocks and delightful Exmoor right on the doorstep of Minehead, where the golf course boasts excellent drainage for all-year-round play. Here, however, you are in the land of literature, for in this western corner of Somerset some of the literary world's most famous names have sought - and found - inspiration. The novelists and poets of the Romantic movement were drawn here around the turn of the 19th century by the bleak beauty of the landscape, and it was at Nether Stowey, on the edge of the Quantocks, where Samuel Taylor Coleridge wrote 'The Rime of the Ancient Mariner.' Both William Wordsworth and Charles Lamb stayed with Coleridge during his three-year sojourn here, and Coleridge's Cottage is now a tourist attraction owned by the National Trust.

A few miles away, a scientist was experimenting with electrical energy at Fyne Court, Broomfield. This strange behaviour created much of a stir among the locals, who believed that these experiments had given rise to live organisms. So taken was she by the rumour that it is said that Mary Shelley based her classic story, Frankenstein, on it. And before we leave the literary world, visit the scenic Doone Valley, west of Minehead, should you get the chance, and you may witness what moved RD Blackmore to pen his romantic novel Lorna Doone. Although the wildlife park has now gone, along with Noel Edmonds' Crinkley Bottom theme park, the Windwhistle estate south of Chard still offers windswept golf, especially if you like to play on a plateau 735 feet above sea level and with panoramic views all round.

That should blow away any cobwebs of history - even off a dragon.

Forde Abbey, Chard

Location of Golf Courses

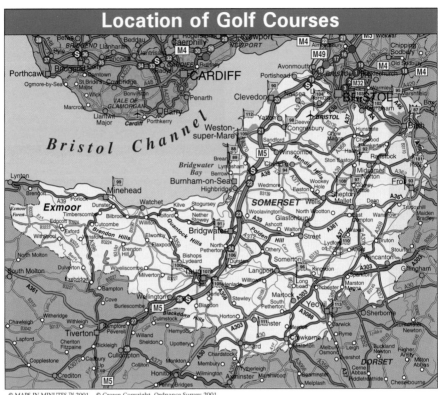

© MAPS IN MINUTES ™ 2001   © Crown Copyright, Ordnance Survey 2001

Bath Golf Club

Sham Castle, North Road, Bath,
Somerset BA2 6JG

Tel: 01225 463834 Fax: 01225 331027

The name of Ralph Allen springs up all over the place in the lovely Georgian city of Bath, such was his impact on the area. The 18th century philanthropist, who made a fortune from improving the fledgling postal service in England, was known as the Man of Bath, famous for his patronage. So it comes as little surprise that he and the Sham Castle site are inextricably linked, for it was his successors who leased the land for the original golf course in 1881.

Ralph was obviously a canny lad when it came to money, because he also invested in stone quarrying, and anyone who knows Bath will know that it was the business to be in during the 1700s. The course even takes its name from the folly he built - now near the clubhouse - to provide him with spectacular views.

The course is set on high ground overlooking the city, and some of the old stone quarries are still in evidence, particularly on the 14th, where tee shots have to carry over the edge of one of the ancient sites. But generally, despite its elevated setting, the course is gently undulating and offers numerous testing holes, not least of which is the 17th, a dog-leg to the right which teases would-be big hitters to cut the corner and risk going out of bounds.

And just to prove its pedigree, Sham Castle is also a regular venue for Somerset county matches and championships

Sec/Manager:	Paul Ware
Professional:	Peter Hancox
Directions:	1¾ miles east of Bath city centre. At Sydney Gardens roundabout (junction of A4 and A36) on northeast side of the city take the A36 (Warminster) and immediately turn right into North Rd. After ½ mile turn left into Golf Course Road. The entrance is at the end.
Date Founded:	1880
Type of Course:	Hilltop Downland
No of Holes:	18
Length:	6442 yds (5946 mtrs)
Par:	71
SSS:	71

Green Fees:	Weekdays: £27; Weekends/ Bank Holidays: £33
Visitors:	Welcome: Contact Club in Advance. Handicap Certificates
Societies:	Welcome: Contact Club in Advance. Restrictions apply
Facilities:	Practice Area, Putting Green, Chipping Green, Driving Range, Club Hire, Trolley Hire, Bar, Restaurant

Accommodation, Food and Drink

Reference numbers below refer to detailed information provided in section 2

Accommodation

The Bear Inn, Holwell, Nr. Frome, Somerset BA11 4PY

Tel: 01373 836585
Unusual structure, built directly into the face of a quarry, cosy interior. Fine ales and wide selection of meals and snacks. Six guest rooms.   444

Ellsworth House, Fosseway, Midsomer Norton, Bath, Somerset BA3 4AU

Tel: 01761 412305
e-mail: accommodation@ellsworth.fsbusiness.co.uk
website: www.ellsworth.fsbusiness.co.uk
Attractive house with a number of comfortable, en-suite guest rooms. Spacious sun lounge and indoor koi carp pond. Non-smoking establishment.   442

Executive Holidays, Whitemill Farm, Iron Mills Lane, Oldford, Frome, Somerset BA11 2NR

Tel: 01373 452907 Fax: 01373 453253
e-mail: info@executiveholidays.co.uk
website: www.executiveholidays.co.uk
Ten different properties of varying sizes all located within the attractive valley of the River Frome. Superb range of leisure activities can be organised .   414

Innlodge at the Bridge Inn, North End Road, Yatton, Nr. Bristol, Somerset BS49 4AU

Tel: 01934 839100 Fax: 01934 839149
e-mail bridgeinn@sfigroup.co.uk
website www.innlodge.com
Modern lodge accommodation with 41 en-suite rooms including some luxurious suites. The Bridge Inn is a popular country inn serving superb home-cooked food.   446

Ston Easton Park, Ston Easton, Nr. Bath, Somerset BA3 4DF

Tel: 01761 241631 Fax: 01761 241377
e-mail: enquiry@stoneaston.co.uk
website: www.stoneaston.co.uk
Grand English country house surrounded by extensive grounds restored to recapture much of the original elegance and splendour. 24 individually-designed en-suite bedrooms. Choice of formal or casual dining, with award-winning cuisine. Superb leisure facilities.   416

Walton's Guest House, 17-19 Crescent Gardens, Upper Bristol Road, Bath BA1 2NA

Tel: 01225 426528 Fax: 01225 420350
Within five minutes walk of City centre, Roman Baths, Pump Rooms and other interesting places, while at the rear of the property is Victoria Park and the Royal Crescent. 15 bedrooms, 2 en-suite. Adjoining public car park.

The White Hart Hotel, 19-21 Sadler Street, Wells, Somerset BA5 2RR

Tel: 01749 672056 Fax: 01749 671074
e-mail: info@whitehart-wells.co.uk
website: www.whitehart-wells.co.uk
Delightful, black and white hotel in the centre of Wells. 13 luxurious bedrooms. Newly refurbished restaurant offers relaxed dining with a more formal Italian restaurant nearby. Function suite.   417

Food and Drink

The Bear Inn, Holwell, Nr. Frome, Somerset BA11 4PY

Tel: 01373 836585
Unusual structure, built directly into the face of a quarry, with cosy interior. Fine ales and wide selection of meals and snacks. Six guest rooms.   444

Innlodge at the Bridge Inn, North End Road, Yatton, Nr. Bristol, Somerset BS49 4AU

Tel: 01934 839100 Fax: 01934 839149
e-mail bridgeinn@sfigroup.co.uk
website www.innlodge.com
Modern lodge accommodation with 41 en-suite rooms including some luxurious suites. The Bridge Inn is a popular country inn serving superb home-cooked food.   446

La Bisalta, 6 Vicarage Street, Frome, Somerset BA11 1PX

Tel: 01373 464238 Fax: 01373 304603
e-mail: luigi@labisalta.fsnet.co.uk
Genuine Italian restaurant, with open veranda and garden area, serving classic Italian cuisine. Long established with popular reputation.   415

Mason's Arms, Marston Gate, Frome, Somerset BA11 4DJ

Tel: 01373 464537 Fax: 01373 455071
Cosy pub with a characterful interior where beams and original fireplaces have been retained. Excellent selection of real ales and delicious menu of tasty dishes.   443

The Somerset Wagon, Broadway, Chilcompton, Radstock, Somerset BA3 4JW

Tel: 01761 232732 Fax: 01761 232522
Former coaching inn that has been transformed into an attractive hostelry. Superb food and ales. Occasional live music.   439

Ston Easton Park, Ston Easton, Nr. Bath, Somerset BA3 4DF

Tel: 01761 241631 Fax: 01761 241377
e-mail: enquiry@stoneaston.co.uk

website: www.stoneaston.co.uk
Grand English country house surrounded by extensive grounds restored to recapture much of the original elegance and splendour. 24 individually-designed en-suite bedrooms. Choice of formal or casual dining, with award-winning cuisine. Superb leisure facilities.   416

Sun Inn, 6 Catherine Street, Frome, Somerset BA11 1DA

Tel: 01373 471913
A 16th-century, town centre inn, and a fine example of a traditional public house. Well-stocked bar and a menu of light meals and snacks. Seven guest rooms, one en-suite.   413

The White Hart Hotel, 19-21 Sadler Street, Wells, Somerset BA5 2RR

Tel: 01749 672056 Fax: 01749 671074
e-mail: info@whitehart-wells.co.uk
website: www.whitehart-wells.co.uk
Delightful, black and white hotel in the centre of Wells. 13 luxurious bedrooms. Newly refurbished restaurant offers relaxed dining with a more formal Italian restaurant nearby. Function suite.   417

Brean Golf Club

Coast Road, Brean, Burnham-on-Sea, Somerset TA8 2RT
Tel: 01278 751595 Fax: 01278 752102

Sec/Manager:	Alex Ferguson
Professional:	David Maines
Directions:	3¾ miles southwest of Weston-super-Mare. From sea front take A370 (M5, Burnham-on-

Sea). After 4 miles at Eastertown turn right onto B road signed Brean. Meander for 4 miles and the entrance is at the end of Pinewood Way in Brean.

Date Founded:	1974
Type of Course:	Meadowland
No of Holes:	18
Length:	5715 yds (5275 mtrs)
Par:	69
SSS:	67
Green Fees:	Weekdays: £15; Weekends/ Bank Holidays: £20
Visitors:	Welcome: Contact Club in Advance. Unable to play before 11.30 am at weekends Handicap Certificates
Societies:	Welcome: Contact Club in Advance
Facilities:	Practice Area, Club Hire, Trolley Hire, Buggy Hire, Bar, Restaurant

Accommodation, Food and Drink

Reference numbers below refer to detailed information provided in section 2

Accommodation

Bella Vista Hotel, 19 Upper Church Road, Weston-super-Mare, Somerset BS23 2DX

Tel: 01934 631931 Fax: 01934 620126
Family-run hotel located just 100 metres from the sea front. Eight spacious en-suite bedrooms. Warm, friendly atmosphere. 408

Beverleigh, Beacon Road, North Hill, Minehead, Somerset TA24 5SF

Tel: 01643 708450
e-mail: beverleigh@talk21.com
Charming Edwardian house, beautifully furnished. Situated on the higher slopes of North Hill where Exmoor meets the sea. Set in lovely gardens with breathtaking views of Minehead and the surrounding hills.

Carefree Holiday Park, 12 Beach Road, Sand Bay, Weston-super-Mare, Somerset BS22 9UZ

Tel: 01934 624541
Beautifully kept, quiet, five-star holiday park situated directly on Sand Bay Beach. Modern caravans offer luxurious four- and six- berth accommodation. Two miles along coast road from Weston-super-Mare and only one mile from Worlebury golf course.

Ellenborough Hall, 15 Ellenborough Park North, Weston-super-Mare, Somerset BS23 1XQ

Tel: 01934 629543
Large Victorian house converted into a family-run hotel with a friendly atmosphere. Four en-suite rooms. Plenty of off-road parking. Within easy reach of the town centre and sea front.

Goodrington Guest House, 23 Charlton Road, Weston-super-Mare, Somerset BS23 4HB

Tel: 01934 623229
e-mail: vera.bishop@btclick.com
website: http://home.btclick.com/vera.bishop
Friendly guest house with just three guest rooms, two with en-suite facilities. One double, one triple and one room with four single beds. Evening meals available on request.

The Greyhound Inn, 1 Lime Street, Stogursey, Bridgwater, Somerset TA5 1QR

Tel: 01278 732490
Traditional rural inn. Bar stocks a range of local real ales, cider, wine and spirits. Good selection of home-cooked food. Bed and breakfast accommodation. 412

The Hawthorne, Crooked Lane, Brent Knoll, Somerset TA9 4BQ

Tel: 01278 760181
Comfortable country house in quiet surroundings. Separate annexe for guests with dining hall and two en-suite bed and breakfast rooms. Close to Berrow golf course.

Innlodge at the Bridge Inn, North End Road, Yatton, Nr. Bristol, Somerset BS49 4AU

Tel: 01934 839100 Fax: 01934 839149
e-mail bridgeinn@sfigroup.co.uk
website www.innlodge.com
Modern lodge accommodation with 41 en-suite rooms including some luxurious suites. The Bridge Inn is a popular country inn serving superb home-cooked food. 446

Laburnum House Lodge Hotel, Sloway Lane, West Huntspill, Highbridge, Somerset TA9 3RJ

Tel: 01278 781830 Fax: 01278 781612
e-mail: laburnumhh@aol.com
website: www.laburnumhh.co.uk
Family-run country lodge hotel. 60 bedrooms, all en-suite, of varying sizes. Peaceful, rural location with clay pigeon shooting, fishing and many other activities available on site. Also holiday complex with superb 80-cover restaurant and two bars open to all visitors. Excellent menus and great pub grub with weekly BBQs and Pig Roasts.

Three Acres Caravan Park, South Road, Brean, Somerset TA8 2RF

Tel: 01278 751313
e-mail: 3acres@ic24.net
15 self-catering six-berth caravans within a couple of miles of Burnham-on-Sea and close to several golf courses. Bar and restaurant within the site for residents' use.

Food and Drink

The Greyhound Inn, 1 Lime Street, Stogursey, Bridgwater, Somerset TA5 1QR

Tel: 01278 732490
Traditional rural inn. Bar stocks a range of local real ales, cider, wine and spirits. Good selection of home-cooked food. Bed and breakfast accommodation. 412

Innlodge at the Bridge Inn, North End Road, Yatton, Nr. Bristol, Somerset BS49 4AU

Tel: 01934 839100 Fax: 01934 839149
e-mail bridgeinn@sfigroup.co.uk
website www.innlodge.com
Modern lodge accommodation with 41 en-suite rooms including some luxurious suites. The Bridge Inn is a popular country inn serving superb home-cooked food. 446

Laburnum House Lodge Hotel, Sloway Lane, West Huntspill, Highbridge, Somerset TA9 3RJ

Tel: 01278 781830 Fax: 01278 781612
e-mail: laburnumhh@aol.com
website: www.laburnumhh.co.uk
Family-run country lodge hotel. 60 bedrooms, all en-suite, of varying sizes. Peaceful, rural location with clay pigeon shooting, fishing and many other activities available on site. Also holiday complex with superb 80-cover restaurant and two bars open to all visitors. Excellent menus and great pub grub with weekly BBQs and Pig Roasts.

Long John Silver, 73 Beach Road, Kewstoke, Weston-super-Mare, Somerset BS22 9UP

Tel: 01934 623367
Characterful inn serving an excellent selection of food ranging from traditional pub fayre to seafood and steak dishes. Vegetarians also catered for.

The Major from Glengarry, 10-14 Upper Church Road, Weston-super-Mare, Somerset BS23 2DT

Tel: 01934 629260
Family-run pub offering a warm welcome to all. Serves Wadsworth Cask Ales and an extensive range of snacks and traditional food prepared by the owner, who is a qualified chef. Regular evening entertainment with live music. Families welcome.

The Market Inn, 1 North End Road, Yatton, Somerset BS49 4AL

Tel: 01934 832209 Fax: 01934 835981
A traditional, country inn located close to the M5. Friendly, warm welcome for locals and visitors to the area. Wide choice of draught ales and fine selection of meals and snacks. 438

The Old Thatched Cottage Restaurant, 14 Knightstone Road, Weston-super-Mare, Somerset BS23 2AN

Tel: 01934 621313
Popular restaurant on seafront serving French, Italian and Greek cuisine from an a la carte menu. Fresh fish is the house speciality. Open every day, all year round. Caters for parties of up to 100.

Burnham & Berrow Golf Club

St. Christopher's Way, Burnham-on-Sea, Somerset TA8 2PE

Tel: 01278 783137 Fax: 01278 795440

How do you like your golf? Does links in the raw suit you? If not, stay away from this, the best-known championship course in the region.

As a measure of the course's stature in the game, five-time Open champion JH Taylor was the club's first professional, and innumerable stars have either twinkled or faded across the sand dunes down the years in an array of regional, national and international events.

And such is its reputation that it regularly hosts a qualifier for the Open each July. It is even rumoured among local golfers that many an aspiring Open champ will even practise on the adjacent and tough little nine-hole course before taking on its big brother.

This is true links golf, with the dunes melting away into the reed beds, from which startled herons can suddenly appear, making equally-startled golfers jump, and where the wind - and therefore the course - can change with the tide.

If all that isn't enough to cope with, there are narrow, ravine-like valleys which are actually fairways, natural hollows and humps, pocket handkerchief greens surrounded by dreaded pot bunkers, and untamed rough which can bring tears to the eyes of the most hardened player.

On top of all that, there are some extremely tough holes as well! But don't let elevated or sloping greens worry you - you may never get that far.

Seriously, this is links golf as good as it gets and, if you can't master the often alien-like landscape, at least enjoy golf as it was meant to be played.

Sec/Manager:	Mrs. Sloman
Professional:	Mark Crowther-Smith
Directions:	1 mile north of Burnham-on-Sea. From centre take Berrow Rd (B3140). After 1 mile, just before Texaco Service Station turn left into St Christophers Way. The entrance is at the end.
Visitors:	Welcome: Contact Club in Advance. Handicap Certificates
Societies:	Welcome: By arrangement with Club
Facilities:	Putting Green, Chipping Green, Club Hire, Trolley Hire, Buggy Hire, Bar, Restaurant

Championship

Date Founded:	1890
Type of Course:	Links
No of Holes:	18
Length:	6606 yds (6097 mtrs)
Par:	71
SSS:	73
Green Fees:	Weekdays: £40; Weekends/ Bank Holidays: £60

Channel

Type of Course:	Links
No of Holes:	9 x 2
Length:	6120 yds (5649 mtrs)
Par:	70
SSS:	69
Green Fees:	Weekdays: £12; Weekends/ Bank Holidays: £12

Accommodation, Food and Drink

Reference numbers below refer to detailed information provided in section 2

Accommodation

Bella Vista Hotel, 19 Upper Church Road, Weston-super-Mare, Somerset BS23 2DX

Tel: 01934 631931 Fax: 01934 620126
Family-run hotel located just 100 metres from the sea front. Eight spacious en-suite bedrooms. Warm, friendly atmosphere. *408*

Beverleigh, Beacon Road, North Hill, Minehead, Somerset TA24 5SF

Tel: 01643 708450
e-mail: beverleigh@talk21.com
Charming Edwardian house, beautifully furnished.

Situated on the higher slopes of North Hill where Exmoor meets the sea. Set in lovely gardens with breathtaking views of Minehead and the surrounding hills.

Carefree Holiday Park, 12 Beach Road, Sand Bay, Weston-super-Mare, Somerset BS22 9UZ

Tel: 01934 624541
Beautifully kept, quiet, five-star holiday park situated directly on Sand Bay Beach. Modern caravans offer luxurious four- and six- berth accommodation. Two miles along coast road from Weston-super-Mare and only one mile from Worlebury golf course.

Ellenborough Hall, 15 Ellenborough Park North, Weston-super-Mare, Somerset BS23 1XQ

Tel: 01934 629543
Large Victorian house converted into a family-run hotel with a friendly atmosphere. Four en-suite rooms. Plenty of off-road parking. Within easy reach of the town centre and sea front.

Goodrington Guest House, 23 Charlton Road, Weston-super-Mare, Somerset BS23 4HB

Tel: 01934 623229
e-mail: vera.bishop@btclick.com
website: http://home.btclick.com/vera.bishop
Friendly guest house with just three guest rooms, two with en-suite facilities. One double, one triple and one room with four single beds. Evening meals available on request.

The Greyhound Inn, 1 Lime Street, Stogursey, Bridgwater, Somerset TA5 1QR

Tel: 01278 732490
Traditional rural inn. Bar stocks a range of local real ales, cider, wine and spirits. Good selection of home-cooked food. Bed and breakfast accommodation. *412*

The Hawthorne, Crooked Lane, Brent Knoll, Somerset TA9 4BQ

Tel: 01278 760181
Comfortable country house in quiet surroundings. Separate annexe for guests with dining hall and two en-suite bed and breakfast rooms. Close to Berrow golf course.

Innlodge at the Bridge Inn, North End Road, Yatton, Nr. Bristol, Somerset BS49 4AU

Tel: 01934 839100 Fax: 01934 839149
e-mail bridgeinn@sfigroup.co.uk
website www.innlodge.com
Modern lodge accommodation with 41 en-suite rooms including some luxurious suites. The Bridge Inn is a popular country inn serving superb home-cooked food. *446*

Laburnum House Lodge Hotel, Sloway Lane, West Huntspill, Highbridge, Somerset TA9 3RJ

Tel: 01278 781830 Fax: 01278 781612
e-mail: laburnumhh@aol.com
website: www.laburnumhh.co.uk
Family-run country lodge hotel. 60 bedrooms, all en-suite, of varying sizes. Peaceful, rural location with clay pigeon shooting, fishing and many other activities available on site. Also holiday complex with

superb 80-cover restaurant and two bars open to all visitors. Excellent menus and great pub grub with weekly BBQs and Pig Roasts.

Three Acres Caravan Park, South Road, Brean, Somerset TA8 2RF

Tel: 01278 751313
e-mail: 3acres@ic24.net
15 self-catering six-berth caravans within a couple of miles of Burnham-on-Sea and close to several golf courses. Bar and restaurant within the site for residents' use.

Food and Drink

The Greyhound Inn, 1 Lime Street, Stogursey, Bridgwater, Somerset TA5 1QR

Tel: 01278 732490
Traditional rural inn. Bar stocks a range of local real ales, cider, wine and spirits. Good selection of home-cooked food. Bed and breakfast accommodation. 412

Innlodge at the Bridge Inn, North End Road, Yatton, Nr. Bristol, Somerset BS49 4AU

Tel: 01934 839100 Fax: 01934 839149
e-mail bridgeinn@sfigroup.co.uk
website www.innlodge.com
Modern lodge accommodation with 41 en-suite rooms including some luxurious suites. The Bridge Inn is a popular country inn serving superb home-cooked food. 446

Laburnum House Lodge Hotel, Sloway Lane, West Huntspill, Highbridge, Somerset TA9 3RJ

Tel: 01278 781830 Fax: 01278 781612
e-mail: laburnumhh@aol.com
website: www.laburnumhh.co.uk
Family-run country lodge hotel. 60 bedrooms, all en-suite, of varying sizes. Peaceful, rural location with clay pigeon shooting, fishing and many other activities available on site. Also holiday complex with superb 80-cover restaurant and two bars open to all visitors. Excellent menus and great pub grub with weekly BBQs and Pig Roasts.

Long John Silver, 73 Beach Road, Kewstoke, Weston-super-Mare, Somerset BS22 9UP

Tel: 01934 623367
Characterful inn serving an excellent selection of food ranging from traditional pub fayre to seafood and steak dishes. Vegetarians also catered for.

The Major from Glengarry, 10-14 Upper Church Road, Weston-super-Mare, Somerset BS23 2DT

Tel: 01934 629260
Family-run pub offering a warm welcome to all. Serves Wadsworth Cask Ales and an extensive range of snacks and traditional food prepared by the owner, who is a qualified chef. Regular evening entertainment with live music. Families welcome.

The Market Inn, 1 North End Road, Yatton, Somerset BS49 4AL

Tel: 01934 832209 Fax: 01934 835981
A traditional, country inn located close to the M5. Friendly, warm welcome for locals and visitors to the

area. Wide choice of draught ales and fine selection of meals and snacks. 438

The Old Thatched Cottage Restaurant, 14 Knightstone Road, Weston-super-Mare, Somerset BS23 2AN

Tel: 01934 621313
Popular restaurant on seafront serving French, Italian and Greek cuisine from an a la carte menu. Fresh fish is the house speciality. Open every day, all year round. Caters for parties of up to 100.

Clevedon Golf Club

Castle Road, Clevedon, Somerset BS21 7AA

Tel: 01275 874057 Fax: 01275 340221

If there is one thing you need to practice before tackling this pretty spectacular course, it is those low, under-the-wind punched iron shots. That is because there are two things you are just about guaranteed at Clevedon - a bad hair day and some terrific views.

The cliff-top course boasts of being one of the most picturesque in the south west, with views across the Severn Estuary to Wales, and with the Second Severn Crossing adding more spectacle to the holes around the middle of the 18.

Although the course has been on the same site since 1898, it has undergone a great deal of re-construction in recent years, with 16 greens rebuilt to USGA standards and the introduction of five new holes. All five are due to be in play by the summer of 2001, increasing the par from 68 to 72 as two par threes are retired, and the yardage will go up from the original 5,641 to 6,483 off the championship tees.

Having negotiated the five newcomers, you arrive at the course's signature hole, and it is sure to be one you will never forget. The par four 16th, or "Castle Hole", has its tee perched some 200 feet above the fairway, affording views over the whole of Clevedon, and seawards to the islands of Flat Holm and Steep Holm (the origin of which will become obvious at first sight), making its 346 yards look quite an awesome task.

Try keeping that tee shot under the wind.

Sec/Manager:	Jim Cunning
Professional:	Rob Scanlan
Directions:	1 mile north of Clevedon. From M5 junction 20 take B3133 (Clevedon). After 200 yds at roundabout turn right into Northern Way (leading to B3214, Portishead). After ¾ mile turn left into Holly Lane leading to Castle Road. The

entrance is after ½ mile in Linkside.

Date Founded: 1891

Type of Course: Parkland

No of Holes: 18

Length: 6500 yds (5169 mtrs)

Par: 72

SSS: 72

Green Fees: Weekdays: £25; Weekends/ Bank Holidays: £40

Visitors: Welcome: Contact Club in Advance. Playing times by arrangement

Societies: Welcome: Contact Club in Advance. Unable to play at weekends

Facilities: Putting Green, Chipping Green, Club Hire, Trolley Hire, Bar, Restaurant

Accommodation, Food and Drink

Reference numbers below refer to detailed information provided in section 2

Accommodation

Innlodge at the Bridge Inn, North End Road, Yatton, Nr. Bristol, Somerset BS49 4AU

Tel: 01934 839100 Fax: 01934 839149
e-mail bridgeinn@sfigroup.co.uk
website www.innlodge.com
Modern lodge accommodation with 41 en-suite rooms including some luxurious suites. The Bridge Inn is a popular country inn serving superb home-cooked food.   446

The Manor Lodge, 21 Station Road, Keynsham Road, Bristol BS31 2BH

Tel: 0117 986 2191
e-mail: jean@themanorlodge.freeserve.co.uk
Impressive Victorian town house offering comfortable bed and breakfast accommodation. Seven en-suite guest rooms.   425

The Prince of Orange, 17 High Street, Yatton, Somerset BS49 4JD

Tel: 01934 832193
Fax: 01934 832193
Popular with locals and tourists for the good range of beers and hearty food. Accommodation available in a self-contained part of the building, with five en-suite rooms.   441

Food and Drink

Innlodge at the Bridge Inn, North End Road, Yatton, Nr. Bristol, Somerset BS49 4AU

Tel: 01934 839100 Fax: 01934 839149
e-mail bridgeinn@sfigroup.co.uk

website www.innlodge.com
Modern lodge accommodation with 41 en-suite rooms including some luxurious suites. The Bridge Inn is a popular country inn serving superb home-cooked food.   446

The Market Inn, 1 North End Road, Yatton, Somerset BS49 4AL

Tel: 01934 832209 Fax: 01934 835981
A traditional, country inn located close to the M5. Friendly, warm welcome for locals and visitors to the area. Wide choice of draught ales and fine selection of meals and snacks.   438

The Prince of Orange, 17 High Street, Yatton, Somerset BS49 4JD

Tel: 01934 832193
Fax: 01934 832193
Popular with locals and tourists for the good range of beers and hearty food. Accommodation available in a self-contained part of the building, with five en-suite rooms.   441

Enmore Park Golf Club

Enmore, Bridgwater, Somerset TA5 2AN

Tel: 01278 671481 Fax: 01278 671740

Sec/Manager: David Weston

Professional: Nigel Wixon

Directions: 4 miles southwest of Bridgwater. Follow signs to Enmore off the A39 to the west of Bridgwater

Date Founded: 1906

Type of Course: Parkland

No of Holes: 18

Length: 6411 yds (5917 mtrs)

Par: 71

SSS: 71

Green Fees: Weekdays: £20; Weekends/ Bank Holidays: £30

Visitors:	Welcome: Contact Club in Advance. Handicap Certificates
Societies:	Welcome: Contact Club in Advance. Unable to play Tues, Wed
Facilities:	Putting Green, Chipping Green, Buggy Hire, Club Hire, Trolley Hire Bar, Restaurant

Accommodation, Food and Drink

Reference numbers below refer to detailed information provided in section 2

Accommodation

Bashfords Farmhouse, West Bagborough, Taunton, Somerset TA4 3EF

Tel: 01823 432015 Fax: 0870 1671587
e-mail: charlieritchie@netscapeonline.co.uk
Non-working farmhouse dating largely from the 18th century. Three comfortable rooms with en-suite facilities or private bathroom. Evening meals available on request.   440

Blackmore Farm, Cannington, Bridgwater, Somerset TA5 2NE

Tel: 01278 653442 Fax: 01278 653427
Historic manor house dating back to the 14th century offering comfortable farmhouse bed and breakfast with four spacious en-suite rooms.   410

The Greyhound Inn, 1 Lime Street, Stogursey, Bridgwater, Somerset TA5 1QR

Tel: 01278 732490
Traditional rural inn. Bar stocks a range of local real ales, cider, wine and spirits. Good selection of home-cooked food. Bed and breakfast accommodation. 412

The Kings Head Inn, 12 High Street, Cannington, Bridgwater, Somerset TA5 2HE

Tel: 01278 652293 Fax: 01278 652293
A 17th-century, former coaching inn with cosy interior. Good selection stocked behind the bar. Lunch time carvery and evening a la carte menu. Bed and breakfast accommodation.   411

Laburnum House Lodge Hotel, Sloway Lane, West Huntspill, Highbridge, Somerset TA9 3RJ

Tel: 01278 781830 Fax: 01278 781612
e-mail: laburnumhh@aol.com
website: www.laburnumhh.co.uk
Family-run country lodge hotel. 60 bedrooms, all en-suite, of varying sizes. Peaceful, rural location with clay pigeon shooting, fishing and many other activities available on site. Also holiday complex with superb 80-cover restaurant and two bars open to all visitors. Excellent menus and great pub grub with weekly BBQs and Pig Roasts.

Marshfield Hotel, 18 Tregonwell Road, Minehead, Somerset TA24 5DU

Tel: 01643 702517 Fax: 01643 702517
e-mail: marshfield.hotel@minehead18.freeserve.co.uk
website: http://welcome.to/marshfieldhotel

Small, family-run hotel providing a relaxed atmosphere in which to enjoy a short break or week-long holiday. Ten en-suite rooms, attractively furnished and decorated. Also a guests' lounge, licensed bar and restaurant.

Promenade Hotel, Esplanade, Minehead, Somerset TA24 5QS

Tel: 01643 702572 Fax: 01643 702572
Lovely seafront hotel in unrivalled location overlooking Minehead harbour. Converted in 1976 into a fully wheelchair-accessible property. 11 en-suite bedrooms.   405

Rose and Crown, St. Mary Street, Nether Stowey, Somerset TA5 1LJ

Tel: 01278 732265
Old coaching inn dating back to the 15th century. Cosy interior with separate restaurant and lounge area. Comfortable en-suite accommodation with rooms of varying sizes.   409

Spears Cross Hotel, 1 West Street, Dunster, Minehead, Somerset TA24 6SN

Tel: 01643 821439
e-mail: mjcapel@aol.com
website: www.smoothhound.co.uk/hotels/
   spearsx.html
A listed 15th-century hotel located in the centre of the medieval village of Dunster. Four en-suite guest rooms. Tasty breakfasts are cooked to order and light meals and packed lunches are also available. Terraced garden features model houses.

Food and Drink

The Bird in Hand, Mount Street, Bishops Lydeard, Taunton, Somerset TA4 3LH

Tel: 01823 432090
Traditional country pub dating to the 18th century. Menu offers a selection of meals and snacks while the bar claims to stock the best beer in the area.   437

The Greyhound Inn, 1 Lime Street, Stogursey, Bridgwater, Somerset TA5 1QR

Tel: 01278 732490
Traditional rural inn. Bar stocks a range of local real ales, cider, wine and spirits. Good selection of home-cooked food. Bed and breakfast accommodation. 412

The Kings Head Inn, 12 High Street, Cannington, Bridgwater, Somerset TA5 2HE

Tel: 01278 652293 Fax: 01278 652293
A 17th-century, former coaching inn with cosy interior. Good selection stocked behind the bar. Lunch time carvery and evening a la carte menu. Bed and breakfast accommodation.   411

Laburnum House Lodge Hotel, Sloway Lane, West Huntspill, Highbridge, Somerset TA9 3RJ

Tel: 01278 781830 Fax: 01278 781612
e-mail: laburnumhh@aol.com
website: www.laburnumhh.co.uk
Family-run country lodge hotel. 60 bedrooms, all en-suite, of varying sizes. Peaceful, rural location with clay pigeon shooting, fishing and many other

activities available on site. Also holiday complex with superb 80-cover restaurant and two bars open to all visitors. Excellent menus and great pub grub with weekly BBQs and Pig Roasts.

Rose and Crown, St. Mary Street, Nether Stowey, Somerset TA5 1LJ

Tel: 01278 732265
Old coaching inn dating back to the 15th century. Cosy interior with separate restaurant and lounge area. Comfortable en-suite accommodation with rooms of varying sizes.   409

Farrington Golf Club

Marsh Lane, Farrington Gurney, Bristol, Somerset BS39 6TS

Tel: 01761 241274 Fax: 01761 451021

This is another of the region's "youngsters", being about eight years old, with USGA spec greens and computerised irrigation to boot! Although in some respects the course is still maturing, it offers a strong test of anyone's game.

The course was designed by Peter Thompson - the club's original owner and professional - and in 2000 was taken over by new a owner with some ideas for development. Thompson, however, did a good job in contouring the course to the landscape, making the most of mature trees and hedgerows plus, of course, the inevitable lakes.

If you don't get any rushes of blood to the head for the first five holes, which are a bit tight and carved into a hillside, there's plenty of opportunity later to open your shoulders - as long as you keep it straight. The seventh allows the big hitters ample opportunity to lose a ball or two in the water, as does the cheeky little par-three 176-yard eighth

The back nine conceals two pretty intimidating holes, both of which could be called the signature holes for the course. The first of these is the 12th, a par four 272-yarder, but the green is about 100 feet below the tee, and guarded by a

lake in front and to one side, and a hedge on the other side. Stroke index 16 - you must be joking! The second is the 17th, which would be a relatively straightforward par four of 360 yards if the fairway didn't arrow between two lakes.

Sec/Manager:	Steve Cook
Professional:	John Cowgill
Directions:	1½ miles west of Midsomer Norton off the A362 from Frome close to its intersection with the A37
Visitors:	Welcome: Contact Club in Advance. Handicap Certificates
Societies:	Welcome: Contact Club in Advance. Unable to play weekends
Facilities:	Putting Green, Chipping Green, Club Hire, Trolley Hire, Buggy Hire, Bar, Restaurant, Driving Range

Course 1

Date Founded:	1992
Type of Course:	Parkland
No of Holes:	18
Length:	6693 yds (6176 mtrs)
Par:	72
SSS:	72

Green Fees: Weekdays: £22; Weekends/
                Bank Holidays: £28

Course 2

Type of Course: Parkland

No of Holes: 9

Length: 3022 yds (2789 mtrs)

Par: 54

SSS: 53

Green Fees: Weekdays: £5.50; Weekends/
                Bank Holidays: £8

Accommodation, Food and Drink

Reference numbers below refer to detailed
information provided in section 2

Accommodation

**The Bear Inn, Holwell, Nr. Frome,
Somerset BA11 4PY**

Tel: 01373 836585
Unusual structure, built directly into the face of a
quarry, with cosy interior. Fine ales and wide selection
of meals and snacks. Six guest rooms.   444

**Castlebrook Holiday Cottages, Castlebrook,
Compton Dundon, Somerton,
Somerset TA11 6PR**

Tel: 01458 841680 Fax: 01458 841680
Two fully-equipped holiday homes located in the
heart of the Polden Hills. Both feature kitchenette,
sitting/dining room, shower room/WC, sleeping three
and five adults. Pets welcome by arrangement.   407

**Ellsworth House, Fosseway, Midsomer Norton,
Bath, Somerset BA3 4AU**

Tel: 01761 412305
e-mail: accommodation@ellsworth.fsbusiness.co.uk
website: www.ellsworth.fsbusiness.co.uk
Attractive house with a number of comfortable, en-
suite guest rooms. Spacious sun lounge and indoor
koi carp pond. Non-smoking establishment.   442

**Executive Holidays, Whitemill Farm, Iron Mills
Lane, Oldford, Frome, Somerset BA11 2NR**

Tel: 01373 452907 Fax: 01373 453253
e-mail: info@executiveholidays.co.uk
website: www.executiveholidays.co.uk
Ten different properties of varying sizes all located
within the attractive valley of the River Frome. Superb
range of leisure activities can be organised.   414

**The Gordons Hotel, Cliff Street, Cheddar,
Somerset BS27 3RD**

Tel: 01934 742497 Fax: 01934 744965
e-mail: gordons.hotel@virgin.net
Owned by the same family for over 25 years and well
liked for its friendly and comfortable atmosphere, The
Gordons Hotel offers 14 bedrooms, mostly en-suite.
Situated at the foot of the famous gorge and an ideal
holiday base. No evening meals.

**Innlodge at the Bridge Inn, North End Road,
Yatton, Nr. Bristol, Somerset BS49 4AU**

Tel: 01934 839100 Fax: 01934 839149
e-mail: bridgeinn@sfigroup.co.uk
website: www.innlodge.com
Modern lodge accommodation with 41 en-suite
rooms including some luxurious suites. The Bridge
Inn is a popular country inn serving superb home-
cooked food.   446

**The Manor Lodge, 21 Station Road, Keynsham
Road, Bristol BS31 2BH**

Tel: 0117 986 2191
e-mail: jean@themanorlodge.freeserve.co.uk
Impressive Victorian town house offering comfortable
bed and breakfast accommodation. Seven en-suite
guest rooms.   425

**Poachers Table, Cliff Street, Cheddar,
Somerset BS27 3PT**

Tel: 01934 742271
A family-run restaurant offering a wide variety of
food, catering to all tastes and appetites. Situated on
the main street, at the foot of Cheddar Gorge, with
ample car parking available opposite.

**The Prince of Orange, 17 High Street, Yatton,
Somerset BS49 4JD**

Tel: 01934 832193 Fax: 01934 832193
Popular with locals and tourists for the good range of
beers and hearty food. Accommodation available in a
self-contained part of the building, with five en-suite
rooms.   441

**Ston Easton Park, Ston Easton, Nr. Bath,
Somerset BA3 4DF**

Tel: 01761 241631 Fax: 01761 241377
e-mail: enquiry@stoneaston.co.uk
website: www.stoneaston.co.uk
Grand English country house surrounded by
extensive grounds restored to recapture much of the
original elegance and splendour. 24 individually-
designed en-suite bedrooms. Choice of formal or
casual dining, with award-winning cuisine. Superb
leisure facilities.   416

**Walton's Guest House, 17-19 Crescent Gardens,
Upper Bristol Road, Bath BA1 2NA**

Tel: 01225 426528 Fax: 01225 420350
Within five minutes walk of City centre, Roman
Baths, Pump Rooms and other interesting places,
while at the rear of the property is Victoria Park and
the Royal Crescent. 15 bedrooms, 2 en-suite.
Adjoining public car park.

**The White Hart Hotel, 19-21 Sadler Street, Wells,
Somerset BA5 2RR**

Tel: 01749 672056 Fax: 01749 671074
e-mail: info@whitehart-wells.co.uk
website: www.whitehart-wells.co.uk
Delightful, black and white hotel in the centre of
Wells. 13 luxurious bedrooms. Newly refurbished
restaurant offers relaxed dining with a more formal
Italian restaurant nearby. Function suite.   417

Food and Drink

The Bear Inn, Holwell, Nr. Frome, Somerset BA11 4PY

Tel: 01373 836585
Unusual structure, built directly into the face of a quarry, with cosy interior. Fine ales and wide selection of meals and snacks. Six guest rooms.	444

Innlodge at the Bridge Inn, North End Road, Yatton, Nr. Bristol, Somerset BS49 4AU

Tel: 01934 839100 Fax: 01934 839149
e-mail bridgeinn@sfigroup.co.uk
website www.innlodge.com
Modern lodge accommodation with 41 en-suite rooms including some luxurious suites. The Bridge Inn is a popular country inn serving superb home-cooked food.	446

Mason's Arms, Marston Gate, Frome, Somerset BA11 4DJ

Tel: 01373 464537 Fax: 01373 455071
Cosy pub with a characterful interior where beams and original fireplaces have been retained. Excellent selection of real ales and delicious menu of tasty dishes.	443

Poachers Table, Cliff Street, Cheddar, Somerset BS27 3PT

Tel: 01934 742271
A family-run restaurant offering a wide variety of food, catering to all tastes and appetites. Situated on the main street, at the foot of Cheddar Gorge, with ample car parking available opposite.

The Prince of Orange, 17 High Street, Yatton, Somerset BS49 4JD

Tel: 01934 832193
Fax: 01934 832193
Popular with locals and tourists for the good range of beers and hearty food. Accommodation available in a self-contained part of the building, with five en-suite rooms.	441

The Somerset Wagon, Broadway, Chilcompton, Radstock, Somerset BA3 4JW

Tel: 01761 232732 Fax: 01761 232522
Former coaching inn that has been transformed into an attractive hostelry. Superb food and ales. Occasional live music.	439

Ston Easton Park, Ston Easton, Nr. Bath, Somerset BA3 4DF

Tel: 01761 241631 Fax: 01761 241377
e-mail: enquiry@stoneaston.co.uk
website: www.stoneaston.co.uk
Grand English country house surrounded by extensive grounds restored to recapture much of the original elegance and splendour. 24 individually-designed en-suite bedrooms. Choice of formal or casual dining, with award-winning cuisine. Superb leisure facilities.	416

Sun Inn, 6 Catherine Street, Frome, Somerset BA11 1DA

Tel: 01373 471913
A 16th-century, town centre inn, and a fine example of a traditional public house. Well-stocked bar and a menu of light meals and snacks. Seven guest rooms, one en-suite.	413

The White Hart Hotel, 19-21 Sadler Street, Wells, Somerset BA5 2RR

Tel: 01749 672056 Fax: 01749 671074
e-mail: info@whitehart-wells.co.uk
website: www.whitehart-wells.co.uk
Delightful, black and white hotel in the centre of Wells. 13 luxurious bedrooms. Newly refurbished restaurant offers relaxed dining with a more formal Italian restaurant nearby. Function suite.	417

Frome Golf Club

Critchill Manor, Frome, Somerset BA11 4LJ
Tel: 01373 453410 Fax: 01373 453410

Sec/Manager:	Juliet Vowell
Professional:	Murdoch McEwan
Directions:	1 mile west of Frome. From A361 (Shepton Mallet to Trowbridge road) on east side of Frome take A362 (Radstock). At Esso Service Station turn left into Nunney Rd leading to Critch Hill. The entrance is on the right hand side 1 mile after Esso Station.
Date Founded:	1992
Type of Course:	Parkland
No of Holes:	18
Length:	5466 yds (5045 mtrs)
Par:	69
SSS:	67
Green Fees:	Weekdays: £13 (round) £18 (day); Weekends/Bank Holidays: £15 (round) £19 (day)
Visitors:	Welcome: Tee times bookable Weekends and Bank Holidays only
Societies:	Welcome: By arrangement with Club
Facilities:	Putting Green, Chipping Green, Driving Range, Club Hire, Trolley Hire, Bar, Restaurant

Accommodation, Food and Drink

Reference numbers below refer to detailed information provided in section 2

Accommodation

The Bear Inn, Holwell, Nr. Frome, Somerset BA11 4PY

Tel: 01373 836585
Unusual structure, built directly into the face of a quarry, with cosy interior. Fine ales and wide selection of meals and snacks. Six guest rooms.   444

Ellsworth House, Fosseway, Midsomer Norton, Bath, Somerset BA3 4AU

Tel: 01761 412305
e-mail: accommodation@ellsworth.fsbusiness.co.uk
website: www.ellsworth.fsbusiness.co.uk
Attractive house with a number of comfortable, en-suite guest rooms. Spacious sun lounge and indoor koi carp pond. Non-smoking establishment.   442

Executive Holidays, Whitemill Farm, Iron Mills Lane, Oldford, Frome, Somerset BA11 2NR

Tel: 01373 452907 Fax: 01373 453253
e-mail: info@executiveholidays.co.uk
website: www.executiveholidays.co.uk
Ten different properties of varying sizes all located within the attractive valley of the River Frome. Superb range of leisure activities can be organised.   414

Innlodge at the Bridge Inn, North End Road, Yatton, Nr. Bristol, Somerset BS49 4AU

Tel: 01934 839100 Fax: 01934 839149
e-mail bridgeinn@sfigroup.co.uk
website www.innlodge.com
Modern lodge accommodation with 41 en-suite rooms including some luxurious suites. The Bridge Inn is a popular country inn serving superb home-cooked food.   446

Ston Easton Park, Ston Easton, Nr. Bath, Somerset BA3 4DF

Tel: 01761 241631 Fax: 01761 241377
e-mail: enquiry@stoneaston.co.uk
website: www.stoneaston.co.uk
Grand English country house surrounded by extensive grounds restored to recapture much of the original elegance and splendour. 24 individually-designed en-suite bedrooms. Choice of formal or casual dining, with award-winning cuisine. Superb leisure facilities.   416

Walton's Guest House, 17-19 Crescent Gardens, Upper Bristol Road, Bath BA1 2NA

Tel: 01225 426528 Fax: 01225 420350
Within five minutes walk of City centre, Roman Baths, Pump Rooms and other interesting places, while at the rear of the property is Victoria Park and the Royal Crescent. 15 bedrooms, 2 en-suite. Adjoining public car park.

The White Hart Hotel, 19-21 Sadler Street, Wells, Somerset BA5 2RR

Tel: 01749 672056 Fax: 01749 671074
e-mail: info@whitehart-wells.co.uk
website: www.whitehart-wells.co.uk
Delightful, black and white hotel in the centre of Wells. 13 luxurious bedrooms. Newly refurbished restaurant offers relaxed dining with a more formal Italian restaurant nearby. Function suite.   417

Food and Drink

The Bear Inn, Holwell, Nr. Frome, Somerset BA11 4PY

Tel: 01373 836585
Unusual structure, built directly into the face of a quarry, with cosy interior. Fine ales and wide selection of meals and snacks. Six guest rooms.   444

Innlodge at the Bridge Inn, North End Road, Yatton, Nr. Bristol, Somerset BS49 4AU

Tel: 01934 839100 Fax: 01934 839149
e-mail bridgeinn@sfigroup.co.uk
website www.innlodge.com
Modern lodge accommodation with 41 en-suite rooms including some luxurious suites. The Bridge Inn is a popular country inn serving superb home-cooked food.   446

La Bisalta, 6 Vicarage Street, Frome, Somerset BA11 1PX

Tel: 01373 464238 Fax: 01373 304603
e-mail: luigi@labisalta.fsnet.co.uk
Genuine Italian restaurant, with open veranda and garden area, serving classic Italian cuisine. Long established with popular reputation.   415

Mason's Arms, Marston Gate, Frome, Somerset BA11 4DJ

Tel: 01373 464537 Fax: 01373 455071
Cosy pub with a characterful interior where beams and original fireplaces have been retained. Excellent selection of real ales and delicious menu of tasty dishes.   443

The Somerset Wagon, Broadway, Chilcompton, Radstock, Somerset BA3 4JW

Tel: 01761 232732 Fax: 01761 232522
Former coaching inn that has been transformed into an attractive hostelry. Superb food and ales. Occasional live music.   439

Ston Easton Park, Ston Easton, Nr. Bath, Somerset BA3 4DF

Tel: 01761 241631 Fax: 01761 241377
e-mail: enquiry@stoneaston.co.uk
website: www.stoneaston.co.uk
Grand English country house surrounded by extensive grounds restored to recapture much of the original elegance and splendour. 24 individually-designed en-suite bedrooms. Choice of formal or casual dining, with award-winning cuisine. Superb leisure facilities.   416

Sun Inn, 6 Catherine Street, Frome, Somerset BA11 1DA

Tel: 01373 471913
A 16th-century, town centre inn, and a fine example of a traditional public house. Well-stocked bar and a menu of light meals and snacks. Seven guest rooms, one en-suite.   413

The White Hart Hotel, 19-21 Sadler Street, Wells, Somerset BA5 2RR

Tel: 01749 672056 Fax: 01749 671074
e-mail: info@whitehart-wells.co.uk
website: www.whitehart-wells.co.uk
Delightful, black and white hotel in the centre of Wells. 13 luxurious bedrooms. Newly refurbished restaurant offers relaxed dining with a more formal Italian restaurant nearby. Function suite.   417

Isle of Wedmore Golf Club

Lineage, Lascots Hill, Wedmore, Somerset BS28 4QT

Tel: 01934 713649 Fax: 01934 713554

Date Founded:	1992
Type of Course:	Parkland
No of Holes:	18
Length:	5850 yds (5399 mtrs)
Par:	70
SSS:	69
Green Fees:	Weekdays: £18; Weekends/ Bank Holidays: £22
Visitors:	Welcome: Contact Club in Advance. Before 9.00 am at weekends
Societies:	Welcome: Contact Club in Advance
Facilities:	Putting Green, Chipping Green, Club Hire, Trolley Hire, Buggy Hire, Bar, Restaurant

Sec/Manager:	Andrew Edwards
Professional:	Graham Coombe
Directions:	¾ mile north of Wedmore. From M5 junction 22 turn left at exit roundabout onto A38 (Bridgewater). After ¼ mile turn left onto B3139 (Wedmore, Wells). On north side of Wedmore turn left off B3139 into Lascot Hill. The entrance is on the right hand side after ¾ mile.

Accommodation, Food and Drink

Reference numbers below refer to detailed information provided in section 2

Accommodation

The Gordons Hotel, Cliff Street, Cheddar, Somerset BS27 3PT

Tel: 01934 742497 Fax: 01934 744965
e-mail: gordons.hotel@virgin.net
Owned by the same family for over 25 years and well liked for its friendly and comfortable atmosphere, The Gordons Hotel offers 14 bedrooms, mostly en-suite. Situated at the foot of the famous gorge and an ideal holiday base. No evening meals.

The Hawthorne, Crooked Lane, Brent Knoll, Somerset TA9 4BQ

Tel: 01278 760181
Comfortable country house in quiet surroundings. Separate annexe for guests with dining hall and two en-suite bed and breakfast rooms. Close to Berrow golf course.

Laburnum House Lodge Hotel, Sloway Lane, West Huntspill, Highbridge, Somerset TA9 3RJ

Tel: 01278 781830 Fax: 01278 781612
e-mail: laburnumhh@aol.com
website: www.laburnumhh.co.uk

Family-run country lodge hotel. 60 bedrooms, all en-suite, of varying sizes. Peaceful, rural location with clay pigeon shooting, fishing and many other activities available on site. Also holiday complex with superb 80-cover restaurant and two bars open to all visitors. Excellent menus and great pub grub with weekly BBQs and Pig Roasts.

Poachers Table, Cliff Street, Cheddar, Somerset BS27 3PT

Tel: 01934 742271
A family-run restaurant offering a wide variety of food, catering to all tastes and appetites. Situated on the main street, at the foot of Cheddar Gorge, with ample car parking available opposite.

Three Acres Caravan Park, South Road, Brean, Somerset TA8 2RF

Tel: 01278 751313
e-mail: 3acres@ic24.net
15 self-catering six-berth caravans within a couple of miles of Burnham-on-Sea and close to several golf courses. Bar and restaurant within the site for residents' use.

The White Hart Hotel, 19-21 Sadler Street, Wells, Somerset BA5 2RR

Tel: 01749 672056 Fax: 01749 671074
e-mail: info@whitehart-wells.co.uk
website: www.whitehart-wells.co.uk
Delightful, black and white hotel in the centre of Wells. 13 luxurious bedrooms. Newly refurbished restaurant offers relaxed dining with a more formal Italian restaurant nearby. Function suite.   417

Food and Drink

Laburnum House Lodge Hotel, Sloway Lane, West Huntspill, Highbridge, Somerset TA9 3RJ

Tel: 01278 781830 Fax: 01278 781612
e-mail: laburnumhh@aol.com
website: www.laburnumhh.co.uk
Family-run country lodge hotel. 60 bedrooms, all en-suite, of varying sizes. Peaceful, rural location with clay pigeon shooting, fishing and many other activities available on site. Also holiday complex with superb 80-cover restaurant and two bars open to all visitors. Excellent menus and great pub grub with weekly BBQs and Pig Roasts.

Poachers Table, Cliff Street, Cheddar, Somerset BS27 3PT

Tel: 01934 742271
A family-run restaurant offering a wide variety of food, catering to all tastes and appetites. Situated on the main street, at the foot of Cheddar Gorge, with ample car parking available opposite.

The White Hart Hotel, 19-21 Sadler Street, Wells, Somerset BA5 2RR

Tel: 01749 672056 Fax: 01749 671074
e-mail: info@whitehart-wells.co.uk
website: www.whitehart-wells.co.uk
Delightful, black and white hotel in the centre of Wells. 13 luxurious bedrooms. Newly refurbished restaurant offers relaxed dining with a more formal Italian restaurant nearby. Function suite.   417

Lansdown Golf Club

Lansdown, Bath, Somerset BA1 9BT

Tel: 01225 422138 Fax: 01225 339252

Sec/Manager:	Terry Mercer
Professional:	None
Directions:	3 miles northwest of Bath City the centre. From centre take Broad St (A4, Chippenham) leading to Lansdown Rd (Lansdown). The entrance is on left hand side at Lansdown.
Date Founded:	1894
Type of Course:	Parkland
No of Holes:	18
Length:	6049 yds (5583 mtrs)
Par:	71
SSS:	70
Green Fees:	Weekdays: £22; Weekends/ Bank Holidays: £28
Visitors:	Welcome: Contact Club in Advance. Unable to play weekends
Societies:	Welcome: By arrangement with the Club
Facilities:	Putting Green, Chipping Green, Driving Range, Trolley Hire, Buggy Hire, Bar, Restaurant

Accommodation, Food and Drink

Reference numbers below refer to detailed information provided in section 2

Accommodation

The Bear Inn, Holwell, Nr. Frome, Somerset BA11 4PY

Tel: 01373 836585
Unusual structure, built directly into the face of a quarry, with cosy interior. Fine ales and wide selection of meals and snacks. Six guest rooms.   444

Ellsworth House, Fosseway, Midsomer Norton, Bath, Somerset BA3 4AU

Tel: 01761 412305
e-mail: accommodation@ellsworth.fsbusiness.co.uk
website: www.ellsworth.fsbusiness.co.uk
Attractive house with a number of comfortable, en-suite guest rooms. Spacious sun lounge and indoor koi carp pond. Non-smoking establishment.   442

Executive Holidays, Whitemill Farm, Iron Mills Lane, Oldford, Frome, Somerset BA11 2NR

Tel: 01373 452907 Fax: 01373 453253

e-mail: info@executiveholidays.co.uk
website: www.executiveholidays.co.uk
Ten different properties of varying sizes all located
within the attractive valley of the River Frome. Superb
range of leisure activities can be organised .   414

Innlodge at the Bridge Inn, North End Road, Yatton, Nr. Bristol, Somerset BS49 4AU

Tel: 01934 839100 Fax: 01934 839149
e-mail bridgeinn@sfigroup.co.uk
website www.innlodge.com
Modern lodge accommodation with 41 en-suite
rooms including some luxurious suites. The Bridge
Inn is a popular country inn serving superb home-
cooked food.   446

Ston Easton Park, Ston Easton, Nr. Bath, Somerset BA3 4DF

Tel: 01761 241631 Fax: 01761 241377
e-mail: enquiry@stoneaston.co.uk
website: www.stoneaston.co.uk
Grand English country house surrounded by
extensive grounds restored to recapture much of the
original elegance and splendour. 24 individually-
designed en-suite bedrooms. Choice of formal or
casual dining, with award-winning cuisine. Superb
leisure facilities.   416

Walton's Guest House, 17-19 Crescent Gardens, Upper Bristol Road, Bath BA1 2NA

Tel: 01225 426528 Fax: 01225 420350
Within five minutes walk of City centre, Roman
Baths, Pump Rooms and other interesting places,
while at the rear of the property is Victoria Park and
the Royal Crescent. 15 bedrooms, 2 en-suite.
Adjoining public car park.

The White Hart Hotel, 19-21 Sadler Street, Wells, Somerset BA5 2RR

Tel: 01749 672056 Fax: 01749 671074
e-mail: info@whitehart-wells.co.uk
website: www.whitehart-wells.co.uk
Delightful, black and white hotel in the centre of
Wells. 13 luxurious bedrooms. Newly refurbished
restaurant offers relaxed dining with a more formal
Italian restaurant nearby. Function suite.   417

Food and Drink

The Bear Inn, Holwell, Nr. Frome, Somerset BA11 4PY

Tel: 01373 836585
Unusual structure, built directly into the face of a
quarry, with cosy interior. Fine ales and wide selection
of meals and snacks. Six guest rooms.   444

Innlodge at the Bridge Inn, North End Road, Yatton, Nr. Bristol, Somerset BS49 4AU

Tel: 01934 839100 Fax: 01934 839149
e-mail bridgeinn@sfigroup.co.uk
website www.innlodge.com
Modern lodge accommodation with 41 en-suite
rooms including some luxurious suites. The Bridge
Inn is a popular country inn serving superb home-
cooked food.   446

La Bisalta, 6 Vicarage Street, Frome, Somerset BA11 1PX

Tel: 01373 464238 Fax: 01373 304603
e-mail: luigi@labisalta.fsnet.co.uk
Genuine Italian restaurant, with open veranda and
garden area, serving classic Italian cuisine. Long
established with popular reputation.   415

Mason's Arms, Marston Gate, Frome, Somerset BA11 4DJ

Tel: 01373 464537 Fax: 01373 455071
Cosy pub with a characterful interior where beams
and original fireplaces have been retained. Excellent
selection of real ales and delicious menu of tasty
dishes.   443

The Somerset Wagon, Broadway, Chilcompton, Radstock, Somerset BA3 4JW

Tel: 01761 232732 Fax: 01761 232522
Former coaching inn that has been transformed into
an attractive hostelry. Superb food and ales.
Occasional live music.   439

Ston Easton Park, Ston Easton, Nr. Bath, Somerset BA3 4DF

Tel: 01761 241631 Fax: 01761 241377
e-mail: enquiry@stoneaston.co.uk
website: www.stoneaston.co.uk
Grand English country house surrounded by
extensive grounds restored to recapture much of the
original elegance and splendour. 24 individually-
designed en-suite bedrooms. Choice of formal or
casual dining, with award-winning cuisine. Superb
leisure facilities.   416

Sun Inn, 6 Catherine Street, Frome, Somerset BA11 1DA

Tel: 01373 471913
A 16th-century, town centre inn, and a fine example
of a traditional public house. Well-stocked bar and a
menu of light meals and snacks. Seven guest rooms,
one en-suite.   413

The White Hart Hotel, 19-21 Sadler Street, Wells, Somerset BA5 2RR

Tel: 01749 672056 Fax: 01749 671074
e-mail: info@whitehart-wells.co.uk
website: www.whitehart-wells.co.uk
Delightful, black and white hotel in the centre of
Wells. 13 luxurious bedrooms. Newly refurbished
restaurant offers relaxed dining with a more formal
Italian restaurant nearby. Function suite.   417

Long Sutton Golf Club

Long Load, Langport, Somerset TA10 9JU
Tel: 01458 241017 Fax: 01458 241022

Sec/Manager: Marlene Cox
Professional: Andrew Hayes

Directions:	3 miles southeast of Langport. From centre take A372 (Huish Episcopi). After 3 miles turn right onto B3165 (Long Sutton). The entrance is on the right hand side after 1 mile having crossed River Yeo.
Date Founded:	1991
Type of Course:	Parkland
No of Holes:	18
Length:	6398 yds (5905 mtrs)
Par:	71
SSS:	70
Green Fees:	Weekdays: £16; Weekends/ Bank Holidays: £20
Visitors:	Welcome: Contact Club in Advance. Tee times bookable at weekends
Societies:	Welcome: By arrangement with the Club
Facilities:	Putting Green, Chipping Green, Driving Range, Club Hire, Trolley Hire, Buggy Hire, Bar, Restaurant, Private Rooms

Accommodation, Food and Drink

Reference numbers below refer to detailed information provided in section 2

Accommodation

'Riverside', Goosebradon Farm, Westport, Nr. Langport, Somerset TA10 0BH

Tel: 01823 680447 Fax: 01823 681008
e-mail: cking@dunnsgreen.fsnet.co.uk
Pretty self-catering cottage in a quiet corner of Somerset. Sleeps eight adults in three bedrooms. Attractive rear garden and off-road parking. 418

Amberley Guest House, Martock Road, Long Load, Langport, Somerset TA10 9LD

Tel: 01458 241542
e-mail: jeanatamberley@talk21.com
An attractive farmhouse-style property with four comfortable guest rooms of varying sizes. Evening meals available on request. Non-smoking. 422

Ash House Country House Hotel and Restaurant, Main Street, Ash, Nr. Martock, Somerset TA12 6PB

Tel: 01935 822036 Fax: 01935 822992
e-mail: reception@ashhousehotel.freeserve.co.uk
website: www.ashhousecountryhotel.co.uk
Small, privately-owned Georgian Country house hotel surrounded by attractive gardens. Popular a la carte restaurant with high standard of cuisine. Eight delightful en-suite rooms. 424

Castlebrook Holiday Cottages, Castlebrook, Compton Dundon, Somerton, Somerset TA11 6PR

Tel: 01458 841680 Fax: 01458 841680
Two fully-equipped holiday homes located in the heart of the Polden Hills. Both feature kitchenette, sitting/dining room, shower room/WC, sleeping three and five adults. Pets welcome by arrangement. 407

East Lambrook Farm, South Petherton, Somerset TA13 5HH

Tel: 01460 240064 Fax: 01460 240064
e-mail: nicolaeeles@supernet.com
A delightful 17th-century house, built of local sandstone with a thatched roof, set within two and a half acres of rolling gardens and woodland. Three en-suite guest rooms. Tennis Courts. 421

The Ilchester Arms, The Square, Ilchester, Nr. Yeovil, Somerset BA22 8LN

Tel: 01935 840220 Fax: 01935 841353
Impressive Georgian building, dominating the main street, offering comfortable en-suite accommodation. High quality restaurant with wide-ranging menu. 434

Northover Manor Hotel, Northover, Ilchester, Somerset BA22 8LD

Tel: 01935 840447 Fax: 01935 840006
e-mail: melhaddigan@compuserve.com
A rambling, 15th-century, former manor house offering comfortable, stylish accommodation in 13 en-suite rooms. Formal restaurant and more casual Village Bar which are both open to non-residents.406

Food and Drink

Ash House Country House Hotel and Restaurant, Main Street, Ash, Nr. Martock, Somerset TA12 6PB

Tel: 01935 822036 Fax: 01935 822992
e-mail: reception@ashhousehotel.freeserve.co.uk
website: www.ashhousecountryhotel.co.uk
Small, privately-owned Georgian Country house hotel surrounded by attractive gardens. Popular a la carte restaurant with high standard of cuisine. Eight delightful en-suite rooms. 424

The Fox and Hounds, Broadway Road, Charlton Adam, Somerset TA11 7AU

Tel: 01458 223466
Small village pub serving traditional, wholesome food and specialising in home-made pies. Real ales served, including local Butcombe Ales. Pool table, function room and can accommodate up to five caravans or motor homes on an adjoining field.

The Ilchester Arms, The Square, Ilchester, Nr. Yeovil, Somerset BA22 8LN

Tel: 01935 840220 Fax: 01935 841353

Impressive Georgian building, dominating the main street, offering comfortable en-suite accommodation. High quality restaurant with wide-ranging menu. 434

Marlborough Tea Rooms, Bow Street, Langport, Somerset TA10 9PR

Tel: 01458 250786 Fax: 01458 250786
Small, charming tea rooms serving morning coffee, light lunches and afternoon tea. Wide ranging menu, mostly home-made, and superb cream teas.   445

Northover Manor Hotel, Northover, Ilchester, Somerset BA22 8LD

Tel: 01935 840447 Fax: 01935 840006
e-mail: melhaddigan@compuserve.com
A rambling, 15th-century, former manor house offering comfortable, stylish accommodation in 13 en-suite rooms. Formal restaurant and more casual Village Bar which are both open to non-residents. 406

The Old Barn Owl, Westport, Nr. Langport, Somerset TA10 0BH

Tel: 01460 281391 Fax: 01460 281995
Good-sized, family pub enjoying a good location. Comfortable interior with relaxed atmosphere. Good range stocked behind the bar and equally excellent selection in the restaurant.   419

The Old Forge Inn, Church Street, Curry Rivel, Nr. Langport, Somerset TA10 0HE

Tel: 01458 251554 Fax: 01458 252847
Grade 2 listed building, providing characterful surroundings. Excellent menu with good fish selection. Public bar open to all. Regular art exhibitions. 5 rooms for bed and breakfast planned for April 2002.   420

The Mendip Golf Club

Gurney Slade, Bath, Somerset BA3 4UT
Tel: 01749 840570 Fax: 01749 841439

Sec/Manager:	J. Scott
Professional:	Adrian Marsh
Directions:	9 miles south of Bristol city centre. From centre take Bath Rd (A4) then Wells Rd

(Shepton Mallet, A37) and follow to Gurney Slade. Turn right just after Gurney Slade near Q8 Service Station into Golf Links Road. The entrance is on the right hand side after 300 yds.

Date Founded:	1908
Type of Course:	Parkland
No of Holes:	18
Length:	6383 yds (5892 mtrs)
Par:	71
SSS:	71
Green Fees:	Weekdays: £21 (round) £26 (day); Weekends/Bank Holidays: £31
Visitors:	Welcome: Contact club in advance. No restrictions.
Societies:	Welcome: Contact club in advance. Unable to play Tuesdays, Wednesdays, Fridays and weekends.
Facilities:	Putting Green, Chipping Green, Club Hire, Trolley Hire, Bar, Restaurant

Accommodation, Food and Drink

Reference numbers below refer to detailed information provided in section 2

Accommodation

The Bear Inn, Holwell, Nr. Frome, Somerset BA11 4PY

Tel: 01373 836585
Unusual structure, built directly into the face of a quarry, with cosy interior. Fine ales and wide selection of meals and snacks. Six guest rooms.   444

Castlebrook Holiday Cottages, Castlebrook, Compton Dundon, Somerton, Somerset TA11 6PR

Tel: 01458 841680 Fax: 01458 841680
Two fully-equipped holiday homes located in the heart of the Polden Hills. Both feature kitchenette, sitting/dining room, shower room/WC, sleeping three and five adults. Pets welcome by arrangement.   407

Ellsworth House, Fosseway, Midsomer Norton, Bath, Somerset BA3 4AU

Tel: 01761 412305
e-mail: accommodation@ellsworth.fsbusiness.co.uk
website: www.ellsworth.fsbusiness.co.uk
Attractive house with a number of comfortable, en-suite guest rooms. Spacious sun lounge and indoor koi carp pond. Non-smoking establishment.   442

Executive Holidays, Whitemill Farm, Iron Mills Lane, Oldford, Frome, Somerset BA11 2NR

Tel: 01373 452907 Fax: 01373 453253
e-mail: info@executiveholidays.co.uk
website: www.executiveholidays.co.uk
Ten different properties of varying sizes all located
within the attractive valley of the River Frome. Superb
range of leisure activities can be organised.   414

The Gordons Hotel, Cliff Street, Cheddar, Somerset BS27 3PT

Tel: 01934 742497 Fax: 01934 744965
e-mail: gordons.hotel@virgin.net
Owned by the same family for over 25 years and well
liked for its friendly and comfortable atmosphere, The
Gordons Hotel offers 14 bedrooms, mostly en-suite.
Situated at the foot of the famous gorge and an ideal
holiday base. No evening meals.

Poachers Table, Cliff Street, Cheddar, Somerset BS27 3PT

Tel: 01934 742271
A family-run restaurant offering a wide variety of
food, catering to all tastes and appetites. Situated on
the main street, at the foot of Cheddar Gorge, with
ample car parking available opposite.

The Prince of Orange, 17 High Street, Yatton, Somerset BS49 4JD

Tel: 01934 832193
Fax: 01934 832193
Popular with locals and tourists for the good range of
beers and hearty food. Accommodation available in a
self-contained part of the building, with five en-suite
rooms.   441

Ston Easton Park, Ston Easton, Nr. Bath, Somerset BA3 4DF

Tel: 01761 241631 Fax: 01761 241377
e-mail: enquiry@stoneaston.co.uk
website: www.stoneaston.co.uk
Grand English country house surrounded by
extensive grounds restored to recapture much of the
original elegance and splendour. 24 individually-
designed en-suite bedrooms. Choice of formal or
casual dining, with award-winning cuisine. Superb
leisure facilities   416

Walton's Guest House, 17-19 Crescent Gardens, Upper Bristol Road, Bath BA1 2NA

Tel: 01225 426528 Fax: 01225 420350
Within five minutes walk of City centre, Roman
Baths, Pump Rooms and other interesting places,
while at the rear of the property is Victoria Park and
the Royal Crescent. 15 bedrooms, 2 en-suite.
Adjoining public car park.

The White Hart Hotel, 19-21 Sadler Street, Wells, Somerset BA5 2RR

Tel: 01749 672056 Fax: 01749 671074
e-mail: info@whitehart-wells.co.uk
website: www.whitehart-wells.co.uk
Delightful, black and white hotel in the centre of
Wells. 13 luxurious bedrooms. Newly refurbished
restaurant offers relaxed dining with a more formal
Italian restaurant nearby. Function suite.   417

Food and Drink

The Bear Inn, Holwell, Nr. Frome, Somerset BA11 4PY

Tel: 01373 836585
Unusual structure, built directly into the face of a
quarry, with cosy interior. Fine ales and wide selection
of meals and snacks. Six guest rooms.   444

Innlodge at the Bridge Inn, North End Road, Yatton, Nr. Bristol, Somerset BS49 4AU

Tel: 01934 839100 Fax: 01934 839149
e-mail bridgeinn@sfigroup.co.uk
website www.innlodge.com
Modern lodge accommodation with 41 en-suite
rooms including some luxurious suites. The Bridge
Inn is a popular country inn serving superb home-
cooked food.   446

Mason's Arms, Marston Gate, Frome, Somerset BA11 4DJ

Tel: 01373 464537 Fax: 01373 455071
Cosy pub with a characterful interior where beams
and original fireplaces have been retained. Excellent
selection of real ales and delicious menu of tasty
dishes.   443

Poachers Table, Cliff Street, Cheddar, Somerset BS27 3PT

Tel: 01934 742271
A family-run restaurant offering a wide variety of
food, catering to all tastes and appetites. Situated on
the main street, at the foot of Cheddar Gorge, with
ample car parking available opposite.

The Prince of Orange, 17 High Street, Yatton, Somerset BS49 4JD

Tel: 01934 832193 Fax: 01934 832193
Popular with locals and tourists for the good range of
beers and hearty food. Accommodation available in a
self-contained part of the building, with five en-suite
rooms.   441

The Somerset Wagon, Broadway, Chilcompton, Radstock, Somerset BA3 4JW

Tel: 01761 232732 Fax: 01761 232522
Former coaching inn that has been transformed into
an attractive hostelry. Superb food and ales.
Occasional live music.   439

Ston Easton Park, Ston Easton, Nr. Bath, Somerset BA3 4DF

Tel: 01761 241631 Fax: 01761 241377
e-mail: enquiry@stoneaston.co.uk
website: www.stoneaston.co.uk
Grand English country house surrounded by
extensive grounds restored to recapture much of the
original elegance and splendour. 24 individually-
designed en-suite bedrooms. Choice of formal or
casual dining, with award-winning cuisine. Superb
leisure facilities   416

Sun Inn, 6 Catherine Street, Frome, Somerset BA11 1DA

Tel: 01373 471913
A 16th-century, town centre inn, and a fine example

of a traditional public house. Well-stocked bar and a menu of light meals and snacks. Seven guest rooms, one en-suite. 413

The White Hart Hotel, 19-21 Sadler Street, Wells, Somerset BA5 2RR

Tel: 01749 672056 Fax: 01749 671074
e-mail: info@whitehart-wells.co.uk
website: www.whitehart-wells.co.uk
Delightful, black and white hotel in the centre of Wells. 13 luxurious bedrooms. Newly refurbished restaurant offers relaxed dining with a more formal Italian restaurant nearby. Function suite. 417

Mendip Spring Golf Club

Honeyhall Lane, Congresbury,
Somerset BS49 5JT

Tel: 01934 852322 Fax: 01934 853021

Sec/Manager:	Mr. A. Melhuish
Professionals:	Robert Moss and John Blackburn
Directions:	7 miles east of Weston-super-Mare. From M5 junction 21 take A370 (Long Ashton). At Congresbury turn right onto B3133 (Lower Langford) and after 1 mile turn right into Brinsea Batch. After ½ mile turn right into Honeyhall Lane and the entrance is on the right hand side.
Visitors:	Welcome: Contact club in advance.
Societies:	Welcome: Contact club in advance.
Facilities:	Putting Green, Chipping Green, Club Hire, Trolley Hire, Buggy Hire, Bar, Restaurant, Driving Range

Brinsea

Date Founded:	1991
Type of Course:	Parkland
No of Holes:	18
Length:	6334 yds (5847 mtrs)
Par:	71
SSS:	70
Green Fees:	Weekdays: £25 -£30; Weekends/Bank Holidays: £25 -£30

Lakeside

Date Founded:	1991
Type of Course:	Parkland
No of Holes:	9
Length:	2260 yds (2086 mtrs)
Par:	34
SSS:	34
Green Fees:	Weekdays: £7-£10; Weekends/Bank Holidays: £7-£10

Accommodation, Food and Drink
Reference numbers below refer to detailed information provided in section 2

Accommodation

The Gordons Hotel, Cliff Street, Cheddar, Somerset BS27 3PT

Tel: 01934 742497 Fax: 01934 744965
e-mail: gordons.hotel@virgin.net
Owned by the same family for over 25 years and well liked for its friendly and comfortable atmosphere, The Gordons Hotel offers 14 bedrooms, mostly en-suite. Situated at the foot of the famous gorge and an ideal holiday base. No evening meals.

Poachers Table, Cliff Street, Cheddar, Somerset BS27 3PT

Tel: 01934 742271
A family-run restaurant offering a wide variety of food, catering to all tastes and appetites. Situated on the main street, at the foot of Cheddar Gorge, with ample car parking available opposite.

The Prince of Orange, 17 High Street, Yatton, Somerset BS49 4JD

Tel: 01934 832193 Fax: 01934 832193
Popular with locals and tourists for the good range of beers and hearty food. Accommodation available in a self-contained part of the building, with five en-suite rooms. 441

The White Hart Hotel, 19-21 Sadler Street, Wells, Somerset BA5 2RR

Tel: 01749 672056 Fax: 01749 671074
e-mail: info@whitehart-wells.co.uk
website: www.whitehart-wells.co.uk
Delightful, black and white hotel in the centre of Wells. 13 luxurious bedrooms. Newly refurbished restaurant offers relaxed dining with a more formal Italian restaurant nearby. Function suite. 417

Food and Drink

Long John Silver, 73 Beach Road, Kewstoke, Weston-super-Mare, Somerset BS22 9UP

Tel: 01934 623367
Characterful inn serving an excellent selection of food ranging from traditional pub fayre to seafood and steak dishes. Vegetarians also catered for.

The Major from Glengarry, 10-14 Upper Church Road, Weston-super-Mare, Somerset BS23 2DT

Tel: 01934 629260
Family-run pub offering a warm welcome to all. Serves Wadsworth Cask Ales and an extensive range of snacks and traditional food prepared by the owner, who is a qualified chef. Regular evening entertainment with live music. Families welcome.

Poachers Table, Cliff Street, Cheddar, Somerset BS27 3PT

Tel: 01934 742271
A family-run restaurant offering a wide variety of food, catering to all tastes and appetites. Situated on the main street, at the foot of Cheddar Gorge, with ample car parking available opposite.

The Prince of Orange, 17 High Street, Yatton, Somerset BS49 4JD

Tel: 01934 832193
Fax: 01934 832193
Popular with locals and tourists for the good range of beers and hearty food. Accommodation available in a self-contained part of the building, with five en-suite rooms.   441

The White Hart Hotel, 19-21 Sadler Street, Wells, Somerset BA5 2RR

Tel: 01749 672056 Fax: 01749 671074
e-mail: info@whitehart-wells.co.uk
website: www.whitehart-wells.co.uk
Delightful, black and white hotel in the centre of Wells. 13 luxurious bedrooms. Newly refurbished restaurant offers relaxed dining with a more formal Italian restaurant nearby. Function suite.   417

Minehead & West Somerset Golf Club

The Warren, Minehead, Somerset TA24 5SJ
Tel: 01643 702057 Fax: 01643 705095

Minehead, the county's oldest club, dating from 1882, is one of only three true links courses in Somerset, yet is different again from its coastal counterparts at Burnham and Weston-super-Mare. Although it does not have the natural splendour

of Burnham, it is more undulating than Weston and, therefore, probably more interesting. This is reflected in the course often being chosen as the venue for the county championships and county trials, its tight and narrow fairways hugging the coastline and offering a test of any player's control and accuracy.

It is also extremely exposed to the winds which can whip off the Bristol Channel and, although you may think as you progress that the wind has changed direction, it is actually the course which turns on itself.

Despite its proximity to the waves, the course - set on a shingle bank - drains amazingly well, and it is the club's boast that not only is it hardly ever closed, but that grass tees are used all year round, as are the exceptional greens. This, of course, makes Minehead an ideal spot for a day's winter golf.

Don't get carried away if your card is looking good, for it finishes with five real toughies, nearly always into the wind, and none of them tougher than the last.

At 215 yards off the whites, it may look a pussy cat. But with that wind in your face, the beach all down one side and out-of-bounds down the other, and bunkers guarding a green right outside the clubhouse windows, you'll need nerves of steel to get your par three.

Sec/Manager:	Mr Rayner
Professional:	Ian Reed
Directions:	1 mile northeast of Minehead. From A39 at Alcombe turn right into Seaward Way. After 1 mile turn right into Warren Road. The entrance is at the end.
Date Founded:	1882
Type of Course:	Links
No of Holes:	18
Length:	6228 yds (5748 mtrs)
Par:	71
SSS:	71
Green Fees:	Weekdays: £24.50; Weekends/ Bank Holidays: £27.50
Visitors:	Welcome: Contact club in advance. No restrictions.
Societies:	Welcome: Contact club in advance. Unable to play Thursday mornings.
Facilities:	Putting Green, Chipping Green, Club Hire, Trolley Hire, Bar, Restaurant

Accommodation, Food and Drink

Reference numbers below refer to detailed
information provided in section 2

Accommodation

Beverleigh, Beacon Road, North Hill, Minehead, Somerset TA24 5SF

Tel: 01643 708450
e-mail: beverleigh@talk21.com
Charming Edwardian house, beautifully furnished. Situated on the higher slopes of North Hill where Exmoor meets the sea. Set in lovely gardens with breathtaking views of Minehead and the surrounding hills.

The Greyhound Inn, 1 Lime Street, Stogursey, Bridgwater, Somerset TA5 1QR

Tel: 01278 732490
Traditional rural inn. Bar stocks a range of local real ales, cider, wine and spirits. Good selection of home-cooked food. Bed and breakfast accommodation. 412

The Kings Head Inn, 12 High Street, Cannington, Bridgwater, Somerset TA5 2HE

Tel: 01278 652293 Fax: 01278 652293
A 17th-century, former coaching inn with cosy interior. Good selection stocked behind the bar. Lunch time carvery and evening a la carte menu. Bed and breakfast accommodation. 411

Marshfield Hotel, 18 Tregonwell Road, Minehead, Somerset TA24 5DU

Tel: 01643 702517 Fax: 01643 702517
e-mail: marshfield.hotel@minehead18.freeserve.co.uk
website: http://welcome.to/marshfieldhotel
Small, family-run hotel providing a relaxed atmosphere in which to enjoy a short break or week-long holiday. Ten en-suite rooms, attractively furnished and decorated. Also a guests' lounge, licensed bar and restaurant.

Promenade Hotel, Esplanade, Minehead, Somerset TA24 5QS

Tel: 01643 702572 Fax: 01643 702572
Lovely seafront hotel in unrivalled location overlooking Minehead harbour. Converted in 1976 into a fully wheelchair-accessible property. 11 en-suite bedrooms. 405

Rose and Crown, St. Mary Street, Nether Stowey, Somerset TA5 1LJ

Tel: 01278 732265
Old coaching inn dating back to the 15th century. Cosy interior with separate restaurant and lounge area. Comfortable en-suite accommodation with rooms of varying sizes. 409

Spears Cross Hotel, 1 West Street, Dunster, Minehead, Somerset TA24 6SN

Tel: 01643 821439
e-mail: mjcapel@aol.com
website: www.smoothhound.co.uk/hotels/
  spearsx.html
A listed 15th-century hotel located in the centre of

the medieval village of Dunster. Four en-suite guest rooms. Tasty breakfasts are cooked to order and light meals and packed lunches are also available. Terraced garden features model houses.

Food and Drink

The Bird in Hand, Mount Street, Bishops Lydeard, Taunton, Somerset TA4 3LH

Tel: 01823 432090
Traditional country pub dating to the 18th century. Menu offers a selection of meals and snacks while the bar claims to stock the best beer in the area. 437

The Greyhound Inn, 1 Lime Street, Stogursey, Bridgwater, Somerset TA5 1QR

Tel: 01278 732490
Traditional rural inn. Bar stocks a range of local real ales, cider, wine and spirits. Good selection of home-cooked food. Bed and breakfast accommodation. 412

The Kings Head Inn, 12 High Street, Cannington, Bridgwater, Somerset TA5 2HE

Tel: 01278 652293 Fax: 01278 652293
A 17th-century, former coaching inn with cosy interior. Good selection stocked behind the bar. Lunch time carvery and evening a la carte menu. Bed and breakfast accommodation. 411

Rose and Crown, St. Mary Street, Nether Stowey, Somerset TA5 1LJ

Tel: 01278 732265
Old coaching inn dating back to the 15th century. Cosy interior with separate restaurant and lounge area. Comfortable en-suite accommodation with rooms of varying sizes. 409

Oake Manor Golf Club

Oake, Taunton, Somerset TA4 1BA

Tel: 01823 461993 Fax: 01823 461995

During the late 1980s and early 1990s, the south west, with plenty of open space to accommodate the developers, saw a bigger boom in new golf courses than anywhere else in the country. Courses and clubs sprang up all over the place to

satisfy the mushrooming demand of the thousands of people who suddenly found the game fashionable.

Many of the new courses were built on farm pastures as farmers and land owners spotted a way to make some money, and some of the courses are now maturing into pleasant parkland outings. Not many, though, really stick in the memory. Oake Manor will.

It's one of Adrian Stiff's designs, and not one of the toughest - unless you take into account the wet stuff. For this delightful course looks and feels - on a good summer day - like a little bit of American golf architecture has been imported from Florida. Although it is not quite 10 years old, it feels it, such is the manner in which the course wanders through the woodlands and the water.

There are several holes that will probably haunt your dreams, none more so than the 15th, one of 10 where water comes into play. This has a healthy stream all the way down the left, from tee to green, with the added bit of interest in that the green itself is an island. If water is a magnet for you, picking up for a 12 might be a smart move! It's a particularly good course for a group of mixed abilities.

Sec/Manager:	Russell Gardner
Professional:	None
Directions:	5½ miles west of Taunton.

From centre take A358 (Williton). After 2 miles turn right onto B3227 (Norton Fitzwarren, Milverton). At Heathfield turn right onto B road signed Oake. The entrance is signed when entering Oake

Date Founded:	1993
Type of Course:	Parkland
No of Holes:	18
Length:	6105 yds (5634 mtrs)
Par:	70
SSS:	69
Green Fees:	Weekdays: £18; Weekends/ Bank Holidays: £24
Visitors:	Welcome: Contact club in advance. No restrictions.
Societies:	Welcome: Contact club in advance. No restrictions.
Facilities:	Putting Green, Chipping Green, Driving Range, Club Hire, Trolley Hire, Bar, Restaurant

Accommodation, Food and Drink

Reference numbers below refer to detailed information provided in section 2

Accommodation

Bashfords Farmhouse, West Bagborough, Taunton, Somerset TA4 3EF

Tel: 01823 432015 Fax: 0870 1671587
e-mail: charlieritchie@netscapeonline.co.uk
Non-working farmhouse dating largely from the 18th century. Three comfortable rooms with en-suite facilities or private bathroom. Evening meals available on request.   440

Beverleigh, Beacon Road, North Hill, Minehead, Somerset TA24 5SF

Tel: 01643 708450
e-mail: beverleigh@talk21.com
Charming Edwardian house, beautifully furnished. Situated on the higher slopes of North Hill where Exmoor meets the sea. Set in lovely gardens with breathtaking views of Minehead and the surrounding hills.

Blackmore Farm, Cannington, Bridgwater, Somerset TA5 2NE

Tel: 01278 653442 Fax: 01278 653427
Historic manor house dating back to the 14th century offering comfortable farmhouse bed and breakfast with four spacious en-suite rooms.   410

The Kings Head Inn, 12 High Street, Cannington, Bridgwater, Somerset TA5 2HE

Tel: 01278 652293 Fax: 01278 652293

A 17th-century, former coaching inn with cosy interior. Good selection stocked behind the bar. Lunch time carvery and evening a la carte menu. Bed and breakfast accommodation.   411

Marshfield Hotel, 18 Tregonwell Road, Minehead, Somerset TA24 5DU

Tel: 01643 702517 Fax: 01643 702517
e-mail: marshfield.hotel@minehead18.freeserve.co.uk
website: http://welcome.to/marshfieldhotel
Small, family-run hotel providing a relaxed atmosphere in which to enjoy a short break or week-long holiday. Ten en-suite rooms, attractively furnished and decorated. Also a guests' lounge, licensed bar and restaurant.

Promenade Hotel, Esplanade, Minehead, Somerset TA24 5QS

Tel: 01643 702572 Fax: 01643 702572
Lovely seafront hotel in unrivalled location overlooking Minehead harbour. Converted in 1976 into a fully wheelchair-accessible property. 11 en-suite bedrooms.   405

Rose and Crown, St. Mary Street, Nether Stowey, Somerset TA5 1LJ

Tel: 01278 732265
Old coaching inn dating back to the 15th century. Cosy interior with separate restaurant and lounge area. Comfortable en-suite accommodation with rooms of varying sizes.   409

Spears Cross Hotel, 1 West Street, Dunster, Minehead, Somerset TA24 6SN

Tel: 01643 821439
e-mail: mjcapel@aol.com
website: www.smoothhound.co.uk/hotels/spearsx.html
A listed 15th-century hotel located in the centre of the medieval village of Dunster. Four en-suite guest rooms. Tasty breakfasts are cooked to order and light meals and packed lunches are also available. Terraced garden features model houses.

Turnpike Cottage, Turnpike, Milverton, Somerset TA4 1LF

Tel: 01823 400492
Cosy cottage providing self-contained accommodation, sleeping up to five adults. Very well equipped. Pets welcome.   404

Food and Drink

The Bird in Hand, Mount Street, Bishops Lydeard, Taunton, Somerset TA4 3LH

Tel: 01823 432090
Traditional country pub dating to the 18th century. Menu offers a selection of meals and snacks while the bar claims to stock the best beer in the area.   437

The Greyhound Inn, 1 Lime Street, Stogursey, Bridgwater, Somerset TA5 1QR

Tel: 01278 732490
Traditional rural inn. Bar stocks a range of local real ales, cider, wine and spirits. Good selection of home-cooked food. Bed and breakfast accommodation. 412

The Kings Head Inn, 12 High Street, Cannington, Bridgwater, Somerset TA5 2HE

Tel: 01278 652293 Fax: 01278 652293
A 17th-century, former coaching inn with cosy interior. Good selection stocked behind the bar. Lunch time carvery and evening a la carte menu. Bed and breakfast accommodation.   411

Rose and Crown, St. Mary Street, Nether Stowey, Somerset TA5 1LJ

Tel: 01278 732265
Old coaching inn dating back to the 15th century. Cosy interior with separate restaurant and lounge area. Comfortable en-suite accommodation with rooms of varying sizes.   409

Orchardleigh Golf Club

Frome, Somerset BA11 2PH

Tel: 01373 454200 Fax: 01373 454202

There are many golf clubs which have impressive entrances and long, sweeping drives to the clubhouse. But there are not many which you feel should be approached on horseback or, at the very least, in a horse-drawn carriage.

That, however, is the feeling you get on passing through the stone gate posts of Orchardleigh. Imagine you are entering a grand, old estate, with ancient woodlands, meadows, even the odd tenant-farmer or two as the meandering track wanders off to the distant clubhouse. Well, that is exactly what you are doing, for the course is set in what was part of the old Orchardleigh estate. Not only is it so evocative that you expect Henry VIII and a hunting party to burst onto the scene chasing a wild boar, but the course can be a bit of a swine, too!

Former Ryder Cup player Brian Huggett originally designed the course as two returning nines, and it is difficult to believe that it is a mere six years old.

The first of half-a-dozen lakes comes into play on the first hole, and water and those huge, mature trees will dog your footsteps all the way round to the 18th. The only way to get off lightly around this one is to keep it short and straight, and stick to the mown surface. Those tactics may cost a shot or two on holes like the majestic 526-yard par-five 12th, but they'll save you just about everywhere else.

Mr Huggett was a wily old pro, so you have to keep an eye out for some of his little tricks, which include bunker placings to trap every handicap, and danger where normally you might expect a little mercy and some safety.

A terrific course and wondrous English countryside.

Sec/Manager:	Trevor Atkinson
Professional:	Ian Ridsdale
Directions:	1½ miles northwest of Frome. From centre take A362 (Radstock). After 1½ miles entrance is on the right hand side just after railway line.
Date Founded:	1996
Type of Course:	Parkland
No of Holes:	18
Length:	6279 yds (5795 mtrs)
Par:	72
SSS:	70
Green Fees:	Weekdays: £22; Weekends/ Bank Holidays: £30
Visitors:	Welcome: Contact club in advance. Unable to play weekends before 11.30 am
Societies:	Welcome: Contact club in advance. No restrictions.
Facilities:	Putting Green, Chipping Green, Driving Range, Club Hire, Trolley Hire, Buggy Hire, Bar, Restaurant

Accommodation, Food and Drink

Reference numbers below refer to detailed information provided in section 2

Accommodation

The Bear Inn, Holwell, Nr. Frome, Somerset BA11 4PY

Tel: 01373 836585
Unusual structure, built directly into the face of a quarry, with cosy interior. Fine ales and wide selection of meals and snacks. Six guest rooms. 444

Ellsworth House, Fosseway, Midsomer Norton, Bath, Somerset BA3 4AU

Tel: 01761 412305
e-mail: accommodation@ellsworth.fsbusiness.co.uk
website: www.ellsworth.fsbusiness.co.uk
Attractive house with a number of comfortable, en-suite guest rooms. Spacious sun lounge and indoor koi carp pond. Non-smoking establishment. 442

Executive Holidays, Whitemill Farm, Iron Mills Lane, Oldford, Frome, Somerset BA11 2NR

Tel: 01373 452907 Fax: 01373 453253
e-mail: info@executiveholidays.co.uk
website: www.executiveholidays.co.uk
Ten different properties of varying sizes all located within the attractive valley of the River Frome. Superb range of leisure activities can be organised. 414

Innlodge at the Bridge Inn, North End Road, Yatton, Nr. Bristol, Somerset BS49 4AU

Tel: 01934 839100 Fax: 01934 839149
e-mail bridgeinn@sfigroup.co.uk
website www.innlodge.com
Modern lodge accommodation with 41 en-suite rooms including some luxurious suites. The Bridge Inn is a popular country inn serving superb home-cooked food. 446

Ston Easton Park, Ston Easton, Nr. Bath, Somerset BA3 4DF

Tel: 01761 241631 Fax: 01761 241377
e-mail: enquiry@stoneaston.co.uk
website: www.stoneaston.co.uk
Grand English country house surrounded by extensive grounds restored to recapture much of the original elegance and splendour. 24 individually-designed en-suite bedrooms. Choice of formal or casual dining, with award-winning cuisine. Superb leisure facilities. 416

Walton's Guest House, 17-19 Crescent Gardens, Upper Bristol Road, Bath BA1 2NA

Tel: 01225 426528 Fax: 01225 420350
Within five minutes walk of City centre, Roman Baths, Pump Rooms and other interesting places, while at the rear of the property is Victoria Park and the Royal Crescent. 15 bedrooms, 2 en-suite. Adjoining public car park.

The White Hart Hotel, 19-21 Sadler Street, Wells, Somerset BA5 2RR

Tel: 01749 672056 Fax: 01749 671074
e-mail: info@whitehart-wells.co.uk

website: www.whitehart-wells.co.uk
Delightful, black and white hotel in the centre of
Wells. 13 luxurious bedrooms. Newly refurbished
restaurant offers relaxed dining with a more formal
Italian restaurant nearby. Function suite.   417

Food and Drink

The Bear Inn, Holwell, Nr. Frome,
Somerset BA11 4PY

Tel: 01373 836585
Unusual structure, built directly into the face of a
quarry, with cosy interior. Fine ales and wide selection
of meals and snacks. Six guest rooms.   444

Innlodge at the Bridge Inn, North End Road,
Yatton, Nr. Bristol, Somerset BS49 4AU

Tel: 01934 839100 Fax: 01934 839149
e-mail bridgeinn@sfigroup.co.uk
website www.innlodge.com
Modern lodge accommodation with 41 en-suite
rooms including some luxurious suites. The Bridge
Inn is a popular country inn serving superb home-
cooked food.   446

La Bisalta, 6 Vicarage Street, Frome,
Somerset BA11 1PX

Tel: 01373 464238 Fax: 01373 304603
e-mail: luigi@labisalta.fsnet.co.uk
Genuine Italian restaurant, with open veranda and
garden area, serving classic Italian cuisine. Long
established with popular reputation.   415

Mason's Arms, Marston Gate, Frome,
Somerset BA11 4DJ

Tel: 01373 464537 Fax: 01373 455071
Cosy pub with a characterful interior where beams
and original fireplaces have been retained. Excellent
selection of real ales and delicious menu of tasty
dishes.   443

The Somerset Wagon, Broadway, Chilcompton,
Radstock, Somerset BA3 4JW

Tel: 01761 232732 Fax: 01761 232522
Former coaching inn that has been transformed into
an attractive hostelry. Superb food and ales.
Occasional live music.   439

Ston Easton Park, Ston Easton, Nr. Bath,
Somerset BA3 4DF

Tel: 01761 241631 Fax: 01761 241377
e-mail: enquiry@stoneaston.co.uk
website: www.stoneaston.co.uk
Grand English country house surrounded by
extensive grounds restored to recapture much of the
original elegance and splendour. 24 individually-
designed en-suite bedrooms. Choice of formal or
casual dining, with award-winning cuisine. Superb
leisure facilities.   416

Sun Inn, 6 Catherine Street, Frome,
Somerset BA11 1DA

Tel: 01373 471913
A 16th-century, town centre inn, and a fine example
of a traditional public house. Well-stocked bar and a
menu of light meals and snacks. Seven guest rooms,
one en-suite.   413

The White Hart Hotel, 19-21 Sadler Street, Wells,
Somerset BA5 2RR

Tel: 01749 672056 Fax: 01749 671074
e-mail: info@whitehart-wells.co.uk
website: www.whitehart-wells.co.uk
Delightful, black and white hotel in the centre of
Wells. 13 luxurious bedrooms. Newly refurbished
restaurant offers relaxed dining with a more formal
Italian restaurant nearby. Function suite.   417

Saltford Golf Club

Golf Club Lane, Saltford, Bristol, BS31 3AA
Tel: 01225 873513 Fax: 01225 873525

Sec/Manager:	Valerie Radnedge
Professional:	Dudley Millenstead
Directions:	To the south of the A4 about halfway between Bath and Bristol.
Date Founded:	1904
Type of Course:	Parkland
No of Holes:	18
Length:	6341 yds (5853 mtrs)
Par:	71
SSS:	71
Green Fees:	Weekdays: £24 (round) £28 (day); Weekends/Bank Holidays: £32
Visitors:	Welcome: Contact Club in Advance. Unable to play Tuesdays and Wednesdays
Societies:	Welcome: Contact Club in Advance. Unable to play Tuesdays, Wednesdays, Fridays and Weekends
Facilities:	Practice Ground, Chipping Green, Putting Green, Trolley Hire, Buggy Hire, Bar, Restaurant

Accommodation, Food and Drink

Reference numbers below refer to detailed
information provided in section 2

Accommodation

The Bear Inn, Holwell, Nr. Frome,
Somerset BA11 4PY

Tel: 01373 836585
Unusual structure, built directly into the face of a
quarry, with cosy interior. Fine ales and wide selection
of meals and snacks. Six guest rooms.   444

Ellsworth House, Fosseway, Midsomer Norton,
Bath, Somerset BA3 4AU

Tel: 01761 412305
e-mail: accommodation@ellsworth.fsbusiness.co.uk
website: www.ellsworth.fsbusiness.co.uk
Attractive house with a number of comfortable, en-
suite guest rooms. Spacious sun lounge and indoor
koi carp pond. Non-smoking establishment.   442

Executive Holidays, Whitemill Farm, Iron Mills Lane, Oldford, Frome, Somerset BA11 2NR

Tel: 01373 452907 Fax: 01373 453253
e-mail: info@executiveholidays.co.uk
website: www.executiveholidays.co.uk
Ten different properties of varying sizes all located
within the attractive valley of the River Frome. Superb
range of leisure activities can be organised.   414

Innlodge at the Bridge Inn, North End Road, Yatton, Nr. Bristol, Somerset BS49 4AU

Tel: 01934 839100 Fax: 01934 839149
e-mail bridgeinn@sfigroup.co.uk
website www.innlodge.com
Modern lodge accommodation with 41 en-suite
rooms including some luxurious suites. The Bridge
Inn is a popular country inn serving superb home-
cooked food.   446

Ston Easton Park, Ston Easton, Nr. Bath, Somerset BA3 4DF

Tel: 01761 241631 Fax: 01761 241377
e-mail: enquiry@stoneaston.co.uk
website: www.stoneaston.co.uk
Grand English country house surrounded by
extensive grounds restored to recapture much of the
original elegance and splendour. 24 individually-
designed en-suite bedrooms. Choice of formal or
casual dining, with award-winning cuisine. Superb
leisure facilities.   416

Walton's Guest House, 17-19 Crescent Gardens, Upper Bristol Road, Bath BA1 2NA

Tel: 01225 426528 Fax: 01225 420350
Within five minutes walk of City centre, Roman
Baths, Pump Rooms and other interesting places,
while at the rear of the property is Victoria Park and
the Royal Crescent. 15 bedrooms, 2 en-suite.
Adjoining public car park.

The White Hart Hotel, 19-21 Sadler Street, Wells, Somerset BA5 2RR

Tel: 01749 672056 Fax: 01749 671074
e-mail: info@whitehart-wells.co.uk
website: www.whitehart-wells.co.uk
Delightful, black and white hotel in the centre of
Wells. 13 luxurious bedrooms. Newly refurbished
restaurant offers relaxed dining with a more formal
Italian restaurant nearby. Function suite.   417

Food and Drink

The Bear Inn, Holwell, Nr. Frome, Somerset BA11 4PY

Tel: 01373 836585
Unusual structure, built directly into the face of a
quarry, with cosy interior. Fine ales and wide selection
of meals and snacks. Six guest rooms.   444

Innlodge at the Bridge Inn, North End Road, Yatton, Nr. Bristol, Somerset BS49 4AU

Tel: 01934 839100 Fax: 01934 839149
e-mail bridgeinn@sfigroup.co.uk
website www.innlodge.com
Modern lodge accommodation with 41 en-suite
rooms including some luxurious suites. The Bridge
Inn is a popular country inn serving superb home-
cooked food.   446

La Bisalta, 6 Vicarage Street, Frome, Somerset BA11 1PX

Tel: 01373 464238 Fax: 01373 304603
e-mail: luigi@labisalta.fsnet.co.uk
Genuine Italian restaurant, with open veranda and
garden area, serving classic Italian cuisine. Long
established with popular reputation.   415

Mason's Arms, Marston Gate, Frome, Somerset BA11 4DJ

Tel: 01373 464537 Fax: 01373 455071
Cosy pub with a characterful interior where beams
and original fireplaces have been retained. Excellent
selection of real ales and delicious menu of tasty
dishes.   443

The Somerset Wagon, Broadway, Chilcompton, Radstock, Somerset BA3 4JW

Tel: 01761 232732 Fax: 01761 232522
Former coaching inn that has been transformed into
an attractive hostelry. Superb food and ales.
Occasional live music.   439

Ston Easton Park, Ston Easton, Nr. Bath, Somerset BA3 4DF

Tel: 01761 241631 Fax: 01761 241377
e-mail: enquiry@stoneaston.co.uk
website: www.stoneaston.co.uk
Grand English country house surrounded by
extensive grounds restored to recapture much of the
original elegance and splendour. 24 individually-
designed en-suite bedrooms. Choice of formal or
casual dining, with award-winning cuisine. Superb
leisure facilities.   416

Sun Inn, 6 Catherine Street, Frome, Somerset BA11 1DA

Tel: 01373 471913
A 16th-century, town centre inn, and a fine example
of a traditional public house. Well-stocked bar and a
menu of light meals and snacks. Seven guest rooms,
one en-suite.   413

The White Hart Hotel, 19-21 Sadler Street, Wells, Somerset BA5 2RR

Tel: 01749 672056 Fax: 01749 671074
e-mail: info@whitehart-wells.co.uk
website: www.whitehart-wells.co.uk
Delightful, black and white hotel in the centre of
Wells. 13 luxurious bedrooms. Newly refurbished
restaurant offers relaxed dining with a more formal
Italian restaurant nearby. Function suite.   417

Stockwood Vale Golf Club

Stockwood Lane, Keynsham, Bristol BS31 2ER

Tel: 0117 986 6505 Fax: 0117 986 8974

The USGA-standard greens are often guarded by natural streams that meander throughout, and the fourth and fifth add further credence to the course's nickname of the "Vale of Tiers".

This is a smashing little course, not overly long at a fraction under 5,800 yards off the yellows, but with several want-to-play-again holes, and one which is little known outside the area.

Standing on the 13th tee at Stockwood Vale, it is very difficult to imagine that you are only three miles from the bustling city centre of Bristol. It is set in 150 acres of breathtaking and wildly natural countryside, and your mind needs little encouragement to imagine, as you weigh up the 330 yards before you, that this hole would feature in Golfing Heaven's Best 18 in Britain.

It is, without doubt, the course's signature hole, with rough and shrubs tumbling down to the inviting fairway way below your spikes and far-reaching views south across Somerset. The Vale is one of the best-kept and immaculately presented courses in the region, yet maintains - indeed employs - the many natural features so well that it belies the fact that it is a mere 10 years old.

The contours of the rolling and at times massively undulating valley must have made the mouth water when the idea of creating a course here was first mooted, and the entire concept has been meticulously designed to make the most of what nature provided.

Sec/Manager:	Martin Edenbough
Professional:	John Richards
Directions:	Stockwood Lane is south off the A4 between Keynsham and Bristol
Date Founded:	1991
Type of Course:	Parkland
No of Holes:	18
Length:	6031 yds (5567 mtrs)
Par:	71
SSS:	69
Green Fees:	Weekdays: £15; Weekends/ Bank Holidays: £17
Visitors:	Welcome: Contact Club in Advance. No restrictions
Societies:	Welcome: Contact Club in Advance. Unable to play weekends
Facilities:	Putting Green, Chipping Green, Driving Range, Club Hire, Trolley Hire, Bar, Restaurant, Private Room

Accommodation, Food and Drink

Reference numbers below refer to detailed information provided in section 2

Accommodation

The Bear Inn, Holwell, Nr. Frome, Somerset BA11 4PY

Tel: 01373 836585
Unusual structure, built directly into the face of a quarry, with cosy interior. Fine ales and wide selection of meals and snacks. Six guest rooms.   444

Castlebrook Holiday Cottages, Castlebrook, Compton Dundon, Somerton, Somerset TA11 6PR

Tel: 01458 841680 Fax: 01458 841680
Two fully-equipped holiday homes located in the heart of the Polden Hills. Both feature kitchenette, sitting/dining room, shower room/WC, sleeping three and five adults. Pets welcome by arrangement.   407

Ellsworth House, Fosseway, Midsomer Norton, Bath, Somerset BA3 4AU

Tel: 01761 412305
e-mail: accommodation@ellsworth.fsbusiness.co.uk
website: www.ellsworth.fsbusiness.co.uk
Attractive house with a number of comfortable, en-suite guest rooms. Spacious sun lounge and indoor koi carp pond. Non-smoking establishment.   442

Executive Holidays, Whitemill Farm, Iron Mills Lane, Oldford, Frome, Somerset BA11 2NR

Tel: 01373 452907 Fax: 01373 453253
e-mail: info@executiveholidays.co.uk
website: www.executiveholidays.co.uk
Ten different properties of varying sizes all located within the attractive valley of the River Frome. Superb range of leisure activities can be organised.   414

The Gordons Hotel, Cliff Street, Cheddar, Somerset BS27 3PT

Tel: 01934 742497 Fax: 01934 744965
e-mail: gordons.hotel@virgin.net
Owned by the same family for over 25 years and well liked for its friendly and comfortable atmosphere, The Gordons Hotel offers 14 bedrooms, mostly en-suite. Situated at the foot of the famous gorge and an ideal holiday base. No evening meals.

The Manor Lodge, 21 Station Road, Keynsham Road, Bristol BS31 2BH

Tel: 0117 986 2191
e-mail: jean@themanorlodge.freeserve.co.uk
Impressive Victorian town house offering comfortable bed and breakfast accommodation. Seven en-suite guest rooms.   425

Poachers Table, Cliff Street, Cheddar, Somerset BS27 3PT

Tel: 01934 742271
A family-run restaurant offering a wide variety of food, catering to all tastes and appetites. Situated on the main street, at the foot of Cheddar Gorge, with ample car parking available opposite.

The Prince of Orange, 17 High Street, Yatton, Somerset BS49 4JD

Tel: 01934 832193 Fax: 01934 832193
Popular with locals and tourists for the good range of

beers and hearty food. Accommodation available in a self-contained part of the building, with five en-suite rooms.   441

Ston Easton Park, Ston Easton, Nr. Bath, Somerset BA3 4DF

Tel: 01761 241631 Fax: 01761 241377
e-mail: enquiry@stoneaston.co.uk
website: www.stoneaston.co.uk
Grand English country house surrounded by extensive grounds restored to recapture much of the original elegance and splendour. 24 individually-designed en-suite bedrooms. Choice of formal or casual dining, with award-winning cuisine. Superb leisure facilities.   416

Walton's Guest House, 17-19 Crescent Gardens, Upper Bristol Road, Bath BA1 2NA

Tel: 01225 426528 Fax: 01225 420350
Within five minutes walk of City centre, Roman Baths, Pump Rooms and other interesting places, while at the rear of the property is Victoria Park and the Royal Crescent. 15 bedrooms, 2 en-suite. Adjoining public car park.

The White Hart Hotel, 19-21 Sadler Street, Wells, Somerset BA5 2RR

Tel: 01749 672056 Fax: 01749 671074
e-mail: info@whitehart-wells.co.uk
website: www.whitehart-wells.co.uk
Delightful, black and white hotel in the centre of Wells. 13 luxurious bedrooms. Newly refurbished restaurant offers relaxed dining with a more formal Italian restaurant nearby. Function suite.   417

Food and Drink

The Bear Inn, Holwell, Nr. Frome, Somerset BA11 4PY

Tel: 01373 836585
Unusual structure, built directly into the face of a quarry, with cosy interior. Fine ales and wide selection of meals and snacks. Six guest rooms.   444

Innlodge at the Bridge Inn, North End Road, Yatton, Nr. Bristol, Somerset BS49 4AU

Tel: 01934 839100 Fax: 01934 839149
e-mail bridgeinn@sfigroup.co.uk
website www.innlodge.com
Modern lodge accommodation with 41 en-suite rooms including some luxurious suites. The Bridge Inn is a popular country inn serving superb home-cooked food.   446

Mason's Arms, Marston Gate, Frome, Somerset BA11 4DJ

Tel: 01373 464537 Fax: 01373 455071
Cosy pub with a characterful interior where beams and original fireplaces have been retained. Excellent selection of real ales and delicious menu of tasty dishes.   443

Poachers Table, Cliff Street, Cheddar, Somerset BS27 3PT

Tel: 01934 742271
A family-run restaurant offering a wide variety of food, catering to all tastes and appetites. Situated on

the main street, at the foot of Cheddar Gorge, with ample car parking available opposite.

The Prince of Orange, 17 High Street, Yatton, Somerset BS49 4JD

Tel: 01934 832193 Fax: 01934 832193
Popular with locals and tourists for the good range of beers and hearty food. Accommodation available in a self-contained part of the building, with five en-suite rooms.   441

The Somerset Wagon, Broadway, Chilcompton, Radstock, Somerset BA3 4JW

Tel: 01761 232732 Fax: 01761 232522
Former coaching inn that has been transformed into an attractive hostelry. Superb food and ales. Occasional live music.   439

Ston Easton Park, Ston Easton, Nr. Bath, Somerset BA3 4DF

Tel: 01761 241631 Fax: 01761 241377
e-mail: enquiry@stoneaston.co.uk
website: www.stoneaston.co.uk
Grand English country house surrounded by extensive grounds restored to recapture much of the original elegance and splendour. 24 individually-designed en-suite bedrooms. Choice of formal or casual dining, with award-winning cuisine. Superb leisure facilities.   416

Sun Inn, 6 Catherine Street, Frome, Somerset BA11 1DA

Tel: 01373 471913
A 16th-century, town centre inn, and a fine example of a traditional public house. Well-stocked bar and a menu of light meals and snacks. Seven guest rooms, one en-suite.   413

The White Hart Hotel, 19-21 Sadler Street, Wells, Somerset BA5 2RR

Tel: 01749 672056 Fax: 01749 671074
e-mail: info@whitehart-wells.co.uk
website: www.whitehart-wells.co.uk
Delightful, black and white hotel in the centre of Wells. 13 luxurious bedrooms. Newly refurbished restaurant offers relaxed dining with a more formal Italian restaurant nearby. Function suite.   417

Tall Pines Golf Club

Cooks Bridle Path, Downside, Backwell, Bristol BS48 3DJ

Tel: 01275 474869 Fax: 01275 474869

Many golfers who tend to enjoy a relaxing walk through the countryside as much as they do the game itself would probably be surprised to know that some of their fellows aren't all that interested in nature and its changing patterns through the seasons, or the peace and tranquillity broken only by the sound of wildlife going about its daily business.

OK, so here's one for them. Not only does Tall Pines offer a grand little game of golf but there are also aeroplanes - lots of them! The course south of Bristol is cheek-by-jowl with the city's international airport, so those with an aeronautical bent will be in their own particular Heaven. But don't let the thought of aerial activity distract you from what is a thinker's course, where down-to-Earth problems start pretty much from the word go.

The second, a par four of 408 yards, sees you shooting blind to a two-tier green, and the third is even worse - the green is on three levels, so you need your wits about you. The biggest hazards on the fourth and fifth holes are jets coming and going just a short iron away, but the highlights are around the turn at nine and 10.

The ninth is a splendid par three, with a raised tee and sloping green separated by about 150 yards of unfriendly terrain, while the 10th has one of those nice countryside-type problems - a large tree in the middle of the fairway. This little trick is repeated on the 14th, where there really is a resplendent tall pine or two, and there is more thought needed at the awkward 17th, a 488-yarder with yet another two-level green, where a six might be a relief.

Sec/Manager:	Terry Murray
Professional:	Alex Murray
Directions:	7¼ miles southwest of Bristol city centre. From centre take A38, Bristol Airport road. After 6½ miles turn right into Downside Road at the bottom of hill just before Airport. After ¾ mile turn left into Cooks Bridle Path. The entrance is on the right hand side after ¼ mile.
Date Founded:	1990
Type of Course:	Parkland
No of Holes:	18
Length:	6067 yds (5599 mtrs)
Par:	70
SSS:	69
Green Fees:	Weekdays: £16; Weekends/ Bank Holidays: £16
Visitors:	Welcome: Contact club in advance. Unable to play mornings on weekends
Societies:	Welcome: Contact club in advance. No restrictions.
Facilities:	Putting Green, Chipping Green, Trolley Hire, Buggy Hire, Bar, Restaurant

Accommodation, Food and Drink

Reference numbers below refer to detailed
information provided in section 2

Accommodation

**Innlodge at the Bridge Inn, North End Road,
Yatton, Nr. Bristol, Somerset BS49 4AU**

Tel: 01934 839100 Fax: 01934 839149
e-mail bridgeinn@sfigroup.co.uk
website www.innlodge.com
Modern lodge accommodation with 41 en-suite
rooms including some luxurious suites. The Bridge
Inn is a popular country inn serving superb home-
cooked food.   446

**The Manor Lodge, 21 Station Road,
Keynsham Road, Bristol BS31 2BH**

Tel: 0117 986 2191
e-mail: jean@themanorlodge.freeserve.co.uk
Impressive Victorian town house offering comfortable
bed and breakfast accommodation. Seven en-suite
guest rooms.   425

**The Prince of Orange, 17 High Street, Yatton,
Somerset BS49 4JD**

Tel: 01934 832193 Fax: 01934 832193
Popular with locals and tourists for the good range of
beers and hearty food. Accommodation available in a
self-contained part of the building, with five en-suite
rooms.   441

Food and Drink

**Innlodge at the Bridge Inn, North End Road,
Yatton, Nr. Bristol, Somerset BS49 4AU**

Tel: 01934 839100 Fax: 01934 839149
e-mail bridgeinn@sfigroup.co.uk
website www.innlodge.com
Modern lodge accommodation with 41 en-suite
rooms including some luxurious suites. The Bridge
Inn is a popular country inn serving superb home-
cooked food.   446

**The Market Inn, 1 North End Road, Yatton,
Somerset BS49 4AL**

Tel: 01934 832209 Fax: 01934 835981
A traditional, country inn located close to the M5.
Friendly, warm welcome for locals and visitors to the
area. Wide choice of draught ales and fine selection of
meals and snacks.   438

**The Prince of Orange, 17 High Street, Yatton,
Somerset BS49 4JD**

Tel: 01934 832193 Fax: 01934 832193
Popular with locals and tourists for the good range of
beers and hearty food. Accommodation available in a
self-contained part of the building, with five en-suite
rooms.   441

Tauton & Pickeridge Golf Club

Corfe, Tauton, Somerset BA3 7BY

Tel: 01823 421537 Fax: 01823 421742

Sec/Manager:	Mike Walls
Professional:	Gary Milne
Directions:	4 miles south of Taunton. From centre take South Rd (B3170), Corfe, Fyfett). Just after Corfe turn left into entrance which is signed.
Date Founded:	1892
Type of Course:	Parkland
No of Holes:	18
Length:	5880 yds (5427 mtrs)
Par:	69
SSS:	68
Green Fees:	Weekdays: £22 (round) £26 (day); Weekends/Bank Holidays: £30
Visitors:	Welcome: Contact club in advance. No restrictions.
Societies:	Welcome: Contact club in advance. Unable to play weekends
Facilities:	Putting Green, Club Hire, Trolley Hire, Buggy Hire, Bar, Restaurant

Accommodation, Food and Drink

Reference numbers below refer to detailed
information provided in section 2

Accommodation

'Riverside', Goosebradon Farm, Westport, Nr. Langport, Somerset TA10 0BH

Tel: 01823 680447 Fax: 01823 681008
e-mail: cking@dunnsgreen.fsnet.co.uk
Pretty self-catering cottage in a quiet corner of
Somerset. Sleeps eight adults in three bedrooms.
Attractive rear garden and off-road parking.   418

Banana Cottage, Greenway, North Curry, Taunton, Somerset TA3 6NJ

Tel: 01823 490100
e-mail: jpaterson@bananacottage.co.uk
website: www.bananacottage.co.uk
Small country bed and breakfast with three guest
bedrooms and self-catering bungalow. Mid-week and
golfing breaks.   402

Bashfords Farmhouse, West Bagborough, Taunton, Somerset TA4 3EF

Tel: 01823 432015 Fax: 0870 1671587
e-mail: charlieritchie@netscapeonline.co.uk
Non-working farmhouse dating largely from the 18th
century. Three comfortable rooms with en-suite
facilities or private bathroom. Evening meals available
on request.   440

Blackmore Farm, Cannington, Bridgwater, Somerset TA5 2NE

Tel: 01278 653442 Fax: 01278 653427
Historic manor house dating back to the 14th century
offering comfortable farmhouse bed and breakfast
with four spacious en-suite rooms.   410

East Lambrook Farm, South Petherton, Somerset TA13 5HH

Tel: 01460 240064 Fax: 01460 240064
e-mail: nicolaeeles@supernet.com
A delightful 17th-century house, built of local
sandstone with a thatched roof, set within two and a
half acres of rolling gardens and woodland. Three en-
suite guest rooms. Tennis Courts.   421

The Kings Head Inn, 12 High Street, Cannington, Bridgwater, Somerset TA5 2HE

Tel: 01278 652293 Fax: 01278 652293
A 17th-century, former coaching inn with cosy
interior. Good selection stocked behind the bar.
Lunch time carvery and evening a la carte menu. Bed
and breakfast accommodation.   411

Turnpike Cottage, Turnpike, Milverton, Somerset TA4 1LF

Tel: 01823 400492
Cosy cottage providing self-contained
accommodation, sleeping up to five adults. Very well
equipped. Pets welcome.   404

The White Hart Inn, 51-52 East Reach, Taunton, Somerset TA1 3EZ

Tel: 01823 254652
A town centre pub offering a friendly welcome to all.
Tea, coffee and home-cooked bar meals and snacks
served each day.   401

Food and Drink

The Bird in Hand, Mount Street, Bishops Lydeard, Taunton, Somerset TA4 3LH

Tel: 01823 432090
Traditional country pub dating to the 18th century.
Menu offers a selection of meals and snacks while the
bar claims to stock the best beer in the area.   437

The Kings Head Inn, 12 High Street, Cannington, Bridgwater, Somerset TA5 2HE

Tel: 01278 652293 Fax: 01278 652293
A 17th-century, former coaching inn with cosy
interior. Good selection stocked behind the bar.
Lunch time carvery and evening a la carte menu. Bed
and breakfast accommodation.   411

Marlborough Tea Rooms, Bow Street, Langport, Somerset TA10 9PR

Tel: 01458 250786 Fax: 01458 250786
Small, charming tea rooms serving morning coffee,
light lunches and afternoon tea. Wide ranging menu,
mostly home-made, and superb cream teas.   445

The Old Barn Owl, Westport, Nr. Langport, Somerset TA10 0BH

Tel: 01460 281391 Fax: 01460 281995
Good-sized, family pub enjoying a good location.
Comfortable interior with relaxed atmosphere. Good
range stocked behind the bar and equally excellent
selection in the restaurant.   419

The Old Forge Inn, Church Street, Curry Rivel, Nr. Langport, Somerset TA10 0HE

Tel: 01458 251554 Fax: 01458 252847
Grade 2 listed building, providing characterful
surroundings. Excellent menu with good fish
selection. Public bar open to all. Regular art
exhibitions. 5 rooms for bed and breakfast planned
for April 2002.   420

Thatchers Pond Restaurant, Donyatt, Ilminster, Somerset TA19 0RG

Tel: 01460 53210
Delightful, thatched building built of local stone. One
of the more well-known restaurants in Somerset,
renowned for its home-produced fare.   403

The White Hart Inn, 51-52 East Reach, Taunton, Somerset TA1 3EZ

Tel: 01823 254652
A town centre pub offering a friendly welcome to all.
Tea, coffee and home-cooked bar meals and snacks
served each day.   401

Taunton Vale Golf Club

Creech, Heathfield, Taunton,
Somerset TA3 5EY

Tel: **01823 412220** Fax: **01823 413583**

Sec/Manager:	Sue Davidige
Professional:	Martin Keitch
Directions:	4½ miles northeast of Taunton. From centre take East Reach (A38, M5). Turn left at roundabout (A38, Bridgewater) and after 3 miles turn right onto A361 (Glastonbury). The entrance is after ½ mile on the left hand side.
Visitors:	Welcome: Contact club in advance.
Societies:	Welcome: Contact club in advance. Unable to play Saturdays
Facilities:	Putting Green, Chipping Green, Club Hire, Trolley Hire, Buggy Hire, Bar, Restaurant, Driving Range, Private Rooms

Charleton

Date Founded:	1991
Type of Course:	Parkland
No of Holes:	18
Length:	5800 yds (5353 mtrs)
Par:	70
SSS:	68
Green Fees:	Weekdays: £19; Weekends/Bank Holidays: £23

Durston

Date Founded:	1991
Type of Course:	Parkland
No of Holes:	9
Length:	2004 yds (1850 mtrs)
Par:	32
SSS:	60
Green Fees:	Weekdays: £9 (round) £13 (day); Weekends/Bank Holidays: £11 (round) £16 (day)

Accommodation, Food and Drink

Reference numbers below refer to detailed information provided in section 2

Accommodation

'Riverside', Goosebradon Farm, Westport, Nr. Langport, Somerset TA10 0BH

Tel: 01823 680447 Fax: 01823 681008
e-mail: cking@dunnsgreen.fsnet.co.uk
Pretty self-catering cottage in a quiet corner of

Somerset. Sleeps eight adults in three bedrooms. Attractive rear garden and off-road parking. 418

Banana Cottage, Greenway, North Curry, Taunton, Somerset TA3 6NJ

Tel: 01823 490100
e-mail: jpaterson@bananacottage.co.uk
website: www.bananacottage.co.uk
Small country bed and breakfast with three guest bedrooms and self-catering bungalow. Mid-week and golfing breaks. 402

Bashfords Farmhouse, West Bagborough, Taunton, Somerset TA4 3EF

Tel: 01823 432015 Fax: 0870 1671587
e-mail: charlieritchie@netscapeonline.co.uk
Non-working farmhouse dating largely from the 18th century. Three comfortable rooms with en-suite facilities or private bathroom. Evening meals available on request. 440

Blackmore Farm, Cannington, Bridgwater, Somerset TA5 2NE

Tel: 01278 653442 Fax: 01278 653427
Historic manor house dating back to the 14th century offering comfortable farmhouse bed and breakfast with four spacious en-suite rooms. 410

East Lambrook Farm, South Petherton, Somerset TA13 5HH

Tel: 01460 240064 Fax: 01460 240064
e-mail: nicolaeeles@supernet.com
A delightful 17th-century house, built of local sandstone with a thatched roof, set within two and a half acres of rolling gardens and woodland. Three en-suite guest rooms. Tennis Courts. 421

The Kings Head Inn, 12 High Street, Cannington, Bridgwater, Somerset TA5 2HE

Tel: 01278 652293 Fax: 01278 652293
A 17th-century, former coaching inn with cosy interior. Good selection stocked behind the bar. Lunch time carvery and evening a la carte menu. Bed and breakfast accommodation. 411

Turnpike Cottage, Turnpike, Milverton, Somerset TA4 1LF

Tel: 01823 400492
Cosy cottage providing self-contained accommodation, sleeping up to five adults. Very well equipped. Pets welcome. 404

The White Hart Inn, 51-52 East Reach, Taunton, Somerset TA1 3EZ

Tel: 01823 254652
A town centre pub offering a friendly welcome to all. Tea, coffee and home-cooked bar meals and snacks served each day. 401

Food and Drink

The Bird in Hand, Mount Street, Bishops Lydeard, Taunton, Somerset TA4 3LH

Tel: 01823 432090
Traditional country pub dating to the 18th century. Menu offers a selection of meals and snacks while the bar claims to stock the best beer in the area. 437

The Kings Head Inn, 12 High Street, Cannington, Bridgwater, Somerset TA5 2HE

Tel: 01278 652293 Fax: 01278 652293
A 17th-century, former coaching inn with cosy interior. Good selection stocked behind the bar. Lunch time carvery and evening a la carte menu. Bed and breakfast accommodation.   411

Marlborough Tea Rooms, Bow Street, Langport, Somerset TA10 9PR

Tel: 01458 250786 Fax: 01458 250786
Small, charming tea rooms serving morning coffee, light lunches and afternoon tea. Wide ranging menu, mostly home-made, and superb cream teas.   445

The Old Barn Owl, Westport, Nr. Langport, Somerset TA10 0BH

Tel: 01460 281391 Fax: 01460 281995
Good-sized, family pub enjoying a good location. Comfortable interior with relaxed atmosphere. Good range stocked behind the bar and equally excellent selection in the restaurant.   419

The Old Forge Inn, Church Street, Curry Rivel, Nr. Langport, Somerset TA10 0HE

Tel: 01458 251554 Fax: 01458 252847
Grade 2 listed building, providing characterful surroundings. Excellent menu with good fish selection. Public bar open to all. Regular art exhibitions. 5 rooms for bed and breakfast planned for April 2002.   420

Thatchers Pond Restaurant, Donyatt, Ilminster, Somerset TA19 0RG

Tel: 01460 53210
Delightful, thatched building built of local stone. One of the more well-known restaurants in Somerset, renowned for its home-produced fare.   403

The White Hart Inn, 51-52 East Reach, Taunton, Somerset TA1 3EZ

Tel: 01823 254652
A town centre pub offering a friendly welcome to all. Tea, coffee and home-cooked bar meals and snacks served each day.   401

Vivary Golf Club

Vivary Park, Taunton, Somerset TA1 3JW

Tel: 01823 289274

Sec/Manager:	Alan Stone
Professional:	Mike Steadman
Directions:	½ mile south of Taunton. From centre take Upper High St (A38, Wellington). Turn left at first roundabout into Trull Rd, then first left Wilton Grove and third left into Fons George. The entrance is on the left hand side after 200 yds.

Date Founded:	1928
Type of Course:	Parkland
No of Holes:	18
Length:	4620 yds (4264 mtrs)
Par:	63
SSS:	63
Green Fees:	Weekdays: £8.50; Weekends/ Bank Holidays: £8.50
Visitors:	Welcome: Contact club in advance. No restrictions.
Societies:	Welcome: Contact club in advance. Unable to play weekends.
Facilities:	Putting Green, Club Hire, Trolley Hire, Bar, Restaurant

Accommodation, Food and Drink

Reference numbers below refer to detailed information provided in section 2

Accommodation

'Riverside', Goosebradon Farm, Westport, Nr. Langport, Somerset TA10 0BH

Tel: 01823 680447 Fax: 01823 681008
e-mail: cking@dunnsgreen.fsnet.co.uk
Pretty self-catering cottage in a quiet corner of Somerset. Sleeps eight adults in three bedrooms. Attractive rear garden and off-road parking.   418

Banana Cottage, Greenway, North Curry, Taunton, Somerset TA3 6NJ

Tel: 01823 490100
e-mail: jpaterson@bananacottage.co.uk
website: www.bananacottage.co.uk
Small country bed and breakfast with three guest bedrooms and self-catering bungalow. Mid-week and golfing breaks.   402

Bashfords Farmhouse, West Bagborough, Taunton, Somerset TA4 3EF

Tel: 01823 432015 Fax: 0870 1671587
e-mail: charlieritchie@netscapeonline.co.uk
Non-working farmhouse dating largely from the 18th century. Three comfortable rooms with en-suite facilities or private bathroom. Evening meals available on request.   440

Blackmore Farm, Cannington, Bridgwater, Somerset TA5 2NE

Tel: 01278 653442 Fax: 01278 653427
Historic manor house dating back to the 14th century offering comfortable farmhouse bed and breakfast with four spacious en-suite rooms.   410

East Lambrook Farm, South Petherton, Somerset TA13 5HH

Tel: 01460 240064 Fax: 01460 240064
e-mail: nicolaeeles@supernet.com
A delightful 17th-century house, built of local

sandstone with a thatched roof, set within two and a half acres of rolling gardens and woodland. Three en-suite guest rooms. Tennis Courts. 421

The Kings Head Inn, 12 High Street, Cannington, Bridgwater, Somerset TA5 2HE

Tel: 01278 652293 Fax: 01278 652293
A 17th-century, former coaching inn with cosy interior. Good selection stocked behind the bar. Lunch time carvery and evening a la carte menu. Bed and breakfast accommodation. 411

Turnpike Cottage, Turnpike, Milverton, Somerset TA4 1LF

Tel: 01823 400492
Cosy cottage providing self-contained accommodation, sleeping up to five adults. Very well equipped. Pets welcome. 404

The White Hart Inn, 51-52 East Reach, Taunton, Somerset TA1 3EZ

Tel: 01823 254652
A town centre pub offering a friendly welcome to all. Tea, coffee and home-cooked bar meals and snacks served each day. 401

Food and Drink

The Bird in Hand, Mount Street, Bishops Lydeard, Taunton, Somerset TA4 3LH

Tel: 01823 432090
Traditional country pub dating to the 18th century. Menu offers a selection of meals and snacks while the bar claims to stock the best beer in the area. 437

The Kings Head Inn, 12 High Street, Cannington, Bridgwater, Somerset TA5 2HE

Tel: 01278 652293 Fax: 01278 652293
A 17th-century, former coaching inn with cosy interior. Good selection stocked behind the bar. Lunch time carvery and evening a la carte menu. Bed and breakfast accommodation. 411

Marlborough Tea Rooms, Bow Street, Langport, Somerset TA10 9PR

Tel: 01458 250786 Fax: 01458 250786
Small, charming tea rooms serving morning coffee, light lunches and afternoon tea. Wide ranging menu, mostly home-made, and superb cream teas. 445

The Old Barn Owl, Westport, Nr. Langport, Somerset TA10 0BH

Tel: 01460 281391 Fax: 01460 281995
Good-sized, family pub enjoying a good location. Comfortable interior with relaxed atmosphere. Good range stocked behind the bar and equally excellent selection in the restaurant. 419

The Old Forge Inn, Church Street, Curry Rivel, Nr. Langport, Somerset TA10 0HE

Tel: 01458 251554 Fax: 01458 252847
Grade 2 listed building, providing characterful surroundings. Excellent menu with good fish selection. Public bar open to all. Regular art exhibitions. 5 rooms for bed and breakfast planned for April 2002. 420

Thatchers Pond Restaurant, Donyatt, Ilminster, Somerset TA19 0RG

Tel: 01460 53210
Delightful, thatched building built of local stone. One of the more well-known restaurants in Somerset, renowned for its home-produced fare. 403

The White Hart Inn, 51-52 East Reach, Taunton, Somerset TA1 3EZ

Tel: 01823 254652
A town centre pub offering a friendly welcome to all. Tea, coffee and home-cooked bar meals and snacks served each day. 401

Wells Golf Club

East Horrington Road, Wells,
Somerset BA5 3DS

Tel: 01749 675005 Fax: 01749 675005

Sec/Manager:	Chris Searle
Professional:	Adrian Bishop
Directions:	2½ miles northeast of Wells. From centre take The Liberty (B3139, Chilcompton). After 2¾ miles turn right onto B road (East Horrington Road). The entrance is on the right hand side after ½ mile.

Date Founded: 1893

Type of Course: Parkland

No of Holes:	18
Length:	6015 yds (5551 mtrs)
Par:	70
SSS:	69
Green Fees:	Weekdays: £20; Weekends/ Bank Holidays: £25
Visitors:	Welcome: Contact club in advance. No restrictions.
Societies:	Welcome: Contact club in advance. Unable to play Mondays, Wednesdays, Fridays and Weekends
Facilities:	Putting Green, Driving Range, Club Hire, Trolley Hire, Buggy Hire, Bar, Restaurant

Accommodation, Food and Drink

Reference numbers below refer to detailed
information provided in section 2

Accommodation

The Bear Inn, Holwell, Nr. Frome, Somerset BA11 4PY

Tel: 01373 836585
Unusual structure, built directly into the face of a
quarry, with cosy interior. Fine ales and wide selection
of meals and snacks. Six guest rooms.   444

Castlebrook Holiday Cottages, Castlebrook, Compton Dundon, Somerton, Somerset TA11 6PR

Tel: 01458 841680 Fax: 01458 841680
Two fully-equipped holiday homes located in the
heart of the Polden Hills. Both feature kitchenette,
sitting/dining room, shower room/WC, sleeping three
and five adults. Pets welcome by arrangement.   407

Ellsworth House, Fosseway, Midsomer Norton, Bath, Somerset BA3 4AU

Tel: 01761 412305
e-mail: accommodation@ellsworth.fsbusiness.co.uk
website: www.ellsworth.fsbusiness.co.uk
Attractive house with a number of comfortable, en-
suite guest rooms. Spacious sun lounge and indoor
koi carp pond. Non-smoking establishment.   442

Executive Holidays, Whitemill Farm, Iron Mills Lane, Oldford, Frome, Somerset BA11 2NR

Tel: 01373 452907 Fax: 01373 453253
e-mail: info@executiveholidays.co.uk
website: www.executiveholidays.co.uk
Ten different properties of varying sizes all located
within the attractive valley of the River Frome. Superb
range of leisure activities can be organised.   414

The Gordons Hotel, Cliff Street, Cheddar, Somerset BS27 3PT

Tel: 01934 742497 Fax: 01934 744965
e-mail: gordons.hotel@virgin.net
Owned by the same family for over 25 years and well

liked for its friendly and comfortable atmosphere, The
Gordons Hotel offers 14 bedrooms, mostly en-suite.
Situated at the foot of the famous gorge and an ideal
holiday base. No evening meals.

Poachers Table, Cliff Street, Cheddar, Somerset BS27 3PT

Tel: 01934 742271
A family-run restaurant offering a wide variety of
food, catering to all tastes and appetites. Situated on
the main street, at the foot of Cheddar Gorge, with
ample car parking available opposite.

The Prince of Orange, 17 High Street, Yatton, Somerset BS49 4JD

Tel: 01934 832193 Fax: 01934 832193
Popular with locals and tourists for the good range of
beers and hearty food. Accommodation available in a
self-contained part of the building, with five en-suite
rooms.   441

Ston Easton Park, Ston Easton, Nr. Bath, Somerset BA3 4DF

Tel: 01761 241631 Fax: 01761 241377
e-mail: enquiry@stoneaston.co.uk
website: www.stoneaston.co.uk
Grand English country house surrounded by
extensive grounds restored to recapture much of the
original elegance and splendour. 24 individually-
designed en-suite bedrooms. Choice of formal or
casual dining, with award-winning cuisine. Superb
leisure facilities.   416

Walton's Guest House, 17-19 Crescent Gardens, Upper Bristol Road, Bath BA1 2NA

Tel: 01225 426528 Fax: 01225 420350
Within five minutes walk of City centre, Roman
Baths, Pump Rooms and other interesting places,
while at the rear of the property is Victoria Park and
the Royal Crescent. 15 bedrooms, 2 en-suite.
Adjoining public car park.

The White Hart Hotel, 19-21 Sadler Street, Wells, Somerset BA5 2RR

Tel: 01749 672056 Fax: 01749 671074
e-mail: info@whitehart-wells.co.uk
website: www.whitehart-wells.co.uk
Delightful, black and white hotel in the centre of
Wells. 13aurant offers relaxed dining with a more
formal Italian restaurant nearby. Function suite.   417

Food and Drink

The Bear Inn, Holwell, Nr. Frome, Somerset BA11 4PY

Tel: 01373 836585
Unusual structure, built directly into the face of a
quarry, with cosy interior. Fine ales and wide selection
of meals and snacks. Six guest rooms.   444

Innlodge at the Bridge Inn, North End Road, Yatton, Nr. Bristol, Somerset BS49 4AU

Tel: 01934 839100 Fax: 01934 839149
e-mail bridgeinn@sfigroup.co.uk
website www.innlodge.com
Modern lodge accommodation with 41 en-suite

rooms including some luxurious suites. The Bridge Inn is a popular country inn serving superb home-cooked food.   446

Mason's Arms, Marston Gate, Frome, Somerset BA11 4DJ

Tel: 01373 464537 Fax: 01373 455071
Cosy pub with a characterful interior where beams and original fireplaces have been retained. Excellent selection of real ales and delicious menu of tasty dishes.   443

Poachers Table, Cliff Street, Cheddar, Somerset BS27 3PT

Tel: 01934 742271
A family-run restaurant offering a wide variety of food, catering to all tastes and appetites. Situated on the main street, at the foot of Cheddar Gorge, with ample car parking available opposite.

The Prince of Orange, 17 High Street, Yatton, Somerset BS49 4JD

Tel: 01934 832193
Fax: 01934 832193
Popular with locals and tourists for the good range of beers and hearty food. Accommodation available in a self-contained part of the building, with five en-suite rooms.   441

The Somerset Wagon, Broadway, Chilcompton, Radstock, Somerset BA3 4JW

Tel: 01761 232732 Fax: 01761 232522
Former coaching inn that has been transformed into an attractive hostelry. Superb food and ales. Occasional live music.   439

Ston Easton Park, Ston Easton, Nr. Bath, Somerset BA3 4DF

Tel: 01761 241631 Fax: 01761 241377
e-mail: enquiry@stoneaston.co.uk
website: www.stoneaston.co.uk
Grand English country house surrounded by extensive grounds restored to recapture much of the original elegance and splendour. 24 individually-designed en-suite bedrooms. Choice of formal or casual dining, with award-winning cuisine. Superb leisure facilities.   416

Sun Inn, 6 Catherine Street, Frome, Somerset BA11 1DA

Tel: 01373 471913
A 16th-century, town centre inn, and a fine example of a traditional public house. Well-stocked bar and a menu of light meals and snacks. Seven guest rooms, one en-suite.   413

The White Hart Hotel, 19-21 Sadler Street, Wells, Somerset BA5 2RR

Tel: 01749 672056 Fax: 01749 671074
e-mail: info@whitehart-wells.co.uk
website: www.whitehart-wells.co.uk
Delightful, black and white hotel in the centre of Wells. 13 luxurious bedrooms. Newly refurbished restaurant offers relaxed dining with a more formal Italian restaurant nearby. Function suite.   417

Weston-super-Mare Golf Club

Uphill Road North, Weston-super-Mare, Somerset BS23 4NQ

Tel: 01934 626968 Fax: 01934 621360

This must be one of the easiest seaside resort courses to find. Walk south from the pier along the prom, past the wide-open Beach Lawns and, in a couple of minutes, you're there, even pulling your trolley!

Weston offers a fairly flattish and compact round of links golf, with some gently undulating fairways and one or two oddities. For instance, access to the fifth and sixth holes takes you across a road and through a little caravan park. Here you'll face two awkward tests, with a 411-yarder seeming innocuous enough apart from some bumps and banks, but with a green snuggling tight into a corner, surrounded by trees. The sixth also looks easy enough, but watch for the out of bounds, too close for comfort down the left.

Other highlights of a pleasant course include the 13th, which has a two-tier green guarded by

a very large greenside bunker, and the 17th, one for the big hitters to challenge with its left-to-right dog-leg, although the smart money wouldn't risk more out of bounds, which stretch just about all the way down the right of each of the 493 yard holes.

With an opening hole almost on the resort's famous flat beach - you can play spot the sea, if you have that much time - and views across the Bristol Channel to South Wales, Weston needs just about the right amount of effort from a holidaymaker.

Sec/Manager:	Karen Drake
Professional:	Mike Laband
Directions:	From the centre of Weston-super-Mare take the Promenade south towards Uphill. The entrance is on the right at the end.
Date Founded:	1892
Type of Course:	Links
No of Holes:	18
Length:	6208 yds (5730 mtrs)
Par:	70
SSS:	70

Green Fees:	Weekdays: £24; Weekends/Bank Holidays: £35
Visitors:	Welcome: Contact Club in Advance. No restrictions
Societies:	Welcome: Contact Club in Advance. Unable to play Weekends
Facilities:	Chipping Green, Putting Green, Trolley Hire, Bar, Restaurant

Accommodation, Food and Drink

Reference numbers below refer to detailed information provided in section 2

Accommodation

Bella Vista Hotel, 19 Upper Church Road, Weston-super-Mare, Somerset BS23 2DX

Tel: 01934 631931 Fax: 01934 620126
Family-run hotel located just 100 metres from the sea front. Eight spacious en-suite bedrooms. Warm, friendly atmosphere.   408

Beverleigh, Beacon Road, North Hill, Minehead, Somerset TA24 5SF

Tel: 01643 708450
e-mail: beverleigh@talk21.com
Charming Edwardian house, beautifully furnished. Situated on the higher slopes of North Hill where Exmoor meets the sea. Set in lovely gardens with breathtaking views of Minehead and the surrounding hills.

Carefree Holiday Park, 12 Beach Road, Sand Bay, Weston-super-Mare, Somerset BS22 9UZ

Tel: 01934 624541
Beautifully kept, quiet, five-star holiday park situated directly on Sand Bay Beach. Modern caravans offer luxurious four- and six- berth accommodation. Two miles along coast road from Weston-super-Mare and only one mile from Worlebury golf course.

Ellenborough Hall, 15 Ellenborough Park North, Weston-super-Mare, Somerset BS23 1XQ

Tel: 01934 629543
Large Victorian house converted into a family-run hotel with a friendly atmosphere. Four en-suite rooms. Plenty of off-road parking. Within easy reach of the town centre and sea front.

Goodrington Guest House, 23 Charlton Road, Weston-super-Mare, Somerset BS23 4HB

Tel: 01934 623229
e-mail: vera.bishop@btclick.com
website: http://home.btclick.com/vera.bishop
Friendly guest house with just three guest rooms, two with en-suite facilities. One double, one triple and one room with four single beds. Evening meals available on request.

The Greyhound Inn, 1 Lime Street, Stogursey, Bridgwater, Somerset TA5 1QR

Tel: 01278 732490
Traditional rural inn. Bar stocks a range of local real
ales, cider, wine and spirits. Good selection of home-
cooked food. Bed and breakfast accommodation. 412

**The Hawthorne, Crooked Lane, Brent Knoll,
Somerset TA9 4BQ**

Tel: 01278 760181
Comfortable country house in quiet surroundings.
Separate annexe for guests with dining hall and two
en-suite bed and breakfast rooms. Close to Berrow
golf course.

**Innlodge at the Bridge Inn, North End Road,
Yatton, Nr. Bristol, Somerset BS49 4AU**

Tel: 01934 839100 Fax: 01934 839149
e-mail bridgeinn@sfigroup.co.uk
website www.innlodge.com
Modern lodge accommodation with 41 en-suite
rooms including some luxurious suites. The Bridge
Inn is a popular country inn serving superb home-
cooked food. 446

**Laburnum House Lodge Hotel, Sloway Lane,
West Huntspill, Highbridge, Somerset TA9 3RJ**

Tel: 01278 781830 Fax: 01278 781612
e-mail: laburnumhh@aol.com
website: www.laburnumhh.co.uk
Family-run country lodge hotel. 60 bedrooms, all en-
suite, of varying sizes. Peaceful, rural location with
clay pigeon shooting, fishing and many other
activities available on site. Also holiday complex with
superb 80-cover restaurant and two bars open to all
visitors. Excellent menus and great pub grub with
weekly BBQs and Pig Roasts.

**Three Acres Caravan Park, South Road, Brean,
Somerset TA8 2RF**

Tel: 01278 751313
e-mail: 3acres@ic24.net
15 self-catering six-berth caravans within a couple of
miles of Burnham-on-Sea and close to several golf
courses. Bar and restaurant within the site for
residents' use.

Food and Drink

**The Greyhound Inn, 1 Lime Street, Stogursey,
Bridgwater, Somerset TA5 1QR**

Tel: 01278 732490
Traditional rural inn. Bar stocks a range of local real
ales, cider, wine and spirits. Good selection of home-
cooked food. Bed and breakfast accommodation. 412

**Innlodge at the Bridge Inn, North End Road,
Yatton, Nr. Bristol, Somerset BS49 4AU**

Tel: 01934 839100 Fax: 01934 839149
e-mail bridgeinn@sfigroup.co.uk
website www.innlodge.com
Modern lodge accommodation with 41 en-suite
rooms including some luxurious suites. The Bridge
Inn is a popular country inn serving superb home-
cooked food. 446

**Laburnum House Lodge Hotel, Sloway Lane,
West Huntspill, Highbridge, Somerset TA9 3RJ**

Tel: 01278 781830 Fax: 01278 781612
e-mail: laburnumhh@aol.com
website: www.laburnumhh.co.uk
Family-run country lodge hotel. 60 bedrooms, all en-
suite, of varying sizes. Peaceful, rural location with
clay pigeon shooting, fishing and many other
activities available on site. Also holiday complex with
superb 80-cover restaurant and two bars open to all
visitors. Excellent menus and great pub grub with
weekly BBQs and Pig Roasts.

**Long John Silver, 73 Beach Road, Kewstoke,
Weston-super-Mare, Somerset BS22 9UP**

Tel: 01934 623367
Characterful inn serving an excellent selection of
food ranging from traditional pub fayre to seafood
and steak dishes. Vegetarians also catered for.

**The Major from Glengarry, 10-14 Upper Church
Road, Weston-super-Mare, Somerset BS23 2DT**

Tel: 01934 629260
Family-run pub offering a warm welcome to all.
Serves Wadsworth Cask Ales and an extensive range of
snacks and traditional food prepared by the owner,
who is a qualified chef. Regular evening
entertainment with live music. Families welcome.

**The Market Inn, 1 North End Road, Yatton,
Somerset BS49 4AL**

Tel: 01934 832209 Fax: 01934 835981
A traditional, country inn located close to the M5.
Friendly, warm welcome for locals and visitors to the
area. Wide choice of draught ales and fine selection of
meals and snacks. 438

**The Old Thatched Cottage Restaurant,
14 Knightstone Road, Weston-super-Mare,
Somerset BS23 2AN**

Tel: 01934 621313
Popular restaurant on seafront serving French, Italian
and Greek cuisine from an a la carte menu. Fresh fish
is the house speciality. Open every day, all year
round. Caters for parties of up to 100.

Wheathill Golf Club

Wheathill, Somerton, Somerset TA11 7HG
Tel: 01963 240667 Fax: 01963 240230

Sec/Manager:	Alan Lidden
Professional:	Andrew England
Directions:	8 miles south of Shepton Mallet. From centre take A361 (Glastonbury). After 2 miles turn left onto A37 (Podimore). After 7 miles turn left onto B3153 (Castle Cary). The entrance is after 1 mile turning right into B road for 500 yds.
Date Founded:	1993
Type of Course:	Parkland

No of Holes:	18
Length:	5351 yds (4938 mtrs)
Par:	68
SSS:	66
Green Fees:	Weekdays: £15; Weekends/Bank Holidays: £20
Visitors:	Welcome: Contact club in advance. No Restrictions.
Societies:	Welcome: Contact club in advance. No Restrictions.
Facilities:	Putting Green, Chipping Green, Club Hire, Trolley Hire, Buggy Hire, Bar, Restaurant, Practice Ground

Accommodation, Food and Drink

Reference numbers below refer to detailed information provided in section 2

Accommodation

'Riverside', Goosebradon Farm, Westport, Nr. Langport, Somerset TA10 0BH

Tel: 01823 680447 Fax: 01823 681008
e-mail: cking@dunnsgreen.fsnet.co.uk
Pretty self-catering cottage in a quiet corner of Somerset. Sleeps eight adults in three bedrooms. Attractive rear garden and off-road parking.   418

Amberley Guest House, Martock Road, Long Load, Langport, Somerset TA10 9LD

Tel: 01458 241542
e-mail: jeanatamberley@talk21.com
An attractive farmhouse-style property with four comfortable guest rooms of varying sizes. Evening meals available on request. Non-smoking.   422

Ash House Country House Hotel and Restaurant, Main Street, Ash, Nr. Martock, Somerset TA12 6PB

Tel: 01935 822036 Fax: 01935 822992
e-mail: reception@ashhousehotel.freeserve.co.uk
website: www.ashhousecountryhotel.co.uk
Small, privately-owned Georgian Country house hotel surrounded by attractive gardens. Popular a la carte restaurant with high standard of cuisine. Eight delightful en-suite rooms.   424

Castlebrook Holiday Cottages, Castlebrook, Compton Dundon, Somerton, Somerset TA11 6PR

Tel: 01458 841680 Fax: 01458 841680
Two fully-equipped holiday homes located in the heart of the Polden Hills. Both feature kitchenette, sitting/dining room, shower room/WC, sleeping three and five adults. Pets welcome by arrangement.   407

East Lambrook Farm, South Petherton, Somerset TA13 5HH

Tel: 01460 240064 Fax: 01460 240064
e-mail: nicolaeeles@supernet.com
A delightful 17th-century house, built of local sandstone with a thatched roof, set within two and a half acres of rolling gardens and woodland. Three en-suite guest rooms. Tennis Courts.   421

The Ilchester Arms, The Square, Ilchester, Nr. Yeovil, Somerset BA22 8LN

Tel: 01935 840220 Fax: 01935 841353
Impressive Georgian building, dominating the main street, offering comfortable en-suite accommodation. High quality restaurant with wide-ranging menu. 434

The Portman Arms, High Street, East Chinnock, Yeovil, Somerset BA22 9DP

Tel: 01935 862227 Fax: 01935 862227
An imposing building dating from the early 1800s providing a spacious eating and drinking area. Good menu. Five, newly-refurbished, en-suite guest rooms. Caravan pitches also available.   429

Richmond House Holiday Accommodation, Barrow Farm, North Barrow, Yeovil, Somerset BA22 7LZ

Tel: 01963 240543 Fax: 01963 240543
e-mail: rhholidays@netscapeonline.co.uk
website: www.rhholidays.co.uk
Eight cottages of varying sizes situated on two sites just 50 metres apart and surrounded by 600 acres of grazing land. Well-maintained and well-equipped.431

The Royal George, West Coker, Yeovil, Somerset BA22 9AN

Tel: 01935 862334 Fax: 01935 864499
18th-century hostelry with a cosy, traditional interior. Menu offers a good selection of dishes. Occasional live music and a regular quiz night. Two en-suite guest rooms.   428

The Walnut Tree, West Camel, Nr. Yeovil, Somerset BA22 7QW

Tel: 01935 851292 Fax: 01935 851292
website: www.thewalnuttreehotel.com
Charming family-run hotel, restaurant and inn. Fine menu of imaginative dishes served both in the bar and restaurant, with fish being a speciality. Thirteen en-suite guest rooms.   426

Weston House Cottages, East Chinnock, Nr. Yeovil, Somerset BA22 9EL

Tel: 01935 863712/863394 Mobile: 07884 214768

e-mail: westonhouseuk@netscapeonline.co.uk
Two cottages converted from former barns located within a working farm. High quality well-equipped accommodation. One cottage sleeps four, the other sleeps five. Dogs welcome. 430

The Yew Tree Inn, Forest Hill, Yeovil, Somerset BA20 2PG

Tel: 01935 476808 Fax: 01935 476808
Former gentleman's residence which was converted into a pub only 30 years ago. Cosy, friendly atmosphere. Excellent food with a menu of traditional pub food. Four guest rooms of varying sizes. 432

Food and Drink

Ash House Country House Hotel and Restaurant, Main Street, Ash, Nr. Martock, Somerset TA12 6PB

Tel: 01935 822036 Fax: 01935 822992
e-mail: reception@ashhousehotel.freeserve.co.uk
website: www.ashhousecountryhotel.co.uk
Small, privately-owned Georgian Country house hotel surrounded by attractive gardens. Popular a la carte restaurant with high standard of cuisine. Eight delightful en-suite rooms. 424

The Fox and Hounds, Broadway Road, Charlton Adam, Somerset TA11 7AU

Tel: 01458 223466
Small village pub serving traditional, wholesome food and specialising in home-made pies. Real ales served, including local Butcombe Ales. Pool table, function room and can accommodate up to five caravans or motor homes on an adjoining field.

The Ilchester Arms, The Square, Ilchester, Nr. Yeovil, Somerset BA22 8LN

Tel: 01935 840220 Fax: 01935 841353
Impressive Georgian building, dominating the main street, offering comfortable en-suite accommodation. High quality restaurant with wide-ranging menu. 434

The Lamb and Lark, Limington, Nr. Yeovil, Somerset

Tel: 01935 840368
e-mail: thelambandlark@cs.com
Pub housed within a 15th-century building that has been carefully restored. Inside there is a piano bar and lounge. Good selection of freshly-prepared food. 433

Marlborough Tea Rooms, Bow Street, Langport, Somerset TA10 9PR

Tel: 01458 250786 Fax: 01458 250786
Small, charming tea rooms serving morning coffee, light lunches and afternoon tea. Wide ranging menu, mostly home-made, and superb cream teas. 445

The Old Barn Owl, Westport, Nr. Langport, Somerset TA10 0BH

Tel: 01460 281391 Fax: 01460 281995
Good-sized, family pub enjoying a good location. Comfortable interior with relaxed atmosphere. Good range stocked behind the bar and equally excellent selection in the restaurant. 419

The Old Forge Inn, Church Street, Curry Rivel, Nr. Langport, Somerset TA10 0HE

Tel: 01458 251554 Fax: 01458 252847
Grade 2 listed building, providing characterful surroundings. Excellent menu with good fish selection. Public bar open to all. Regular art exhibitions. 5 rooms for bed and breakfast planned for April 2002. 420

The Portman Arms, High Street, East Chinnock, Yeovil, Somerset BA22 9DP

Tel: 01935 862227 Fax: 01935 862227
An imposing building dating from the early 1800s providing a spacious eating and drinking area. Good menu. Five, newly-refurbished, en-suite guest rooms. Caravan pitches also available. 429

The Royal George, West Coker, Yeovil, Somerset BA22 9AN

Tel: 01935 862334 Fax: 01935 864499
18th-century hostelry with a cosy, traditional interior. Menu offers a good selection of dishes. Occasional live music and a regular quiz night. Two en-suite guest rooms. 428

The Royal Marine, St. Weston Terrace, Yeovil, Somerset BA21 5AA

Tel: 01935 474350 Fax: 01935 474350
Popular inn just a short walk from the centre of Yeovil. Sensibly priced menu of meals and snacks and a selection of real ales on tap. 435

The Royal Oak, Stoford, Yeovil, Somerset BA22 9UD

Tel: 01935 475071
Quiet village location just a couple of miles from the centre of Yeovil. Cosy interior with separate restaurant. Well-priced menu of traditional dishes. Occasional quiz and theme nights. 427

Rusty Axe, Stembridge, Somerset

Tel: 01460 240109
Friendly, cosy country pub. Popular for food with a wide ranging menu offering excellent choice. Live music on Saturday evenings. 423

The Walnut Tree, West Camel, Nr. Yeovil, Somerset BA22 7QW

Tel: 01935 851292 Fax: 01935 851292
website: www.thewalnuttreehotel.com
Charming family-run hotel, restaurant and inn. Fine menu of imaginative dishes served both in the bar and restaurant, with fish being a speciality. Thirteen en-suite guest rooms. 426

The Yew Tree Inn, Forest Hill, Yeovil, Somerset BA20 2PG

Tel: 01935 476808 Fax: 01935 476808
Former gentleman's residence which was converted into a pub only 30 years ago. Cosy, friendly atmosphere. Excellent food with a menu of traditional pub food. Four guest rooms of varying sizes. 432

Windwhistle Golf Club

Cricket St Thomas, Chard, Somerset TA20 4DG
Tel: 01460 30231 Fax: 01460 30055

Sec/Manager:	Ian Dodd
Professional:	Duncan Driver
Directions:	2½ miles east of Chard. From centre take Fore St (A30, Crewkerne). The entrance is on the left hand side of main road after 2½ miles.
Date Founded:	1932
Type of Course:	Parkland
No of Holes:	18
Length:	6510 yds (6009 mtrs)
Par:	73
SSS:	71
Green Fees:	Weekdays: £18; Weekends/Bank Holidays: £22
Visitors:	Welcome: Contact club in advance. No restrictions.
Societies:	Welcome: Contact club in advance. No restrictions.
Facilities:	Putting Green, Chipping Green, Driving Range, Club Hire, Trolley Hire, Buggy Hire, Bar, Restaurant

Accommodation, Food and Drink

Reference numbers below refer to detailed information provided in section 2

Accommodation

'Riverside', Goosebradon Farm, Westport, Nr. Langport, Somerset TA10 0BH

Tel: 01823 680447 Fax: 01823 681008
e-mail: cking@dunnsgreen.fsnet.co.uk
Pretty self-catering cottage in a quiet corner of Somerset. Sleeps eight adults in three bedrooms. Attractive rear garden and off-road parking. 418

Kersbrook Hotel, Pound Road, Lyme Regis, Dorset DT7 3HX

Tel: 01297 442596 Fax: 01297 442596
A family-run bed and breakfast establishment housed within an historic, listed building. Ten en-suite guest bedrooms with many enjoying fine views.

The Portman Arms, High Street, East Chinnock, Yeovil, Somerset BA22 9DP

Tel: 01935 862227 Fax: 01935 862227
An imposing building dating from the early 1800s providing a spacious eating and drinking area. Good menu. Five, newly-refurbished, en-suite guest rooms. Caravan pitches also available. 429

The Royal George, West Coker, Yeovil, Somerset BA22 9AN

Tel: 01935 862334 Fax: 01935 864499
18th-century hostelry with a cosy, traditional interior. Menu offers a good selection of dishes. Occasional live music and a regular quiz night. Two en-suite guest rooms. 428

Weston House Cottages, East Chinnock, Nr. Yeovil, Somerset BA22 9EL

Tel: 01935 863712/863394 Mobile: 07884 214768
e-mail: westonhouseuk@netscapeonline.co.uk
Two cottages converted from former barns located within a working farm. High quality well-equipped accommodation. One cottage sleeps four, the other sleeps five. Dogs welcome. 430

Food and Drink

The Crown Inn, 59 West Bay Road, Bridport, Dorset DT6 4AX

Tel: 01308 422037 Fax: 01308 458875
e-mail: enquiries@thecrowninn.org.uk
website: www.thecrowninn.org.uk
Situated midway between Bridport and West Bay, The Crown Inn offers classic Irish hospitality in a traditional English setting. A full menu is always available, and parties can be catered for. Children are welcomed and there is a special children's menu.

The Old Barn Owl, Westport, Nr. Langport, Somerset TA10 0BH

Tel: 01460 281391 Fax: 01460 281995
Good-sized, family pub enjoying a good location. Comfortable interior with relaxed atmosphere. Good range stocked behind the bar and equally excellent selection in the restaurant. 419

The Portman Arms, High Street, East Chinnock, Yeovil, Somerset BA22 9DP

Tel: 01935 862227 Fax: 01935 862227
An imposing building dating from the early 1800s providing a spacious eating and drinking area. Good menu. Five, newly-refurbished, en-suite guest rooms. Caravan pitches also available. 429

The Royal George, West Coker, Yeovil, Somerset BA22 9AN

Tel: 01935 862334 Fax: 01935 864499
18th-century hostelry with a cosy, traditional interior. Menu offers a good selection of dishes. Occasional live music and a regular quiz night. Two en-suite guest rooms. 428

Rusty Axe, Stembridge, Somerset

Tel: 01460 240109
Friendly, cosy country pub. Popular for food with a wide ranging menu offering excellent choice. Live music on Saturday evenings. 423

Thatchers Pond Restaurant, Donyatt, Ilminster, Somerset TA19 0RG

Tel: 01460 53210

Delightful, thatched building built of local stone. One of the more well-known restaurants in Somerset, renowned for its home-produced fare. 403

Worlebury Golf Club

Monks Hill, Worlebury, Weston-Super-Mare, Somerset BS22 9SX

Tel: 01934 623214 Fax: 01934 621935

Sec/Manager:	Mike Wake
Professional:	Gary Marks
Directions:	1¾ miles northeast of Weston-super-Mare. From M5 junction 21 take A370 (Weston-super-Mare). After 2¼ miles turn right into Baytree Rd, leading to Milton Hill. The entrance is at the junction of Milton Hill and Wonsbury Hill Rd, 900 yds from the A370.
Date Founded:	1908
Type of Course:	Clifftop
No of Holes:	18
Length:	5850 yds (5399 mtrs)
Par:	70

SSS:	69
Green Fees:	Weekdays: £20; Weekends/ Bank Holidays: £30
Visitors:	Welcome: Contact club in advance. Unable to play Tuesday morning.
Societies:	Welcome: Contact club in advance. No restrictions.
Facilities:	Putting Green, Chipping Green, Club Hire, Trolley Hire, Bar, Restaurant

Accommodation, Food and Drink

Reference numbers below refer to detailed information provided in section 2

Accommodation

Bella Vista Hotel, 19 Upper Church Road, Weston-super-Mare, Somerset BS23 2DX

Tel: 01934 631931 Fax: 01934 620126
Family-run hotel located just 100 metres from the sea front. Eight spacious en-suite bedrooms. Warm, friendly atmosphere. 408

Beverleigh, Beacon Road, North Hill, Minehead, Somerset TA24 5SF

Tel: 01643 708450
e-mail: beverleigh@talk21.com
Charming Edwardian house, beautifully furnished. Situated on the higher slopes of North Hill where Exmoor meets the sea. Set in lovely gardens with breathtaking views of Minehead and the surrounding hills.

Carefree Holiday Park, 12 Beach Road, Sand Bay, Weston-super-Mare, Somerset BS22 9UZ

Tel: 01934 624541
Beautifully kept, quiet, five-star holiday park situated directly on Sand Bay Beach. Modern caravans offer luxurious four- and six- berth accommodation. Two miles along coast road from Weston-super-Mare and only one mile from Worlebury golf course.

Ellenborough Hall, 15 Ellenborough Park North, Weston-super-Mare, Somerset BS23 1XQ

Tel: 01934 629543
Large Victorian house converted into a family-run hotel with a friendly atmosphere. Four en-suite rooms. Plenty of off-road parking. Within easy reach of the town centre and sea front.

Goodrington Guest House, 23 Charlton Road, Weston-super-Mare, Somerset BS23 4HB

Tel: 01934 623229
e-mail: vera.bishop@btclick.com
website: http://home.btclick.com/vera.bishop
Friendly guest house with just three guest rooms, two with en-suite facilities. One double, one triple and one room with four single beds. Evening meals available on request.

The Greyhound Inn, 1 Lime Street, Stogursey, Bridgwater, Somerset TA5 1QR

Tel: 01278 732490
Traditional rural inn. Bar stocks a range of local real ales, cider, wine and spirits. Good selection of home-cooked food. Bed and breakfast accommodation. 412

The Hawthorne, Crooked Lane, Brent Knoll, Somerset TA9 4BQ

Tel: 01278 760181
Comfortable country house in quiet surroundings. Separate annexe for guests with dining hall and two en-suite bed and breakfast rooms. Close to Berrow golf course.

Innlodge at the Bridge Inn, North End Road, Yatton, Nr. Bristol, Somerset BS49 4AU

Tel: 01934 839100 Fax: 01934 839149
e-mail bridgeinn@sfigroup.co.uk
website www.innlodge.com
Modern lodge accommodation with 41 en-suite rooms including some luxurious suites. The Bridge Inn is a popular country inn serving superb home-cooked food. 446

Laburnum House Lodge Hotel, Sloway Lane, West Huntspill, Highbridge, Somerset TA9 3RJ

Tel: 01278 781830 Fax: 01278 781612
e-mail: laburnumhh@aol.com
website: www.laburnumhh.co.uk
Family-run country lodge hotel. 60 bedrooms, all en-suite, of varying sizes. Peaceful, rural location with clay pigeon shooting, fishing and many other activities available on site. Also holiday complex with superb 80-cover restaurant and two bars open to all visitors. Excellent menus and great pub grub with weekly BBQs and Pig Roasts.

Three Acres Caravan Park, South Road, Brean, Somerset TA8 2RF

Tel: 01278 751313
e-mail: 3acres@ic24.net
15 self-catering six-berth caravans within a couple of miles of Burnham-on-Sea and close to several golf courses. Bar and restaurant within the site for residents' use.

Food and Drink

The Greyhound Inn, 1 Lime Street, Stogursey, Bridgwater, Somerset TA5 1QR

Tel: 01278 732490
Traditional rural inn. Bar stocks a range of local real ales, cider, wine and spirits. Good selection of home-cooked food. Bed and breakfast accommodation. 412

Innlodge at the Bridge Inn, North End Road, Yatton, Nr. Bristol, Somerset BS49 4AU

Tel: 01934 839100 Fax: 01934 839149
e-mail bridgeinn@sfigroup.co.uk
website www.innlodge.com
Modern lodge accommodation with 41 en-suite rooms including some luxurious suites. The Bridge Inn is a popular country inn serving superb home-cooked food. 446

Laburnum House Lodge Hotel, Sloway Lane, West Huntspill, Highbridge, Somerset TA9 3RJ

Tel: 01278 781830 Fax: 01278 781612
e-mail: laburnumhh@aol.com
website: www.laburnumhh.co.uk
Family-run country lodge hotel. 60 bedrooms, all en-suite, of varying sizes. Peaceful, rural location with clay pigeon shooting, fishing and many other activities available on site. Also holiday complex with superb 80-cover restaurant and two bars open to all visitors. Excellent menus and great pub grub with weekly BBQs and Pig Roasts.

Long John Silver, 73 Beach Road, Kewstoke, Weston-super-Mare, Somerset BS22 9UP

Tel: 01934 623367
Characterful inn serving an excellent selection of food ranging from traditional pub fayre to seafood and steak dishes. Vegetarians also catered for.

The Major from Glengarry, 10-14 Upper Church Road, Weston-super-Mare, Somerset BS23 2DT

Tel: 01934 629260
Family-run pub offering a warm welcome to all. Serves Wadsworth Cask Ales and an extensive range of snacks and traditional food prepared by the owner, who is a qualified chef. Regular evening entertainment with live music. Families welcome.

The Market Inn, 1 North End Road, Yatton, Somerset BS49 4AL

Tel: 01934 832209 Fax: 01934 835981
A traditional, country inn located close to the M5. Friendly, warm welcome for locals and visitors to the area. Wide choice of draught ales and fine selection of meals and snacks. 438

The Old Thatched Cottage Restaurant, 14 Knightstone Road, Weston-super-Mare, Somerset BS23 2AN

Tel: 01934 621313
Popular restaurant on seafront serving French, Italian and Greek cuisine from an a la carte menu. Fresh fish is the house speciality. Open every day, all year round. Caters for parties of up to 100.

Yeovil Golf Club

Sherbourne Road, Yeovil, Somerset BA21 5BW
Tel: 01935 475949 Fax: 01935 411283

Now pay attention, this might get complicated. For if ever a course suffered from a split personality, it is Yeovil. As every football fan will tell you, Yeovil is in Somerset but, tucked up so close is it to the county border that the club's 18-hole **Old Course** lies entirely on the Dorset side of the River Yeo, while the nine-hole **Newton Course** is all in Somerset. And although the club is affiliated to the Dorset Golf Uionn, it is only historic, and could equally affiliate to Somerset. Got that ?

The 6,144-yard Old Course is also a real Jekyll and Hyde teaser. The par-three second soon tests your mettle, playing uphill between the trees to a blind green. That is swiftly followed by one you wouldn't want to play so early in the round, the 405-yard third which plays a lot longer, and which has a regiment of bunkers across the fairway just short of 300 yards.

If your card isn't already ruined and your confidence in tatters, the course is pleasantly picturesque for the most part, with the 14th affording fine views over the town.

Then it turns nasty again, with a long (232 yards) par three swinging left to right downhill to a two-tier green at 15, followed by a par five at 16 down towards the river and a valley of willow trees, but both played into the prevailing south-westerly winds.

But despite its two-faced nature, it is nevertheless a pleasing course, where all standard of golfers feel in with a chance. And isn't that really what it is all about?

Sec/Manager:	Graham Dodd
Professional:	Geoff Kite
Directions:	1¾ miles southeast of Yeovil. From centre take A30 (Sherborne). The entrance is on the right hand side after 1¾ miles.
Visitors:	Welcome: Contact club in advance. Unable to play Tuesdays before 1.00 pm
Societies:	Welcome: Contact club in advance. Unable to play weekends.

Facilities: Putting Green, Chipping Green, Club Hire, Trolley Hire, Buggy Hire, Bar, Restaurant, Driving Range

Old

Date Founded: 1908
Type of Course: Parkland
No of Holes: 18
Length: 6150 yds (5676 mtrs)
Par: 72
SSS: 70
Green Fees: Weekdays: £25 (round) £30 (day); Weekends/Bank Holidays: £30 (round) £40 (day)

Newton

Date Founded: 1908
Type of Course: Parkland
No of Holes: 9
Length: 4891 yds (4514 mtrs)
Par: 68
SSS: 65
Green Fees: Weekdays: £18; Weekends/Bank Holidays: £18

Accommodation, Food and Drink

Reference numbers below refer to detailed information provided in section 2

Accommodation

Amberley Guest House, Martock Road, Long Load, Langport, Somerset TA10 9LD

Tel: 01458 241542
e-mail: jeanatamberley@talk21.com
An attractive farmhouse-style property with four comfortable guest rooms of varying sizes. Evening meals available on request. Non-smoking.   422

Ash House Country House Hotel and Restaurant, Main Street, Ash, Nr. Martock, Somerset TA12 6PB

Tel: 01935 822036 Fax: 01935 822992
e-mail: reception@ashhousehotel.freeserve.co.uk
website: www.ashhousecountryhotel.co.uk
Small, privately-owned Georgian Country house hotel surrounded by attractive gardens. Popular a la carte restaurant with high standard of cuisine. Eight delightful en-suite rooms.   424

Castlebrook Holiday Cottages, Castlebrook, Compton Dundon, Somerton, Somerset TA11 6PR

Tel: 01458 841680 Fax: 01458 841680

Two fully-equipped holiday homes located in the heart of the Polden Hills. Both feature kitchenette, sitting/dining room, shower room/WC, sleeping three and five adults. Pets welcome by arrangement. 407

East Lambrook Farm, South Petherton, Somerset TA13 5HH

Tel: 01460 240064 Fax: 01460 240064
e-mail: nicolaeeles@supernet.com
A delightful 17th-century house, built of local sandstone with a thatched roof, set within two and a half acres of rolling gardens and woodland. Three en-suite guest rooms. Tennis Courts. 421

Eastbury Hotel, Long Street, Sherborne, Dorset DT9 3BY

Tel: 01935 813131 Fax: 01935 817296
e-mail: eastbury.sherborne@virgin.net
An elegant Georgian hotel surrounded by fine gardens. Award-winning Conservatory Restaurant enjoys a fine reputation serving mainly English cuisine. 15 en-suite bedrooms. 307

The Ilchester Arms, The Square, Ilchester, Nr. Yeovil, Somerset BA22 8LN

Tel: 01935 840220 Fax: 01935 841353
Impressive Georgian building, dominating the main street, offering comfortable en-suite accommodation. High quality restaurant with wide-ranging menu. 434

Northover Manor Hotel, Northover, Ilchester, Somerset BA22 8LD

Tel: 01935 840447 Fax: 01935 840006
e-mail: melhaddigan@compuserve.com
A rambling, 15th-century, former manor house offering comfortable, stylish accommodation in 13 en-suite rooms. Formal restaurant and more casual Village Bar which are both open to non-residents. 406

The Portman Arms, High Street, East Chinnock, Yeovil, Somerset BA22 9DP

Tel: 01935 862227 Fax: 01935 862227
An imposing building dating from the early 1800s providing a spacious eating and drinking area. Good menu. Five, newly-refurbished, en-suite guest rooms. Caravan pitches also available. 429

Quiet Woman House, Halstock, Dorset BA22 9RX

Tel: 01935 891218
e-mail: quietwomanhouse@ukonline.com
Newly converted bed and breakfast offering high quality accommodation in traditional surroundings. Three guest rooms of varying sizes and two self-catering cottages. Evening meals on request. 315

Richmond House Holiday Accommodation, Barrow Farm, North Barrow, Yeovil, Somerset BA22 7LZ

Tel: 01963 240543 Fax: 01963 240543
e-mail: rhholidays@netscapeonline.co.uk
website: www.rhholidays.co.uk
Eight cottages of varying sizes situated on two sites just 50 metres apart and surrounded by 600 acres of grazing land. Well-maintained and well-equipped.431

The Royal George, West Coker, Yeovil, Somerset BA22 9AN

Tel: 01935 862334 Fax: 01935 864499
18th-century hostelry with a cosy, traditional interior. Menu offers a good selection of dishes. Occasional live music and a regular quiz night. Two en-suite guest rooms. 428

The Walnut Tree, West Camel, Nr. Yeovil, Somerset BA22 7QW

Tel: 01935 851292 Fax: 01935 851292
website: www.thewalnuttreehotel.com
Charming family-run hotel, restaurant and inn. Fine menu of imaginative dishes served both in the bar and restaurant, with fish being a speciality. Thirteen en-suite guest rooms. 426

Weston House Cottages, East Chinnock, Nr. Yeovil, Somerset BA22 9EL

Tel: 01935 863712/863394 Mobile: 07884 214768
e-mail: westonhouseuk@netscapeonline.co.uk
Two cottages converted from former barns located within a working farm. High quality well-equipped accommodation. One cottage sleeps four, the other sleeps five. Dogs welcome. 430

The Yew Tree Inn, Forest Hill, Yeovil, Somerset BA20 2PG

Tel: 01935 476808 Fax: 01935 476808
Former gentleman's residence which was converted into a pub only 30 years ago. Cosy, friendly atmosphere. Excellent food with a menu of traditional pub food. Four guest rooms of varying sizes. 432

Food and Drink

Ash House Country House Hotel and Restaurant, Main Street, Ash, Nr. Martock, Somerset TA12 6PB

Tel: 01935 822036 Fax: 01935 822992
e-mail: reception@ashhousehotel.freeserve.co.uk
website: www.ashhousecountryhotel.co.uk
Small, privately-owned Georgian Country house hotel surrounded by attractive gardens. Popular a la carte restaurant with high standard of cuisine. Eight delightful en-suite rooms. 424

The Chetnole Inn, Chetnole, Nr. Sherborne, Dorset DT9 6NU

Tel: 01935 872337
Popular local's inn, well-liked for top-quality real ales, fine food and its fabulous atmosphere. Cosy music-free lounge bar, spacious restaurant and friendly public bar. 308

Eastbury Hotel, Long Street, Sherborne, Dorset DT9 3BY

Tel: 01935 813131 Fax: 01935 817296
e-mail: eastbury.sherborne@virgin.net
An elegant Georgian hotel surrounded by fine gardens. Award-winning Conservatory Restaurant enjoys a fine reputation serving mainly English cuisine. 15 en-suite bedrooms. 307

The Fox and Hounds, Broadway Road, Charlton Adam, Somerset TA11 7AU

Tel: 01458 223466
Small village pub serving traditional, wholesome food and specialising in home-made pies. Real ales served, including local Butcombe Ales. Pool table, function room and can accommodate up to five caravans or motor homes on an adjoining field.

The Ilchester Arms, The Square, Ilchester, Nr. Yeovil, Somerset BA22 8LN

Tel: 01935 840220 Fax: 01935 841353
Impressive Georgian building, dominating the main street, offering comfortable en-suite accommodation. High quality restaurant with wide-ranging menu. 434

The Lamb and Lark, Limington, Nr. Yeovil, Somerset

Tel: 01935 840368
e-mail: thelambandlark@cs.com
Pub housed within a 15th-century building that has been carefully restored. Inside there is a piano bar and lounge. Good selection of freshly-prepared food. 433

Marlborough Tea Rooms, Bow Street, Langport, Somerset TA10 9PR

Tel: 01458 250786 Fax: 01458 250786
Small, charming tea rooms serving morning coffee, light lunches and afternoon tea. Wide ranging menu, mostly home-made, and superb cream teas.   445

Northover Manor Hotel, Northover, Ilchester, Somerset BA22 8LD

Tel: 01935 840447 Fax: 01935 840006
e-mail: melhaddigan@compuserve.com
A rambling, 15th-century, former manor house offering comfortable, stylish accommodation in 13 en-suite rooms. Formal restaurant and more casual Village Bar which are both open to non-residents. 406

The Old Barn Owl, Westport, Nr. Langport, Somerset TA10 0BH

Tel: 01460 281391 Fax: 01460 281995
Good-sized, family pub enjoying a good location. Comfortable interior with relaxed atmosphere. Good range stocked behind the bar and equally excellent selection in the restaurant. 419

The Old Forge Inn, Church Street, Curry Rivel, Nr. Langport, Somerset TA10 0HE

Tel: 01458 251554 Fax: 01458 252847
Grade 2 listed building, providing characterful surroundings. Excellent menu with good fish selection. Public bar open to all. Regular art exhibitions. 5 rooms for bed and breakfast planned for April 2002. 420

The Portman Arms, High Street, East Chinnock, Yeovil, Somerset BA22 9DP

Tel: 01935 862227 Fax: 01935 862227
An imposing building dating from the early 1800s providing a spacious eating and drinking area. Good menu. Five, newly-refurbished, en-suite guest rooms. Caravan pitches also available. 429

The Royal George, West Coker, Yeovil, Somerset BA22 9AN

Tel: 01935 862334 Fax: 01935 864499
18th-century hostelry with a cosy, traditional interior. Menu offers a good selection of dishes. Occasional live music and a regular quiz night. Two en-suite guest rooms. 428

The Royal Marine, St. Weston Terrace, Yeovil, Somerset BA21 5AA

Tel: 01935 474350 Fax: 01935 474350
Popular inn just a short walk from the centre of Yeovil. Sensibly priced menu of meals and snacks and a selection of real ales on tap. 435

The Royal Oak, Stoford, Yeovil, Somerset BA22 9UD

Tel: 01935 475071
Quiet village location just a couple of miles from the centre of Yeovil. Cosy interior with separate restaurant. Well-priced menu of traditional dishes. Occasional quiz and theme nights. 427

Rusty Axe, Stembridge, Somerset

Tel: 01460 240109
Friendly, cosy country pub. Popular for food with a wide ranging menu offering excellent choice. Live music on Saturday evenings. 423

The Walnut Tree, West Camel, Nr. Yeovil, Somerset BA22 7QW

Tel: 01935 851292 Fax: 01935 851292
website: www.thewalnuttreehotel.com
Charming family-run hotel, restaurant and inn. Fine menu of imaginative dishes served both in the bar and restaurant, with fish being a speciality. Thirteen en-suite guest rooms. 426

The White Hart, Bishops Caundle, Sherborne, Dorset DT9 5ND

Tel: 01963 23301 Fax: 01963 23301
Popular inn serving a full range of traditional meals ranging from bar snacks to a la carte. The bar stocks range of locally brewed real ales.

The Yew Tree Inn, Forest Hill, Yeovil, Somerset BA20 2PG

Tel: 01935 476808 Fax: 01935 476808
Former gentleman's residence which was converted into a pub only 30 years ago. Cosy, friendly atmosphere. Excellent food with a menu of traditional pub food. Four guest rooms of varying sizes. 432

ACCOMMODATION, FOOD AND DRINK

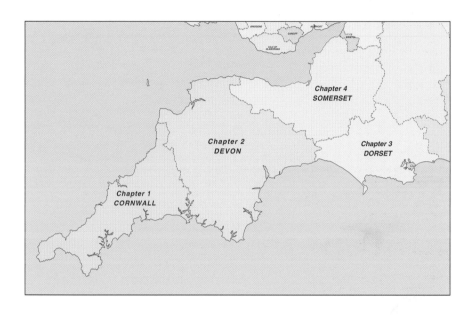

RUTHERN VALLEY HOLIDAYS 101

Small holiday park

Accommodation in delightful woodland setting

Credit Cards: All the major cards

Ruthern Bridge, Nr. Bodmin, Cornwall PL30 5LU
Tel: 01208 831395 Fax: 01208 832324
website: www: self-catering-ruthern.co.uk

A peaceful, relaxing holiday retreat set in seven and a half acres of park and woodland abundant with wildlife and within easy reach of the North and South coasts. The range of trees and shrubs reflect the high level of expertise which went into landscaping this beautiful undulating site some 30 years ago. A perfect setting for the small family run site of lodges and caravans and caravan/campsite. An ideal central location for the wide ranging attractions of Cornwall including the nearby Eden Project.

Local Golf Courses: Lanhydrock, Lostwithiel, St. Austell

THE GLOBE INN 102

Pub with food.

Friendly inn with relaxed atmosphere

Credit cards: All the major cards.

3 North Street, Lostwithiel, Cornwall PL22 0EG
Tel: 01208 872501

Tucked away on a small side street, **The Globe Inn** is well worth hunting out. This is a cosy, friendly, traditional inn offering a warm welcome to all who pass through the doors. Inside visitors will find an open plan bar area furnished with easy chairs and comfy sofas with a separate restaurant area, patio and beer garden. Here you can enjoy a refreshing drink and tasty home-cooked, freshly-prepared food from a good menu which offers plenty of choice. Ensuite B&B accommodation available.

Local Golf Courses: Lostwithiel, Carolyn Bay, St. Austell, Looe

MARCORRIE HOTEL 103

20 Falmouth Road, Truro, Cornwall TR1 2HX
Tel: 01872 277374 Fax: 01872 241666
e-mail: marcorrie@aol.com website: www.cornwall.net/marcorrie

Situated in the heart of the city of Truro, the **Marcorrie Hotel** can be found in a delightful Victorian and Edwardian street just five minutes walk from the cathedral and city centre. This is a small, family-run hotel offering traditional Cornish hospitality with true personal service from the friendly, local staff. The welcoming atmosphere is enhanced with comfortable furnishings throughout, and the guest bedrooms are a cosy haven at the end of a long day. Generous Continental and

cooked breakfasts are served each morning giving you plenty of energy for a day sightseeing or at the beach.

The Marcorrie Hotel would provide an ideal base for a short break, or more lengthy holiday in this corner of England. Cornwall has plenty to offer to visitors, with many attractions and places of interest within easy reach. The city of Truro itself is well worth exploring and a boat trip along the river Fal, to Falmouth, would make a refreshing change to driving. There are numerous safe, sandy beaches in the area with water sports being widely available.

Hotel

Small, charming hotel in city centre location

Credit Cards: All the major cards.

There is a wealth of natural beauty, with the stunning coastline and many superb gardens to visit. The famous Eden Project is also within easy reach at nearby St. Austell.

Local Golf Courses: Truro, Falmouth, Newquay

CORNWALL

CORNWALL

THE WILSEY DOWN 104

Hallworthy, Camelford, Cornwall PL32 9SH
Tel: 01840 261205
e-mail: jane@greatbidlake.farmcom.net

The Wilsey Down is a comfortable, welcoming establishment with two bars, each with an open fireplace, where visitors can enjoy a game of pool or darts while savouring a pint of real ale. There is a separate restaurant, though meals can also be taken in the bar, and the menu offers a good selection of traditional English dishes and light snacks. There are regular home-made specials and a number of vegetarian options. Bed and breakfast accommodation is available with six rooms, two en-suite, ranging from a single to a family room.

Inn, Restaurant, B&B
Friendly atmosphere

Credit Cards: All the major cards.

Local Golf Courses: Bowood Park, St. Enodoc, Trevose, Trethorne

MAYROSE FARM HOLIDAY COTTAGES 105

Helstone, Camelford, Cornwall PL32 9RN
Tel: 01840 213509 Fax: 01840 213509
e-mail: mayrosefarm@hotmail.com

Converted from former farm buildings, **Mayrose Holiday Cottages** comprise five, very different properties each with its own unique charm. The cottages vary in size, sleeping between two and six adults, and have been individually decorated while the furniture and fittings are of a very high standard. Outside, tucked away, is the walled and terraced, large heated outdoor pool with its backdrop of exotic plants. Another feature of the farm is the paddock of animals, including goats, rabbits and pigs, and a short walk leads to a private lake which is a haven for wildfowl. All in all, a super holiday base.

Holiday Cottages.
Five super cottages, outdoor pool

Credit Cards: None.

Local Golf Courses: Bowood Park, St. Enodoc, Trevose

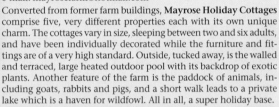

CAMELOT HOTEL & HAWKERS RESTAURANT 106

Downs View, Bude, Cornwall EX23 8RE
Tel: 01288 352361 e-mail: stay@camelot-hotel.co.uk
Fax: 01288 355470 website: www.camelot-hotel.co.uk

The Camelot Hotel enjoys a fine situation on the edge of Bude and North Cornwall Golf Course with many of the rooms offering uninterrupted views across the fairways to the sea. Surrounded by its own private grounds, in a residential area, this is a delightfully quiet and secluded spot for a weekend break or longer holiday. The stylish property has recently undergone a extensive programme of redecoration and refurbishment throughout, ensuring that every area is up to the high standards that the owners, the Naylor family, expect to maintain, and making this possibly the best two star hotel in the West Country. From the light and airy, glass-ceilinged reception area to the spacious bar and lounges, you will certainly feel relaxed and comfortable here. Guests can enjoy an afternoon cup of tea or early evening drink on the decking area adjoining the lounge or perhaps venture into the games room for a game of pool, darts or table tennis.

Every comfort has been thought of in the 24 bedrooms, with each having en-suite facilities, controllable heating, TV, telephone and a hot drinks tray, with top quality beds and elegant decor helping to ensure a restful night. For today's 'high tech' traveller there is also a modem socket in every room. The popular restaurant, named after a celebrated local parson, serves fine food in comfortable, stylish surroundings. The dinner menu changes daily to make the most of seasonal produce and offers plenty of choice, catering to all tastes. Table d'hote and a la carte menus are available and the management pride themselves on offering high quality food and good value for money. The Camelot specialises in golfing breaks for individuals or groups, and has connections with 16 golf courses in the surrounding area. Ask for the Golf Information Guide for further details.

Hotel and Restaurant
Super hotel in great location.

Credit Cards: All the major cards.

Local Golf Courses: Bude, Holsworthy, St. Mellion, Bowood Park

INN ON THE GREEN 107

Crooklets Beach, Bude, Cornwall EX23 8NF
Tel: 01288 356013 e-mail: innonthegreen46@btinternet.com
Fax: 01288 356244 website: www.innonthegreen46.co.uk

This family-run Victorian hotel has a reputation for comfort, service and value for money, combined with a friendly, relaxed atmosphere. It is 100 metres from the beach and only a short walk from the town centre. The attractive restaurant serves wholesome, home produced food while a fully stocked bar, including real ales, is open all day. The accommodation comprises 17 en-suite rooms with the premier rooms all having glorious views over the golf course.

Restaurant, Bar and Hotel
Super eating and drinking place with friendly owners.

Credit Cards: All the major cards.

Local Golf Courses: Bude & North Cornwall, Holsworthy, Launceston

LINKS SIDE 108

7 Burn View, Bude, Cornwall EX23 8BY
Tel: 01288 352410

You can be assured of a warm, friendly welcome at **Link's Side Guest House** under the new ownership of former farming wife, Beryl Thomas. The bright, Victorian style house is kept in pristine order, with colour co-ordinated furnishings and a high standard of decor maintained throughout. The rooms vary in size, with most having en-suite facilities. The colourful gardens that surround the house have won awards in 'Bude in Bloom'.

Bed and Breakfast
Small, cosy B&B in popular resort.

Credit Cards: None

Local Golf Courses: Bude & North Cornwall, Holsworthy, Launceston

THE BRENDON ARMS 109

Vicarage Road, Bude, Cornwall EX23 8SD
Tel: 01288 354542 Fax: 01288 354542
e-mail: sophia@sophiafrbrendon.demon.co.uk
website: www.north-cornwall.co.uk/client/brendon-arms/

Situated in a picturesque part of town, here at **The Brendon Arms** you can enjoy a good selection of local seafood, among many other menu options, with the fish often caught by the pub's landlord! The bar stocks a good range of real ales and drinks can be enjoyed at the many outside tables in warm weather. Comfortable bed and breakfast accommodation is available with seven en-suite guest rooms.

Pub with food, B&B
Traditional Cornish inn near to town centre.

Credit Cards: All the major cards

Local Golf Courses: Bude & North Cornwall, Holsworthy, St. Mellion

TREWITHEN RESTAURANT 110

3 Fore Street, Lostwithiel, Cornwall PL22 0BP
Tel: 01208 872373

In the heart of the pretty town of Lostwithiel, just 200 metres from the main through road and near to the river, you will find the super Trewithen Restaurant. The cosy, cottage style adds to the relaxed and comfortable atmosphere while the menus offer traditional, English cuisine. The selection on offer is wide-ranging, with the most popular dishes being lobster, seafood, crispy duckling and prime fillet of beef. The a la carte menu is complemented by a range of daily specials.

Restaurant
Award-winning, high quality restaurant

Credit Cards: All the major cards.

Local Golf Courses: Lostwithiel, Carolyn Bay, St. Austell, Looe

CORNWALL

WHITE HOUSE COURT HOLIDAY COTTAGES `111`

Penhallow, Cornwall
Tel: 01752 873128 Fax: 01752 873128
e-mail: whitehouse.cotts@barclay.net
www. whitehousecourt.co.uk

White House Court, in the village of Penhallow, has been created from what was once a number of traditional Cornish farm buildings. To create these delightful holiday cottages, the

original buildings have been substantially redesigned and rebuilt, to ensure that there are no low ceilings or steep stairs, while retaining the olde worlde character and charm. The result is an enclosed courtyard of cottages around a large lawned area, with ample car parking, which is kept well lit at night by old Cornish street lamps. There is a total of eleven self contained properties, some single storey and some two storey, sleeping from between two and ten people. Each has been furnished in a cosy, cottage style and is very well equipped, with a fully fitted kitchen, colour TV and electric log-effect fire. In addition to the cottages, there is a central facility called the 'round house' where visitors will find the reception, a pay phone and coin operated laundry facilities.

Just 100 yards away from the cottages is the newly refurbished White House Inn, a convenient hostelry serving excellent food and fine ales. It has children's play areas both inside and out, a regular programme of evening entertainment and an outdoor swimming pool. The cottages are just two miles from the coastal town of Perranporth, famous for its surfing and beautiful sandy beach. There are a number of activities available here to suit all the family including a boating lake, tennis courts, pitch and putt, bowls, fishing and riding. There is also this spectacular coastline to be explored, with the cliff top paths being ideal for spotting the wealth of local wildlife, rare birds and wild flowers.

Holiday Cottages
Eleven cottages of varying sizes set around private courtyard.

Credit Cards: None

Local Golf Courses: Perranporth, Newquay, Truro, Falmouth

THE SUNDECK RESTAURANT `112`

East Quay, Mevagissy, Cornwall PL26 6QQ
Tel: 01726 843051

The Sundeck restaurant is a real surprise and delight, with the feel more of a classy hotel than an sea front establishment. It can be located at the east end of the quay in the heart of Mevagissy, above a small gift and souvenir shop, and is reached up a set of steps. Inside, the first impression of how bright and airy the dining area is, combined with a stylish decor in a Mediterranean theme, with which there have clearly been no short cuts.

Discreet lighting is in the form of blue glass uplighters and luxurious drapes divide up the space and hang at the windows. A waiting area has three comfortable sofas, while the dining is at a variety of square and round wooden tables with pretty wooden Captain's and Bosun's chairs. Large picture windows look out onto the terrace, which is reached by French doors, and here there are further tables with parasols. There are superb views out to sea and from the terrace, directly onto the craggy rock shoreline below.

Furnishings aside, here you can enjoy good home-cooked food throughout the day and in to the evening. Opening at 10am the menu offers a wide selection of drinks, snacks and hot meals, with evening meals served from 6pm until 10pm. The food is a cross section of English and European cuisine, with a strong Mediterranean influence with fresh local produce, including fish, featuring prominently. The friendly staff offer silver service, with the popular Sunday carvery and tempting dessert selection being self service.

Restaurant
High quality sea front restaurant

Credit Cards: All the major cards

Local Golf Courses: St. Austell, Falmouth, Truro

THE BROOKDALE HOTEL　　113

Tregolls Road, Truro, Cornwall TR1 1JZ
Tel: 01872 273513 Fax: 01872 272400
e-mail: brookdale@hotelstruro.com
website: www.hotelstruro.com/brookdale

The Brookdale Hotel is a large, privately owned and run hotel set in its own grounds off the main A39 road on the outskirts of Truro. Set back from the road on a small rise, the surrounding gardens are beautifully landscaped in a tropical style.

The Brookdale is well known for its warmth and friendliness and the high quality of personal service. Centuries of family tradition and hospitality can be savoured during an overnight stop, short break or a more lengthy stay.

Within the hotel there is an Italian Ristorante, San Carlo, which is open Monday to Saturday evenings to hotel guests and non-residents and the spacious dining area has a relaxed, comfortable ambience making it very popular. The varied menus offer a wide range of freshly prepared dishes in a Continental style with both table d'hote and a la carte options. You can enjoy a simple meals of pasta with fresh sauce or something much more exotic, complemented by a bottle of wine from the extensive wine list. On Sunday evenings, when the San Carlo is closed, cold suppers are available to guests.

The accommodation comprises comfortable, elegantly furnished rooms of varying sizes, with singles, doubles and twins being available. All the bedrooms have recently been refurbished to a tourist board three star quality and are provided with a direct dial computer ported phone. Each room also features en-suite facilities, tea- and coffee-making tray, colour TV, trouser press and hairdryers. Guests can also make use of the comfortable lounge areas and in the evenings, the well-stocked, licensed bar.

Within The Brookdale Hotel there are three function rooms of varying sizes, suitable for small conferences, meetings and private parties. Easily located by car, Truro can also be reached by other transport methods with the bus depot and train station within an easy walk. If you do choose to drive yourself, there is a large car park with some covered spaces available.

The city of Truro is only a few minutes walk from the hotel and provides a compact shopping centre with a wide range of retail outlets. For those with more cultural interests, there is a fine Cathedral, an interesting museum, an excellent entertainment venue in the Hall for Cornwall and some delightful art galleries. Truro also hosts various festivals and events during the year.

The Brookdale is well situated for touring Cornwall which has a wealth of beautiful places and attractions. There are numerous gardens, golf courses and safe, sandy beaches reached within a short drive. Reasonable rates for bed and breakfast, with rates on request for dinner included, or for an extended stay of four or more nights.

Hotel and Restaurant
Family-run, friendly hotel with popular restaurant
Credit Cards: All the major cards.

Local Golf Courses: Truro, Falmouth, Newquay

CORNWALL

Guest House

Cosy and friendly. Six rooms

Credit Cards: All the major cards

WYVERN HOUSE 114

7 Downs View, Bude, Cornwall EX23 8RF
Tel: 01288 352205 e-mail: eileen@wyvernhouse.co.uk
Fax: 01288 356802 website: www.wyvernhouse.co.uk

Located on the edge of Bude, **Wyvern House** enjoys a pleasant situation just five minutes walk from the sandy beaches. Six guest rooms, some with en-suite facilities, and all being provided with a TV and hot drinks tray. There is a licensed bar, guests' lounge and the restaurant serves excellent home cooked breakfasts and evening meals. Guests can be sure of a friendly welcome from the resident owners, Eileen and Michael Luxton.

Local Golf Courses: Bude & North Cornwall, Holsworthy, St. Mellion

Hotel and Restaurant

Country house hotel, all rooms en-suite, some larger superior rooms.

Credit Cards: All the major cards

FIELDHEAD HOTEL 115

Portuan Road, Hannafore, West Looe, Cornwall PL13 2DR
Tel: 01503 262689 Fax: 01503 264114
e-mail: field.head@virgin.net website: www.fieldheadhotel.co.uk
The Fieldhead Hotel is situated in West Looe, just a short walk from the harbour and looking out to sea. Built in 1896 as a grand private residence it has since been converted into a country house style hotel offering a very high standard of comfort and service. The comfortable guest rooms are all en-suite, many enjoy unrivalled sea views, and guests can also make use of the elegant lounges and bar. The restaurant serves a menu of mainly English and French dishes, with freshly-caught fish featuring widely.

Local Golf Courses: Looe, St. Mellion, Lostwithiel

Pub with food

Sea front pub serving home-cooked food. Live entertainment at weekends

Credit Cards: All the major cards.

THREE PILCHARDS 116

Quay Street, Polperro, Looe, Cornwall PL13 2QZ
Tel: 01503 272233
The Three Pilchards is a traditional Cornish pub offering a warm and friendly welcome to all. Located on The Quay, in the heart of the village of Polperro, the views over the village are magnificent at any time of year. Visitors will find a good range of refreshment stocked behind the bar, with home-cooked food served each day. The house specialities are locally-caught fish and steak dishes. There's never a dull moment at the Three Pilchards with live entertainment most weekends

Local Golf Courses: Lostwithiel, St Mellion, Whitsand Bay

Pub with food, B&B

Typical Cornish pub serving tasty food

Credit Cards: All the major cards.

THE CARPENTERS ARMS 117

Metherell, Nr. Callington, Cornwall PL17 8BJ
Tel: 01579 350242 Fax: 01579 350242
Dating back to the 15th century, the picturesque **Carpenters Arms** takes its name from the carpenters who stayed here while constructing nearby Cotehele House, now a National Trust property. The cosy interior retains many original features, such as the flagstone floor and low, beamed ceilings, and the service is friendly and welcoming. Customers can enjoy a refreshing pint from the well-stocked bar while food is served from a wide-ranging menu of home-cooked bar meals and snacks. Barbecues are a popular option in summer months and a traditional roast lunch is available on Sundays. Bed and breakfast accommodation.

Local Golf Courses: Tavistock, Yelverton, St. Mellion Hotel G&CC

TAVISTOCK ARMS `118`

Fore Street, Gunnislake, Cornwall PL18 9BN
Tel: 01822 832217

The Tavistock Arms is a traditional, country pub located within the village of Gunnislake on the A390, to the Southwest of Tavistock, and directly on the Devon/Cornwall border. Visitors will find both a public and lounge bar in which to enjoy a drink while food is served both in the bar and a separate restaurant. A menu of tasty hot meals and bar snacks is served all day. Bed and breakfast accommodation is also available.

Pub with food, B&B

Traditional country pub serving tasty food.

Credit Cards: All the major cards

Local Golf Courses: St Mellion, Tavistock, Yelverton, Hurdwick

MEUDON HOTEL `119`

Mawnan Smith, Nr. Falmouth, Cornwall TR11 5HT
Tel: 01326 250541 Fax: 01326 250543
website: www.meudon.co.uk

Unique, superior retreat, a family-run country house hotel, set in a sub-tropical garden paradise with private beach. Specialists in local seafood, traditional service, cosseted comforts - antiques, log fires and fresh flowers. FREE golf at host club Falmouth and a further 6 clubs throughout Cornwall included in high and mid-season rates. Also a self-catering cottage available. Recommended by Johansens, Michelin and Which? Hotel Guide among others.

Hotel and Restaurant.

Country house hotel surrounded by superb gardens.

Credit Cards: All the major cards.

Local Golf Courses: Falmouth, Mullion, Truro, Cape Cornwall

TRETHIN MANOR HOLIDAY COTTAGES `120`

Advent, Camelford, Cornwall PL32 9QW
Tel: 01840 213522 Fax: 01840 212898

In the heart of the Cornish countryside north of Bodmin Moor, just two miles from Camelford and within the parish of Advent, is **Trethin Manor Holiday Cottages**. Once a working farm, the former mill, granary, stables and other buildings have been converted into comfortable self-catering holiday accommodation. The ten cottages are surrounded by landscaped grounds with lawned areas, shrubs and trees. There is plenty of space for quiet relaxation and children will find a separate play area in an adjoining field where there is also a large shared barbecue. A games rooms with table tennis and a pool table can also be found within the site.

The cottages are simply and comfortably furnished with a fully equipped kitchen, complete with microwave, comfortable lounge with colour TV, and each enjoys a natural spring water supply. There are varying sizes of property ranging from The Coach House which sleeps two, to Drovers which can sleep six. Most cottages sleep four. Additional facilities within the site include a laundry room and public telephone.

This is a superb part of Cornwall with the nearby coast being wild and rugged in parts and with sandy beaches in others. There are a number of pretty fishing villages and fishing trips and boat hire can be easily arranged. There is plenty of spectacular countryside to be explored, both along the coast and further inland, and there is an abundance of visitor attractions throughout the area. All in all, this would be an ideal base for a holiday for all ages.

Holiday Cottages

Attractive site with ten cottages

Credit Cards: None.

Local Golf Courses: St. Enodoc, Trevose, St. Mellion Hotel G&CC

CORNWALL

CORNWALL

CHYNOWETH LODGE | 121

1 Eliot Gardens, Newquay, Cornwall TR7 2QE
Tel: 01637 876684
e-mail: reg@chynowethlodge.co.uk
website: www.chynowethlodge.co.uk

Chynoweth Lodge is the home of Reg and Diana Evans, and here they offer comfortable hotel accommodation. Each of the nine en-suite rooms has been individually styled and each is provided with a colour TV and tea and coffee making facilities. There is a comfortable lounge area, while breakfast and evening meals are served in the attractive dining room. All food is home cooked and served in ample portions.

Bed and Breakfast
Cosy accommodation, nine en-suite rooms

Credit Cards: None

Local Golf Courses: Newquay, Merlin, Perranporth, Trevose

BEWDLEY HOTEL | 122

Pentire Road, Newquay, Cornwall TR7 1NX
Tel: 01637 872883
Fax: 01637 872883

Bewdley Hotel enjoys a fine location, overlooking the links golf course and beach beyond, at one end of the town of Newquay. A good-sized property, there are 29 en-suite rooms, and the hotel restaurant prides itself on offering the best in traditional Cornish cuisine. Live entertainment is provided most evenings through the summer and guests can also enjoy the heated outdoor pool.

Hotel
Friendly, family-run hotel. 29 rooms, all en-suite.
Credit Cards:Visa, Mastercard, Switch

Local Golf Courses: Newquay, Merlin, Trevose, Perranporth

PORTH LODGE HOTEL | 123

Porthbean Road, Newquay, Cornwall TR7 3TL
Tel: 01637 874483

A cosy hotel tucked away in a corner of Newquay, yet within two minutes' walk of the sands of Porth Bay. Built around a 17th-century inn, the bars are popular with holiday makers and locals. Reasonably-priced bar food is served, while there is also an a la carte menu. The hotel accommodation comprises 20 en-suite rooms and there are also six self-catering apartments available. The complex also houses a four-lane 10-pin bowling alley which is free to residents.

Hotel, Pub with food.
Popular hostelry, 20 en-suite rooms, bowling alley.

Credit Cards: All the major cards.

Local Golf Courses: Newquay, Merlin, Perranporth, Trevose

TRENANCE LODGE HOTEL AND RESTAURANT | 124

Trenance Road, Newquay, Cornwall TR7 2HW
Tel: 01637 876702 e-mail: info@trenance-lodge.co.uk
Fax: 01637 878772 website: www.trenance-lodge.co.uk

Trenance Lodge is located within its own spacious, beautifully landscaped grounds, in a part of Newquay where the pace of life is a little slower. The property has a calm, relaxing atmosphere, enhanced both by the elegant decor and the welcoming staff. Primarily a restaurant, Trenance Lodge has an enviable reputation for serving fine local produce in a modern British style. The five en-suite bedrooms are of an equally high quality, being stylishly furnished and well-appointed.

Restaurant & Accommodation
Fine restaurant, excellent food, 5 en-suite rooms

Credit Cards: All the major cards.

Local Golf Courses: Newquay, Merlin, Trevose, Perranporth

PORTH VEOR MANOR 125

Porth Way, Nr. Newquay, Cornwall TR7 3LW
Tel: 01637 873274 Fax: 01637 873274

This 'Cornish Country House on the Coast', as **Porth Veor Manor** describes itself, stands in three acres of terraced lawned gardens overlooking the spectacular Cornish coast. Every room, including the 22 individually styled en-suite bedrooms, seems to have fine views towards the cliffs, sea, surrounding fields or the elegant gardens. Guests can also make use of the quiet lounge, enjoy a drink in the Aviators Cocktail Bar or dine in the AA Red Rosette, award-winning Officers Mess restaurant which is also open to non-residents.

Hotel and Restaurant.
Friendly hotel enjoying superb views. 22 en-suite rooms.

Credit Cards: All the major cards.

Local Golf Courses: Newquay, Merlin, Perranporth, Trevose

SMUGGLERS DEN INN 126

Cubert, Newquay, Cornwall TR8 5PY
Tel: 01637 830209
Fax: 01637 830580

Tucked away down a narrow lane, behind high hedges, in a beautiful valley in the heart of the Cornish countryside, you may be lucky enough to stumble across the 400-year old **Smugglers Den Inn**. This quaint, thatched hostelry has a popular reputation for serving fine food and well-kept ale. The menu offers a good selection of fresh, home-cooked dishes with seafood and steaks being the specialities. But be warned, the pub is reputedly haunted!

Pub with food.
400-year old, Cornish inn serving excellent food.

Credit Cards: All the major cards.

Local Golf Courses: Newquay, Merlin, Perranporth, Truro

BUDE HAVEN HOTEL & ANNABELS RESTAURANT 127

Flexbury Avenue, Bude, Cornwall EX23 8NS
Tel: 01288 352305 Fax: 01288 352305
e-mail: enquiries@budehavenhotel.co.uk
website: www.budehavenhotel.co.uk

In a quiet corner of Bude you will find the tourist board two star and AA four diamond **Bude Haven Hotel** where a warm welcome awaits you. The attractive Georgian building is beautifully decorated throughout and offers a comfortable, relaxed atmosphere in which visitors are encouraged to feel right at home.

The hotel offers eleven individually furnished en-suite bedrooms of varying sizes and each is provided with a TV and tea and coffee making facilities. Guests can also make use of a non-smoking lounge and a cosy bar furnished with leather sofas, ideal for an afternoon cup of tea with the newspaper, or a pre-dinner drink with friends.

The highlight of the hotel is the superb, Annabel's Restaurant, which is open to residents and non residents and is described as an elegant, exotic and unforgettable experience. It serves a wide-ranging menu, from local seafood to the finest steaks, all prepared by the resident chef using fresh locally-sourced produce.

Bude Haven Hotel is within easy walking distance of the town and beaches, and overlooks the Bude and North Cornwall golf course. Special green fee rates can be arranged. Ample car parking.

Hotel
Small, friendly hotel in good location.

Credit Cards: All the major cards

Local Golf Courses: Bude & North Cornwall, Holsworthy, Hartland Forest

CORNWALL

CORNWALL

Hotel

Stylish hotel with Victorian charm. 58 en-suite rooms.

Credit Cards: All the major cards.

THE BEACONSFIELD HOTEL 128

The Crescent, Newquay, Cornwall TR7 1DT
Tel: 01637 872172 Fax: 01637 850711

The Beaconsfield Hotel enjoys one of the finest locations in the heart of Newquay, overlooking the sandy beach and open sea beyond. Retaining a Victorian elegance that is rarely found these days, this friendly hotel offers comfortable accommodation with a total of 58 bedrooms, all attractively furnished and with en-suite facilities. Guests can also make use of the many lounge areas for relaxing and enjoy a fine meal in the oak-panelled dining room. The ballroom is used for live entertainment in the summer season and is also available for private hire.

Local Golf Courses: Newquay, Merlin, Perranporth, St. Enodoc

Hotel and Restaurant

Relaxing atmosphere, friendly service, 15 en-suite rooms.

Credit Cards: All the major cards.

PENDEEN HOTEL 129

7 Alexandra Road, Porth, Newquay, Cornwall TR7 3ND
Tel: 01637 873521 Fax: 01637 873521
e-mail: pendeen@cornwall.net

The aim of the owners of the **Pendeen Hotel** is to provide a relaxing and peaceful holiday with friendly and caring service. The hotel is situated on the North Cornwall coastal path and is just two minutes from the fabulous Porth Beach. There are 15 light and airy rooms, all with en-suite facilities. The restaurant serves a good range of traditional English and international cuisine, with the focus being on fresh fish and seafood.

Local Golf Courses: Newquay, Merlin, Perranporth, St. Enodoc

CAWSAND BAY HOTEL & RESTAURANT 130

The Bound, Cawsand, Nr. Torpoint, Cornwall PL10 1PG
Tel: 01752 822425 Fax: 01752 823527
e-mail: sales@cawsandbay.co.uk
website: www.cawsandbay.co.uk

The unspoilt fishing village of Cawsand can be found right at the mouth of the Plymouth South, and is reputed to have had smuggling connections in days gone by. There is just one road into the village and if you follow this right to the sea's edge there you will find the **Cawsand Bay Hotel and Galleon Restaurant.**

The beach is sandy and there are superb views across the Sound towards the hills of Dartmoor, and all of the bedrooms in the hotel overlook the beach. There is a total of 10 comfortable rooms of varying sizes and this would form an ideal base for a family holiday. Non-residents are most welcome in the hotel's pub-style Galleon Bar and there is plenty of outdoor seating for making the most of the warm weather. The outside balcony with its spectacular sea views is ideal for an evening's relaxation. The Galleon Restaurant is open each day serving a wide range meals and snacks from a varied a la carte menu. There are plenty of fresh, home-cooked dishes with local seafood featuring widely.

Situated directly on the bay, you would not need to stray far for an enjoyable holiday. There is a wide range of marine activities readily available such as fishing, water skiing and boating. Horse riding, golf

and picturesque walks are also within easy reach. If you want to venture further afield then Plymouth is easily accessed via the Tamar Bridge or Torpoint Ferry, and Cawsand is an ideal base for exploring Bodmin Moor and Dartmoor.

Hotel, Restaurant, Bar

Sea front location, great facilities

Credit Cards: All the major cards.

Local Golf Courses: St. Mellion, Lostwithiel, Whitsand Bay Hotel

WOODLANDS HOTEL — 131

38-40 Pentire Crescent, Newquay, Cornwall TR7 1PU
Tel: 01637 852229 Fax: 01637 852227

From the road, you perhaps wouldn't guess that the **Woodlands Hotel** looks out over the pretty River Gannel estuary and the open countryside beyond. This feature is maximised with most of the bedrooms, the restaurant, and large patio with outdoor pool, all being south-facing and enjoying the spectacular views. There are 54 bedrooms in total, all with en-suite facilities, and available in varying sizes from singles, to rooms sleeping four.

Hotel

Quiet setting with stunning views. 54 bedrooms.

Credit Cards: All the major cards.

Local Golf Courses: Newquay, Merlin, Perranporth, Trevose, Truro

WHIDBORNE MANOR — 201

Ashill, Bishopsteignton, Devon TQ14 9PY
Tel: 01626 870177
e-mail: nicky.dykes@btinternet.com

Despite the grand name, this is a traditional 15th-century Devon longhouse built of cob and stone, with a thatched roof and is conveniently located on the edge of the village, close to the ruins of the Bishop's palace and just a mile from Teignmouth Golf Club. It is a spacious house, attractively furnished with many original beams and timbers throughout, and can offer two double rooms for bed and breakfast accommodation. The guest rooms are of a good size and share a 'four poster' bathroom. Good pubs for food close by.

Bed and breakfast

Cosy, 15th-century longhouse, two double rooms

Credit Cards: None

Local Golf Courses: Teignmouth, Warren, Torquay

CHIMNEYS OF STARCROSS — 202

Starcross, Nr. Exeter, Devon EX6 8PA
Tel: 01626 890813

Chimneys of Starcross is an imposing detached house, located on the A379, overlooking the Exe estuary. Built in 1888 many of the original features have been preserved with the most impressive being the stained glass window on the main staircase. The accommodation comprises seven rooms, of which five are en-suite, with a four poster room available for special occasions. Evening meals are available on request.

Guest House

Charming Victorian house, seven rooms

Credit Cards: All the major cards

Local Golf Courses: Warren, Exeter G&CC, Teignmouth

THE WHITE HOUSE — 203

Chillington, Nr. Kingsbridge, Devon TQ7 2JX
Tel: 01548 580580 Fax: 01548 581124
e-mail: tinawhthse@cs.com

The White House is a small, high quality hotel enjoying a rural location near to Kingsbridge. The charming Georgian house is set in an acre of landscaped grounds and offers seven luxuriously furnished bedrooms including two suites. The Copper Beach Restaurant serves an equally high standard of cuisine with freshly prepared table d'hote menus available each day. This family-run hotel is recommended by the Johansen Hotel Guide.

Hotel and Restaurant

Small, high quality hotel and restaurant.

Credit Cards: All the major cards

Local Golf Courses: Dartmouth G&CC, Thurlestone, Churston

CORNWALL

DEVON

THE BEAUFORT HOTEL   204

Hotel

Elegant hotel with pool. 12 en-suite rooms.

Credit Cards: All the major cards.

Torrs Park, Ilfracombe, Devon EX34 8AY
Tel: 01271 866556

The Beaufort Hotel is situated in the delightful Torrs Park area of Ilfracombe. Built in the 1840's, it has been carefully restored to its present glory, while retaining much of its original character and elegance. Each of the rooms in this family run Hotel have colour TV, tea and coffee making faclities, hair dryers etc. There is an outdoor heated pool, or for the less energetic a well stocked bar and games room. Golf, horse riding ,fishing and pleasure trips can be arranged. Evening meals can be provided by arrangement.

Local Golf Courses: Ilfracombe, Saunton, Royal North Devon

SOUTH LEIGH HOTEL   205

Hotel

Friendly, family-run hotel. 26 guest rooms.

Credit Cards: All the major cards.

Runnacleave Road, Ilfracombe, Devon EX34 8AQ
Tel: 01271 863976
Fax: 01271 863322

South Leigh is a family-run hotel, situated in its own grounds close to the beach. The hotel is comfortably furnished with a very pleasant atmosphere and the proprietors and staff make every effort to ensure guests feel at home. Each of the 26 bedrooms have en-suite shower, colour TV with access to Sky channels, and a hot drinks tray. There is a hotel bar and entertainment is arranged most nights.

Local Golf Courses: Ilfracombe, Saunton, Royal North Devon

THE HALFWAY HOUSE INN   206

Grenofen, Tavistock, Devon PL19 9ER
Tel: 01822 612960 Fax: 01822 617697

The Halfway House Inn is ideally situated for golfers who wish to play the beautiful moorland courses of Tavistock and Yelverton, the attractive parkland course at Launceston and the championship course at St Mellion. But for those who wish to have a break from golf the inn is also a perfect base for walking, with a number of scenic paths close by, or for touring the local area with the ancient towns of Tavistock and Launceston and the historic city of Plymouth only a few miles away.

A spacious black and white building, The Halfway House Inn has an immediate feeling of warmth and friendliness with its old beamed ceilings and open log fire in the lounge bar. Outside there is an attractive garden with glorious views across Dartmoor to Hessary Tor. The pub was originally built in the 16th century as eight cottages, a fact which becomes more apparent when you go upstairs where there are four guest bedrooms with ensuite or private facilities including a large family room.

A major attraction at this appealing old hostelry is the quality of food available in the smoking and non-smoking restaurants both offering an extensive a la carte menu as well as a blackboard listing daily specials and special wine offers. In the bar you'll find an equally wide choice of meals and snacks and an excellent selection of real ales. A substantial traditional English or continental breakfast is included in the bed & breakfast tariff.

Inn with food, B&B

Characterful inn serving excellent food.

Credit Cards: All the major cards

Local Golf Courses: Tavistock, St. Mellion Hotel G&CC, Yelverton

SUNNYMEADE COUNTRY HOTEL — 207

Country Hotel

Friendly hotel with award-winning chef. Six en-suite rooms.

Credit Cards: All the major cards.

Dean Cross, West Down, Nr. Ilfracombe, Devon EX34 8NT
Tel: 01271 863668
e-mail: info@sunnymeade.co.uk
website: www.sunnymeade.co.uk

Surrounded by rolling green hills, **Sunnymeade** enjoys a spectacular location amidst North Devon's natural beauty and wildlife. Your host is a professionally trained chef and has won awards for the excellent standard of his home-cooked, regional specialities and traditional English dishes. Meal times can be arranged to suit guests' requirements. Sunnymeade specialises in shooting breaks.

Local Golf Courses: Ilfracombe, Saunton, Royal North Devon

GLEN TOR HOTEL — 208

Hotel

Small, cosy family-run hotel.
ETC 4 diamonds

Credit Cards: Most major cards.

Torrs Park, Ilfracombe, Devon EX34 8AZ
Tel: 01271 862403 Fax: 01271 862403
e-mail: info@glentorhotel.co.uk
website: www.glentorhotel.co.uk

A warm welcome awaits at the **Glen Tor Hotel**, a small, family-run establishment in a quiet corner of Ilfracombe. There are seven en-suite guest bedrooms all tastefully decorated and provided with those little extras that help make your stay a relaxing one. Guests can enjoy the comfortable lounge with adjoining licensed bar and make use of the extensive library. Evening meals available on request.

Local Golf Courses: Ilfracombe, Saunton, Royal North Devon

EPCHRIS HOTEL — 209

ETC - 3 Diamonds Guest Accommodation
Torrs Park, Ilfracombe, Devon EX34 8AZ
Tel: 01271 862751 Fax: 01271 879077
e-mail: epchris-hotel@ic24.net
website: www.epchris-hotel.co.uk

The Epchris Hotel is the oldest building on the Torrs, offering the comfortable charm and intimate atmosphere of a large, former country residence. A family run hotel, The Epchris is set within two acres, close to the National Trust Torrs walks, coastal paths and Exmoor. You can relax here and enjoy the outdoor heated swimming pool or only a short stroll away is the new Landmark Theatre on the Ilfracombe sea front with its cinema and the rendezvous cafe bar.

All the twin/family bedrooms are en-suite and have direct dial telephone, colour TV, tea/coffee making facilities and one of the rooms is on the ground floor.

COSY LICENSED BAR
LARGE PRIVATE PARKING
GAMES CHALET
FULL CENTRAL HEATING
OUTDOOR HEATED SWIMMING POOL
SECURE GUN CABINETS

Hotel

Hotel in private grounds. Nine bedrooms.

Credit Cards: All the major cards.

Local Golf Courses: Ilfracombe, Saunton, Royal North Devon

DEVON

DEVON

WENTWORTH HOUSE HOTEL   210

2 Belmont Road, Ilfracombe, Devon EX34 8DR
Tel: 01271 863048 Fax: 01271 863048

Enjoying a central location in the heart of Ilfracombe, **Wentworth House Hotel** was built in 1857 as a gentleman's residence. It has since been lovingly restored and furnished and now offers comfortable accommodation with a total of nine spacious guest rooms. The residents' lounge overlooks the hotel garden and the bedrooms also have fine views over the sea or surrounding countryside. Evening meals available on request.

Hotel
Centrally located hotel. Nine rooms.

Credit Cards: None.

Local Golf Courses: Ilfracombe, Saunton, Royal North Devon

THE COLLINGDALE HOTEL   211

Larkstone Terrace, Ilfracombe, Devon EX34 9NU
Tel: 01271 863770 Fax: 01271 863770
e-mail: collingdale@onet.co.uk

The Collingdale is a small, comfortable hotel with a relaxed, happy atmosphere located within a few minutes walk of the beach, harbour and town centre of Ilfracombe. The comfortable guests' lounge overlooks the coast while the dining room and sun patio enjoy views of the harbour. Many guests book for sports orientated breaks and your hosts will happily book you a slot at a local golf course.

Hotel
Small, comfortable hotel. Eight en-suite rooms.

Credit Cards: All the major cards.

Local Golf Courses: Ilfracombe, Saunton, Royal North Devon

BRUNSWICK HOUSE   212

5 Brunswick Street, Teignmouth, South Devon TQ14 8AE
Tel: 01626 774102 e-mail: peterhockings@hotmail.com

Teignmouth lies at the estuary of the River Teign from which it takes its name and a sandy beach reaches all along the front of the town around to the back where boats are moored at the river mouth. Across the other side of the estuary is the village of Shaldon and a passenger ferry provides a five-minute crossing, although the road bridge is not too far away.

Just 100 metres from the sea front, tucked into a quiet side street, is **Brunswick House**, whose proprietors are Margrethe & Pete Hockings. This luxury bed and breakfast is housed within a tall, three-storey Victorian terrace and offers comfortable, spacious accommodation. The period property features high-ceilinged rooms and superb, new decor and furnishing throughout. There are a total of eight rooms, three triples (one being a 4-person family room), four doubles and a single. Each has an en-suite bathroom, with power shower, and is provided with a colour TV and tea- and coffee-making tray. The breakfasts are a sumptuous offering, with no distinction made between Continental and English - there is plenty of everything to choose from. Vegetarian and other special dietary requirements can be accommodated on request.

Teignmouth itself is a charming and fascinating town and the shops, and many other facilities it offers, can be reached on foot from Brunswick House. There is superb bathing, boating and numerous other leisure facilities to suit all ages and interests. The magnificent scenery of Dartmoor is within a short drive as well as many other delightful coastal and inland towns that the area has to offer. Inspected and approved by Teignmouth & District Hotels & Caterers Association.

Bed and Breakfast
Good sized property with eight rooms

Credit Cards: Visa, Mastercard

Local Golf Courses: Teignmouth, Warren, Torquay

ST. BRANNOCKS HOUSE HOTEL — 213

61-62 St. Brannocks Road, Ilfracombe, Devon EX34 8EQ
Tel: 01271 863873 Fax: 01271 863873
e-mail: stbrannocks@aol.com website: www. stbrannocks.co.uk

Ilfracombe is situated in one of the most beautiful areas of Britain and it is easy to see why it is the leading holiday resort in North Devon. Visitors to this corner of England have the best of both worlds, with the sea and the wilds of Exmoor literally on the doorstep. There are trips by boat and easy drives to many places of interest on the coast and inland.

St. Brannocks House is a detached Victorian Hotel set in its own grounds, just a few minutes walk from the town, sea front and many visitor attractions. Whether you are planning a holiday or just a short break, then here you will find a successful mix of first class accommodation, good home cooking and service with a smile.

The guests' lounge is the ideal place to catch up on the evening news, or just to relax after a day out. There is also a cosy bar area where you can enjoy a quiet drink, or socialise with other guests. In the pleasant dining room residents can enjoy generous portions of good, home-cooked food from a varied menu, with a fine choice both at breakfast and also for the optional evening meals. A selection of table wines is available to complement your evening meal and special diets can be catered for. The comfortable accommodation comprises 14 tastefully decorated bedrooms, all with en-suite bath or shower-room, and all have a television and complimentary tea and coffee making facilities. Open all year including Christmas and New Year. Special short breaks, walking and golfing breaks available. Dogs welcome free of charge.

Hotel

Comfortable accommodation. 14 bedrooms. ETC 2 Stars

Credit Cards: All the major cards.

Local Golf Courses: Ilfracombe, Saunton, Royal North Devon

THE RED BARN RESTAURANT — 214

Woolacombe, Devon EX34 7DF
Tel: 01271 870264

The family-run **Red Barn Restaurant and Bar** stands just 100 metres from the fabulous beach of Woolacombe. The owner and several of the staff are keen surfers and this is the theme adopted throughout the establishment with trophies and other interesting items on display. Catering to all appetites, you will find the menu offering a wide selection of tasty dishes to suit all tastes, together with a good choice of ales and cider. Ideal for families.

Restaurant and Bar

Unusual sea-front eatery.

Credit Cards: All the major cards

Local Golf Courses: Ilfracombe, Saunton, Royal North Devon

PRESTON HOUSE HOTEL — 215

Saunton, Braunton, Devon EX33 1LG
Tel: 01271 890472   Fax: 01271 890555
e-mail: prestonhouse-saunton@zoom.co.uk

The Preston House Hotel enjoys a unrivalled location high up above the coast, looking down on the open sea and the three mile stretch of Saunton Sands. This elegant hotel maximises its position with the terrace, restaurant and gardens looking out over the breathtaking views. There are 12 guest rooms, all with en-suite facilities, and some having a Jacuzzi and four poster beds. The stylish restaurant, which is also open to non-residents, serves a delicious selection of freshly prepared dishes and has an AA Rosette for its food.

Hotel and Restaurant

12 en-suite rooms. Elegant restaurant. Cliff top location.

Credit Cards: All the major cards.

Local Golf Courses: Saunton, Ilfracombe, Royal North Devon

DEVON

YEOLDON HOUSE HOTEL 216

Durrant Lane, Northam, Nr. Bideford, Devon EX39 2RL
Tel: 01237 474400 e-mail: yeoldonhouse@aol.com
Fax: 01237 476618 website: www.yeoldonhousehotel.co.uk

Enjoying an unrivalled position on the banks of the River Torridge, not far from the north Devon coast you will find the delightful **Yeoldon House Hotel**. This imposing house is surrounded by lawns and colourful flower beds that slope gently down to the river and visitors are welcome to explore and enjoy a quiet drink here should they wish.

Inside, visitors will quickly become aware of the quiet charm that pervades the atmosphere, while their every comfort is being well looked after by friendly and efficient hosts Brian and Jennifer Steele. Downstairs are the guests' lounge and the elegant "Soyer's" Restaurant both of which look out over the lawns and down to the river. The restaurant takes its name from a famous Victorian chef, Alexis Soyer, and serves an imaginative menu of freshly prepared dishes that incorporate a variety of locally-sourced produce. The resident chef takes great pride in presenting good food in a relaxing atmosphere and every meal can be complemented by a selection from a fine range of international wines.

The accommodation comprises ten en-suite rooms each having been individually designed and furnished - many have a charming, country style while there is also a grand four poster room and a split level suite with its own balcony and lounge area. The surrounding area has much to offer visitors to the area with an exceptional range of things to do. The coast offers some magnificent scenery and a steamer trip could take you out to Lundy Island while inland there is the whole of Exmoor to be explored.

Country House Hotel
Elegant, riverside hotel. 10 en-suite rooms.

Credit Cards: All the major cards.

Local Golf Courses: Royal North Devon, Saunton, Chulmleigh

SHUNA GUEST HOUSE 217

Downend, Croyde, Devon EX33 1QE
Tel: 01271 890537
Fax: 01271 890537

Shuna is a small, luxurious, family-run guest house situated at the southern end of Croyde Bay. From the front of the house there are spectacular views across the sea to Baggy Point and from the rear, views over the beautiful Devon countryside. There is ample private parking and the house is within easy walking distance of the beach, picturesque Croyde village and the coastal footpaths. Saunton Golf course is only two miles away.

Guest House
Family-run guest house. Five en-suite rooms.

Credit Cards: None

Local Golf Courses: Saunton, Ilfracombe, Royal North Devon

MOLE COTTAGE 218

Chittlehamholt, Devon EX37 9HF
Tel: 01769 540471 Fax: 01769 540471
e-mail: relax@moley.uk.com website: www.moley.uk.com

You can expect a warm, friendly welcome at **Mole Cottage**, a 17th century thatched cottage situated within the magical Mole Valley. This friendly home from home offers bed and breakfast accommodation, with guests being welcome to enjoy the surrounding gardens which extend to the river. The proprietors also run a thriving pottery, No 9 Studio, which specialises in Architectural Ceramics. A gallery in the old coach house displays a wide range of items made on the premises, where you purchase a small memento. Residential Pottery courses available.

B&B, Pottery, Gallery
Romantic, thatched cottage in riverside location. 3 rooms, 1 en-suite.
Credit Cards: None.

Local Golf Courses: Royal North Devon, Chulmleigh, Saunton

AUTUMN LODGE 219

Victoria Street, Combe Martin, Devon EX34 0JS
Tel: 01271 883558
e-mail: lespallatt@supanet.com

Combe Martin lies in a deep sheltered valley, and the **Autumn Lodge Hotel** is situated at the top end of the village about a mile from the sea. There are eight guest bedrooms, of which six have en-suite facilities. Guests can meet for drinks in the cocktail bar and an excellent standard of cuisine can be enjoyed in the restaurant. A large heated, outdoor pool is available to residents.

Hotel

Friendly, comfortable hotel with eight bedrooms.

Credit Cards: None.

Local Golf Courses: Ilfracombe, Saunton, Royal North Devon

WATERFRONT INN 220

Golf Links Road, Westward Ho!, Devon EX39 1LH
Tel: 01237 474737
Fax: 01237 471719

Just yards from the beach, the **Waterfront Inn** has much to offer visitors to the area. There is a large, comfortable lounge bar, or the more lively Sportsman's Bar, in which to enjoy a drink. Food is available from a menu of bar meals and snacks, and these can be enjoyed either in the bar or the stylish restaurant. Bed and breakfast accommodation is offered with eight en-suite light and airy rooms, all newly decorated and furnished.

Pub, Restaurant, B&B

Modern, friendly inn with 8 en-suite bedrooms.

Credit Cards: All the major cards.

Local Golf Courses: Royal North Devon, Saunton, Chulmleigh

WOODLANDS HOTEL 221

51 Barnpark Road, Teignmouth, Devon TQ14 8PN
Tel: 01626 773094

Just on the outskirts of the popular seaside town of Teignmouth, **Woodlands Hotel** can found at the end of a private, tree-lined drive. This delightful hotel was built in Regency times and still retains a great deal of elegance of that period. The architecture is grand, with an impressive sweeping staircase dominating the entrance hall, while the decor and furnishings are fresh and modern. Surrounding the house is a large lawned garden with plenty of trees and shrubs and guests are more than welcome to sit outside and enjoy the superb views across to the town and sea beyond.

Inside, the stylish feel continues through to the comfortable guest rooms, which are available in various sizes, with some rooms also having the superb views out to sea. Accommodation is on a bed and breakfast basis. The food is all freshly prepared using locally-sourced produce, and the cuisine is mainly a traditional English style.

This is an ideal base for exploring much of Devon, with Dartmoor and many other popular sites within easy reach. This stretch of coast is popular for bathing and surfing with a number of award-winning Blue Flag beaches. Groups can be catered for and ample car parking is available on the drive.

Hotel

Impressive Regency property in super location

Credit Cards: None

Local Golf Courses: Teignmouth, Warren, Dainton Park

DEVON

WHEEL FARM COUNTRY COTTAGES   222

Holiday Cottages

Complex of ten cottages and apartments

Credit Cards: None.

Wheel Farm, Berry Down, Combe Martin, Devon EX34 0NT
Tel: 01271 882100 Fax: 01271 883120
website: www.wheelfarmcottages.co.uk

Nestling in a sheltered valley, close to Combe Martin, with views of Exmoor, **Wheel Farm Country Cottages** provide the perfect holiday setting. Surrounded by 11 acres of Gold award winning gardens and grounds, the eight cottages and two apartments, sleeping from 2 to 6 persons, have been converted to a high standard from an old watermill and barns, creating cosy, centrally heated and well equipped accommodation. Special features include an impressive indoor pool, sauna, LTA standard tennis court, fitness room, four poster beds and log fires. ETB 4 star

Local Golf Courses: Ilfracombe, Saunton, Royal North Devon

HOME FARM HOTEL AND RESTAURANT   223

Hotel and Restaurant

Characterful hotel and cosy restaurant. 13 en-suite rooms.

Credit Cards: All the major cards.

Wilmington, Honiton, Devon EX14 9JR
Tel: 01404 831278 e-mail: homefarmhotel@breathemail.net
Fax: 01404 831411 website: www.homefarmhotel.co.uk

Home Farm was built in the 16th century and, together with the surrounding buildings, has been extended and converted into an intimate hotel and restaurant with a cosy, olde worlde charm throughout. There are a total of 13 individually-styled, en-suite bedrooms of varying sizes, with some on the ground floor. The restaurant has a far-reaching reputation for the high quality of its food and service. The menus offer a comprehensive a la carte or table d'hote menu, while in the adjoining lounge you can enjoy a selection of lighter meals or snacks.

Local Golf Courses: Honiton, Axe Cliff, Sidmouth

MARLBOROUGH HOTEL   224

The Esplanade, Sidmouth, Devon EX10 8AR
Tel: 01395 513320

The Marlborough Hotel is truly a sea front property, being just a stone's throw from one of Sidmouth's superb beaches. Open all year round this historic hotel and pub is thought to date back, in parts, to the 14th century. The superb location makes this an ideal base for exploring the delightful surrounding countryside and many attractions that this part of Devon has to offer.

Family-run, you can be assured of a friendly welcome on your arrival, with high levels of service being continued throughout the establishment. As a hostelry, the Marlborough is popular both with the locals and many holiday makers. The large patio area to the front is packed with tables and chairs in summer, so you can enjoy a drink at the same time as enjoying the views. Inside there is an open plan bar lounge which is bright and clean and an ideal spot for a quiet drink or a bite to eat. Food is available throughout the day with the menu offering a good range of bar meals and snacks. An a la carte selection is available in the hotel's sea-front restaurant, which is open to non-residents from April to the end of September. The food is good, home-cooked English cuisine with the varied menu featuring local produce and fresh fish.

The accommodation comprises 18 bedrooms, which have recently been refurbished and redecorated, and many have stunning views over the beach and sea front. Varying in size, all are en-suite and include some family rooms. Rates are reasonable for B&B, with special short breaks and off-season offers too.

Hotel and Restaurant

Sea front hotel and pub. 18 en-suite rooms.

Credit Cards: All the major cards.

Local Golf Courses: Sidmouth, Woodbury Park, Axe Cliff, East Devon

THE ILFRACOMBE REGAL HOTEL | 225

19 Gilbert Grove, Ilfracombe, Devon EX34 9BG
Tel: 01271 866799

The Ilfracombe Regal is a small, privately-run hotel in the heart of the town of Ilfracombe. All the rooms are en-suite and provided with tea and coffee making facilities and a colour TV. There is a licensed bar and this provides a ideal place to enjoy a drink at the end of the day and to make plans for the next. Breakfast and the three-course evening meals are served in the spacious dining room with all food being freshly prepared to order.

Hotel

Small, privately-run hotel.

Credit Cards: None

Local Golf Courses: Ilfracombe, Saunton, Royal North Devon

WATERLOO HOUSE HOTEL | 226

Waterloo Terrace, Fore Street, Ilfracombe, Devon EX34 9DJ
Tel: 01271 863060 e-mail: info@waterloohousehotel.co.uk
Fax: 01272 863060 website: www.waterloohousehotel.co.uk

Waterloo House Hotel is in the heart of the old town, just 200 metres from the harbour and a short stroll from the main shops and restaurants. Dating back to 1820 the hotel was originally three cottages built to commemorate the Battle of Waterloo. Many of the original period features of the building have been retained while the property has been converted to offer stylish hotel accommodation. There are ten individually styled guest rooms, most with en-suite facilities, and some having sea views. The superb Bonapartes Restaurant, which is also open to non-residents, prides itself on serving a fine menu of high quality cuisine.

Hotel and Restaurant

Characterful accommodation, superb restaurant

Credit Cards: All the major cards.

Local Golf Courses: Ilfracombe, Saunton, Royal North Devon

THE LAUGHING MONK RESTAURANT | 227

Totnes Road, Strete, Nr. Dartmouth, Devon TQ6 0RN
Tel: 01803 770639

The Laughing Monk is one of the most highly respected restaurants in the whole of the south west of England and indeed the reputation of the owners, David and Trudy Rothwell, extends world-wide. The couple have been here for over fourteen years and have become known for serving excellent meals with consistently courteous service. Over the years they have been the recipients of many awards including the 'Best Restaurant in the West' Gold Award.

The restaurant is housed within a 160-year old former church school which has been converted to provide a characterful, L-shaped dining area. The interior has recently been refurbished and features pine polished tables and a variety of wooden seating. A large wood burner keeps the whole building warm, while individual table lamps and candles help to create an intimate atmosphere. Part of the dining area is curtained off for private parties and functions.

Open Tuesday to Saturday for dinner, the menu is a regularly changing selection of imaginative dishes featuring the best of local produce. Inevitably there is often a number of fresh fish dishes though everyone can be sure of finding something to suit their particular taste and appetite. During Autumn and Winter, on the last Sunday in every month, a traditional lunch menu is served.

The Laughing Monk is one of those special places that one constantly seeks but rarely finds. The location is ideal for anyone visiting Devon and regular customers travel from far and wide. Highly recommended.

Restaurant

Award-winning restaurant, open for dinner throughout the year.

Credit Cards: All the major cards

Local Golf Courses: Dartmouth G&CC, Churston, Thurleston

DEVON

CLIFFE HYDRO HOTEL — 228

Hillsborough Road, Ilfracombe, Devon EX34 9NP
Tel: 01271 863606 Fax: 01271 879019

The **Cliffe Hydro Hotel** enjoys a superb location in the heart of Ilfracombe, high up on a cliff looking down onto the harbour. Medium-sized, the accommodation is clean, simply furnished and sensibly priced with the en-suite rooms available in varying sizes. Within the hotel there is a excellent indoor leisure complex with heated indoor pool, gymnasium, sauna, solarium and much more. The hotel restaurant serves traditional English cuisine with a menu catering to all tastes and appetites.

Hotel
Medium sized hotel with superb leisure facilities

Credit Cards: All the major cards

Local Golf Courses: Ilfracombe, Saunton, Royal North Devon

VICTORIAN PANTRY — 229

Museum Courtyard, West Street, Okehampton,
Devon EX20 1HQ
Tel: 01837 53988

Located just off the main street the **Victorian Pantry Tea Rooms** are housed within an historic building which was once the town's courthouse, not far from the Dartmoor Museum. The quaint tea room and restaurant has a charming atmosphere and is a most delightful place in which to enjoy a leisurely drink or meal. The menu offers a good selection of drinks and fresh, home-cooked cakes and hot meals, all prepared on the premises by the owner, Margaret Allin.

Tea rooms
Cosy tea rooms in historic corner of town

Credit Cards: None

Local Golf Courses: Okehampton, Ashbury, Tavistock

PRESSLAND COUNTRY HOUSE HOTEL — 230

Hatherleigh, Nr. Okehampton, Devon EX20 3LW
Tel: 01837 810871 Fax: 01837 810303
e-mail: graham@presslandhouse.co.uk
website: www.presslandhouse.co.uk

Pressland Country House Hotel is a Victorian manor house built in local stone, set back from the main road surrounded by lawns and woodland, with superb views of Dartmoor and the surrounding countryside. The house is attractively decorated and furnished throughout and there are five spacious guest rooms, most with en-suite facilities. Guests can enjoy superb three-course evening meals, should they wish, with the dishes freshly prepared from locally-sourced, seasonal ingredients.

Hotel
Delightful Victorian manor house

Credit Cards: All the major cards

Local Golf Courses: Okehampton, Ashbury, Tavistock

THE BRIDGE INN — 231

Bridge Street, Hatherleigh,
Nr. Okehampton, Devon EX20 3JA
Tel: 01837 810947 Fax: 01837 810614

Located at one end of the village of Hatherleigh, **The Bridge Inn** dates from the 16th century and is one of the oldest buildings to be found in the area. This is very much a rural, village pub and it has a well-used and well-loved feel to it. The cosy interior has a bar and separate 40-seater restaurant where the menu offers a fine selection including fresh fish and 'sizzling' dishes. Bed and breakfast accommodation is also available with six en-suite rooms of varying sizes.

Pub with food, B&B
Cosy, village pub serving good food

Credit Cards: All the major cards

Local Golf Courses: Okehampton, Ashbury, Chulmleigh

DEVON

THE TORRS | 232

Belstone, Okehampton, Devon EX20 1QZ
Tel: 01837 840689

The village of Belstone, just three miles from Okehampton, is surrounded by rolling hills and moors, with fine views to be enjoyed in most directions. In the heart of the village, in an unusual corner site, is **The Torrs**. Housed within a Victorian building, constructed of local stone, the interior is simply furnished in a clean, bright, comfortable style. Popular with locals and visitors, here you can enjoy a refreshing drink and a tasty, home-cooked meal with the pies and smoked fish platter being strongly recommended. Bed and breakfast accommodation available with three en-suite guest rooms.

Pub with food, B&B

Small, cosy inn, three en-suite rooms

Credit Cards: All the major cards

Local Golf Courses: Okehampton, Ashbury, Tavistock

'THE OYSTER' | 233

Colebrooke, Devon EX17 5JQ
Tel: 01363 84576

Next to the village church, in the tiny village of Colebrooke, is the cosy modern bungalow that is **The Oyster**. Taking its unusual name from the owner, Pearl, the comfortable house offers three guest bedrooms, each having en-suite or private facilities. A former farmer's wife, Pearl knows how to look after her guests with a super traditional English or Continental breakfast served each morning. The local hostelry, open for lunch and dinner, is just a short walk away. It is no surprise to learn that many visitors return time and again.

Bed and breakfast

Homely, modern bungalow.

Credit Cards: None.

Local Golf Courses: Downes Crediton, Okehampton, Exeter G&CC

TIDES REACH HOTEL | 234

South Sands, Salcombe, Devon TQ8 8LJ
Tel: 01548 843466 Fax: 01548 843954
e-mail: enquire@tidesreach.com website: www.tidesreach.com

Tides Reach is an elegant, luxurious hotel owned and personally-run by Mr and Mrs Roy Edwards for over twenty five years. In that time they have built up an enviable reputation for the high standards of service offered by the friendly staff and the high quality of cuisine served in the restaurant. The location of Tides Reach is an impressive one, positioned at the mouth of the scenic Salcombe estuary, in the tree-lined cove of South Sands. South facing, the hotel and most of the rooms look out over the river mouth and the sea beyond. It is hard to imagine a more idyllic setting for a short break or relaxing holiday.

Elegantly and stylishly furnished, the guests' lounges and cocktail bar have a relaxing atmosphere in which to enjoy the full range of services available throughout the day. In the Garden Room restaurant the standard of cuisine is superb and will surely satisfy the most discerning of diners. Carefully selected local produce and freshly caught fish are expertly prepared by a team of resident chefs to create a delicious selection of dishes. To complement your meal, the well-stocked cellar features wines from around the world. There are 38 guest bedrooms, individually designed, and all but four having a view over the estuary. Some rooms have balconies while a small number of Premier Rooms are even more luxurious and spacious and have some of the best views. In addition to the water sports that are available within the bay, there are a variety of activities provided within the hotel. The heated indoor pool is the focus of a leisure complex with guests having use of a gym, squash court, sauna, solarium and much more. There is also a hair and beauty salon which is ideal for extra pampering before a night out.

Hotel and Restaurant

Luxurious hotel with excellent facilities. 38 en-suite rooms.

Credit Cards: All the major cards.

Local Golf Courses: Thurlestone, Bigbury, Dartmouth G&CC

DEVON

ROYAL STANDARD INN | 235

Mary Tavy, Nr. Tavistock, Devon PL19 9QB
Tel: 01822 810289 Fax: 01822 810615

The Royal Standard Inn can be found on the main A386 Tavistock to Okehampton road. Dating from the mid-1700s this former coaching inn has changed much over the centuries resulting in the spacious establishment you find today. Inside the atmosphere is one of character and charm, with plenty of corners in which to enjoy a quiet drink, while there is also a good-sized restaurant. There was once a brewery next door and to this day the inn claims to serve the best beer in the area. The food comprises a good selection of traditional meals and snacks, served all day.

Pub with food

Excellent real ales and tasty food

Credit Cards: All the major cards

Local Golf Courses: Tavistock, Yelverton, St. Mellion Hotel G&CC

THE OLD COACH HOUSE | 236

Ottery, Tavistock, Devon PL19 8NS
Tel: 01822 617515 Fax: 01822 617515
e-mail: eddie@coachhouseone.supanet.com

The Old Coach House can be found in the tiny hamlet of Ottery just a couple of miles from Tavistock. It dates back to 1857 when it was built for the Duke of Bedford, and was substantially renovated in 1989 to create this delightful establishment. A high standard of decor can be found throughout, with wooden floors and sumptuous furnishings in both the restaurant and guest accommodation. Food can be enjoyed from a superb a la carte menu with all dishes being freshly prepared to order, and there is a comprehensive wine list.

Hotel and Restaurant

Comfortable accommodation and good restaurant

Credit Cards: All the major cards

Local Golf Courses: Tavistock, Yelverton, St. Mellion Hotel G&CC

LANGSTONE CLIFF HOTEL | 237

Dawlish, Devon EX7 0NA
Tel: 01626 868000 Fax: 01626 868006
e-mail: reception@langstone-hotel.co.uk

The Langstone Cliff Hotel is one of Devon's premier hotels, having opened in 1947, and has been run by the same family ever since. The location is unbeatable with the hotel and surrounding grounds overlooking the sea and red cliffs of this stretch of coastline. The extensive lawns are ideal for sunbathing, while the veranda that surrounds the hotel offers some shade should you prefer. In the grounds visitors will also find hard tennis courts, woodland walks, an outdoor pool and a golf practice area. Warren Golf Club is located just 100 metres from the hotel and guests can enjoy concessionary fees. Inside, the hotel offers numerous large, public rooms, with no less than three comfortable lounges for enjoying some TV, reading the paper, or a quiet chat with friends. There are two games rooms and an indoor pool if it isn't warm enough to venture outdoors. The large Washington Ballroom is used for a variety of dance and cabaret evenings with a full programme being presented throughout the year. A choice of entertainment is also offered in the smaller Lincoln Ballroom and there is often live music in the Poolside Room.

The accommodation comprises 67 bedrooms with 9 of these at ground floor level. Every room has an en-suite bathroom, colour TV, hot drinks tray and many other small essentials to help make your stay more comfortable. Lincoln Restaurant and Bar, right in the heart of the hotel, are open all day every day. Guests can enjoy breakfast, lunches on request and table d'hote dinner menus. The menus offer a wide choice of dishes at every course and there is also a very popular carvery option. Vegetarian dishes are always available and special diets can be catered for. A coffee-shop style service for drinks and snacks is also available throughout the day and can be enjoyed in the grounds, on the veranda or in any of the public rooms.

Hotel and Restaurant

Superb hotel with excellent facilities. 67 rooms.

Credit Cards: All the major cards.

Local Golf Courses: Warren, Teignmouth, Exeter G&CC

THE WALKHAMPTON INN 238

Walkhampton, Nr. Yelverton, Devon PL20 6JY
Tel: 01822 855556 Fax: 01822 855556
e-mail: info@walkhamptoninn.co.uk
There has been a hostelry on the site of **The Walkhampton Inn**
since the 15th-century, with the present establishment dating back
to the 17th century. Over the years the structure has been substantially rebuilt and, in recent years, completely refurbished ensuring
that the original features are complemented by modern furnishings and facilities. The inn is popular in the area for serving a good

Pub with food, B&B

Historic pub offering traditional
hospitality and real ales

range of beer and traditional pub fayre and the home-made Jail
Ale pies are to be particularly recommended. Bed and breakfast
accommodation can also be found here with two guest rooms, both
of which are en-suite and with TV and tea/coffee making facilities.

Credit Cards: All the major cards

Local Golf Courses: Yelverton, Tavistock, Staddon Heights

THE LAURELS 239

Huckworthy Bridge, Yelverton, Devon PL20 6LP
Tel: 01822 853622
The Laurels can be found just over a narrow bridge, on the banks
of the River Walkham, surrounded by trees. This charming old cottage has been lovingly restored, while retaining the original stone
structure, and is now the home of June and Derek Lavers. Here
they offer bed and breakfast accommodation together with a completely self-contained holiday cottage. The spacious three-

Holiday Cottage, B&B

Pretty cottage in riverside setting

bedroomed property is very well-equipped and so popular that many
guests return again and again. Situated in the heart of the Dartmoor National Park this makes an ideal holiday base.

Credit Cards: None

Local Golf Courses: Yelverton, Tavistock, Staddon Heights

LIFTON HALL HOTEL 240

Lifton, Devon PL16 0DR
Tel: 01566 784863 Fax: 01566 784770
e-mail: mail@liftonhall.co.uk
Lifton Hall is a traditional Country House hotel enjoying a peaceful village location in the heart of the West Country. The charming
250-year old manor house has a comfortable, relaxed ambience
while the owners provide the highest levels of personal service.
The accommodation comprises ten spacious, en-suite rooms with

Hotel and Restaurant

Charming country house hotel,
ten rooms

two twins, six doubles and two family-sized rooms. High quality
home-cooked food can be enjoyed in either the formal restaurant
or the more casual bistro with fresh, locally-caught fish a speciality.

Credit Cards: All the major cards

Local Golf Courses: Launceston, Okehampton, Tavistock

THE DUCHESS RESTAURANT 241

Duke Street, South Molton, Devon EX36 3AL
Tel: 01769 573123

The Duchess Restaurant can be found in a quiet street, behind an
unpretentious Victorian frontage marked only by a discreet sign
over the door. Inside you will find a calm, relaxing atmosphere,
enhanced by unfussy, elegant decor. Open Wednesday to Saturday
lunch time and evening, here you can enjoy a light snack or a la

Restaurant

Small charming restaurant.

carte meal with a fully licensed bar serving wine, draught and
bottled beers to enjoy with your meal. Owned and personally run
by Chris and Jane McKeown.

Credit Cards: All the major cards.

Local Golf Courses: Downes Crediton, Okehampton, Royal North Devon

DEVON

LOWER SOUTHBROOK FARM 242

Southbrook Lane, Whimple, Exeter, Devon EX5 2PG
Tel: 01404 822989 Fax: 01404 822989

Lower Southbrook Farm offers delightful self-catering accommodation in the heart of the Devon countryside. Three single-storey cottages, converted from former farm buildings, adjoin the main house and are surrounded by agricultural land. The accommodation is comfortable, with a fully fitted kitchen, ensuring that every stay is relaxing one. Each cottage sleeps six. Heated swimming pool.

Self-catering cottages
Holiday cottages converted from farm buildings.

Credit Cards: None

Local Golf Courses: Honiton, East Devon, Sidmouth

THE HALFWAY INN 243

Sidmouth Road, Aylesbeare, Devon EX5 2JP
Tel: 01395 232273 Fax: 01395 516398

The Halfway Inn at Aylesbeare is a former coaching inn, and takes its unusual name from its position 'halfway' along the once busy London-Penzance coaching route. A popular country pub it offers a fine selection of refreshments to all who visit. The menu is of epic proportions, and plenty of time should be allowed to make a choice, even before each dish is freshly prepared to order. Four comfortable guest rooms for bed and breakfast, of which two are en-suite.

Pub, Restaurant, B&B
Country pub offering excellent selection of food. Four rooms, two en-suite.

Credit Cards: all except amex

Local Golf Courses: Woodbury Park, Exeter, Sidmouth

THE RED LION 244

Shobrooke, Nr. Crediton, Devon EX17 1AT
Tel: 01363 772340

If you like a traditional country pub, then you need look no further than **The Red Lion** in the village of Shobrooke. The cosy interior offers a lounge and public bar, with a separate 40-seater restaurant. In addition there is a patio and beer garden. The pub is open for fine ales and good food each day of the week. Entertainment is provided in the form of darts, pool, skittles and a regular Sunday night quiz. Bed and breakfast accommodation with three, double, en-suite rooms with a three diamond tourist board grading.

Pub with food, B&B
Friendly pub with emphasis on good service.

Credit Cards: All the major cards.

Local Golf Courses: Downes Crediton, Okehampton, Exeter G&CC

THE COFFEE POT 245

14 St. James Street, Okehampton, Devon EX20 1DA
Tel: 01837 52988

Just off the main thoroughfare, in the heart of Okehampton, you will find the conveniently located **The Coffee Pot.** Exactly as its name suggests this is a traditional coffee shop, open daily serving early breakfast, coffee, lunches and afternoon teas. Immaculately presented and kept spotlessly clean, The Coffee Pot is popular both with shoppers and office workers who all enjoy the freshly prepared food and drinks that are available at reasonable prices.

Coffee Shop
Traditional coffee shop

Credit Cards: None.

Local Golf Courses: Okehampton, Ashbury, Tavistock

BENNETTS COURT COTTAGES · 246

Whitstone, Holsworthy, Devon EX22 6UD
Tel: 01288 341370 Fax: 01288 341370
e-mail: helen@bennettscourt.co.uk
website: www.bennettscourt.co.uk

Positioned at the end of a tree-lined drive, surrounded by 12 acres of gardens and open pasture, **Bennetts Court Cottages** comprises five self-catering cottages. This family-run operation offers superb, well-equipped properties converted from former farm buildings and sleeping between two and six people. Guests are invited to make full use of various facilities, including the outdoor heated pool, children's play area, play barn and table tennis barn. Great holiday location with plenty to do in the surrounding area.

Holiday Cottages

Family-run complex of five cottages

Credit Cards: None.

Local Golf Courses: Bude , Holsworthy, Okehampton

'OAKLANDS' · 247

Black Dog, Nr. Crediton, Devon EX17 4QJ
Tel: 01884 860645 Fax: 01884 861030

In the unusually named village of Black Dog you will find **Oaklands**, the lovely home of Janet Bradford. This super house was built to the highest possible standards of craftsmanship. Here you can enjoy comfortable accommodation in one of three en-suite rooms with the surrounding gardens enjoying some stunning views. The local hostelry, which is open for lunch and dinner, is just a short walk away.

Bed and breakfast

Superb house, with stunning views and garden

Credit Cards: None.

Local Golf Courses: Downes Crediton, Okehampton, Royal North Devon

DARTMOOR RAILWAY INN · 248

Station Road, Crediton, Devon EX17 3BX
Tel: 01363 724989

In the heart of Crediton, at a junction of the Exeter road, visitors will find the **Dartmoor Railway Inn**. It lies next to the former British Rail station, from which it takes its name, and dates back to the mid-1850's. This traditional public house offers a warm, friendly welcome to customers old and new and everyone can be sure of finding a refreshing drink and tasty bite to eat here.

The open plan bar area leads through to a restaurant while the adjoining skittle alley doubles as a function room. To the rear there is a stone-flagged courtyard where drinks can be enjoyed al fresco in warmer weather. Here you will also find an aviary which is a useful distraction for younger guests.

Food is served each day with fresh locally-sourced produce converted into a delicious selection of dishes by the resident chef, Rosemary. The regular menu is supplemented by daily specials, which change regularly, with a highly popular roast lunch served on Sundays.

If you are looking to while away a summer's evening, or a wet afternoon, then the dart board or the skittle alley could take your fancy and you can be sure that there will always be someone to take you on! There are also regular quiz nights if want to tax the 'little grey cells'.

Statue of St Boniface, Crediton

Bed and breakfast accommodation is available with three comfortable, en-suite rooms. Rates are reasonable, and this could be a convenient central base for exploring the whole of Devon.

Pub with food, B&B

Home-cooked food. 1 twin room, two doubles

Credit Cards: All the major cards.

Local Golf Courses: Downes Crediton, Okehampton, Exeter

DEVON

DEVON

ALEXANDRA LODGE HOLIDAY APARTMENTS 249

Grafton Road, Torquay, South Devon TQ1 1QJ
Tel: 01803 213465 Fax: 01803 390933
e-mail: armes@fsbdial.co.uk
website: www.alexandra-lodge.co.uk
Alexandra Lodge is a lovely detached Georgian villa set in its own quiet, secluded grounds and enjoying picturesque views over Torbay and Dartmoor, yet within walking distance of the town, harbour and other amenities. There are seven self-catering apartments sleeping between two and eight people, and all are comfortably furnished and well maintained. Week long and short breaks.

Holiday Apartments
Georgian villa divided into self-catering apartments of varying sizes.
Credit Cards: Visa, Mastercard

Local Golf Courses: Torquay, Churston, Dainton Park

EXMOUTH VIEW HOTEL 250

St. Albans Road, Babbacombe, Torquay, Devon TQ1 3LQ
Tel: 0800 7817817 / 01803 327307 Fax: 01803 329967
e-mail: relax@exmouth-view.co.uk
website: www.exmouth-view.co.uk
The Exmouth View hotel is a modern hotel located in a quiet area on the corner of the beautiful Babbacombe Downs. This stylish hotel offers comfortable accommodation at an affordable price with many of the en-suite rooms enjoying coastal views. There is a lounge bar and home-cooked food can be enjoyed in the light and airy dining room. Regular party nights, live music and cabaret acts.

Hotel
Modern hotel enjoying seaside views.

Credit Cards: All the major cards.

Local Golf Courses: Torquay, Warren, Royal North Devon

SHELL COVE HOUSE APARTMENTS & COTTAGES 251

Old Teignmouth Road, Dawlish, Devon EX7 0NJ
Tel: 01626 862523 Fax: 01626 862523
In an idyllic setting, a choice of cottages or apartments in a beautiful Georgian Country House with breathtaking sea views and a virtually private beach. Nestling in 4 acres of grounds of outstanding natural beauty, the many facilities include heated swimming pool, tennis court, badminton,croquet lawns and bird hide gazebo. Well equipped attractively furnished accommodation with central heating, dishwashers, linen, fresh flowers and all comforts provided. Laundry room. Resident family owners. Tourist Board rating 4 stars

Self catering apts and cotts
Superb holiday complex on the coast, excellent accommodation and facilities.
Credit Cards: All the major cards.

Local Golf Courses: Teignmouth, Warren, Newton Abbot

SIR WALTER RALEIGH 252

22 High Street, East Budleigh, Devon EX9 7EB
Tel: 01395 442510

The **Sir Walter Raleigh** dates back to the 16th century and takes its names from the famous adventurer who was born in the nearby village of Hayes Barton. The charming, traditional, thatched building offers fine local ales to locals and visitors to the area. Food is served each day from a menu offering light snacks through to an a la carte selection, with fresh fish being served on Fridays. There is bed and breakfast accommodation also available.

Pub with food, B&B
Historic, country inn serving good food.

Credit Cards: All the major cards.

Local Golf Courses: East Devon, Sidmouth, Woodbury Park

BABBACOMBE HALL HOTEL 253

17 Manor Road, Babbacombe, Torquay, Devon TQ1 3JX
Tel: 01803 325668 Fax: 01803 325668
website: www.babbacombehall.co.uk
e-mail: glyn.aida.rees@lineone.net

Babbacombe, just to the north of Torquay, is where you will find the most delightful of establishments, the **Babbacombe Hall Hotel**. Built in
the early 1900s, recent renovations have ensured that the accommodation is of the highest standard, while a traditional Victorian style has been retained both inside and out. The decor uses bright, pastel shades throughout creating a light airy feel from the guest bar and lounges through to the guest bedrooms.

There are seven rooms in all, four doubles and three twins, six with en-suite facilities and one with it's own private bathroom opposite. All the rooms are provided with hot drinks tray and colour TV. The standard of the accommodation is such that it is the equivalent of a tourist board four diamond grading.

The bar and restaurant are open to residents only, and here you can enjoy breakfast, lunch and an evening meal should you wish. The food is freshly prepared and is usually of a traditional, English cuisine. In the summer season afternoon cream teas are served, either in the dining room or the hotel garden. In the warmer weather, guests can also enjoy the heated outdoor pool and sun terrace. Ample car parking.

Seaside Hotel.
Victorian Hotel, four double, three twin rooms, six en-suite, one with private bathroom.
Credit Cards: All the major cards

Local Golf Courses: Torquay, Teignmouth, Dainton Park

THE DEVON ARMS 254

Kenton, Nr. Exeter, Devon EX6 8LD
Tel: 01626 890213 Fax: 01626 891678
e-mail: devon.arms@ukgateway.net

Next to Powderham Castle, the seat of the Earl and Countess of Devon in the village of Kenton, is **The Devon Arms**. This former coaching inn is a friendly, family-run pub with a dining area serving a good range of home-cooked bar meals and snacks. There are six en-suite letting rooms available for bed and breakfast. Outside there is a patio and garden.

Pub with food, B&B
Family run pub serving home-cooked food. Six en-suite rooms.

Credit Cards: All the major cards

Local Golf Courses: Exeter G&CC, Dawlish Warren, East Devon

WESTBURY 255

51 New Road, Brixham, Devon TQ5 8NL
Tel/Fax: 01803 851684   e-mail: ann.burt@lineone.net

Just a short level walk from the shops and harbour in the attractive port of Brixham will bring you to the delightful guest house of **Westbury**. The charming Georgian house offers accommodation in one of six guest rooms, all tastefully furnished to ensure that every stay is a comfortable one. A delightful conservatory overlooks the patio and colourful garden. Full English breakfast. Private parking.

Guest House
Stylish, Georgian house with six guest rooms.

Credit House: None

Local Golf Courses: Churston, Dainton Park, Torquay

DEVON

COLLINGWOOD HOTEL 256

Braddons Hill Road East, Torquay, Devon TQ1 1HB
Tel: 01803 293448 Fax: 01626 400221
e-mail: bookings@collingwood-hotel.co.uk

A short distance from the sea front you will find the charming **Collingwood Hotel** which dates back to the early 1800s when it was once a grand family residence. Many original features have been retained, giving this medium-sized hotel an elegant style throughout. There is a bar and restaurant, offering traditional English cuisine, dance floor and evening entertainment in season. Regular themed breaks throughout the year. Sun terrace and a heated outdoor pool.

Hotel with Restaurant

Elegant Georgian hotel enjoying fine sea views.
Credit Cards: Visa, Mastercard, Switch, Solo

Local Golf Courses: Torquay, Teignmouth, Dainton Park

THE ANCHORAGE GUEST HOUSE 257

170 New Road, Brixham, Devon TQ5 8DA
Tel/Fax: 01803 852960

Situated on the main road into Brixham is the colourful **Anchorage Guest House.** Owned and personally run by Carolyn Rose, her garden has won Torbay in Bloom awards each year since 1995. There are a total of seven letting rooms, mostly en-suite and on the ground floor, together with a comfortable lounge available for guests to relax in. Brixham's Best Kept Secret - Daily Telegraph June 1999. ETB 3 diamonds

Guest House

Comfortable, friendly guest house with a fabulous garden.

Credit Cards: All the major cards

Local Golf Courses: Torquay, Churston, Dainton Park, Newton Abbot

THE ROYAL OAK 258

The Square, Dolton, Winkleigh, Devon EX19 8QF
Tel: 01805 804288

The Royal Oak can be readily located on the main square in the heart of the village of Dolton, in the depths of the Devon countryside. The imposing 16th-century building is constructed of the traditional local materials of cob, stone and slate and the attractive black and white front is enlivened with planted troughs, window boxes and colourful flower beds.

Inside a warm welcome awaits one and all, with the main lounge area having an open fire to help make the atmosphere even more inviting. The spacious interior means that there are plenty of nooks and crannies in which to enjoy an intimate drink, though there is plenty of room at the bar as well. The separate restaurant provides 24 covers, with the atmosphere here being one of refined elegance, the tables being set with linen cloths and crystal wine glasses. The superb food is a good mix of traditional English and more varied international flavours with a wide ranging menu catering to all. The tempting dishes include a popular 'sizzling' range, and seafood features widely.

Great fun can be had at the skittle alley, which is occasionally converted into a music room where twice-monthly

jazz nights are hosted. The room is also made available for private hire. Comfortable bed and breakfast accommodation can also be found here at The Royal Oak. There are five guest rooms in all, some with en-suite facilities, and all newly refurnished and redecorated by the present owners.

Pub with food, B&B

Friendly pub with superb restaurant.

Credit Cards: All the major cards.

Local Golf Courses: Libbaton, Holsworthy, Royal North Devon

THE PLOUGH INN 259

Fore Street, Ipplepen, Devon TQ12 5RP
Tel: 01803 812118 Fax: 01803 814278
website: www.ipplepen.com

Dating back to the 18th century, **The Plough Inn** is an attractive old inn with a great deal of character. The cosy, intimate interior has a welcoming atmosphere warmed by open log fires in winter, while in the summer visitors can enjoy the secluded beer garden. As well as stocking a good range of drinks, the menu offers a tempting range of dishes to suit all tastes and appetites.

Pub with food

Attractive old inn with great atmosphere.

Credit Cards: None.

Local Golf Courses: Newton Abbott, Dainton Park, Torquay

THE WELCOME STRANGER 260

Liverton, Nr. Newton Abbott, Devon TQ12 6JA
Tel: 01626 821224
e-mail: welcomestranger@talk21.com

As its name suggests, **The Welcome Stranger** is a friendly country pub offering a warm welcome and good service. Here you can enjoy a refreshing drink, with the bar stocking a reasonable selection, together with some tasty home cooked food. The menu is wide ranging, with plenty of choice to suit all tastes, and is sensibly priced. Bed and breakfast accommodation available with two en-suite, twin rooms.

Pub, Restaurant, B&B

Friendly, country pub offering sensibly priced, tasty food. Two twin rooms.

Credit Cards: None.

Local Golf Courses: Dainton, Newton Abbott, Torquay

THE STEAM PACKET INN 261

St. Peter's Quay, Totnes, Devon TQ9 5EN
Tel: 01803 863880 Fax: 01803 862754

An elegant riverside hostelry with accommodation, **The Steam Packet Inn** enjoys a delightful location with stunning views over the River Dart. With the feel more of a hotel than a public house, inside visitors will find an open plan lounge bar with settees and easy chairs and plenty of nooks and crannies in which to enjoy an intimate drink. The lounge leads to an elegant, conservatory dining area where the tables are set with fine linen and crystal. The lunch time menu offers a good choice of meals and snacks, with a small selection designed for business-men and those who would prefer a quick meal, rather than an extended lunch. The dishes available range from fresh sandwiches and jacket potatoes to pasta dishes. In the evening, the a la carte menu caters to a variety of tastes and appetites with fresh fish and sea-food featuring prominently. The variety of interesting dishes is impressive, and all are freshly prepared to order using local produce as widely as possible. To enjoy with your meal there is a carefully selected wine list offering excellent value.

There are ten en-suite guest bedrooms furnished to a very high standard offering comfortable accommodation for a single night or short break. The rooms are of varying sizes, all have a hot drinks tray and colour TV, and some enjoy river views. Private moorings adjoining the inn, for up to four boats, are available.

Inn & Accommodation

Stylish, riverside inn with elegant restaurant. Ten guest rooms.

The motto of The Steam Packet Inn is "Enter a stranger - leave a friend" and the staff definitely make every effort to ensure that this is the case for every visitor who passes through the doors.

Credit Cards: All the major cards

Local Golf Courses: Newton Abbott, Dainton Park, Torquay

DEVON

CHUCKLE TOO　262

Blackawton, Totnes, Devon TQ9 7BG
Tel: 01803 712455

Chuckle Too is a modernised and completely self contained wing of Chuckle Cottage (in which the owner lives). This pretty and cosy annexe includes a cot and sleeps up to three adults, with a double bedroom and separate sofa bed. The kitchen is fully equipped and even tea towels, picnic rugs, cool box, maps and walking sticks are provided. Guests need only bring clothes, food and a beach towel. There is also a garden and barbecue available for residents' use. Your pet dog is welcome for a small additional charge.

Holiday Cottage.

Self-contained, modernised and sleeping up to 3.

Credit Cards: None

Local Golf Courses: Dartmouth G&CC, Thurlestone, Torquay

THE SINGING KETTLE　263

6 Smith Street, Dartmouth, Devon TQ6 9QR
Tel: 01803 832624

The Singing Kettle is a traditional English tea room with a popular local reputation, tucked away up a little side street in the centre of Dartmouth. The building dates back to the 1500s and the interior has a cosy, welcoming feel. Open all day, here you can enjoy a fresh cup of coffee, a light lunch, sandwich or a traditional cream tea, should you wish. All the produce is home baked and every dish is freshly prepared to order.

Tea room

Cosy tea room serving home-made food.

Credit Cards: none

Local Golf Courses: Dartmouth G&CC, Thurlestone, Churston

CAMPBELLS　264

5 Mount Boone, Dartmouth, Devon TQ6 9PB
Tel: 01803 833438 Fax: 01803 833438
website: www.webmachine.co.uk/campbells

Campbells is an award-winning bed and breakfast, where a high standard of excellence can be perceived in every area. The 1930s house is home to Angie and Colin Campbell who are friendly and thoughtful hosts, and the location provides the most stunning views over the town of Dartmouth and to the river beyond. There are just two elegant, double bedrooms both provided with an en-suite bathroom and all those little extras that help to make a holiday a special one. Superb breakfasts with excellent choice.

Bed and breakfast

Two double rooms, superb breakfasts, stunning views.

Credit Cards: None.

Local Golf Courses: Dartmouth G&CC, Thurlestone, Churston

YEALM HOLIDAYS　265

8 Whittingham Road, Collaton Park, Yealmpton, Plymouth, Devon PL8 2NF
Tel: 01752 872712 Fax: 01752 873173
e-mail: info@yealm-holidays.co.uk
website: www.yealm-holidays.co.uk

Self-catering properties are located at the Barbican in Plymouth and the villages of Newton Ferrers and Noss Mayo, at the estuary of the River Yealm (pronounced 'Yam'). All the properties are Tourist Board inspected and rated 2-4 stars.

Holiday Cottages

A range of size and types of self catering properties

Credit Cards: All the major cards

Local Golf Courses: Staddon Heights, Bigbury, Wrangaton

FLOATING BRIDGE & FLOATERS RESTAURANT 266

Sandquay, Dartmouth, Devon TQ6 9PQ
Tel: 01803 832354 Fax: 01803 832354

Enjoying a riverside setting overlooking the yacht moorings and mouth of the River Dart, **The Floating Bridge** has been the watering hole for seafarers and day trippers for centuries. Recorded history shows that it became a pub in 1720, though the building is thought to be even older than that. The

patio to the front of the pub extends right to the waters' edge and in summer can seat up to 60 at the outside tables. Inside there is an open plan bar area with the views from the windows looking out towards the river. The decor is cosy and traditional, with seating available both on high stools at the bar or at small wooden tables, and the walls are decorated with prints depicting the town of Dartmouth through the centuries.

There is a separate dining room with a total of 44 covers and the award-winning cuisine is served throughout the day, seven days a week. The varied menu features imaginative dishes, all prepared to order, and fresh, locally-caught fish is a speciality. In addition to the restaurant menu, there is also a full bar menu and daily specials board. The managers organise a regular programme of themed nights, such as the popular 'Sizzling Steak Bonanza' and special menus for events such as Valentine's Day and Mother's Day.

Pub with food.	This is a popular hostelry, both with the locals and visitors to
Fine riverside pub, award-winning food.	the town, and is a delightful spot in summer in which to enjoy a drink and watch the comings and goings in the harbour. Well worth a detour.
Credit Cards: All the major cards	**Local Golf Courses:** Dartmouth G&CC, Thurlestone, Churston

HOLE MILL 267

Branscombe, Seaton, Devon EX12 3BX
Tel: 01297 680314
website: www.users.globalnet.co.uk/~branscombe/hole1.htm

Hole Mill was once a working watermill, located in a pretty valley just outside the village centre, which used to grind corn until the early part of the 20th century. The mill building and adjoining cottage have since been converted into a most charming house, on many levels, with an abundance of exposed wooden beams throughout. Here you will be able to find comfortable bed and breakfast accommodation with three guest rooms available.

Bed and Breakfast	
Charming former mill with colourful gardens.	
Credit Cards: None	**Local Golf Courses:** Axe Cliff, Woodbury Park, Sidmouth, Honiton

GORWELL FARM COTTAGES 301

Abbotsbury, Weymouth, Dorset DT3 4JX
Tel: 01305 871401 Fax: 01305 871441
e-mail: mary@gorwellfarm.co.uk website: www.gorwellfarm.co.uk

Gorwell Farm is located about 2 miles to the north of Abbotsbury in beautiful chalk downlands only a few miles from Came Down Golf Course and the historic town of Dorchester. The self-catered accommodation offers 8 double or twin rooms (each with ensuite or private bathroom) contained in 4 attractively refurbished cottages, all with living room, well-equipped kitchen, laundry facilities, central heating, television and ample parking. Special prices are available for golfers between October and April. English Tourism Council 5 star award.

Self Catering Holiday Cottages	
4 self-catering cottages with 8 double or twin rooms (each with en suite) in rural setting	
Credit Cards: All the major cards	**Local Golf Courses:** Weymouth, Bridport & West Dorset, Came Down

DEVON

DORSET

THE ANGLEBURY HOUSE AND RESTAURANT 302

15/17 North Street, Wareham, Dorset BH20 4AB
Tel: 01929 552988 Fax: 01929 554665
e-mail: anglebury@btconnect.com

Located on the main road through Wareham, visitors will find a warm welcome at the charming **Anglebury House** which offers guest house accommodation, a coffee shop and restaurant. This is one of the few houses within the walled town of Wareham to survive the great fire of 1762 and the ambience and decor is in keeping with its age. The accommodation comprises seven letting rooms, all but one with en-suite facilities, each comfortably furnished. The traditional coffee shop is open during the day serving hot drinks, cakes and light snacks. In the Tudor-style restaurant there is a choice of a la carte or fixed price menus with a wide variety of dishes to appeal to all tastes.

Hotel, Coffee Shop, Restaurant

Cosy guest house with long-established coffee shop

Credit Cards: All the major cards.

Local Golf Courses: Wareham, Bournemouth, Ferndown Forest

BOURNE DENE HOTEL 303

12 Manor Road, Bournemouth, Dorset BH1 3HU
Tel: 01202 553127
e-mail: enquiries@bournedene.co.uk
website: www. bournedene.co.uk

Bourne Dene is a deceptively large country house hotel, conveniently located just a little way from the sea front, and enjoying a delightful setting surrounded by landscaped gardens. Family-owned, this twenty-one bedroomed hotel enjoys a fine reputation for comfort and excellent cuisine. In the evenings guests can make use of the licensed bar and private restaurant where the menus offer genuine home-style cooking.

Hotel

Within short walk of beach. 21 rooms.

Credit Cards: Mastercard, Visa

Local Golf Courses: Parkstone, Bournemouth, Queens Park

THE GREYHOUND 304

North Street, Winterbourne Kingston, Blandford Forum, Dorset DT11 9AZ
Tel: 01929 471332 Fax: 01929 427610
website: www.greyhoundinnwk.co.uk

The village of Winterbourne Kingston can be found just to the Southwest of Blandford Forum, between the A354 and A31 roads. Located on the main street, **The Greyhound** is a traditional, country inn with a spacious, comfortable interior. Inside is it quite open with plenty of seating available, in both the bar and restaurant area, at small wooden tables and chairs. A traditional style has been retained with the use of exposed brickwork and wooden timbers, with a most attractive wooden bar as a main feature. A warm, welcoming atmosphere is immediately apparent, complemented by friendly service from the helpful staff.

This is a popular watering hole for locals, with many regular customers being drawn from the surrounding towns. They come for the real ales, of which there is usually a small selection, and the tasty home-cooked food. The menu is extensive, with a wideranging selection of meals and snacks, and there is a carvery served each evening as well. In addition to the restaurant, there is also a popular skittle alley which double as a function room and is made available for private hire. Outside there is a good-sized beer garden, with pretty fish pond, and children's play area.

Comfortable bed and breakfast accommodation is offered with four comfortable, en-suite rooms, two doubles and two twins. Each is provided with colour TV and hot drinks tray and meals can be taken in the pub restaurant. This would be an ideal overnight stop and would also be a good base for a few days exploring the area. Reasonable rates.

Pub with food, B&B

Good-sized pub with four guest rooms.

Credit Cards: All the major cards

Local Golf Courses: East Dorset, The Bulbury Club, Ashley Wood

DORSET

KENT HOUSE HOTEL 305

Silver Street, Lyme Regis, Dorset DT7 3HT
Tel: 01297 443442 Fax: 01297 444626
e-mail: thekenthouse@talk21.com

Kent House was taken over by the present owners in 1999 and the large Victorian property has since undergone an extensive programme of renovation and refurbishment both inside and out to provide bright, airy and well-appointed accommodation. There are nine rooms in all, of varying sizes, and most are en-suite. Each has T.V. and tea/coffee making facilities. The restaurant, which overlooks the gardens and Lyme Valley, is open to non-residents for evening meals and Sunday lunches. Parking available

Hotel and Restaurant

Recently refurbished with nine rooms. AA 3 diamonds

Credit Cards: All the major cards. | **Local Golf Courses:** Lyme Regis, Axe Cliff, Bridport & West Dorset

COVERDALE GUEST HOUSE 306

Woodmead Road, Lyme Regis, Dorset DT7 3AB
Tel: 01297 442882 Fax: 01297 444673
e-mail: coverdale@tinyworld.co.uk

Coverdale offers spacious non-smoking accommodation in the heart of an area renowned for its beauty. The house enjoys spectacular views to the coast and overlooks woodland trust land which adjoins the rear of the property. The house is warm and welcoming with eight comfortable bedrooms and an attractive dining room which overlooking the pretty cottage garden. The centre of the town of Lyme Regis, pubs and restaurants and sea front are just a few minutes walk.

Guest House

Friendly, welcoming guest house, good home cooking

Credit Cards: None. | **Local Golf Courses:** Lyme Regis, Bridport & West Dorset, Axe Cliff

EASTBURY HOTEL 307

Long Street, Sherborne, Dorset DT9 3BY
Tel: 01935 813131 Fax: 01935 817296
e-mail: eastbury.sherborne@virgin.net

A prominent landmark in the quiet, lower part of Old Sherborne is the imposing **Eastbury Hotel and Restaurant**. Built in the Georgian period as a private Gentleman's residence it has, in more recent years, been lovingly converted into an elegant ho-

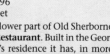

tel making full use of the light, spacious rooms and enhancing the many original architectural features. The grounds are a peaceful haven in a busy world and are a delightful setting in which to enjoy dinner on a summer's evening. If you have the chance to explore the walled gardens that surround the property you can almost imagine yourself transported back in time...

Inside, the calm, tranquil atmosphere continues through the many public rooms with comfortable lounges and a cosy bar available to guests. Here you can enjoy an afternoon cup of tea, or perhaps an aperitif before dinner. The award-winning Conservatory Restaurant has a reputation that extends far beyond the borders of Dorset, with the resident chefs having been awarded a coveted AA Rosette. The style of the cuisine is mainly English, with an excellent selection of imaginative and interesting dishes available at every course. Using the freshest local ingredients with the seafood dishes in particular receiving much acclaim. To accompany your meal there is an admirable selection of wines available from the extensive cellar. The 15 private guest

Hotel and Restaurant

Elegant, Georgian hotel with fine restaurant.

bedrooms, all named after traditional English flowers, have been individually decorated and furnished and all feature en-suite facilities. Each room is also provided with remote control colour TV, hot drinks tray, direct dial telephone and luxury bathrobes.

Credit Cards: All the major cards. | **Local Golf Courses:** Sherborne, Yeovil, Lyme Regis, Isle of Purbeck

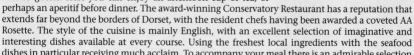

DORSET

THE CHETNOLE INN — 308

Chetnole, Nr. Sherborne, Dorset DT9 6NU
Tel: 01935 872337

This is a popular local's inn, well-liked for the top-quality real ales, fine food and fabulous atmosphere. Several small breweries are represented behind the bar, while the menus offer an outstanding selection ranging from snacks to gourmet dinners. Converted from 19th-century cottages, inside you will find a cosy, music-free, lounge bar, spacious restaurant and a warm, friendly public bar complete with darts, pool and shove ha'penny. Also a favourite stopping place for walker, cyclists and tourists - and it's easy to see why.

Pub with food
Friendly, well-liked hostelry

Credit Cards: All the major cards

Local Golf Courses: Sherborne, Halstock, Yeovil

CHIDEOCK HOUSE HOTEL — 309

Main Street, Chideock, Dorset DT6 6JN
Tel: 01297 489242 Fax: 01297 489184
website: www.chideockhousehotel.com

Chideock House has the honour of being the oldest property in a village of pretty thatched, sandstone cottages and many of its unique features have been preserved throughout, while sensitive conversions within this fabulous hotel and restaurant provide every modern comfort. There are nine, individual en-suite rooms all doubles, with some superior rooms available. The restaurant, open to non-residents Tuesday to Saturday, serves an unpretentious variety of mainly English and French dishes.

Hotel and Restaurant
Casually elegant hotel and restaurant.

Credit Cards: All the major cards.

Local Golf Courses: Bridport & W Devon, Lyme Regis, Chedington Court

THE SHEAF OF ARROWS — 310

4 The Square, Cranborne, Dorset BH21 5PR
Tel: 01725 517456

Located in the heart of the pretty village of Cranborne, is a traditional village hostelry, **The Sheaf of Arrows**. Popular with locals and visitors to the area, here you will find a warm welcome together with efficient, friendly service. There is always a choice of real ales on tap while a good selection of sensibly priced meals and snacks are served each lunch time and evening. Bed and breakfast accommodation comprises five en-suite rooms. The excellent Rushmore Park Golf Club at Tollard Royal, Wiltshire is within a few miles.

Pub with food, B&B
Popular hostelry with five guest rooms.

Credit Cards: All the major cards.

Local Golf Courses: Crane Valley, Dudsbury, Moors Valley

THE BEACH HOUSE — 311

Brunswick Terrace, Weymouth, Dorset DT4 7RW
Tel: 01305 789353

Just ten metres from the sea front, **The Beach House** enjoys a prime location at one end of Weymouth's esplanade. The whole of the Beach House is comfortable and cosy, a real home from home, and many of the bedrooms enjoy full en-suite facilities. The fabulous site means that there are some superb views over the sea front. Full English breakfasts are served each morning, there is a licensed bar and a variety of eating places are within a short walk.

Bed and Breakfast
Prime, sea front location

Credit Cards: All the major cards

Local Golf Courses: Weymouth, East Dorset, Came Down

DORSET

Holiday Park.

Selection of 45 caravans and 19 chalets

Credit Cards: All the major cards

COBBS HOLIDAY PARK 312

32 Gordon Road, Highcliffe on Sea,
Christchurch, Dorset BH23 5HN
Tel: 01425 273301/275313 Fax: 01425 276090

Cobbs is a long established family-run holiday park enjoying a fine location between Bournemouth and the New Forest. The accommodation ranges from a four berth chalet to a selection of six berth chalets and caravans, all distributed across an attractive site. For the entertainment of residents there is a fully licensed social club while additional facilities include a shop, laundrette and children's play area. All caravans are fitted with a toilet, shower, fridge and colour TV. Ideal for a family holiday.

Local Golf Courses: Highcliffe Castle, Queens Park, Bournemouth

Restaurant

Superb menu specialising in fresh seafood

Credit Cards: All the major cards

SWANSON'S RESTAURANT 313

Lakeside Walk, Weymouth, Dorset DT4 7AW
Tel: 01305 776740 Fax: 01305 776740

Not far from the centre of Weymouth, located on the edge of a small lake with swans, is the unusual **Swanson's Restaurant**. Built over the water, with a structure reminiscent of a boat, there is a open, conservatory feel about the restaurant. The decor is superb, with elegant tables and chairs for dining, and comfortable loungers and sofas for enjoying a pre-dinner drink. The menu is of a very high standard, with freshly prepared, delicious dishes to suit all tastes. The speciality is seafood, especially scallops, which are served when available.

Local Golf Courses: Weymouth, Came Down, East Dorset

Hotel and Restaurant

Stylish accommodation and elegant dining

Credit Cards: All the major cards

BELVEDERE HOTEL 314

14 Bath Road, Bournemouth, Dorset BH1 2EU
Tel: 01202 293336 e-mail: enquiries @belvedere-hotel.co.uk
Fax: 01202 294699 website: www.belvedere-hotel.co.uk

The Belvedere Hotel is ideally located close to the town centre yet within reach of the beach and other amenities. Described as one of the finest of Bournemouth's three star hotels here you will find comfortable, stylish accommodation with a total of 60 en-suite rooms of varying sizes. The Belvedere Restaurant provides elegant dining with a superb a la carte menu of international cuisine freshly prepared to order. There are two bars, one featuring regular musical entertainment, and both offer more casual dining.

Local Golf Courses: Bournemouth, Queen's Park, Isle of Purbeck

Bed & Breakfast

Newly converted property, three guest rooms and 2 self catering cottages

Credit Cards: None

QUIET WOMAN HOUSE 315

Halstock, Dorset BA22 9RX
Tel: 01935 891218
e-mail: quietwomanhouse@ukonline.co.uk

This unusually-named establishment is a delightful bed and breakfast run by husband and wife team, Paul and Gill Tebano. Dating back to the 1700s the property was formerly a pub and has been converted into high quality accommodation while retaining many features of the original building. Here visitors will find three guest rooms, a twin, a double and a family-sized room, all en-suite, and there are also two self-catering cottages available. Evening meals on request. Taxi service to and from local hostelries is available by arrangement. E.T.C. applied for.

Local Golf Courses: Halstock, Yeovil, Sherborne, Bridport & W Dorset

SUNNYDENE HOTEL 316

11 Spencer Road, Bournemouth, Dorset BH1 3TE
Tel: 01202 552281

Located close to the heart of Bournemouth is the **Sunnydene Hotel**, a good-sized, family-run establishment offering comfortable bed and breakfast accommodation. The spacious, Victorian building has recently been refurbished and redecorated throughout and the large guest rooms have been attractively furnished retaining a light and airy feel. Most of the ten rooms have en-suite facilities and are also provided with a colour TV and hot drinks tray. Evening meals available on request.

Bed and Breakfast
Comfortable accommodation, 10 guest rooms

Credit Cards: None

Local Golf Courses: Queens Park, Bournemouth, Knighton Heath

PEAR TREE COTTAGE 317

248 Wimborne Road West, Stapehill,
Wimborne, Dorset BH21 2DZ
Tel: 01202 890174

Pear Tree Cottage really is one of those exceptionally pretty Dorset cottages that should feature on postcards or chocolate boxes! It would be a real treat to be able to stay here, in the home of Caroline Whiteman, where she offers comfortable bed and breakfast accommodation in three cosy rooms. None of the rooms enjoy full en-suite facilities which is reflected in the very reasonable room rate. The property is furnished throughout in a traditional style, reflecting the character of the building, and guests are free to enjoy the fine gardens which surround the cottage.

Bed and breakfast
Pretty, picture postcard cottage with three rooms

Credit Cards: None

Local Golf Courses: Ferndown, Ferndown Forest, Dudsbury

THE MOUNT 318

49 Blandford Road, Corfe Mullen,
Wimbourne, Dorset BH21 3HD
Tel: 01202 693908

You could easily drive past **The Mount** and think it was a rather un-inspiring looking place, though we would strongly recommend making a stop here and venturing inside as we think you will be pleasantly surprised. The atmosphere is relaxed and comfortable and this pub is popular for the fine ales that are served together with a selection of tasty meals and snacks. There is karaoke every Thursday together with regular live music and pub quizzes. In summer the large rear gardens can be enjoyed to the full.

Pub with food
Popular pub with excellent ales

Credit Cards: None

Local Golf Courses: The Bulbury Club, Parkstone, Wareham

HIGH TOR 319

Worgret Hill, Wareham, Dorset BH20 6AD
Tel: 01929 556869 Fax: 01929 555068
e-mail: jeannie@innerpower.freeserve.co.uk

High Tor is a most unusual house, set in acres of rambling lawns and woodland just two miles from Wareham. Here you will find an holistic health centre which calls itself 'a new concept in complementary medicine'. It incorporates a number of major therapies, sixteen in total, into one all-encompassing system which treats the whole person. Further details can be found in the highly informative leaflet which is available on request. The couple that run the centre also offer bed and breakfast accommodation with one room which can sleep up to four.

Holistic Health Clinic, B&B
A new concept in complementary medicine

Credit Cards: All the major cards

Local Golf Courses: Wareham, East Dorset, Isle of Purbeck

Bed and Breakfast

Charming conversion of former granary

Credit Cards: None

THE OLD GRANARY 320

West Holme Farm, Wareham, Dorset BH20 6AQ
Tel: 01929 552972 Fax: 01929 551616

The Old Granary is a modern conversion of a former farm building in which much of the rustic character and traditional charm has been retained. The result is the delightful home of Venn Goldsack and here she offers comfortable bed and breakfast accommodation in two twin-bedded, en-suite rooms. Both rooms have direct access and the downstairs room is equipped for category 3 disabled visitors. Ample, freshly cooked breakfasts are served each morning and a two-course evening meal is available by prior arrangement. Also a farm shop and plant nursery.

Local Golf Courses: Wareham, East Dorset, Isle of Purbeck

Pub with food.

Town centre pub offering selection of drinks, Bar meals and snacks.

Credit cards: All the major cards.

THE WHITE HART INN 401

51-52 East Reach, Taunton, Somerset TA1 3EZ
Tel: 01823 254652

Enjoying a central location, **The White Hart Inn** is conveniently located close to all the facilities that town of Taunton has to offer. Popular with locals and visitors to the area, the inn has recently been refurbished offering new and improved customer facilities throughout. Here you can enjoy a refreshing drink from the fine selection stocked behind the bar, with soft drinks, tea and real coffee also served throughout the day. Home-cooked food is available with a menu offering a good selection of meals and snacks to suit all appetites. Live music Fridays and regular quiz nights. Children welcome.

Local Golf Courses: Taunton Vale, Taunton & Pickeridge, Vivary

Bed & Breakfast, Self-Catering

Three guest rooms and self-catering bungalow.

Credit Cards: None

BANANA COTTAGE 402

Greenway, North Curry, Taunton, Somerset TA3 6NJ
Tel: 01823 490100 e-mail: jpaterson@bananacottage.co.uk
website: www.bananacottage.co.uk

Banana Cottage is a delightful country bed and breakfast establishment, conveniently located just a few miles east of Taunton between the A361 and the A378. The 300-year old, stone-built cottage stands in one acre of grounds and is surrounded by mature lawns and colourful gardens. There are three guest bedrooms of varying sizes, of which one is en-suite, together with a self-catering bungalow. Full English breakfasts are served each morning. Midweek and golfing breaks available. Residents can enjoy reduced green fees at local courses.

Local Golf Courses: Taunton Vale, Taunton & Pickeridge, Vivary

Restaurant

Charming, traditional building housing popular restaurant.

Credit Cards: Visa, Mastercard.

THATCHERS POND RESTAURANT 403

Donyatt, Ilminster, Somerset TA19 0RG
Tel: 01460 53210

Thatchers Pond Restaurant is a delightful, thatched building constructed of local Hamstone, and thought to date back, in part, to 1480. For many years it has been one of the main restaurants in Somerset, and is renowned for its home-produced fare. It serves a full range of traditional meals from a menu offering something to suit all tastes and appetites, with daily specials also available. The proprietors, Linda and Pete Williams, are keen golfers.

Local Golf Courses: Windwhistle, Taunton Vale, Taunton & Pickeridge

DORSET

SOMERSET

TURNPIKE COTTAGE 404

Turnpike, Milverton, Somerset TA4 1LF
Tel: 01823 400492

This cottage is thought to be well over 100 years old and was probably originally built to house servants from the 'grand' houses in Milverton. It has in recent years been carefully converted to provide self-contained accommodation sleeping up to five adults. The property extends to three floors with a steep staircase making it unsuitable for young children or less agile guests. Very well equipped, there is even a washing machine. The owner lives next door, so you can be assured of a friendly welcome.

Holiday Cottage
Cosy cottage, pets welcome, rural location.

Credit Cards: None.

Local Golf Courses: Oake Manor, Vivary, Taunton Vale

PROMENADE HOTEL 405

Esplanade, Minehead, Somerset TA24 5QS
Tel: 01643 702572 Fax: 01643 702572
The Promenade Hotel is positioned close to the centre of the Minehead and enjoys an unrivalled location overlooking the harbour. The restaurant serves superb breakfasts, delicious dinners and wicked cream teas with plenty of choice of freshly-prepared options. The 11 en-suite bedrooms all feature wheel-in shower and are linked to an emergency call system. Visitors will also find the usual comforts of a colour TV and hot drinks tray. A 12-seater minibus is available for excursions. The Promenade Hotel is part of Grooms Holidays, registered charity no. 212463.

Hotel
Elegant hotel, fully wheelchair accessible

Credit Cards: All the major cards.

Local Golf Courses: Minehead, Enmore Park, Oake Manor

NORTHOVER MANOR HOTEL 406

Northover, Ilchester, Somerset BA22 8LD
Tel: 01935 840447 Fax: 01935 840006
e-mail: melhaddigan@compuserve.com
Northover Manor Hotel and Restaurant is housed within a rambling 15th-century house and offers comfortable, stylish accommodation in 13 en-suite guest rooms. The restaurant serves a full a la carte menu while there is also the Village Bar which serves a more informal menu of snacks and bar meals. Both are open to non-residents. To the rear there is large garden which stretches down to the River Yeo and this is popular for 'al fresco' drinking and dining when the sun shines. Also an outdoor children's play area.

Hotel, Restaurant, Bar
High quality, friendly establishment

Credit Cards: All the major cards.

Local Golf Courses: Yeovil, Sherbourne, Long Sutton

CASTLEBROOK HOLIDAY COTTAGES 407

Castlebrook, Compton Dundon,
Somerton, Somerset TA11 6PR
Tel: 01458 841680 Fax: 01458 441680
Set amid extensive enclosed gardens, **Castlebrook Holiday Cottages** are two fully equipped self-catering homes located in the heart of the Polden Hills. Recently refurbished, each of the two cottages has a well-appointed kitchenette, cosy sitting/dining room, shower room/WC and a wooden staircase built of reclaimed timber. Upstairs Pool Hay has a double, a twin and a single bedroom while Press Bars has a double and a single. Pets welcome by arrangement.

Holiday Cottages.
Two pretty cottages, varying sizes.

Credit Cards: None

Local Golf Courses: Wheathill, Long Sutton, Wells, Yeovil

BELLA VISTA HOTEL 408

Hotel

Family-run hotel with warm, friendly feel

Credit Cards: All the major cards

19 Upper Church Road, Weston-super-Mare, Somerset BS23 2DX
Tel: 01934 631931 Fax: 01934 620126

This family-run hotel, located just 100 metres from the sea front, offers a friendly welcome with high standards of service. The eight spacious bedrooms are comfortable and tastefully furnished, with all having en-suite or private facilities, TV and hot drinks tray. A full English breakfast is served each morning with packed lunches available on request.

Local Golf Courses: Worlebury, Weston-super-Mare, Burnham & Berrow

ROSE AND CROWN 409

Pub with food, B&B

Cosy, olde worlde inn

Credit Cards: All the major cards.

St. Mary Street, Nether Stowey, Somerset TA5 1LJ
Tel: 01278 732265

The Rose and Crown is old coaching inn dating back to the 15th century and retains a great deal of olde worlde charm. The cosy interior is furnished with wooden tables and chairs and decorated with copper and brasses. There is a separate restaurant and lounge area and discreet music is played throughout. The bar stocks a good range of liquid refreshment while the menu offers an excellent selection of meals and snacks to suit all. Comfortable en-suite accommodation with rooms of varying sizes.

Local Golf Courses: Enmore Park, Oake Manor, Minehead & W. Somerset

BLACKMORE FARM 410

Farmhouse B&B

Historic house on working farm

CreditCards:Visa,Delta,Mastercard

Cannington, Bridgwater, Somerset TA5 2NE
Tel: 01278 653442 Fax: 01278 653427

Blackmore Farm has a long history stretching back to the 14th century when it was built by the local Tremayle family. The present structure retains many of the original features including stone archways, garderobes and oak beams. Still a working farm, the present owners now offer comfortable farmhouse bed and breakfast with four, spacious en-suite rooms available. The Stable, is on the ground floor and has full disabled facilities. Breakfast is served in the Great Hall around a 16 foot long carved oak table.

Local Golf Courses: Enmore Park, Oake Manor, Taunton & Pickeridge

THE KINGS HEAD INN 411

Pub with food, B&B

Former coaching inn, good food

Credit Cards: All the major cards.

12 High Street, Cannington, Bridgwater, Somerset TA5 2HE
Tel: 01278 652293 Fax: 01278 652293

The Kings Head Inn is a 17th-century, former coaching inn, situated in the foothills of the picturesque Quantock Hills, in the centre of the village of Cannington. The interior is in Tudor style and the restaurant is dated 1642. The food is of a high standard and reasonably priced offering a daily lunchtime menu with a carvery and a full a-la-carte where the char-grilled steaks are the speciality.Comfortable en-suite bed and breakfast accommodation is available and there is a beer garden with skittle alley and a function room to suit 75 people. Awarded 'Inn of the Year 1999' with Les Routiers for outstanding quality, value and hospitality.

Local Golf Courses: Enmore Park, Oake Manor, Taunton & Pickeridge

SOMERSET

THE GREYHOUND INN 412

1 Lime Street, Stogursey, Bridgwater, Somerset TA5 1QR
Tel: 01278 732490

The Greyhound Inn is a traditional rural inn located in the heart of the village of Stogursey. Visitors will find a main bar with an open fire, a lounge bar furnished with comfortable easy chairs and a separate dining area, while outside there is a beer garden. The bar stocks a range of local real ales, cider, wine and spirits with hot drinks served throughout the day. A good selection of home-cooked food is available and offers terrific value for money. Bed and breakfast accommodation.

Pub with food, B&B

Traditional inn, good food and ales

Credit Cards: None.

Local Golf Courses: Enmore Park, Burnham and Berrow, Brean

THE SUN INN 413

6 Catherine Street, Frome, Somerset BA11 1DA
Tel: 01373 471913

A 16th-century, town centre inn, and a fine example of a traditional public house, **The Sun Inn** is popular with a wide variety of clientele ranging from local residents to business men. A cosy, friendly atmosphere pervades and the uncluttered interior retains a great deal of character. The bar stocks a good selection of liquid refreshment while the food menu offers a range of snacks and light meals. Bed and breakfast accommodation with seven guest rooms.

Pub

Traditional, town centre pub

Credit Cards: All the major cards

Local Golf Courses: Orchardleigh, Frome Golf Centre, The Mendip

EXECUTIVE HOLIDAYS 414

Whitemill Farm, Iron Mills Lane, Oldford, Frome,
Somerset BA11 2NR Tel: 01373 452907 Fax: 01373 453253
e-mail: info@executiveholidays.co.uk
website: www.executiveholidays.co.uk

Executive Cottages comprises ten different properties, of varying sizes, all located within a valley of outstanding natural beauty alongside the River Frome. The two largest properties are detached homes, set in their own gardens, while the eight Oldford Farm cottages have been converted from former farm buildings. All are furnished to the highest standards. Overall the properties range from sleeping four to twelve adults. Additional facilities available to guests include river fishing within the grounds.

Holiday Cottages

Varied properties located in pretty valley

Credit Cards: All the major cards.

Local Golf Courses: Orchardleigh, Frome Golf Centre, The Mendip

LA BISALTA 415

6 Vicarage Street, Frome, Somerset BA11 1PX
Tel: 01373 464238 Fax: 01373 304603
e-mail: luigi@labisalta.fsnet.co.uk

A genuine Italian restaurant situated in the heart of the quaint town of Frome. **La Bisalta** is easily identified by the covered canvas entrance and ivy clad upper storey. The interior is equally delightful with the tables being presented with linen tablecloths and crystal ware. To the rear there is a open veranda and garden area which is very popular on summer evenings. The cuisine is classic Italian in style with a wide range of delicious dishes on the menu, all prepared with the freshest of local ingredients. The restaurant is well-established with the owner, Luigi, having earned a far-reaching reputation for friendly service.

Restaurant

Genuine Italian restaurant

Credit Cards: All the major cards.

Local Golf Courses: Frome, Orchardleigh, Lansdown

SOMERSET

Hotel and Restaurant

Palladian mansion surrounded by landscaped grounds

Credit Cards: All the major cards.

STON EASTON PARK `416`

Ston Easton, Nr. Bath, Somerset BA3 4DF
Tel: 01761 241631 Fax: 01761 241377
e-mail: enquiry@stoneaston.co.uk website: www.stoneaston.co.uk
Ston Easton Park is a grand English country house surrounded by extensive grounds. Guests are welcome to explore the gardens and a leaflet describing the highlights is available from reception. Many of the state rooms are open to residents and the 24 bedrooms have been individually designed in the 18th-century style with many featuring four poster beds and antique furniture. There are three dining rooms, offering a choice of formal or casual dining, with award-winning cuisine being served throughout. Leisure facilities available to guests include hot air ballooning, shooting, fishing, tennis and much more.

Local Golf Courses: Farrington, Wells, Bath

Hotel and Restaurant

High quality hotel in central location

Credit Cards: All the major cards

THE WHITE HART HOTEL `417`

19-21 Sadler Street, Wells, Somerset BA5 2RR
Tel: 01749 672056 e-mail: info@whitehart-wells.co.uk
Fax: 01749 671074 website: www.whitehart-wells.co.uk
The delightful, black and white timbered **White Hart Hotel** can be found on the main street in the centre of Wells opposite the famous Cathedral. The thirteen bedrooms are all luxuriously furnished and provided with the usual extras including hot drinks tray, direct dial telephone and modem socket. The newly refurbished restaurant offers relaxed dining with a menu of traditional English cuisine. Just over the road is a more formal Italian restaurant under the same management. A function suite is available for conferences or private parties of up to 70.

Local Golf Courses: Wells, Farrington, Mendip Spring, Isle of Wedmore

Holiday Cottage

Good sized cottage in lovely location

Credit Cards: None

'RIVERSIDE' `418`

Goosebradon Farm, Westport, Nr. Langport, Somerset TA10 0BH
Tel: 01823 680447 Fax: 01823 681008
e-mail: cking@dunnsgreen.fsnet.co.uk
A delightful detached cottage refurbished and converted into a self-catering gem overlooking the rolling fields of this quiet corner of Somerset. Good size, sleeping up to six adults in three bedrooms, with a well equipped kitchen and comfortable furnishings throughout. Ideal base for golfers with good fishing also available nearby. The surrounding countryside offers some lovely walks and there is a super pub, The Old Barn Owl, just a short stroll away. Attractive rear garden and off-road parking.

Local Golf Courses: Long Sutton, Taunton & Pickeridge, Wheathill

Pub with food

Good sized pub to suit all ages

Credit Cards: All the major cards.

THE OLD BARN OWL `419`

Westport, Nr. Langport, Somerset TA10 0BH
Tel: 01460 281391 Fax: 01460 281995
Good-sized, family pub, once an 18th-century coaching inn, enjoying a good location in pretty village between Taunton and Yeovil. Recently refurbished throughout the interior is comfortable, welcoming and has a very relaxed atmosphere. The bar stocks a good range of house wines and the home brew, Barn Owl Ale, is recommended. The food is a popular draw with a good sized restaurant offering a wide-ranging menu of fresh meals and bar snacks. The shoulder of lamb is one of the specialities. Outdoor beer garden and children's play area.

Local Golf Courses: Taunton & Pickeridge, Wheathill, Yeovil

SOMERSET

Restaurant and Bar

Characterful surroundings

Credit Cards: All the major cards.

THE OLD FORGE INN   420

Church Street, Curry Rivel, Nr. Langport,
Somerset TA10 0HE
Tel: 01458 251554 Fax: 01458 252847

Housed within a Grade 2 listed building, **The Old Forge Inn** is an ideal place for a special occasion, a party or simply an evening meal for two. The excellent menu caters for all tastes and features a good range of fresh fish and vegetarian dishes. There is also a comprehensive wine list. The bar is open to the public and the adjoining 14th-century Cellar bar can be booked for private parties. Regular art exhibitions are hosted here. From April 2002 there will be five rooms for bed and breakfast.

Local Golf Courses: Taunton & Pickeridge, Wheathill, Yeovil

Bed and breakfast

Charming, historic property

Credit Cards: None

EAST LAMBROOK FARM   421

South Petherton, Somerset TA13 5HH
Tel: 01460 240064 Fax: 01460 240064
e-mail: nicolaeeles@supernet.com

This really is a delightful hidden gem, well worth seeking out. The pretty 17th-century house, built of local sandstone with a thatched roof, is set within two and a half acres of rolling gardens. Built in a traditional style the present property retains many original features and much of the historic character. There are just three comfortable guest rooms available for bed and breakfast, with two private bathrooms and evening meals are provided on request. Tennis court available to guests.

Local Golf Courses: Yeovil, Wheathill, Taunton & Pickeridge

Guest House

Non-smoking guest house, three rooms

Credit Cards: None.

AMBERLEY GUEST HOUSE   422

Martock Road, Long Load, Langport, Somerset TA10 9LD
Tel: 01458 241542
e-mail: jeanatamberley@talk21.com

Amberley is located within a rural farming community, literally mid-way between the north and south coasts of Somerset and Devon. An attractive farmhouse-style property there are some superb views over open countryside towards the Quantock Hills. The accommodation is made up of three comfortable rooms of varying sizes, with one having en-suite facilities. There is a cosy sitting room and large conservatory where meals are served. Evening meals available on request. E.T.C. grading 4 diamonds.

Local Golf Courses: Long Sutton, Yeovil, Wheathill

Pub with food

Friendly, cosy country pub

Credit Cards: All the major cards.

RUSTY AXE   423

Stembridge, Somerset
Tel: 01460 240109

Situated in the heart of one of Somerset's nicest villages is the rather unusually-named **Rusty Axe** public house. A cosy, thatched property dating back to the 1600s the pub is popular with locals and passing trade with the food being very much in demand. The wide ranging menu offers an excellent choice of steaks and other hot dishes together with lighter bar snacks. Live music on most Saturday evenings with other entertainment in the form of a skittle alley, dart board and pool table.

Local Golf Courses: Yeovil, Sherbourne, Wheathill

SOMERSET

ASH HOUSE COUNTRY HOTEL & RESTAURANT | 424

Hotel and Restaurant

High quality food and accommodation

Credit Cards: All the major cards.

Main Street, Ash, Nr. Martock, Somerset TA12 6PB
Tel: 01935 822036 Fax: 01935 822992
e-mail: reception@ashhousehotel.freeserve.co.uk
website: www.ashhousecountryhotel.co.uk

Ash House is a small, privately-owned Georgian Country house hotel set in over one acre of attractive gardens in the heart of rural Somerset. The a la carte restaurant is a popular draw for many visitors, and is open to non-residents. The high standard of cuisine is seasonally updated and holds a Heartbeat award for offering healthy dietary options. There are eight delightful en-suite rooms and guests can also enjoy the sunny lounge and conservatory for afternoon tea or a pre-dinner drink. E.T.C. 3 stars and a Silver award.

Local Golf Courses: Yeovil, Sherborne, Wheathill

THE MANOR LODGE | 425

Guest House

Seven en-suite guest rooms

Credit Cards: None

21 Station Road, Keynsham Road, Bristol BS31 2BH
Tel: 0117 986 2191
e-mail: jean@themanorlodge.freeserve.co.uk

The Manor House is an impressive Victorian town house dating from the 1860s. Privately owned, here you can enjoy comfortable bed and breakfast accommodation in one of seven en-suite rooms with one single, one twin, one family and four doubles. Each is provided with a colour TV and hot drinks tray and residents can also make use of the elegant lounge and pleasant dining room where breakfast is served.

Local Golf Courses: Stockwood Vale, Tall Pines, Saltford

THE WALNUT TREE | 426

Hotel, Restaurant & Inn

Cosy, candlelit restaurant serving superb food

Credit Cards: All the major cards

West Camel, Nr. Yeovil, Somerset BA22 7QW
Tel: 01935 851292 Fax: 01935 851292
website: www.thewalnuttreehotel.com

The Walnut Tree is a charming family-run hotel, restaurant and inn providing warm, friendly hospitality. The inn is open each day and many visitors come to enjoy the fine menu which offers a wide choice of imaginative dishes, prepared using fresh local ingredients, and been recognised with an Egon Ronay award for a number of years in succession. There are thirteen individually-styled, comfortable en-suite guest rooms with a four poster room available for a special stay.

Local Golf Courses: Yeovil, Sherborne, Wheathill

THE ROYAL OAK | 427

Pub with food

Well-liked pub in good position

Credit Cards: None

Stoford, Yeovil, Somerset BA22 9UD
Tel: 01935 475071

The Royal Oak is housed within a stylish, sandstone building, dating back to 1837, that is Grade 2 listed. The quiet village location is just a couple of miles from the centre of Yeovil, and very easily located. The traditional, compact interior is neat, clean and well decorated with a separate, 24-cover restaurant. The menu offers a good selection of traditional, wholesome fayre with all the dishes being reasonably priced. Well-liked by the locals, the Royal Oak is a popular pub and a fine example of friendly Somerset hospitality. Occasional quiz and theme nights.

Local Golf Courses: Yeovil, Sherborne, Wheathill

SOMERSET

THE ROYAL GEORGE 428

West Coker, Yeovil, Somerset BA22 9AN
Tel: 01935 862334 Fax: 01935 864499

The Royal George is a long-established hostelry, dating back to the early 1700s, and the interior retains some original features, including a stone slab floor and exposed oak beams, helping to create a welcoming atmosphere. Open daily, food is served each lunch time and evening with a menu offering a good selection of dishes to suit all. Occasional live music is arranged and a quiz night is held each Thursday. Bed and breakfast accommodation is available with two, en-suite guest rooms.

Pub with food, B&B

18th-century, traditional inn. Two guest rooms

Credit Cards: All the major cards

Local Golf Courses: Yeovil, Sherborne, Wheathill

THE PORTMAN ARMS 429

High Street, East Chinnock, Yeovil, Somerset BA22 9DP
Tel: 01935 862227 Fax: 01935 862227

Dominating the small village of East Chinnock, just a couple of miles from Yeovil, is the former ale house of **The Portland Arms**. The imposing building dates from the early 1800s and provides a spacious eating and drinking area with separate bar and restaurant. Food is available from a sensible menu offering a varied selection of meat, poultry, fish and vegetarian dishes, supplemented by daily specials. Bed and breakfast accommodation is offered in five, newly-refurbished, en-suite guest rooms. Overnight caravan pitches also available.

Pub with food, B&B

Impressive building housing friendly inn

Credit Cards: All the major cards

Local Golf Courses: Yeovil, Sherborne, Wheathill

WESTON HOUSE COTTAGES (ETC 4 STARS) 430

East Chinnock, Nr. Yeovil, Somerset BA22 9EL
Tel: 01935 863712/ 863394 Mobile: 07884 214768
e-mail: westonhouseuk@netscapeonline.co.uk

Weston House Farm is located just outside the village of East Chinnock and here you will find two cottages which have been attractively converted from stone-built, former barns. Both cottages are of an exceptional quality, with the accommodation being of a very high standard and furnished in a cosy, country style with attractive personal touches. The Byre offers a twin room plus double sofa bed while The Dairy can sleep up to five in three bedrooms. Well-behaved dogs welcome by prior arrangement.

Holiday Cottages

High quality, well-equipped accommodation

Credit Cards: None

Local Golf Courses: Yeovil, Sherborne, Wheathill, Chedington

RICHMOND HOUSE HOLIDAY ACCOMMODATION 431

Barrow Farm, North Barrow, Yeovil, Somerset BA22 7LZ
Tel: 01963 240543 e-mail: rhholidays@netscapeonline.co.uk
Fax: 01963 240543 website: www.rhholidays.co.uk

Richmond House Holiday Accommodation comprises eight cottages situated on two sites located just 50 metres apart and surrounded by 600 acres of grazing land. Richmond House is a former Victorian rectory which has been cleverly converted into three self-contained units, two sleeping up to seven and the third sleeping up to three. The two larger units can also be let together. A short distance away is Barrow Farm, the home of the owner, and here there are a further five cottages sleeping between four and eight. All the properties are well-maintained and well equipped.

Holiday Cottages

Well equipped properties of varying sizes

Credit Cards: None

Local Golf Courses: Yeovil, Sherborne, Wheathill

THE YEW TREE INN | 432

Forest Hill, Yeovil, Somerset BA20 2PG
Tel: 01935 476808 Fax: 01935 476808

The Yew Tree Inn is housed within a former gentleman's residence built in the early-19th century and only converted into a pub 30 years ago. The impressive structure is enhanced by its elevated site, though inside you will find a cosy, friendly atmosphere that is typical of the best Somerset inns. Here visitors can enjoy excellent fayre, with the menu offering a range of freshly-prepared, traditional English pub food with great value lunch specials and a more extensive evening selection. Regular Sunday quiz. Bed and breakfast accommodation available in four guest rooms of varying sizes.

Pub with food, B&B

Popular pub with friendly atmosphere

Credit Cards: None

Local Golf Courses: Yeovil, Sherborne, Wheathill

THE LAMB AND LARK | 433

Limington, Nr. Yeovil, Somerset
Tel: 01935 840368
e-mail: thelambandlark@cs.com

The Lamb and Lark is housed within a charming 15th-century building that at one time was a cottage and stables and has in recent years been carefully restored to create an appealing, characterful hostelry. Here you can enjoy a refreshing drink from the selection behind the bar, with up to four real ales kept on tap, and this can be enjoyed in the piano bar, lounge or the beer garden in fine weather. Food is served from a traditional menu of classic dishes, with fresh, locally-sourced meat used widely.

Pub with food

Pretty, cosy inn serving good food

Credit Cards: All the major cards

Local Golf Courses: Yeovil, Sherborne, Wheathill

THE ILCHESTER ARMS | 434

The Square, Ilchester, Nr. Yeovil, Somerset BA22 8LN
Tel: 01935 840220 Fax: 01935 841353

In the heart of this historic town you will readily locate **The Ilchester Arms Hotel and Country Restaurant**, which dominates the main street. This impressive Georgian building offers comfortable en-suite accommodation in characterful surroundings with many original features having been preserved both inside and out. The restaurant serves freshly-prepared local produce with a menu offering traditional English, modern European dishes and Caribbean dishes, all complemented by an extensive wine list. Ideal for those looking for a small, discreet, high quality establishment.

Hotel and Restaurant

High quality restaurant, comfortable accommodation

Credit Cards: All the major cards

Local Golf Courses: Wheathill, Yeovil, Sherborne

THE ROYAL MARINE | 435

St. Weston Terrace, Yeovil, Somerset BA21 5AA
Tel: 01935 474350 Fax: 01935 474350

The Royal Marine is a popular inn, located just a short walk from the centre of Yeovil, and set back behind a row of fashionable Victorian houses. The corner site dates back to 1896 and the pub retains a traditional feel while being well-maintained and neatly kept. Inside there is a public bar and lounge/dining room where food can be enjoyed from a sensibly priced menu of meals and snacks. Limited accommodation is available.

Pub with food

Friendly, town centre pub

Credit Cards: None

Local Golf Courses: Yeovil, Sherborne, Wheathill

SOMERSET

SOMERSET

THE BIRD IN HAND 437

Mount Street, Bishops Lydeard, Taunton, Somerset TA4 3LH
Tel: 01823 432090

Located in the quiet village of Bishops Lydeard, between Taunton and Minehead, **The Bird in Hand** public house dates back to the early 18th century. The pretty frontage is freshly painted and decorated in the summer months with colourful hanging baskets. Inside you will find a good-sized lounge with plenty of little nooks and crannies in which to enjoy a quiet drink. The menu offers a selection of basket meals, curries and snacks while the bar claims to stock the best beer in the area.

Pub with food
Traditional country pub

Credit Cards: All the major cards

Local Golf Courses: Enmore Park, Oake Manor, Taunton Vale

THE MARKET INN 438

1 North End Road, Yatton, Somerset BS49 4AL
Tel: 01934 832209 Fax: 01934 835981

The Market Inn is a pretty example of a traditional, country inn and is easily located at the north end of town, close to the M5. Dating back to the 18th century the property has a great deal of character and offers a friendly, warm welcome to locals and visitors to the area. The bar stocks a wide choice of draught ales while the menu offers an equally fine selection of meals and snacks. In fine weather, food and drink can be enjoyed in the beer garden.

Pub with food.
Friendly, welcoming pub

Credit Cards: All the major cards

Local Golf Courses: Clevedon, Weston-super-Mare, Burnham & Berrow

THE SOMERSET WAGON 439

Broadway, Chilcompton, Radstock, Somerset BA3 4JW
Tel: 01761 232732 Fax: 01761 232522

Dating from 1750, **The Somerset Wagon** is a former coaching inn that has been transformed into the pretty, bright and airy hostelry you find today. Presenting an attractive, neatly painted exterior surrounded by colourful shrubs and flower beds, inside you will find cosy furnishings and a friendly welcome. The food is superb, with the menu offering freshly prepared, classic dishes to suit all tastes, and the bar stocks some of the best ales around. Occasional live music.

Pub with food
Pretty pub, friendly welcome, excellent food.

Credit Cards: All the major cards.

Local Golf Courses: The Mendip, Lansdown, Bath

BASHFORDS FARMHOUSE 440

West Bagborough, Taunton, Somerset TA4 3EF
Tel: 01823 432015 Fax: 0870 1671587
e-mail: charlieritchie@netscapeonline.co.uk
Bashfords Farmhouse is at the centre of a non-working farm located on the southern slopes of the Quantock Hills. The house dates largely from the 18th century, although parts are over 400 years old, and the present owners carried out extensive renovations when they moved here nine years ago. The result is a charming house which has been beautifully decorated throughout. There are three comfortable rooms each with en-suite facilities or private bathroom. Evening meals available on request.

Bed and Breakfast
Cosy farmhouse accommodation

Credit Cards: None

Local Golf Courses: Enmore Park, Oake Manor, Taunton Vale

THE PRINCE OF ORANGE — 441

17 High Street, Yatton, Somerset BS49 4JD
Tel: 01934 832193 Fax: 01934 832193

The Prince of Orange is a long-established hostelry that has been serving the local community and visitors to the area for over 300 years. Enjoying a good sized site, positioned within easy reach of the motorway, the property is well-maintained and neatly presented with a colourful profusion of hanging baskets throughout the summer. The pub is popular for the good range of beers stocked behind the bar, while food can be enjoyed from a wide-ranging menu of hearty dishes. there is a large beer garden and Bed and breakfast accommodation is available in a self-contained part of the building with five en-suite rooms. 15 minutes from Bristol airport.

Pub with food, B&B

Popular pub with good range of beer

Credit Cards: All the major cards

Local Golf Courses: Mendip Springs, The Mendip, Tall Pines

ELLSWORTH HOUSE — 442

Fosseway, Midsomer Norton, Bath, Somerset BA3 4AU
Tel: 01761 412305
e-mail: accommodation@ellsworth.fsbusiness.co.uk
website: www.ellsworth.fsbusiness.co.uk

Ellsworth House is ideally situated on the Somerset borders surrounded by beautiful countryside and within easy reach of the many places of interest in this corner of England. Within the attractive house there are a number of comfortable, en-suite guest rooms with double and family-sized rooms available. Guests can relax in the spacious sun lounge beyond which is a superb koi carp pond, which may wall be of interest to the fish enthusiast. This is a non-smoking establishment.

Bed and breakfast

Comfortable, homely accommodation.

Credit Cards: All the major cards

Local Golf Courses: The Mendip, Farrington, Lansdown, Bath

MASON'S ARMS — 443

Marston Gate, Frome, Somerset BA11 4DJ
Tel: 01373 464537 Fax: 01373 455071

An attractive inn that at first glance appears to be three cottages - which it was until converted into a pub! Entering through any of the three front doors, the cosy interior is a labyrinth of small rooms where the beams and original fireplaces have been retained throughout. Here visitors can enjoy an excellent selection of real ales with local brewery, Ushers, on offer. There is also a delicious menu of tasty dishes, including sumptuous grills served on a hot skillet, with the mixed grill being very popular. Regular live music and karaoke nights.

Pub with food

Great menu with popular sizzling dishes.

Credit Cards: All the major cards

Local Golf Courses: Frome Golf Centre, Orchardleigh, The Mendip

THE BEAR INN — 444

Holwell, Nr. Frome, Somerset BA 11 4PY
Tel: 01373 836585

Just a few miles from Frome, located directly on the Glastonbury road, you will find **The Bear Inn**, an unusual structure which is built directly into the face of a quarry. Inside visitors will find a large log fire, lit when the weather is cool, and a compact lounge with ar adjoining public and games room. The bar stocks a range of fine ales and the menu offers a wide selection of traditional meals and snacks. There is a beer garden and outdoor children's play area which are popular in fine weather. Bed and breakfast accommodation is available with six guest rooms.

Pub with food, B&B

Cosy pub with friendly service

Credit Cards: None

Local Golf Courses: Frome Golf Centre, Orchardleigh, The Mendip

SOMERSET

Tea Rooms

Small, charming tea room with 26 covers, including tables in the very pretty garden

Credit Cards: None

MARLBOROUGH TEA ROOMS 445

Bow Street, Langport, Somerset TA10 9PR
Tel: 01458 250786 Fax: 01458 250786

In the centre of Langport, on a quiet street, you will find the small and charming **Marlborough Tea Rooms**. Run by a husband and wife team here you can enjoy morning coffee, a light lunch or afternoon tea Tuesday to Saturday and Bank Holidays between 10am and 5pm. The wide ranging menu includes home-baked bread, cakes and scones and all the hot dishes are home-made too. The cream teas have a reputation all of their own and are well worth a try. Wheat-free diets are catered for.

Local Golf Courses: Wheathill, Yeovil, Taunton Vale

Hotel, Pub with food

Modern lodge accommodation and popular pub

Credit Cards: All the major cards

INNLODGE 446

North End Road, Yatton, Nr. Bristol, Somerset BS49 4AU
Tel: 01934 839100 Fax: 01934 839149
e-mail: bridgeinn@sfigroup.co.uk website: www.innlodge.com
The Innlodge is part of a small chain of properties and here at The Bridge you will find they offer rooms ranging from a standard room through to more luxurious suites. Newly built, the 41 en-suite rooms are attractively furnished and comfortable and the room rates are reasonable. The Innlodge is attached to the Bridge Inn, a delightful country inn which is renowned for its superb home-cooked food. Children can also be well-occupied here with an indoor Action Zone and outdoor adventure play area.

Local Golf Courses: Clevedon, Weston-super-Mare, Farrington

Alphabetic List of Golf Courses